**Transforming** our **Teaching** through

**Reading/Writing Connections**

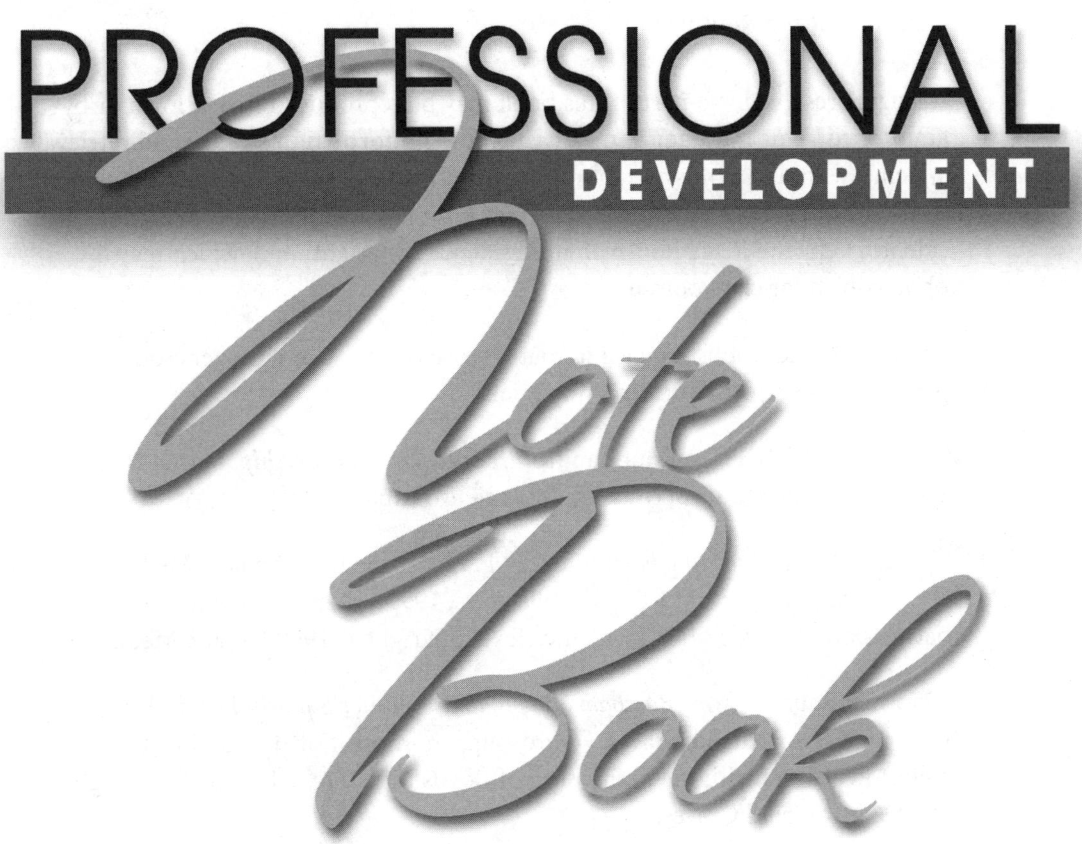

**HEINEMANN**
Portsmouth, NH

**Heinemann**
361 Hanover Street
Portsmouth, NH 03801–3912
www.heinemann.com

*Offices and agents throughout the world*



The author and publisher wish to thank those of you who have generously given permission to reprint borrowed material:

"Teacher Talk" by Regie Routman from *Educational Leadership*, March 2002, Vol. 59, No. 6. Used by permission of Regie Routman.

"T-Shirt" from *My Name Is Jorge on Both Sides of the River* by Jane Medina. (Wordsong, an imprint of Boyds Mills Press, 1999.) Reprinted with the permission of Boyds Mills Press, Inc. Text copyright © 1990 by Jane Medina.

"Summer Squash" from *Baseball, Snakes, and Summer Squash: Poems About Growing Up* by Donald Graves. (Wordsong, an imprint of Boyds Mills Press, 1996.) Reprinted with the permission of Boyds Mills Press, Inc. Text copyright © 1996 by Donald Graves.

ISBN 13: 978-0-325-01243-8
ISBN 10: 0-325-01243-1

*Editor:* Wendy Murray
*Development editor:* Alan Huisman
*Production service:* DB Publishing Services, Inc.
*Production supervisor:* Patty Adams
*Writers/Collaborators:* Sandra Garcia with JoAnne Piccolo
*Typesetting:* Gina Poirier Design
*Cover and interior design:* Lisa Fowler
*Manufacturing:* Louise Richardson

Printed in the United States of America on acid-free paper

12 11 10 09 08 VP 1 2 3 4 5

# Contents for Resources

## Session 11



## Session 12



## Session 13



## Session 14

*Many of the resources in the sessions are also available on the website. These resources have a globe icon next to their heading. See, also, the website for a complete listing of downloadable resources by session.*

# Acknowledgments

My heartfelt thanks go to the many teachers, principals, and students who have been intimately involved in this project and made it a reality. Most of all, I want to thank Sandra Garcia, my dear friend, colleague, and collaborator, who worked by my side on this project the past two years. From drafting and revising the session guides to selecting the video clips and writing lesson plans, Sandy applied both her expertise as an administrator and her deep sensitivity to what's best for all children at every turn. She has worked as a K–12 Literacy Director in an affluent district, and currently is a literacy coach in a school where all the students are English language learners and from low-income families, and it was Sandy who taught me that whether set amidst affluent populations or impoverished ones, *all* schools need to continue asking themselves, *How can we do this better? How can we raise our expectations and the achievement of all students?* Sandy's knowledge of teaching and assessment issues and her savvy about how to best present professional development to teachers, principals, administrators, coaches, and specialists, informed and enriched this project. For her deep commitment, brilliant ideas, common sense, and loving friendship, I am most grateful. For her sense of humor, generosity, and all the laughter we continue to share—along with Seattle's best coffee—I am most fortunate. I could not have completed the project without her.

Special thanks go to all the educators and students in the videos and photographs on the covers, inside pages of the guides, and website who come from schools across the country and in Canada where I have conducted residencies, including Arapahoe Ridge Elementary School in Westminster, CO; Ardmore Elementary School in Bellevue, WA; Audubon Elementary School in Spokane, WA; Lakeview Design Center in Nashville, TN; and White Center Heights Elementary School in Seattle, WA. To the principals and teachers of those schools, I am greatly indebted; I am thankful for the leadership and support of principals, former principals, and literacy leaders Barb Ide, Marilyn Jerde, Dana Myers, Kathleen Poole, and Greta Salmi. Each of them collaborated with me as we worked side by side to raise expectations and results for their students. Equally important are the many talented and dedicated teachers in those schools who welcomed me into their classrooms and shared their students with me. Warmest thanks and appreciation go to those teachers: Nicole Akerson, Christine Axel, Darcy Ballentine, Whitney Clark, Marlene Ellis, Amanda Martinka, Nancy McLean, Gwen Sanders, Judy Sipiora, Ginny Vale, and Mary Yuhas. I am grateful for their smartness, their collaboration, their risk taking, their reviewing parts of this project, and, not least of all, their many kindnesses. As well, thanks go to all the marvelous students in those classrooms who showed what was possible and to the capable videographers who captured them on video: Gary Burlingame, Matt Enigh, Craig Owensby, and Dan Steinke. Grateful thanks, too, to Judy Wallis who skillfully compiled the annotated professional and personal book list on the reading/writing connection and who continues to contribute her expertise in so many ways.

JoAnne Piccolo, teacher of extraordinary talents, as well as my dear friend and colleague was integral to the successful completion of this project. JoAnne reviewed sessions and lesson plans, created charts, wrote parts of sessions, and was always available to do whatever was necessary. I can still hear her voice through email and on the phone, "What else do you need? Just call me." For her selfless efforts, creative ideas, unflinching honesty, and high standards, I am greatly indebted. Simply put, JoAnne is the best there is.

The magnificent team at Heinemann has put forth extraordinary efforts to design, produce, and publish a beautiful, original, and easy-to-use project. Executive editor Wendy Murray, dear editor and friend, has expertly contributed to every part of this project, adding superb ideas and language every step of the way, making the project far richer. As well, gifted development editor Alan Huisman carefully edited the guides and offered graceful revisions. Patty Adams, multi-talented production editor, has left no detail unattended and has worked tirelessly with the marvelous production assistance of Gina Poirier and Denise Botelho to review, typeset, edit, and produce a beautiful and readable project in a timely manner. Abby Heim, production supervisor, helped coordinate all pieces, as she always does, with great aplomb. President Lesa Scott was an early champion of this project and I am so grateful to all she does to make sure teachers and administrators everywhere know about it. Editorial director/vice president Leigh Peake has also been a staunch supporter and spearheaded the far-reaching vision for the website, sparing no efforts to bring it all to wonderful fruition. Lisa Fowler brilliantly created all the covers, video screens, and website designs with panache and elegance, aided by the team of Nicole Russell and Marla Berry. Talented Kevin Carlson—ably assisted by Tom Meegan, Sherry Day, and Pip Clews—expertly edited every video, helped create and place voiceovers, and did whatever it took to produce the DVDs, which are the centerpiece of this project. Pat Carls, excellent director of marketing—along with her marketing team of Erik Chalek, Doria Turner, Janet Taylor, Kim Cahill, and Jenny Jensen Greenleaf—and the sales group, ably led by Buzz Rhodes, innovatively worked and continue to work to translate and promote the project's vision to educators everywhere. Maura Sullivan, managing editor, brought her great instincts about the needs of schools to the table, helping us refine so many aspects of this project, from cover colors to titles. Her humor cheered me on at crucial junctures. As well, special thanks go to others who greatly assisted in this project: Jillan Scahill, Karyn Morrison, Vicki Boyd, and Louise Richardson. For all the extraordinary talents of the Heinemann team, as well as their perseverance and dedication to excellence, I am most fortunate and grateful.

In closing, as always, my deepest thanks go to my loving and patient husband Frank and to all my family and friends who continued to offer support and love throughout the years it took to complete this project.

**Transforming** our **Teaching** through
**Reading/Writing Connections**

# Welcome to Regie Routman in Residence

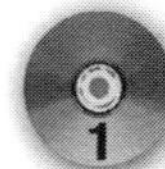

**View Video** (30 min.)

**Welcome to Regie Routman in Residence**

- **Overview of the Professional Development Program**
- **Core Beliefs About Teaching and Learning**

## 1. Engage, Reflect, Assess

- Flip through your *Professional Development Notebook.*
- Read and comment on the Welcome Letter from Regie Routman on p. 1–7.
- Think about a class or professional development opportunity that either had a lasting impact on your teaching—or that disappointed you.
    - *What was the class/session about?*
    - *What changes in your teaching did you make as a result?*
    - *Describe the lasting impact—or why you think the professional development failed.*
    - *What made the sessions/class effective? Or what turned you off?*
- ***Small-Group Share:*** Share this experience with your grade-level team. Determine what you appreciate—and don't appreciate—about the professional development you've had.

**RESOURCES**

*The globe icon indicates a resource is also available on the website.*

- ***Whole-Group Share:*** Contribute your ideas to a chart of "Characteristics of Effective Professional Development" and "Characteristics of Ineffective Professional Development."
- Preview the agenda and routines for all professional development sessions.

## 2. Discuss Professional Reading

- Read (silently) "Teacher Talk," a short article enclosed on p. 1–16 related to the power of schoolwide/districtwide professional conversations. (Or, if this is not your first project, read "Finding Meaning and Purpose Together" [Socol 2007, pp. 616–619], downloadable from the website.)
- Turn-and-talk to a partner about the article.
    - Share a question that you have about one or more points the article makes about the importance of professional conversations.

## 3. Goals

- Learn to value how the reading/writing connection can accelerate and improve teaching and learning.
- Develop a shared sense of what makes professional development effective—and the kinds of things that get in the way of it working well.
- Learn about the beliefs, practices, and development of an effective professional development model.
- Begin to think about core beliefs about teaching and learning.
- Understand the session agenda and the role of professional conversations for long-lasting positive change.
- Set goals for your own learning (schoolwide, classroom, and personal).
- Establish vertical teams as a major professional development structure for ongoing professional conversations.

## 4. View Video and Take Notes

- Turn to the Notecatcher to take notes.

## 5. Respond to the Video

- What are some of the things that struck you as you observed Regie Routman introduce the professional development program?
- What did you hear in the video that relates to your needs as a teacher and learner?
- What do you hope to gain from participating in this professional development program?

- Read the "Professional Development Program Goals" on p. 1–13, and be prepared to highlight and share important ideas.

## 6. Achieve a Deeper Understanding

- Review the purpose and format of the Deeper Understanding charts on p. 1–21.
- Using the example, review the following:

**Video Scenes:**

- Each video is divided into scenes.
- The title of the scene captures the main content of the scene.
- The time notation indicates the running time.
- The navigation system on the DVD promotes easy re-viewing.

**Setting, Notes, and Explicit Teaching Points:**

- Provide background and instructional information.
- Recount actual teaching (including some of the language) that occurred, in sequence.
- Make it easy to revisit and analyze the lesson with or without viewing it again.

**Ongoing Assessment:**

- Itemize the actual assessments, primarily through responsive questioning, used in the video scenes.
- Demonstrate how to continuously embed assessment within teaching.
- Show how assessment and instruction are interconnected.

**Questions/Reflections:**

- Are designed to encourage deep thinking about the teaching and learning depicted in the videos as well as your own teaching.
- Motivate and stimulate professional conversations in whole-group sessions or in weekly team (vertical, grade-level, or partner) meetings.

**Learning Outcomes:**

- Identify the skills and strategies the students will learn.
- Connect to most state standards.

## 7. *Try It/Apply It* in the Classroom

- Research shows that if we don't apply our new learning within a few days we lose it. Studies (Moffett 2000) have also demonstrated that in schools and districts with strong professional learning communities teachers respond more successfully to the needs of students and sustain positive change. These studies also confirm that schools and districts with weak professional learning communities are instructionally ineffective.

  - Sign-up in your vertical teams (facilitator will post or provide a Vertical Team Sign-Up Sheet).
  - Think about what you hope to accomplish through this professional development program—at the classroom level, grade level, school level, and perhaps, the district level. Read the Program Overview and review the broad goals and the goals specific to this professional development program. Write down those goals that are most important to you. Plan to share those goals at the next session.
- Plan how your grade-level team might implement and organize ongoing professional conversations.
- Plan to bring to the next session your plan for getting professional conversations going in your district, at your school, with your grade-level colleagues, or with a partner.
- Plan for ongoing professional conversations using the following resources:
  - "Make Time for Professional Conversations" (p. 1–20).
  - *Conversations* (Routman 2000, pp. 520–527).
  - "Teacher Talk" (see p. 1–16).

## 8. Wrap-Up

- Before the next session, read "Making Professional Development a Priority" (*Conversations* excerpt, pp. 520–527 and downloadable from the website) and be prepared to discuss it at the next session.

- Schedule time to meet with your vertical, grade-level, and/or partner teams in between whole-group sessions to revisit the videos on the website and the Deeper Understanding charts and/or plan together and try out new learning.
- Remember to bring any charts, lessons, writing, or student work samples from the *Try It/Apply It* to the next session.

SESSION 1

# NOTECATCHER

| KEY WORDS | NOTES & REFLECTION |
| --- | --- |
| Joy in learning | |
| Celebration | |
| Focus on the child | |
| An interesting life | |
| Planning | |
| Expert at smartness | |
| Optimal Learning Model | |

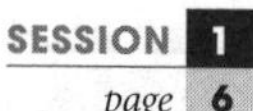

SESSION 1

# NOTECATCHER

| KEY WORDS | NOTES & REFLECTION |
| --- | --- |
| Success and confidence | |
| High expectations | |
| Common sense | |
| The power of writing | |
| Authenticity | |

# *Welcome Letter*

## Welcome to Regie Routman in Residence

*Dear Colleague,*

Since 1997, I have been teaching and coaching in weeklong reading and writing residencies in schools around the country. I created the job when I realized that too few staff developers were providing the demonstration teaching and coaching so crucial to effective professional development. Teachers were expected to implement the latest curriculum or program and improve their teaching practice, but in general, no one was stepping in to model *how* to teach more effectively and *how* to give teachers ongoing support. When I work in schools, I *show* teachers by working with their students and with them for a week in their own classrooms. I demonstrate, explain, collaborate, co-teach, and coach; I facilitate professional conversations; and I support teachers as they observe, try out, rethink, discuss, and collaborate. I show them how to build into their daily teaching life the authentic practices and routines that engage students and help them become independent—to take the reins of their own learning, if you will.

Over time, I was invited back to do additional residencies in schools, and I discovered that the weekly schoolwide professional conversations I modeled and advocated for had become part of the fabric of school life. In these schools, teachers were more confident and knowledgeable than they had been a few years earlier, and most importantly, there had been great gains in student achievement. The transformation was palpable. After several years, a few districts asked me to expand my work from one school—which served as a literacy lab for the district—to all schools in the district. The only way to fulfill that request without my spending too much time away from my home was to replicate, as best I could, the ongoing professional development (PD) model I had been implementing in schools. ***Regie Routman in Residence*** is the result. Not surprisingly, it's video-based, because there is no better way to convey what good teaching, assessing, and sustained professional development look and sound like than to show them in action. These videos and their corresponding guides bring my residency work into your classroom and school. The

website, www.regieroutman.com, provides ongoing support and interaction with me and other colleagues.

Everything that I believe is important in professional development is embedded in this professional development program:

- ***A theory of learning.*** Unless we articulate for ourselves and others what we believe about how children learn, our teaching may lack coherence. I embrace an Optimal Learning Model (OLM) that begins with demonstration, continues with shared experiences, provides lots of time for guided practice, and then gradually hands over responsibility to the learner. I continually show how the Optimal Learning Model can apply to teachers and to students and to all we do in our classrooms and in professional development. This elegantly simple approach ("*I do it,*" "*We do it,*" "*You do it*") applies to how we all learn, children and adults alike.

- ***Simplicity.*** The essence of this program is straightforward: watch and analyze the videos; use them as the basis of personal reflection and conversation with colleagues to arrive at deeper understanding; try out what you have just observed, discussed, and read about; apply learning to new contexts.

- ***Embedded assessment.*** Ongoing assessment—before, during, and after instruction—is part of all effective teaching. That embedded assessment is made explicit in the Deeper Understanding charts that participants begin to review during each session.

- ***Demonstrations.*** The demonstration teaching and assessment you see me do is grounded in theory and current research, as well as in standards, curriculum requirements, and students' needs and interests. I want to convey through my demonstration teaching that you can "have it all"—authentic practices, required curriculum, attention to skills, explicit teaching, student engagement, higher achievement, and enjoyment.

- ***Professional conversations.*** Ongoing conversations with colleagues—both whole-school and small-group—are built into this program in myriad ways, from turn-and-talk exchanges during sessions to the website, where you can engage in local and national conversations with teachers. It's easier to achieve deeper understanding when we exchange ideas about our practice, rather than try to go it alone.

- ***Structured practice.*** After each session, it's your turn to demonstrate, to apply what you have learned with your own students. You have opportunities to try out and practice new understandings and processes with structured feedback.

- ***Collaboration and coaching.*** We teachers are social creatures. No matter what new technology may come along to enhance professional development, we can't forget how much we love to be in a room with our colleagues, exploring how to help particular students, swapping great new books we've read, and just talking. But we also relish our independence. With this in mind, I've tried to balance the need for solo practice with opportunities to share and try new things with colleagues at your grade level. I'm also aware of the potential pitfalls of coaching as it's executed in schools today, and so here and in my professional book, *Teaching Essentials,* I provide the coaching specifics you need to move forward with competence and confidence.

- ***Student learning.*** Students, and their needs, take center stage throughout. Why? Because at the end of the day, the gold standard by which this or any professional development program is evaluated is, *do the students in our schools demonstrate increased knowledge and understanding as a result of this effort?* As you watch the videos, I hope you'll notice the way students demonstrate their independence and joy as learners by choosing to read and write, applying their learning to new contexts, problem solving on their own, monitoring and evaluating their own work, and setting new goals. I model how to use work samples, conferences, record keeping, interviews with students and teachers, and self-evaluations to increase students' confidence and achievement.

- ***Enjoyment.*** Teachers who engage in the approach offered here—who embrace the Optimal Learning Model, and who try out lessons they have observed on the videos—rediscover the joy of teaching. They rediscover the thrill of seeing all their students being successful, right from the start. Celebration—consciously noting strengths and successes—is part of every lesson with students and teachers.

Teachers have always been the most important factor in student achievement. My hope is that this professional development program will help you solidify your beliefs about teaching and learning. I also hope you'll become more confident in your teaching and assessment practices and become part of a vibrant, professional learning community.

I will be by your side as your partner and colleague.
Enjoy teaching and learning!

Regie Routman

# Program Overview

## A Model for Effective Instruction and Whole-School Achievement

### Purposeful, Authentic Teaching

This professional development program provides teachers and schools with a common purpose, process, and language to span across the grades. It is designed to simplify our professional lives, not complicate them, by showing what effective teaching looks like and sounds like, no matter where you are or who you teach. In each of the three projects available in *Regie Routman in Residence—Transforming Our Teaching Through Reading/Writing Connections, Transforming Our Teaching Through Writing for Audience and Purpose,* and *Transforming Our Teaching Through Reading to Understand*—I show what it means to teach any subject with an authenticity and ease that engages and challenges students. By authenticity, I mean that for everything we do in our classrooms, we know—and our students sense—the meaningful big-picture "whole" behind the activity as well as its real-world purpose.

*Regie Routman in Residence* is about effective, efficient, and enjoyable teaching and learning. I want to show others how to teach and assess skills and strategies, meet required standards within challenging and relevant curriculum, and at the same time ensure that all students learn and enjoy doing so. This whole-part-whole teaching (which is how the brain learns most easily) stands in sharp contrast to an isolated focus—and often an overemphasis—on distinct literacy skills and individual components. Perhaps as important, this professional development program is also designed to make professional development meaningful and enjoyable without adding to your workload.

### Proven Results

This model of professional development offers an easy-to-use teaching structure and process that is replicable, sustainable, and applicable at all grade levels, in all classrooms, and in all schools. It is based on an Optimal Learning Model of teaching and learning that applies to all teachers, all students, and all contexts. In a yearlong pilot study implementing *Transforming Our Teaching Through Writing for Audience and Purpose,* teachers and administrators found that they and their students became more effective, knowledgeable, and confident as thinkers, problem solvers, and writers. In addition to attaining higher student achievement, both teachers and students were able to apply and transfer their learning to new areas of teaching and learning. They found that what they learned applied not just to writing but across the curriculum. In schools that implemented *Transforming*

*Our Teaching Through Reading/Writing Connections* and *Transforming Our Teaching Through Reading to Understand* sessions, standardized test scores in reading greatly increased and have so far been maintained for four consecutive years.

## Unparalleled Support

I have worked hard to provide unprecedented guidance for participants, whether district-level administrators or classroom teachers. How? By building all the professional development work around video clips of my classroom teaching in action, day by day. Viewing these 30-minute segments (in connection with detailed guides for both facilitators and participants) serves as the central activity of each professional development session. The session's discussion and collaborative work correspond exactly to what is taking place on the video, so session leaders have a powerful scaffold for guiding teachers to "try it/apply it" in their classrooms. Participants can also go to the website for further support, re-viewing additional video footage and joining professional conversations with colleagues. Viewing and reflecting on the videos with the support of the facilitators' guides and the accompanying book *Teaching Essentials* (2008), along with *Conversations* (2000), *Reading Essentials* (2003), and *Writing Essentials* (2005), encourages high-level, ongoing professional conversations about what effective instruction looks and sounds like.

## Authentic Classroom Settings

The students in the videos are the ones I teach in typical classrooms during my week-long residencies in schools throughout the United States and Canada. The majority of these students are nonwhite and low-income. Many are English language learners. In most of the schools, many languages are spoken (29 in one school). At my request, none of the students—special education students, English language learners, or those with "behavior problems"—are removed when I am teaching. All the schools have struggled with such crucial issues as low expectations, flat achievement and test scores, and lack of enjoyment in teaching and learning. All strive to do better and get better results.

## A Unified Learning Model Across All Levels

The Optimal Learning Model *("I do it," "We do it," "You do it")* is the foundation of all instruction, not just for children but for adults as well. The sessions in *Regie Routman in Residence* individually and collectively reflect this model's flow from demonstration to collaborative work to independent application. See Session 2, p. 2–6.

In order for the model to work well and bring about long-lasting change, it is critical to form varied professional development teams (see p. 1–13). These teams pool knowledge and resources, orchestrate collaboration, and seed professional conversations among all involved. These teams ensure that the Optimal Learning Model continually flows in an "*I do it,*" "*We do it,*" "*You do it*" cycle of professional development throughout the year.

## Common Language, Content, and Goals

What we teach in grades K–8—and by extension, K–12—needs to be framed within common goals articulated in a common language, districtwide. This unified approach makes it possible to devise a philosophy of teaching and learning that has coherence and can be communicated clearly to parents and other stakeholders. Most important of all, it leads to high student achievement.

In reading, for example, we want all students to be able to apply reading strategies—to infer, summarize, choose books they can read and understand, monitor their own comprehension—that will allow them to enjoy reading. In writing, for example, we want all students to write with audience and purpose in mind, to write an engaging lead and satisfying conclusion, to assume increasing responsibility for revising and editing, to publish, to choose to write.

What is taught and assessed is constant throughout the grades. What changes are the duration, depth, amount, and intricacy of the:

- Demonstrations and thinking aloud.
- Scaffolding and "hand-holding."
- Complexity, variety, form, and length of the texts.
- Learner's level of independence.

## Whole-School, On-Site, Professional Development

The role of the administrator, as instructional leader, is an integral part of the success of this and any professional development program. *Regie Routman in Residence* was designed to provide district- and schoolwide leaders with the support they need to implement ongoing professional conversations, to sustain professional growth, and to increase student achievement. It's clear that superficial "one-shot" professional development workshops aren't the answer; they're costly and yet show very little evidence of sustained student achievement and application of new learning. By contrast, my goal here is to provide cost-effective, yearlong—or multiyear—"in-house" professional development, to have all teachers participate in the professional development experience together. I know from my work in schools all around the country that teachers grow, and their practice improves, when the staff development occurs in their own backyard, in the context of their unique school culture. Pilot studies of the projects in *Regie Routman in Residence* result in effective literacy practices and higher achievement that are sustainable and replicable from year to year in classrooms, schools, and districts for all students and all teachers.

# PROFESSIONAL DEVELOPMENT PROGRAM GOALS FOR *REGIE ROUTMAN IN RESIDENCE*

### Transforming Our Teaching Through

- ***Reading/Writing Connections***
- ***Writing for Audience and Purpose***
- ***Reading to Understand***

For detailed goals related to specific projects, see individual sessions in each of the three professional development programs.

## Goals for Educators

- To provide on-site, schoolwide professional development that is easy to implement with new and experienced teachers.
- To provide a professional development framework that is equally accessible and relevant to teachers, principals, and coaches.
- To connect meaningful teaching across the curriculum with standards and student learning outcomes.
- To make ongoing professional conversations part of the fabric of school life.
- To show how to overlay an Optimal Learning Model onto instructional planning, so that students are assured the demonstrations, shared experiences, and guided and independent practice they need in order to learn.
- To show how a whole-part-whole approach to teaching elevates and accelerates learning.
- To show how members of a school community can use a coaching model to improve instruction and assessment.
- To show teachers how to embed ongoing assessment into all teaching and to use that assessment—before, during, and after instruction—to inform instruction.
- To have teachers become more knowledgeable about their practice and more intentional, efficient, and effective day to day.

## Goals for Students

- To raise expectations for what all learners can accomplish.
- To provide success for all learners, including English language learners and those who struggle.
- To make curriculum relevant and meaningful to all learners.
- To read and write texts that recognize, respect, and celebrate students' diverse language and cultures.
- To give learners the tools to become independent readers, writers, and thinkers who create, revise, and comprehend texts and who can apply and transfer their new learning to new contexts.
- To make celebration of learners' strengths and accomplishments part of all teaching and learning.
- To show how the respectful and responsive language we use with students can affirm them, provide useful and specific feedback, and push them to think more deeply.
- To have students transfer what they learn as readers and writers, across the curriculum, to all texts.

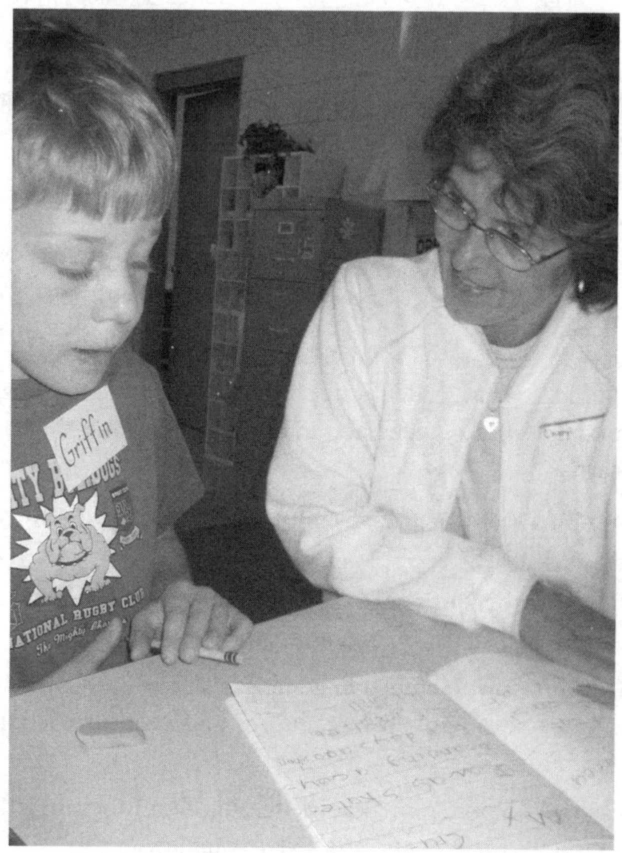

# Specific Professional Development Goals for *Reading/Writing Connections*

- To demonstrate that when we interconnect reading and writing meaningful texts, students' achievement and engagement increases.
- To understand how shared reading and shared writing fit into the "*I do it*"/"*We do it*" phases of the Optimal Learning Model, and see that these "teacher-in-charge" demonstrations and shared experiences are vital to students' learning and becoming independent.
- To share our reading and writing lives and our life stories with our students so they view us as readers and writers.
- To examine current beliefs about reading/writing connections with an eye to developing a consistent set of beliefs and practices across the grades; high schoolwide expectations are more likely to bring high student achievement.
- To learn to bring the voices of all students into the fabric of our teaching through responsive teaching, shared and guided experiences, turn-and-talk, and ongoing assessment.
- To show how to accelerate the reading achievement of English language learners and learners who struggle by having them use their own written texts as an entryway into reading.
- To demonstrate how reading lots of nonfiction texts can positively impact the quality of students' writing and their reading achievement.
- To detail how to set up excellent classroom libraries with and for students for maximum access, relevance, and enjoyment.
- To use shared writing as a scaffold for writing and reading class-authored texts.
- To learn to use scaffolded conversations with students to help them successfully write and read texts.
- To learn how to embed word work in the process of teaching reading and writing.
- To teach students to write with elaboration and detail.
- To appreciate how reading and writing book reviews with students is a powerful way to teach them that one always writes for a purpose and an audience of some kind.
- To understand how free-verse poetry writing can ensure immediate success and enjoyment for *all* learners.
- To show how you can help students write excellent nonfiction reports through lots of shared experiences ("*We do it*" phase of the Optimal Learning Model) and by keeping the reports short and focused.

# Teacher Talk

***Even the best professional development may fail to create meaningful and lasting changes in teaching and learning—unless teachers engage in ongoing professional dialogue to develop a reflective school community***

When the news media and policymakers talk about school improvement, they often mean spending large amounts of money for the "right" program to manage instruction and raise test scores. Rarely do they identify excellent and experienced teachers as the solution to education's problems.

Teacher expertise is routinely devalued. In a recent example, the U.S. Congress mandated the convening of an influential National Reading Panel to determine the best ways to teach reading, especially at the early levels. The 12-member panel included experts from the fields of cognitive psychology, medicine, and higher education, but only two school-based members—an elementary school principal and a middle school reading teacher. This influential, highly publicized report is being used to determine reading practices in U.S. schools, yet no practitioners of beginning reading were included in writing the report. The clear message to the public is that teacher expertise and classroom-based research do not matter.

This notion runs contrary to everything we know about successful education. Knowledgeable, well-informed teachers make a greater difference than do specific programs. Linda Darling-Hammond, who champions the importance of teachers as professionals, states,

> My research and personal experience tell me that the single most important determinant of success for a student is the knowledge and skills of that child's teacher. (Goldberg, 2001, p. 689)

Yet every time a new national report emerges, it creates a crisis of confidence among teachers. Too many teachers assume that "experts" outside the classroom somehow know more than they do. Even seasoned, knowledgeable teachers are quick to question what they believe is right and best for students.

When teachers are well informed—by learning theory and relevant research, as well as by careful reflection on their own experiences—they can make confident decisions about teaching practices. And one of the most powerful approaches to developing this kind of confidence is ongoing professional conversation among colleagues, built into a school's professional development expectations for staff.

## Conversation to Sustain Change

For more than 30 years, I have taught in public schools. For about a decade, I facilitated weekly language arts support groups for teachers, which took the form of conversations—informal, nonjudgmental, exploratory dialogue, often with a common goal in mind. These weekly conversations, along with professional study, gave participating teachers the research, practical ideas, and confidence to move forward in a variety of areas, such as using portfolios and student-led conferences to report progress to parents, improving the teaching of spelling, teaching guided reading, and organized writing workshops.

Since the fall of 1998, I have been teaching in public schools around the country in weeklong school residencies. I spend most of the week demonstrating techniques and strategies in classrooms. For the first three or four days in a school, I demonstrate lessons in the classroom for teachers released to observe. On the last day or two, the teachers try the strategies as I coach and support them. Each teacher can choose to have fellow teachers observe or not. Even though it is difficult for teachers to do so, most agree to have their peers observe because they recognize the value of continued questioning and learning for all teacher learners.

In past school residencies—on the bases of the questions, conversations, and new activities being tried during the week of my visit—it certainly looked as if teachers were in the midst of real change. But return visits were disappointing. I saw new skills and strategies being taught, but with limited connections to big ideas and key concepts in the curriculum.

Although my work in a school had included multiple demonstrations with students, daily conversations with teachers, and coaching several teachers, it still turned out to be a "one-shot deal"—just a longer one. Teachers learned new strategies, skills, and activities, but not necessarily with the understanding and rationale necessary for meaningful application. Experience suggested that the impact on student learning and achievement would remain very limited without ongoing professional reading, reflection, sharing, thinking, collaboration, practice, revision, and continual discussion about all aspects of teaching, learning and evaluating.

**Teachers need time to develop in-depth knowledge through professional conversations, and time is in short supply.**

Finally, I decided not to return to a school unless weekly professional conversations became part of that school's culture. I was no longer willing to put my energies into a school and not have the work and conversations continue after I left. On the last afternoon of a school residency, when meeting with teachers to discuss future goals, I strongly encouraged the staff to begin weekly professional conversations. I told the teachers that they were ready for such conversations, they needed dialogue to remain professional, and conversation would change their teaching practice.

## One School's Story

To my delight and surprise, in each of the schools where I urged teachers to begin ongoing professional conversations, teachers and administrators have taken up the challenge. At Huntsville Elementary School in Huntsville, Ohio, where Diane Gillespie is principal, 30-year veteran teacher Linda Benedict volunteered to spearhead the effort and facilitate weekly meetings.

Last spring, 90 percent of the staff came to each meeting. As is typical when such groups begin, they started by sharing ideas and talking about various teaching concerns. Linda has commented on the impact of the meetings:

> Everyone seemed to get along better. When you see everyone each week and sit down together—instead of teachers just staying in their classrooms—people share more. It definitely pulled our staff closer together.

About six teachers also decided to meet weekly over the summer to discuss professional books. This past fall, the staff chose to focus in depth on teaching reading, especially to struggling readers. Diane Gillespie bought copies of *What Really Matters for Struggling Readers* by Richard Allington (2000), and teachers decided how much they would read each week for discussion. Linda has noted that teachers are thinking more about teaching and what they are doing in their classrooms and that weekly attendance continues to exceed 90 percent of the faculty.

Each meeting still begins with Linda asking, "Did anyone bring anything to share?" but now the staff is also beginning to look carefully at theory and research and to make connections to their own beliefs and practices. During my next residency at this school to demonstrate teaching reading—with a focus on strategies for struggling readers—I expect that the "why" will now connect with the "how" and that teachers will connect the demonstrated strategies to their evolving beliefs about how students learn.

Professional conversations have sparked an interest in learning. More of the teachers are reading professional journals. Whereas no teacher at

Huntsville Elementary had previously belonged to a national teachers' organization or been to a national conference, now about one-third of the staff are members of the International Reading Association (IRA). Gillespie has made a commitment to send several staff members each year to the annual meeting of the IRA.

Although the teachers have not been meeting long enough to assess the impact of teacher conversation on student achievement, I believe that the increased staff collegiality will positively enhance student learning. Third grade teacher Carol Fleece recently commented,

> There is a unity of teachers in our building that wasn't there before. We are open to new ideas and always looking for a good "professional read." We have grown professionally as a staff.

And as Moffett (2000) has noted,

> More than almost any other factor, the sense of a professional community in schools enhances student achievement. (p. 36)

## Developing Good Conversations

As teachers start meeting regularly, typical conversations may be superficial and touch on all aspects of teaching. Initially, many teachers use the time to air their feelings about school life. Because they aren't used to "conversing," they may have to get these general concerns out of the way first. It often takes more than a year for meetings to focus on curriculum and improving student learning.

Additionally, many teachers are embarrassed to admit that they need help. They believe that everyone else must be a successful practitioner who already knows how to teach a particular skill or discipline. In one district, it took six years before an intermediate grade teacher felt safe enough to say, "I don't know how to teach reading when I get students who don't know how to read." That opened the floodgates, and teacher after teacher began to express similar concerns, which led to a three-month focus on how to teach reading in the upper grades.

Loretta Martin, a literacy coach with almost 30 years of experiences as a primary grades teacher, says she needed help when her district moved from a basal to a literature-based approach, but she was afraid to ask for it:

> I knew in my gut that I was not using my reading time to really teach my students to become readers. Seeking advice from my administrator seemed like admitting failure. Finally, I said, "I need help. Can you recommend a recourse or professional conference to learn more about the teaching of reading?"

She attended a week-long literacy conference out of state and began to take responsibility for her own learning. She returned more knowledgeable about the reading process, the research on reading, and the way students learn. Years later, she continues to learn through observing students, having conversations with colleagues, attending conferences, and reading professionally. For the past 13 years, Loretta has been intimately involved in professional development and has become a valued teacher leader and mentor teacher in her school district.

## Moving Beyond Superficial Change

Most change that occurs in our schools is only surface level. It is possible to walk into a classroom that appears to be based on the latest theory and practice—desks grouped in clusters, small groups of students working together, learning centers and computers in place—only to discover that the change is cosmetic. The rationale for and understanding of the physical and learning configurations are missing.

This surface level change is not surprising. In one school I visited, teachers had worked with outside experts in math, behavior management, writing, standards, spelling, and portfolios—all in the past two years! How could teachers be expected to understand the "why" of their practice when so much was being piled onto their teaching? There was no time for the reflection that is vital for all meaningful and lasting change.

In this particular school, the reason for my weeklong visit was primarily concern about the low test scores on the statewide grade 4 writing test—that is, systematically teaching the students to write a paragraph with a topic sentence and supporting details—students' writing, including spelling and grammar, had not improved. In fact, some teachers told me that the quality of the writing had declined.

No surprise here. Students learn to write well when they engage in creating authentic texts for a purpose and an audience that matter. Then revision and editing make sense, not the other way around. But without professional conversations and reflection about how real writers work, it's impossible to teach writing well.

We need to be continually asking:

- Why am I teaching this way?
- How will this activity or lesson contribute to students' literacy and growing independence?
- How do I know whether my students are learning?

If we don't ask these questions, we are just going through the motions. Our students may learn the skills and strategies that we teach them, but application to meaningful contexts will be limited.

**SOME GUIDELINES FOR WEEKLY PROFESSIONAL CONVERSATIONS**

- Make meetings voluntary and invitational
- Survey the staff for interests
- Begin on time
- Post an agenda
- Take minutes and distribute them to the entire staff
- Read and discuss professional articles and books
- Have a specific curricular focus
- Encourage a knowledgeable teacher or co-teachers to facilitate
- Request that the principal attend as a learner and equal group member
- Allow time for sharing ideas

## Making Time for Conversations

Teachers need time to develop in-depth knowledge through professional conversations, and time is in short supply. In one district where I worked for more that 20 years, there was only one required professional development day, and the teachers' union consistently resisted adding more days. Although we had well-attended, voluntary, weekly professional conversations in place in each K–4 elementary school—our "language arts support group"—some teachers noted that these meetings took place before school, on our own time.

Some possibilities for creating time for weekly professional meetings are to:

- Establish before-school support groups.
- Start school late or dismiss students early one day each week.
- Devote faculty meetings to issues of the profession.
- Create common planning times.
- Hire roving substitutes.
- Add paid days to the school calendar.
- Add more time to the school day.

Making a commitment to weekly professional meetings is not easy, but it is one of the best ways to develop thoughtful practice schoolwide and to improve teaching and learning. Ongoing, onsite professional development through reflective, self-guided weekly conversations about teaching practice is a necessity for sustained growth and transformation for both students and teachers.

## References

Goldberg, M. (2001, May). An interview with Linda Darling-Hammond: Balanced optimism. *Phi Delta Kappan,* 82(9), 687–690.

Moffett, C. (2000, April). Sustaining change: The answers are blowing in the wind. *Educational Leadership,* 57(7), 35–38.

# Make Time for Professional Conversations

## SOME **POSSIBILITIES**

- ☐ Before-school support-group meetings
- ☐ Before students arrive on late-start days
- ☐ Early dismissal days
- ☐ Faculty meetings devoted to issues of the profession
- ☐ Common planning times
- ☐ Time freed by roving substitute teachers
- ☐ Ongoing mentoring
- ☐ Videotaped lessons
- ☐ Paid days added to school calendar
- ☐ More time added to the school day

## SOME **GUIDELINES** FOR WEEKLY **PROFESSIONAL CONVERSATIONS**

- ☐ Make meetings voluntary and invitational
- ☐ Survey staff for interests
- ☐ Begin on time
- ☐ Post an agenda
- ☐ Take minutes and distribute to entire staff
- ☐ Read and discuss professional articles and books
- ☐ Have a curricular focus
- ☐ Encourage a knowledgeable teacher or co-teachers to facilitate
- ☐ Maintain a positive tone
- ☐ Have principal attend as a learner and equal group member
- ☐ Allow time for sharing of ideas

SESSION 1

Explanation

# DEEPER UNDERSTANDING

The globe icon indicates that the example is also available when you visit www.regieroutman.com.

## *Video* SCENES

| | Setting, Notes, and Explicit Teaching Points<br>The What, Why, and How of Teaching | Ongoing Assessment<br>Informing Our Instruction | Questions/Reflections<br>For Professional Conversations | Learning Outcomes<br>What Students Know and Are Able To Do |
|---|---|---|---|---|
| | The **SETTING** provides the basic information about the classroom teacher, students, grade, and demographics of the school and student population. | | | |
| **Each video scene is listed by title and scene length and can be easily revisited with the navigation system. Some scenes also have subtitles. All titles and subtitles appear as headings on the videos as you are viewing.** | The **NOTES** provide the background to understand the context of the video scenes and session as well as provide teaching ideas and tips for optimal instruction and learning.<br>The explicit **TEACHING POINTS** name the actual teaching that occurred in sequence, moment by moment, making it easy to revisit and analyze the lesson at any time and to construct a similar lesson plan of your own.<br>The teaching and assessing points reflect the total lesson but all of these points are not on the edited videos. However, the major points are represented on the edited videos.<br> | The **ONGOING ASSESSMENT** provides you with the actual assessments and language used in the video scenes as the assessment occurs, in sequence. The ongoing assessment is placed adjacent to the related teaching points so you can see the interconnectedness between assessment and instruction.<br>You will notice that most of this ongoing assessment is questioning that is meant to get students to think further, to explain their thinking, and to clarify their thinking. This questioning is a prime example of "responsive teaching" (vs. telling teaching). | The **QUESTIONS/REFLECTIONS** for Professional Conversations are designed to encourage thinking deeply about the teaching and learning you are observing. The goal of this section is for you to use the questions to guide your conversations in your whole-group professional development sessions and/or in your weekly vertical teams.<br> | The **LEARNING OUTCOMES** will provide you with the skills and strategies students will be able to know and do as a result of the teaching and learning in the video scenes.<br>These student learning goals align with most state and national standards. |

SESSION 1

# RESPONSENOTES

*Engage, Reflect, Assess, Celebrate!*

REGIE ROUTMAN in RESIDENCE

# SESSION 2

Transforming our Teaching through
**Reading/Writing Connections**

# Applying an Optimal Learning Model to Your Teaching

**View Video** (11 min.)

**Applying an Optimal Learning Model to Your Teaching**

- **Understanding the Optimal Learning Model**

## Agenda

### 1. Engage, Reflect, Assess

- Review the *Try It/Apply It* activity from last session with your vertical team.
- ***Whole-Group:*** Share your plan for organizing ongoing professional conversations in your grade level, school, or district.

### 2. Discuss Professional Reading

- Discuss "Making Professional Development a Priority" (*Conversations*, pp. 520–527 and downloadable from the website) as a whole group, with your vertical team, or with a partner. Perhaps also read and discuss "The Residency Model" p. 2–12 during the session.

### 3. Goals

- Explore your own beliefs about teaching and learning, and consider how they may dovetail with Regie Routman's beliefs.
- Begin to understand the Optimal Learning Model as an instructional framework for real-world learning.

**RESOURCES**

- Optimal Learning Model Across the Curriculum *2–6*
- Abridged Optimal Learning Model Across the Curriculum, *2–7*
- Optimal Learning Model in a Daily Literacy Block *2–8*
- Examining Your Instruction with the Optimal Learning Model (sample lesson) (not available on website) *2–9*
- Examining Your Instruction with the Optimal Learning Model (blank form) *2–10*
- Planning with the OLM in Mind (blank form) *2–11*
- The Residency Model *2–12*

- Begin to think about and apply the Optimal Learning Model in daily instruction.
- Understand the importance of demonstration and of scaffolding students' experience of a new process before releasing responsibility to students to try it independently. Using real-world incidents, Regie Routman explains and demonstrates how application of the Optimal Learning Model positively impacts and accelerates all successful learning.

## 4. View Video and Take Notes

- Turn to the Notecatcher to take notes.

## 5. Respond to the Video

- ***Small-Group Share:*** Respond to the following discussion questions.
  - What did you see in the video that made an impact on you?
  - Think about your teaching. What key teaching practice aligns with your core belief? What are some others?
  - What is your understanding of the Optimal Learning Model (*"I do it," "We do it," "You do it"*)?

## 6. Achieve a Deeper Understanding

- Turn to the Optimal Learning Model on p. 2–6.
- ***Turn-and-talk:*** Share with a partner a real-world example of learning a skill or how to do something where the Optimal Learning Model can be used to describe how you were taught. Perhaps use the graphic organizer below to organize your thoughts.

| Demonstration<br>I DO IT | Shared Demonstration<br>WE DO IT | Guided Practice<br>YOU DO IT/WE DO IT | Independent Practice<br>YOU DO IT |
|---|---|---|---|
| | | | |
| | | | |
| | | | |

- Share your stories with the whole group.

## 7. *Try It/Apply It* in the Classroom

- Choose one of two options that will have you analyze your instruction with the Optimal Learning Model in mind. In both options, examine your lesson plans to see if you have provided a sufficient amount of demonstration and shared demonstration ("handholding") before releasing responsibility to the student (*"You do it"*).

- **Explain Shared Experiences:** Shared experiences, or "*We do it,*" have many advantages to the learner, yet they are left out of lesson plans more often than demonstration ("*I do it*"), guided practice ("*You/We do it*"), and/or independent practice ("*You do it*"). Typically, students have been expected to complete a task independently following an explanation and/or brief demonstration. Shared experiences provide students with additional demonstrations, scaffolded conversations, and support before students are expected to "do it," which makes success more likely.
  - In a shared demonstration ("*We do it*") lesson, teacher and students work *together* to create a text, solve a math problem, or possibly write up a science experiment. The teacher holds their hands—leading, encouraging, affirming, acknowledging. The handholding provides students the opportunity to try things out without fear of failure.
  - Shared experiences help students figure out questions they need to ask in the *process* of participating, thinking, and problem solving.
  - Shared experiences help students develop the skills, and most importantly the confidence, to begin to master a task successfully.
- Turn to the Optimal Learning Model planning chart enclosed, "Examining Your Instruction with the Optimal Learning Model" sample lesson plus blank form, and "Planning with the OLM in Mind," and review the following options:
  - ***Option 1:*** Use the charts on p. 2–9 to analyze and/or plan: 1) a recent lesson plan from a subject of your choice, 2) a lesson plan in progress, or 3) a lesson plan presented in a teachers' manual that you have used or plan to use. Use the following questions to inspire your thinking:
    - Does my plan provide for one or more demonstrations of the task ("*I do it*")?
    - Does my plan provide multiple opportunities for shared experiences ("*We do it*"—shared writing, shared reading, interactive writing, shared read-aloud)?
    - Does my plan provide opportunities for student/teacher interaction and interaction with peers to practice a skill (guided and independent practice)?
    - Do I have assessments (questions, observations, notes) built into my plan that allow me to know when students are ready for guided practice or independent practice (handover of responsibility)?
  - ***Option 2:*** Keep track of the instructional/learning contexts of an Optimal Learning Model (demonstration, shared learning experiences, guided practice, independent practice, assessment, and celebration) that you include in your instruction.

- Choose a subject (reading, writing, math, science, or social studies) and examine the sequence of your instruction over time (perhaps three days to a week).
- Keep an Optimal Learning Model Log. You may choose to use the one like the table below or design your own.

| Lesson | Teaching/learning context | Result |
|---|---|---|
| | | |
| | | |

- You may want to use the following questions to help write a short reflection in your log or Response Notes page.
  - What went well?
  - What did you notice about your students? Their level of engagement? The quality of their engagement? Their learning?
  - What do you notice about your instruction with regard to the Optimal Learning Model?
  - How does what you notice align (or not align) with your beliefs about teaching and learning?
  - What accommodations did you or do you need to make for struggling, gifted, or English language learners?
  - What changes, if any, do you need to make?
- **Encourage:** Be prepared to share your lesson plan, samples of student work, and your notes, or log, and reflections with your team during the next session.

## 8. Wrap-Up

- Before the next session, read "Apply the Optimal Learning Model" (*Teaching Essentials* excerpt, pp. 88–94 and downloadable from the website) and be prepared to discuss it during the next session.
- Read "The Residency Model" on p. 2–12.

- Schedule time to meet with your vertical, grade-level, and/or partner teams in between whole-group sessions to revisit the videos on the website and the Deeper Understanding charts and/or plan together and try out new learning.
- Remember to bring any charts, lessons, writing, or student work samples from the *Try It/Apply It* to the next session.

SESSION 2

# NOTECATCHER

| KEY WORDS | NOTES & REFLECTION |
|---|---|
| **Optimal Learning Model** *("I do it," "We do it," "You do it")* | |
| **Beliefs about learning** | |
| **Real-world** | |
| **Big picture** | |
| **Whole-part-whole** | |
| **Demonstration** | |
| **Gradual release of responsibility** | |
| **Background experience/ vocabulary** | |
| **Shared demonstration** | |
| **Scaffolding** | |
| **Frontloading** | |
| **Handover of responsibility** | |
| **Enjoyment** | |

# Optimal Learning Model Across the Curriculum

| **Who** Holds Book/Pen | Degree of Explicitness/Support |
|---|---|
| **Teacher**/Student | **Demonstration** |
| **Teacher**/Student | **Shared Demonstration** |
| *gradual handover of responsibility* | |
| **Student**/Teacher | **Guided Practice** |
| **Student**/Teacher | **Independent Practice** |

**DEPENDENCE** → **INDEPENDENCE**

**Ongoing Assessment & Celebration**

| *To Learners* | *With Learners* | | | *By Learners* |
|---|---|---|---|---|
| **I DO IT** | **WE DO IT** | | **WE DO IT** | **YOU DO IT** |
| **Demonstration** | **Shared Demonstration** | handover of responsibility | **Guided Practice** | **Independent Practice** |
| *teacher* | *teacher* | | *student* | *student* |
| • initiates<br>• models<br>• explains<br>• thinks aloud<br>• shows how to "do it" | • demonstrates<br>• leads<br>• negotiates<br>• suggests<br>• supports<br>• explains<br>• responds<br>• acknowledges | | • applies learning<br>• takes charge<br>• practices<br>• problem solves<br>• approximates<br>• self-corrects | • initiates<br>• self-monitors<br>• self-directs<br>• applies learning<br>• problem solves<br>• confirms<br>• self-evaluates |
| *student* | *student* | | *teacher* | *teacher* |
| • listens<br>• observes<br>• may participate on a limited basis | • listens<br>• interacts<br>• questions<br>• collaborates<br>• responds<br>• tries out<br>• approximates<br>• participates as best he can | | • scaffolds<br>• validates<br>• teaches as necessary<br>• evaluates<br>• observes<br>• encourages<br>• clarifies<br>• confirms | • affirms<br>• assists as needed<br>• responds<br>• acknowledges<br>• coaches<br>• evaluates<br>• sets goals |
| *instructional context* | *instructional context* | | *instructional context* | *instructional context* |
| • thinking aloud<br>• reading and writing aloud<br>• direct explanation | • shared reading and writing<br>• interactive reading and writing<br>• shared read aloud<br>• scaffolded conversations | | • guided reading and writing experiences<br>• partner reading and writing<br>• reciprocal teaching<br>• literature conversations | • independent reading and writing<br>• informal conferences<br>• partner reading and writing<br>• homework and assignments |

**Ongoing Assessment & Celebration**

# Abridged Optimal Learning Model Across the Curriculum

| Teaching and Learning Contexts | Who Holds Book/Pen | Degree of Explicitness/Support |
|---|---|---|
| **Celebration & Assessment Are Embedded** | | |
| Reading and Writing Aloud | **Teacher**/Student | **Demonstration** |
| Shared Reading and Writing<br>Scaffolded Conversations | **Teacher**/Student | **Shared Demonstration** |
| *gradual handover of responsibility* | | |
| Guided Reading<br>Literature Conversations<br>Reading/Writing Conferences | **Student**/Teacher | **Guided Practice** |
| Independent Reading/Writing | **Student**/Teacher | **Independent Practice** |
| **Celebration & Assessment Are Embedded** | | |

**Use this condensed version of the Optimal Learning Model for quick reference or as a handy desk reference.**

# Optimal Learning Model in a Daily Literacy Block

## *Thinking, Listening, Speaking, Writing, Reading*

(Includes the minimal 90-minute time requirement for most states)
**End Goal:** Learners *choose* to do meaningful reading and writing activities for their own purposes and audiences, set new goals, take new actions, and learners are able to transfer their learning to new contexts across the curriculum.

Assess

**READING**
**(40–60 minutes)**

**Learning to Read and Reading to Learn Meaningful Texts**

- **Demonstration ("I do it")**
  - Thinks aloud while reading
  - Shows how to read a text
- **Shared Experiences ("We do it")**
  - Shared reading
  - Shared read aloud
  - Scaffolded conversations
- **Guided Practice ("You do it, We do it")** (students try out with support)
  - Sustained reading practice (e.g., guided small-group reading, independent reading practice)
  - Reading conferences (Whole group, small group, partner, one-on-one)
- **Independent Practice ("You do it")**
  - Sustained independent reading (Applies learning, independently problem solves, self-monitors, and self-evaluates

**WORD WORK +**
**(10–30 minutes)**

**(The contextual glue that binds reading and writing)**

*May include:*

**phonemic awareness,**
**phonics,**
**spelling,**
**word study,**
**morphology,**
**and/or vocabulary**

**WRITING**
**(40–60 minutes)**

**Learning to Write and Writing to Learn Meaningful Texts**

- **Demonstration ("I do it")**
  - Thinks aloud while writing
  - Shows how to write a text (e.g., writing aloud)
- **Shared Experiences ("We do it")**
  - Shared writing
  - Interactive writing
  - Scaffolded conversations
- **Guided Practice ("You do it, We do it")** (students try out with support)
  - Sustained writing practice (e.g., small-group support, independent writing practice)
  - Writing conferences (Whole group, small group, partner, one-on-one)
- **Independent Practice ("You do it")**
  - Sustained independent writing (Applies learning, independently problem solves, self-monitors, and self-evaluates)

Celebrate

**Note:** Guided practice is most effective immediately following (on the same day) the demonstration and/or shared demonstration. Most time needs to be spent in guided and independent practice.

# Examining Your Instruction with the Optimal Learning Model

## *Sample Lesson:* Writing Friendly Letters

| ***Who** Holds Book/Pen* | *Degree of Explicitness/Support* | | *Planning Notes* |
|---|---|---|---|
| | **How will I assess the learners? How will I celebrate the learner?** | | |
| **Teacher**/Student | Demonstration | Teaching/Learning Context | |
| **I DO IT** | • **explains**<br>• **shows how to do it (demonstrates)**<br>• **tells** | • **reading aloud**<br>• **writing aloud**<br>• **thinking aloud** | *Read Aloud (Ask: What do you notice about these letters?)*<br>• *Letter models from books by Alma Flor Ada*<br>  • *Yours Truly, Goldilocks*<br>  • *With Love, Little Red Hen*<br>• *Letters from my friends (holiday, thank-you note)*<br>• *Writing Aloud (writing demonstration)*<br>• *Think aloud and write a letter to someone. Demonstrate content and conventions.* |
| **Teacher**/Student | Shared Demonstration | Teaching/Learning Context | |
| **WE DO IT** | • **invites student participation**<br>• **scaffolds**<br>• **negotiates**<br>• **shapes thinking**<br>• **supports** | • **shared reading**<br>• **shared writing**<br>• **shared read-aloud**<br>• **shared experiences**<br>• **scaffolded conversations** | *Shared Experiences*<br>• *Chart students' responses to the question: What do you notice about these letters? (content, format)*<br>*Shared Reading/Shared Writing*<br>• *Project one of the letters from the book or my own letter and read together (continue to notice the characteristics of a friendly letter with students; add to chart)*<br>• *Write a class letter to the principal, another class, or a secretary*<br>• *Have public scaffolded conversations with one or more students before students are released to write on their own* |
| gradual handover of responsibility | | | |
| **Student**/Teacher | Guided Practice | Teaching/Learning Context | |
| **YOU DO IT/ WE DO IT** | • **scaffolds**<br>• **coaches**<br>• **negotiates**<br>• **focuses instruction**<br>• **observes**<br>• **demonstrates as needed** | • **guided reading**<br>• **guided experiences**<br>• **small-group work**<br>• **partner work**<br>• **informal conferences** | *Guided Practice*<br>• *Students talk about their intended letter to a partner before writing*<br>• *Students write letters to friends or relatives*<br>• *Confer with students—affirm, assess, teach what's needed—content and conventions* |
| **Student**/Teacher | Independent Practice | Teaching/Learning Context | |
| **YOU DO IT** | • **assists as needed**<br>• **coaches**<br>• **evaluates** | • **independent reading**<br>• **independent writing**<br>• **independent problem-solving**<br>• **small-group work**<br>• **partner work**<br>• **informal conferences** | • *Students choose to write letters to friends or relatives*<br>• *Students self-monitor, set goals at conference, take over revision and editing*<br>• *Students write letters with a reader in mind* |

# EXAMINING YOUR INSTRUCTION WITH THE OPTIMAL LEARNING MODEL

| *Who Holds Book/Pen* | *Degree of Explicitness/Support* | | *Planning Notes* |
|---|---|---|---|
| | **How will I assess the learners? How will I celebrate the learner?** | | |
| **Teacher**/Student | Demonstration | Teaching/Learning Context | |
| **I DO IT** | • **explains**<br>• **shows how to do it (demonstrates)**<br>• **tells** | • **reading aloud**<br>• **writing aloud**<br>• **thinking aloud** | |
| **Teacher**/Student | Shared Demonstration | Teaching/Learning Context | |
| **WE DO IT** | • **invites student participation**<br>• **scaffolds**<br>• **negotiates**<br>• **shapes thinking**<br>• **supports** | • **shared reading**<br>• **shared writing**<br>• **shared read-aloud**<br>• **shared experiences**<br>• **scaffolded conversations** | |
| gradual handover of responsibility | | | |
| **Student**/Teacher | Guided Practice | Teaching/Learning Context | |
| **YOU DO IT/ WE DO IT** | • **scaffolds**<br>• **coaches**<br>• **negotiates**<br>• **focuses instruction**<br>• **observes**<br>• **demonstrates as needed** | • **guided reading**<br>• **guided experiences**<br>• **small-group work**<br>• **partner work**<br>• **informal conferences** | |
| **Student**/Teacher | Independent Practice | Teaching/Learning Context | |
| **YOU DO IT** | • **assists as needed**<br>• **coaches**<br>• **evaluates** | • **independent reading**<br>• **independent writing**<br>• **independent problem-solving**<br>• **small-group work**<br>• **partner work**<br>• **informal conferences** | |

# Planning with the OLM in Mind

DEPENDENCE → INDEPENDENCE

| TEACHING/LEARNING CONTEXT | TEACHER SELF-ASSESSMENT |
|---|---|
| **Demonstration**<br>I DO IT<br>*(To learners)* | |
| **Shared Demonstration**<br>WE DO IT<br>*(With learners)* | |
| handover of responsibility | |
| **Guided Practice**<br>YOU DO IT/WE DO IT<br>*(With learners)* | |
| **Independent Practice**<br>YOU DO IT<br>*(By learners)* | |

# THE RESIDENCY MODEL

The videos for this professional development program were filmed during my residencies in schools in Colorado, Tennessee, and Washington state. The videos are intentionally low-tech because I didn't want to detract from the authenticity with lights, additional cameras, and microphones everywhere.

Why a one-week residency model? By working with teachers over five consecutive days, I can recreate the same model for teachers that excellent teachers provide for students. That is, a teaching/learning model that includes much scaffolding and builds confidence and competence through demonstrations, shared demonstrations, guided practice, and independent practice—all with challenging and relevant curriculum and content. This learning model is really a coaching model that gradually releases responsibility to the learner so that the learner eventually self-directs, self-evaluates, and sets worthwhile goals. By extension, the professional development that you are now involved in is a coaching model. The *Try It/Apply It* exploration given to you at the end of each session is the "you do it" phase of the Optimal Learning Model. In your session evaluation, be candid if you feel you need more opportunities for independence and choice during and outside of sessions. The whole goal of this professional development program is to have it meet the needs of individual teachers.

Here is more background about my residencies so you'll know the full context of what you are viewing on the videos:

Before my visit, the principal or an instructional leader in the school surveys teachers for interests, needs, questions, and concerns regarding the chosen residency focus, usually reading or writing. The principal or instructional leader makes me aware of goals at each grade level and across grade levels, and together we draft a weekly plan and determine necessary resources.

The plan usually includes:

- A weekly teaching plan and focus in both a primary classroom (A.M.) and an intermediate classroom (P.M.) that involves a daily 2½ hour flexible block with the same students and teacher, in their respective classrooms.
- Demonstration teaching (each day).
- Following the Optimal Learning Model: Gradually moving to coaching each of the host teachers in their classrooms—by teaching alongside them (by the end of the week) and by guiding and supporting them as they try out what I have been demonstrating.
- Daily, voluntary after-school professional conversations. (Some of these may be reserved for a particular grade level where I have not done classroom demonstrations.)
- One whole-staff, interactive literacy workshop (2 hours) on our curriculum focus.

- Time on the first day to tour the school, meet teachers and students, and finalize planning by meeting one-on-one for 30 minutes with each host teacher.

For each demonstration lesson in a classroom, teachers at the grade level and adjacent grade levels are released to observe in the host classroom. (The principal or instructional leader works out a plan, often using roving substitutes to make this observation possible.) Teachers have an opportunity, before and after the lesson, to comment and raise questions. Teachers are encouraged to try out what I have been demonstrating.

Each 2½ hour literacy block is flexibly structured as follows:

- 30–45 minutes to meet with teachers and discuss lesson purpose and contents, what to watch for, answer questions, clarify thinking.
- 60–75 minutes of demonstration teaching and working with students (with teachers and the principal observing) in the host classroom.
- 30–45 minutes debriefing (explaining why I did what I did—for example, changing my initial plan to meet students' needs; or answering teachers' questions; or asking them, "What did you notice?" and discussing the next day's plan and the rationale for it).

This residency model, combining dialogue and demonstrations, supports the importance of collegial conversation, which is where the bulk of the learning for teachers occurs.

After several years of doing this sustained professional development work, I've augmented my residency model with a stronger coaching strand for principals. Schoolwide high achievement does not occur without strong principal leadership and knowledge. Thus, in year two and beyond I coach the principal for at least 1 hour each day, usually in the afternoons. (That means we have shortened each of the two literacy blocks, one primary and one intermediate, to 1½ hours or 2 hours.) I demonstrate what to look for in students and in classrooms, how to assume the role of coach and co-teacher (and not evaluator, at this time), how to recognize and comment on each teacher's strengths, and how to identify schoolwide issues to be addressed by the whole staff. When possible, the principal often has her or his assistant principal and literacy coach join us so they can continue to work together as a leadership team after the residency.

SESSION 2

# RESPONSENOTES

***Engage, Reflect, Assess, Celebrate!***

REGIE ROUTMAN in RESIDENCE

**Transforming** our **Teaching** through
**Reading/Writing Connections**

# Examining Our Beliefs About Reading/Writing Connections

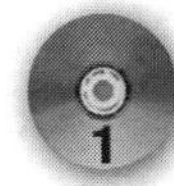

**View Video** (18 min.)

**Examining Our Beliefs About Reading/Writing Connections**

- **Interview with a First-Grade Teacher**
- **Interview with a Fourth-Grade Teacher**

## 1. Engage, Reflect, Assess

- *Small-Group Share:* Share with your vertical team the results of examining the sequence of your instruction over time. Did you notice the components of the Optimal Learning Model (demonstration, shared learning experiences, guided practice, independent practice, assessment, and celebration) in your plans?
- *Whole-Group Share:* Discuss your findings.
    - How did your lesson go?
    - When you taught your lesson with the Optimal Learning Model in mind:
        - What did you notice?
        - How did your students respond?
        - Were there any surprises?
        - What changes, if any, do you need to make?
        - What accommodations did you need to make for struggling, gifted or English language learners?

**RESOURCES**

- Group Process for Examining Our Beliefs About Reading/Writing Connections (options 1 and 2) *3–6*

- Beliefs About Reading/ Writing Connections *3–8*
- Favorite Books on the Reading/Writing Connection *3–10*

## 2. Discuss Professional Reading

- Discuss "Apply the Optimal Learning Model" (*Teaching Essentials* excerpt, pp. 88–94 and downloadable from the website) as a whole group, with your vertical team, or with a partner.

## 3. Goals

- Use the video as a catalyst for thinking about how to apply the Optimal Learning Model to your teaching of reading/writing connections.
- See how continually moving back and forth between reading and writing in your teaching helps students make greater gains in literacy and become more engaged.
- Identify personal beliefs about the reading/writing connection.
- Identify beliefs about reading/writing connections that teachers in your school or district hold in common.
- Identify beliefs about reading/writing connections that the teachers in your school or district **do not** hold in common.
- Begin to align school-/districtwide reading/writing beliefs with teaching practices.

## 4. View Video and Take Notes

- Turn to the Notecatcher to take notes. Also review "Group Process for Examining Our Beliefs About Reading/Writing Connections (options 1 and 2)" on p. 3–6. In vertical teams, explore your beliefs about reading/writing connections. Note that you can decide which option works best for your team.

## 5. Respond to the Video

- Respond to the conversation between the teachers and Regie Routman. Ask yourself:
    - Why is it essential to maximize reading/writing connections across the curriculum for optimal instruction, learning, and achievement?
    - What did these teachers change in their practice that impacted their teaching and, in turn, their students?
    - How did both teachers begin to incorporate the Optimal Learning Model into their daily teaching? What were the outcomes?
    - What have you learned that you can apply to your own beliefs and practices about reading/writing connections?

## 6. Achieve a Deeper Understanding

- ***Whole-Group Share:*** Create a consensus beliefs statement about reading/writing connections for the entire staff to adopt.
- Your facilitator will choose one of the two group share options on p. 3–6 and 3–7.
  - Look at the charts created by the vertical teams during the group process. What do you see?
  - What aspects of teaching reading/writing connections engender the most agreement? Disagreement?

## 7. *Try It/Apply It* in the Classroom

- Reflect on your core beliefs about reading/writing connections and how they drive your teaching practices.
- Think about several practices that are working schoolwide to promote high achievement and several practices that are impeding schoolwide achievement:
  - *How do schoolwide beliefs impact your teaching?*
  - *What have you noticed?*
  - *What are some possible suggestions for raising achievement?*
  - *How might strengthening reading/writing connections improve instruction and student achievement?*
- Be prepared to share your reflections with your team or with the whole group in the next session.

## 8. Wrap-Up

- Before the next session, read "Align Your Beliefs with Your Practices" (*Teaching Essentials* excerpt, pp. 37–39) and "Capitalize on the Reading–Writing Connection" (*Writing Essentials* excerpt, pp. 119–120 and downloadable from the website).

- Schedule time to meet with your vertical, grade-level, and/or partner teams in between whole-group sessions to revisit the videos on the website and the Deeper Understanding charts and/or plan together and try out new learning. You can jot down your ideas and thinking on your Response Notes page for easy reference later.
- Remember to bring any charts, lessons, writing, or student work samples from the *Try It/Apply It* to the next session.

SESSION **3**

# **NOTE**CATCHER

| KEY WORDS | NOTES & REFLECTION |
| --- | --- |
| **Shared demonstrations** | |
| **Scaffolding** | |
| **Shared writing** | |
| **Negotiating** | |

SESSION 3

# NOTECATCHER

| KEY WORDS | NOTES & REFLECTION |
|---|---|
| More demonstrations | |
| Efficiency | |
| Whole-part-whole teaching | |

# Group Process for Examining Our Beliefs About Reading/Writing Connections

## *(Option 1)*

### PURPOSE OF THE ACTIVITY

- To think about and challenge individual and group beliefs about teaching and learning.
- To establish consensus on group's common beliefs (a prerequisite for improving instruction and raising achievement), whether it's a couple of beliefs held in common or many.
- To begin building a schoolwide team that has a high level of trust and collaboration.
- To use the group's consensus of beliefs held in common as a self-assessment for what the staff knows and understands about teaching reading and writing as well as for the status of collegial conversations.

### OPTION 1

***In small-group teams (vertical, grade level, or partner):***

- Give participants time to individually, silently read through the lists of beliefs (pp. 3–8 and 3–9) and note those they feel most strongly about (positive or negative).
- Ask participants to freely discuss those beliefs with their team and/or partners.
- Ask each group to select a scribe.
- Have groups discuss beliefs while the scribe records the group's points of agreement/disagreement.
- Bring the whole group together. Take one or more of each groups' most important, agreed-upon beliefs and write them on a chart so they are visible to all participants.
- Note and discuss key areas of agreement and/or disagreement.
- Ask participants to pinpoint what was most striking for them to discover. Ask them to consider what it means for their daily instruction.
- Encourage them to continually think about how beliefs impact teaching practices.
- Revisit individual and group beliefs at the end of the professional development program.

# Group Process for Examining Our Beliefs About Reading/Writing Connections

## (Option 2)

### PURPOSE OF THE ACTIVITY

- To think about individual and group beliefs about teaching and learning.
- To establish consensus on group's common beliefs (a prerequisite for improving instruction and raising achievement).
- To begin building a schoolwide team that has a high level of trust and collaboration.

### OPTION 2

***In vertical teams or grade-level teams:***

- Participants identify one of the statements that struck them from the lists of beliefs (pp. 3–8 and 3–9).
- The first person begins by choosing a statement about which she feels strongly.
- Each person responds to the statement by saying, "I agree or I disagree with the statement" and tells why.
- The purpose of the response is to expand on the colleague's thinking about the issues, to provide a different look at the issue, to clarify thinking about the issues, and to question the colleague's assumptions about the issue.
- After going around the circle with each person responding, the first person shares whether he chose the statement because he agreed or disagreed with it and why.
- Write every statement the whole team agrees with on the chart paper provided. These statements will be brought back to the whole group.
- This process continues until everyone has had the opportunity to share their statements or until the time is over. (Typically, each participant gets to share 3–4 beliefs.)
- Meet together as a whole group. Share charts of agreement.
- Put an asterisk next to areas of agreement that are in common on all of the charts.
- You will revisit your core beliefs at the end of the professional development program as one way to assess your growth as a teacher and as a school.

# Beliefs About Reading/Writing Connections

Read, think about, and discuss the following statements with your colleagues. (There are no right or wrong answers.) Use these beliefs to get conversations going in your school and to begin to develop a common belief system about reading/writing connections.

Please read the following statements and write an "A" if you agree with the statement or a "D" if you disagree with the statement.

1. ____ For struggling readers, reading their own writing is often their first successful reading experience.

2. ____ Students who write more nonfiction texts have higher reading comprehension.

3. ____ Young children need to know all their letters and sounds before they can write stories and read back their writing.

4. ____ Taking dictation of a child's story can lead to reading that story.

5. ____ A child's written story can be used to teach phonics and skills.

6. ____ You can assess a child's phonemic awareness by examining his/her journal writing.

7. ____ Kindergarten students who write meaningful text daily learn to read faster.

8. ____ The purpose of shared writing is to focus on teaching conventions.

9. ____ English language learners can more easily read a written text that deals with familiar concepts.

10. ____ Explaining vocabulary through interactive read-aloud can lead to students applying that vocabulary in their reading and writing.

11. ____ Students who use graphic organizers before they write have higher reading comprehension.

**12.**_____ The more writing students do, the better readers they become.

**13.**_____ Reading achievement is higher when students read and write more nonfiction texts.

**14.**_____ Kindergarten students can write with elaboration, detail, and voice and read back their writing.

**15.**_____ A good way to work on a child's reading is to help him/her become a strong writer.

**16.**_____ Students who are fluent, comprehending readers easily internalize the rules of grammar, punctuation, and spelling.

**17.**_____ Interactive writing and shared writing are the same and serve the same purpose.

**18.**_____ Shared writing is an excellent way to record common experiences and connect to reading.

**19.**_____ Shared writing texts that evolve from common experiences are often the easiest texts to read.

**20.**_____ Taking notes while reading aids reading comprehension.

**21.**_____ Reading excellent literature and/or hearing quality literature read aloud positively influences students' writing quality.

# Favorite Books on the Reading/Writing Connection

We have long embraced the idea that reading and writing are inextricably linked. However, little has been written to actually help us connect the two. We know that inviting students to see the complementary relationship between reading and writing and to mine the treasures at that intersection is valuable. Because so few texts richly explore this topic, we've listed only the best. See the website for new favorites as we discover them.

- The first edition of ***Creating Classrooms for Authors and Inquirers*** by Jerome Harste, Kathy Short, and Carolyn Burke presents engaging ways to plan thoughtful instruction. In it, the authors suggest a variety of ways that naturally connect reading and writing. In the second edition, they use inquiry as a metaphor for creating curriculum. As in the first edition, the same tried-and-true invitations are described that facilitate students transitions from reader to writer and back again. (Heinemann, 2nd Edition, 1995)
- ***Reading and Writing Informational Text in the Primary Grades*** by Nell Duke and V. Susan Bennett-Armistead presents a comprehensive look at both the challenges and possibilities of encouraging children to read and write informational texts. This accessible resource offers book lists and a thorough discussion of genres, as well as practical suggestions for weaving this important (and sometimes neglected) genre into classroom routines and structures. While the title suggests it is for primary teachers, the ideas are applicable well beyond the primary grades. (Scholastic, 2003)
- Tony Stead's ***Is That a Fact? Teaching Nonfiction Writing K–3*** links the purposes and forms of writing to the personal interests of children. Stead's attention to details, such as how to organize informational texts in the classroom, ensures that teachers will be able to quickly put to use the bounty of ideas presented in this text. The ideas presented in the book are easily adapted for older students. In addition to the book, several video series further illuminate and extend these ideas. (Stenhouse, 2001)
- Laura Robb creates a remarkable text in ***Nonfiction Writing from the Inside Out: Writing Lessons Inspired By Conversations with Leading Authors.*** By connecting children to the inside story of how the people they read write, students gain insights into both reading and writing. Not only will their understanding of reading deepen, they will also sharpen their attention to the craft inherent in quality writing. (Scholastic, 2004)

- There are times when educators must turn to reading to renew their own passion and spirit. These books often come from outside education, but they nurture us and energize our professional lives by offering wisdom and understanding. Francine Prose's ***Reading Like a Writer: A Guide for People Who Love Books and Want to Write Them*** is such a book. Both educative and inspirational, the book contains both sound advice and an insider's perspective on both reading and writing. The book includes not only how to read closely, but it also examines the craft of writing. Prose admonishes readers "to slow down and pay attention..." and engage in careful, close reading. (Harper Collins, 2006)

*—Compiled by Judy Wallis with Regie Routman*

SESSION 3

# RESPONSE NOTES

*Engage, Reflect, Assess, Celebrate!*

REGIE ROUTMAN in RESIDENCE

**Transforming** our **Teaching** through
**Reading/Writing Connections**

# Setting Up the Classroom for Independent Readers and Writers

**View Video** (35 min.)

**Setting Up the Classroom for Independent Readers and Writers**

- **Start with Your Own Stories**
- **Organize an Outstanding Classroom Library**
- **Let Assessment Inform You: What Do Good Readers and Writers Do?**
- **Connect Real-World Writing and Reading**
- **Independent Practice: Students Writing and Reading**
- **Celebration/Evaluation: Fourth-Grade Writing**

## 1. Engage, Reflect, Assess

- Review the *Try It/Apply It Activity.*
- *Small-Group Share*
  - Share your thoughts and ideas with a partner and/or your vertical teams.
- *Whole-Group Share*
  - *Identify several schoolwide practices that promote high achievement and several that impede achievement.*
  - *How do schoolwide beliefs impact your teaching?*
  - *What have you noticed?*
  - *What are some possible suggestions for raising schoolwide achievement?*

**RESOURCES**

**In this Session**

- What to Look for in a Classroom: Self-Evaluation and/or Observation Checklist *4–6*

**On the Website**

- Using the Goldilocks Strategy to Choose Books
- Choosing Books for Independent Reading
- Photographs of Classroom Libraries
- Observation Checklist
- Sharing My Reading and Writing Life *(optional video)*

## 2. Discuss Professional Reading

- Discuss "Align Your Beliefs with Your Practices" (*Teaching Essentials*, pp. 37–39) and "Capitalize on the Reading–Writing Connection" (*Writing Essentials* excerpt, pp. 119–120 and downloadable from the website).

## 3. Goals

- Begin to establish and set expectations for a self-sustaining, independent classroom environment for readers and writers.
- Begin to establish and organize, with considerable student input, an excellent classroom library and reading area.
- Assess what your students know and do relative to choosing books to read.
- Use a shared writing assessment to find out what your students know about reading and writing. Ask: "*What do good readers do? What do good writers do?*" then adjust your instruction accordingly.
- Assess what your students know about why people write in their daily lives and what forms that writing takes. Ask: "*Why do people write? What do people write?*"

## 4. View Video and Take Notes

- Turn to the Notecatcher to take notes.

## 5. Respond to the Video

- ***Small Group or Whole Group:*** Respond to the discussion questions.
  - *What did you notice and wonder about when you observed the teachers share how they set up their classroom libraries?*
  - *What did you observe being taught and assessed?*
  - *What was each teacher doing to begin to help students become independent and successful readers and writers?*
  - *What parts of the Optimal Learning Model* ("I do it," "We do it," "You do it") *did you observe?*

## 6. Achieve a Deeper Understanding

- Read and review the Deeper Understanding charts.
- The Notes, Teaching Points, and Ongoing Assessments in the charts include the language the teacher in the video used.
- In your teams, use the Deeper Understanding charts as a basis for discussing the video scenes.
- Remember that the charts are designed to help you connect more deeply with your own notes, observations, and ideas.

## 7. *Try It/Apply It* in the Classroom

Between this session and the next session:

PART 1:

- Share your reading life with your students (by sharing or starting a reading log or by talking about how you choose the kinds of books and other materials you read) and/or share your writing life (by sharing samples of things you've written recently, such as emails, letters, postcards, to-do lists).

PART 2:

- Examine your classroom library collection for balance of genres and student appeal: narrative, fiction, poetry, nonfiction, favorite authors, a variety of interesting reading materials.
- Notice how your classroom library organization impacts students' access to books and motivation to read.
- Refer to the "What to Look for in a Classroom" checklist and assess and adjust your classroom's learning environment.

PART 3:

- Select one or all of the following topics to write about with your students (shared writing):
  - *How do we choose books to read from the classroom library?*
  - *What do good writers do?*
  - *What do good readers do?*
  - *Why do people write? What do people write?*

- Use the information gathered from this shared writing to adjust and guide your teaching. Refer to the resources on the website: "Using the Goldilocks Strategy to Choose Books" and "Choosing Books for Independent Reading" for assistance and ideas.
- Notice what your students know about authors, genres, reading for understanding, and so on.
- Be prepared to share your class-generated shared writings (and your observations about them) with your team at the next session.

## 8. Wrap-Up

- Before the next session, read "Organize an Outstanding Classroom Library" (*Reading Essentials* excerpt, pp. 63–77 and downloadable from the website) and be prepared to discuss it during next session.
- Schedule time to meet with your vertical, grade-level, and/or partner teams in between whole-group sessions to revisit the videos on the website and the Deeper Understanding charts and/or plan together and try out new learning. You can jot down your ideas and thinking on your Response Notes page for easy reference later.
- Remember to bring any charts, lessons, writing, or student work samples from *Try It/Apply It* to the next session.

SESSION **4** **NOTE**CATCHER

| VIDEO SCENES | LENGTH | NOTES & REFLECTION |
|---|---|---|
| **Start with Your Own Stories** | 2:57 min. | |
| **Organize an Outstanding Classroom Library**<br>• Getting Started: Organizing and Choosing Books to Read from the Classroom Library, Grade 1<br>• Getting Started: Organizing and Choosing Books to Read from the Classroom Library, Grade 4<br>• How Do We Choose Books to Read from the Classroom Library? Grade 1 (Shared Writing Chart) | 12:06 min. | |

## SESSION 4 NOTECATCHER

| VIDEO SCENES | LENGTH | NOTES & REFLECTION |
|---|---|---|
| **Let Assessment Inform You: What Do Good Readers and Writers Do?**<br>• What Do Good Readers Do? Grade 1<br>• What Do Good Writers Do? Grade 1 | 8:56 min. | |
| **Connect Real-World Writing and Reading**<br>• Teacher as Writer<br>• Why Do People Write? What Do People Write? | 8:08 min. | |
| **Independent Practice: Students Writing and Reading** | 0:45 min. | |
| **Celebration/Evaluation: Fourth-Grade Writing** | 2:01 min | |

# What to Look for in a Classroom

## *Self-Evaluation and/or Observation Checklist*

*You can use this form for collegial observations, ongoing conversations, and self-evaluation.*

### THE **CLASSROOM**

- ☐ **Are the bulletin boards or wall and hall displays by and for the students and other audiences?** Is student work labeled and displayed everywhere, and is each student's work unique? Are displays and classroom procedure lists mostly created with and by students, and do they include samples of writing, illustrations, and projects (as opposed to commercial materials)? Is written work error-free or appropriately labeled as "unedited"? Are students using classroom resources for reading, writing, and problem solving? Are visuals such as word walls appropriate and useful, at eye level, or otherwise easily accessible to all students?
- ☐ **Is there a classroom library and cozy reading corner?** Is there a balance of fiction, nonfiction, highly engaging books, and other texts attractively displayed and easily accessible? Have the students had a say in organizing the library? Are there classroom procedures in place for choosing books and returning them to the proper place? Is there an attractive reading area where students can read comfortably with a friend? Are there reference books and dictionaries available?
- ☐ **Is there a writing center?** Is there an area where students can easily find different kinds of paper and writing supplies? Are there many opportunities for written explorations of a topic of study?
- ☐ **Does the seating and room arrangement allow for collaboration?** Are students grouped so they can assist and confer with one another? Is the structure heterogeneous—that is, are students grouped to reflect the total makeup of the classroom?
- ☐ **Is there a meeting area for the class to work as a whole group?** Is this area supplied with an easel, chart paper, markers, an author's chair, and so on?
- ☐ **Does the room look and feel inviting?** Are there touches that make the room unique and appealing, such as lamps, cushions in the reading area, an author's chair, welcome messages by the students, the attractive arrangement and organization of desks, books, and materials?
- ☐ **Would a visitor understand and value the posted work?**

## THE **TEACHER**

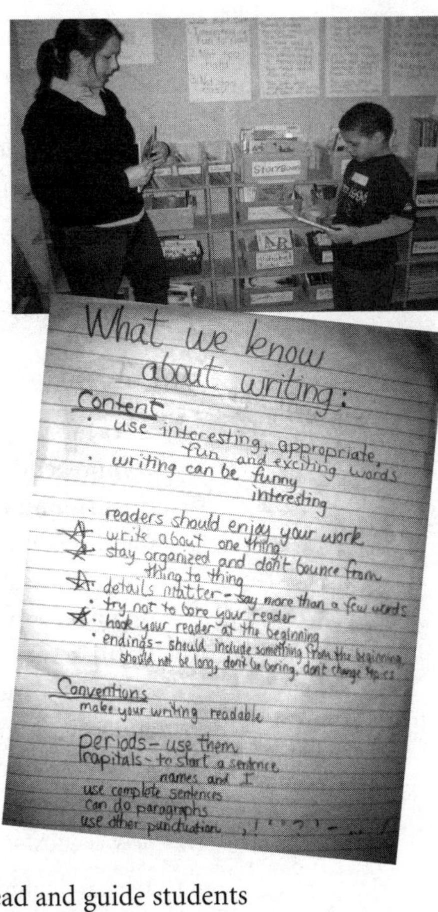


- ☐ **Are the daily reading and writing opportunities meaningful and relevant?** Do students know, understand, and value the purpose of and audience for the activity? Do students take responsibility for doing their best work? Is the quality of much of the work excellent?
- ☐ **Is the teacher ensuring success for every student?** Is the teacher demonstrating and explaining what students are to do? Are students supported, through shared and guided experiences and appropriate resources, in trying out a task or activity before they are expected to attempt it on their own? Is instruction adjusted and differentiated according to students' needs and interests? Are English language learners, gifted learners, typical and struggling students, all being challenged and helped to meet their full potential? Are expectations high enough?
- ☐ **Does the teacher value conversation with students and among students?** Does the teacher promote purposeful, open-ended talk that is more conversational than interrogational? Does the teacher speak with authority and at the same time respectfully lead and guide students to respond thoughtfully? Are there opportunities for students to turn-and-talk during demonstrations? Is the teacher mostly among students, demonstrating, guiding, and conferring?
- ☐ **Does the teacher use a balance of assessment and evaluation practices?** Does the teacher evaluate students regularly, giving them feedback and helping them set goals? Does she use mostly formative assessments (daily work samples, observational data, teacher-made tests) as well as required summative assessments (standardized tests, district assessments)? Are the students shown how and are they able to do self-assessments so they learn to evaluate their own work against a set of criteria (rubric), problem-solve, and set new learning goals?
- ☐ **Does the teacher provide opportunities during the day to celebrate students' work?** Does he focus on students' strengths before suggesting improvement?

## THE **STUDENTS**

- ☐ **Do the students know and apply the routines and procedures?** Do they help establish some routines and procedures with the teacher, assume responsibility for following all of them, use peers as helpers, and undertake some self-management? Is there a well-planned flow from one activity to another? Does the classroom run smoothly even when the teacher is absent?

- ☐ **Are there opportunities for students to work together as well as individually?** Are pairs and small groups of students reading, writing, and problem-solving together? Have students been taught and had guided practice in how to work well in a group? Is there time for sharing every day? Do students have ongoing opportunities in various group structures to participate and deliberate and make their voices heard?
- ☐ **Are the children excited about the opportunities for learning in their classroom?** Is the tone of the classroom peaceful, happy, and energized? Do students take initiative and choose to go on learning even when it's not required?

## THE **WORK**

- ☐ **Is teaching and learning focused on comprehending?** Do students have frequent opportunities to respond to open-ended questions and participate in high-level discussions? Are reading and writing focused on understanding content as well as on learning sounds, letters, and words? Are children spending most of their time reading and writing meaningful texts (and not only in activities centered on reading and writing)? Can students apply what they are learning to new contexts?  
- ☐ **Are curriculum and standards being addressed in a relevant and meaningful way?** Is content presented in an interesting and relevant manner, with accommodations made to meet the needs of all students? Is background knowledge provided and vocabulary explained so content to be read, studied, and written makes sense? Is test preparation appropriate—that is, are students taught how to be test wise without being asked to spend an excessive amount of time responding to prompts and taking practice tests?
- ☐ **Is reading focused on a variety of genres and authors, highly engaging texts, and students' interests?** Is there evidence that students are able to select *just right* books to read independently? How can you tell if students are understanding what they are reading and not just reading words? Is there evidence that students are doing a great deal of focused and intentional reading for enjoyment?
- ☐ **Do students use, apply, and transfer word work to reading and writing across the curriculum?** What evidence of this do you see?
- ☐ **Is writing focused on purpose, audience, and content?** Are students creating texts with purpose for an authentic audience? Are students learning to respect the reader by focusing on meaning and editing carefully for conventions and spelling? Are students given the opportunity to write in a variety of genres?

- ☐ **Is the independent work the students are doing worthwhile?** Are students given purposeful activities that encourage open-ended responses that require them to think and apply their experience and knowledge? If there are learning centers, are they worth the students' time and is the teacher taking the time to evaluate the work students do?

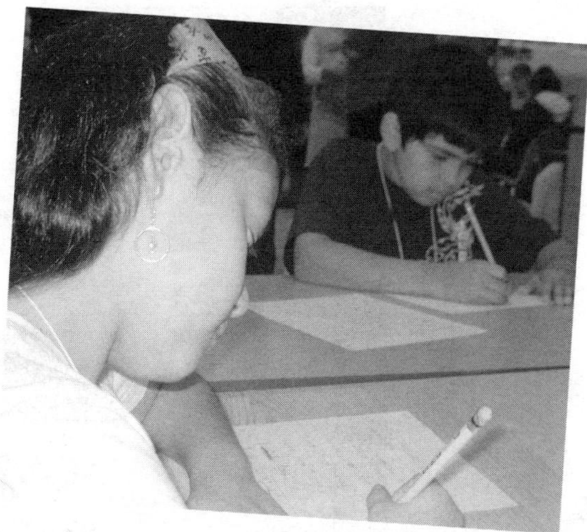

- ☐ **Do the students have enough choices?** Are there opportunities for students to make decisions about their work for the day? Are there some reading and writing activities they can choose themselves? Can students choose their writing topics much of the time?

SESSION 4

Setting Up the Classroom for Independent Readers and Writers

# DEEPER UNDERSTANDING

*The teaching and assessing points reflect the total lesson but not all of these points are on the edited videos you are watching. However, the major points are represented on the edited videos.*

The globe icon indicates that the example is also available when you visit www.regieroutman.com.

| *Video* SCENES | Setting, Notes, and Explicit Teaching Points<br>The What, Why, and How of Teaching | Ongoing Assessment<br>Informing Our Instruction | Questions/Reflections<br>For Professional Conversations | Learning Outcomes<br>What Students Know and Are Able to Do |
|---|---|---|---|---|
| | **SETTING**<br>The scenes in this session come from five classrooms in four schools where I was conducting weeklong demonstration teaching and coaching residencies. Each school has a large number of low-income students and students for whom English is a second language. In each school, reading and writing were being taught with a variety of approaches, programs, and materials with a heavy emphasis on skills in isolation (part-to-whole teaching). | | | **First-grade teacher Mary Yuhas coaches a student as he selects a book from the classroom library.** |
| **Start with Your Own Stories**<br>(2:57 min.) | **NOTES**<br>Bond with your students by sharing your own stories. Let yourself be known. Our students are much more likely to trust us and to take risks in their writing and verbal expression when we tell stories that let them know who we are and that show we care about them. I start with a story whenever I am teaching a new group of students and whenever I want to engage them immediately. | **Regie tells the class about her cat Norman.** | • What are the benefits of connecting personally to students? | |
| **Organize an Outstanding Classroom Library**<br>(12:06 min.) | We begin with organizing the classroom library because in order for students to become independent readers and writers they must do a great deal of reading (and writing), have access to texts they can and want to read, and have lots of time to read them. This reading time must include teaching, guiding, and especially offering students the opportunity to practice and apply what they are learning. An excellent classroom library, especially when it is well organized with and by students, encourages lots of free choice. In these first scenes, I am talking with first-grade teacher Mary Yuhas, and then, fourth-grade teacher Ginny Vale, who discuss and show | Find out what students know (check for understanding). *"Tell how your library is organized. Did your teacher leave anything out?"*<br><br>Check that students know what to do and can use appropriate strategies (check for application).<br>• *"Can you read all the categories* [on the bin]? *What could you do as a good reader if you can't read the words* | • How can an excellent library lessen the need to create "seat work"? (During guided reading and when meeting with small groups or individuals.)<br><br>• Why is it essential to check for understanding before, during, and after a lesson? | • Understand how to use classroom resources (classroom library).<br><br>• Begin to self-manage classroom library and organization. |

**Video SCENES**

**DEEPER UNDERSTANDING: Setting Up the Classroom for Independent Readers and Writers**

| | Setting, Notes, and Explicit Teaching Points<br>The What, Why, and How of Teaching | Ongoing Assessment<br>Informing Our Instruction | Questions/Reflections<br>For Professional Conversations | Learning Outcomes<br>What Students Know and Are Able to Do |
|---|---|---|---|---|
| • Getting Started: Organizing and Choosing Books to Read from the Classroom Library, Grade 1 | how their libraries are getting organized at the start of the school year. In past years, both teachers had previously done all the organizing for students; now students own the process.<br><br>Levels help the teacher select guided reading books. However, books are not leveled in libraries in real life. My recommendation is to give children free and open access to your classroom library and to teach children how to choose *just right* books. The exception would be those few struggling readers who are not yet ready to select appropriate books on their own.<br><br>**TEACHING POINTS**<br>• Set up an excellent classroom library to increase students' reading comprehension, reading choices, and access to books.<br>• Organize books, with student input, so students can access them easily.<br>• Help students categorize books, put them in bins, and label the bins (perhaps with picture cues on labels).<br>• When choosing a book (if you can't read the titles) look at the cover of the books and look through the books in the bins to help determine the category (counting, rhyming, animals, and so on).<br>• Think out loud as you determine a bin's category: *"This is a book about birds. Here are some animals at the ocean. Here are some cats and pandas. Oh! This is the animals bin."* | *category* [label] *on the bin?"*<br>*"Sound it out."*<br>*"But what if you couldn't sound it out? What else could you do?"*<br>*"Look at the first word and see what would make sense."*<br>*"OK . . . how else can you tell what it's about? This is really important. What do you know about all the books that are in the box? How are they organized? Let's have somebody come up here and help us with that."*<br><br>Teach what students need. Because students don't mention using the illustrations to help find/choose a book (or difficulty of reading level), we need to model that next. *"The pictures didn't come out* [in student responses]. *So let's do a demonstration about how important it is to look at that* [the pictures]*."* | <br><br>• Think about your classroom library. Is it central and vital to your reading lessons?<br>• Do your students know how to choose books they can read? How do you know?<br>• Are students selecting books based on topics and interest, or is there an overemphasis on book levels?<br><br> | **Regie tells the class that she's impressed at how well the students did in organizing their library. "I could tell right away that this was your library."**<br><br>• Begin to use features of fiction and nonfiction texts.<br>• Use reading strategies in selecting text. |
| • Getting Started: Organizing and Choosing Books to Read from the Classroom Library, Grade 4 | **NOTES**<br>The way the classroom library looks and is organized is a strong indicator of what the teacher values, who the classroom belongs to, and how much students choose to read. Aim for a beautiful library that is content-rich and part of a cozy, eye-catching reading area. Have students carefully write the labels on the bins that house books and reading materials (this provides a more child-centered, unique feel than a word-processed label). | | | |

continues

## Video SCENES

**DEEPER UNDERSTANDING: Setting Up the Classroom for Independent Readers and Writers**

| Video Scenes | Setting, Notes, and Explicit Teaching Points<br>The What, Why, and How of Teaching | Ongoing Assessment<br>Informing Our Instruction | Questions/Reflections<br>For Professional Conversations | Learning Outcomes<br>What Students Know and Are Able to Do |
|---|---|---|---|---|
| **Organize an Outstanding Classroom Library, *continued*** | **TEACHING POINTS**<br>• Organize the classroom library by the categories kids come up with (with teacher guidance): sort classroom books first into fiction and nonfiction and then by topic. Place books in bins by category.<br>• Have bins for favorite authors (students' and teacher's).<br>• With students, make a genre chart as part of your library to ensure kids know the characteristics of different types of books.<br>• Check that students are understanding what they read and are reading mostly *just right* books. (See *Reading Essentials,* pp. 94–95.) | • What important categories, authors, genres, are underrepresented in the classroom library (for students' interests, for the teacher's needs)? Aim for about 50 percent nonfiction titles/authors.<br>• Check to be sure students know how to find the reading materials they seek.<br>• Ask students: *"How is your library organized? How do you find the books you need or want? What is missing?"*<br>• Use student responses to help you stock and organize your library. | • How can a library organized with and by students impact students' desire to read and their access to books and other reading materials?<br>• How might you as a staff learn about new books and magazines?<br>• How might you as a staff acquire books for your classroom libraries? | • Identify and sort text by fiction and nonfiction. |
| • How Do We Choose Books to Read from the Classroom Library? Grade 1 (Shared Writing Chart) | **NOTES**<br>*Plan for and Monitor Independent Readers and Writers: Start with Assessment.* This is the broader heading for the next clip, which is almost entirely about first checking what students know about choosing a book to read from the classroom library before teaching them what they need to know. This gentle, specific, and affirming questioning and response is an example of responsive teaching (primarily active involvement, which leads to higher achievement) versus telling teaching (primarily passive listening, which leads to lower achievement). | Think about the students who concern you most. Ask yourself: How did I give them opportunities to talk today? Did they seem actively engaged? | • What are the qualities of responsive teaching that might lead to higher student engagement and achievement?<br>• How would you characterize your school's culture? Is it a responsive teaching culture or a telling teaching culture? | |
| | **TEACHING POINTS**<br>• Connect the classroom library to becoming a good reader and choosing books to read.<br>• Connect writing to reading. *"See if you can figure it out* [begins to write title of chart, How Do We Choose Books to Read?]. *Watch me write. Now I have to see if I got it right* [rereading title]. *I've got to check my writing. Read it with me."* And, later on, *"When you're writing, you always have to reread. I left out a word. I'm going to put a caret here."*<br>• Record and make visible (on a chart) students' thinking in order to assess what they know about choosing books to read (so you can validate what they know and see what's needed for instruction). | Use shared writing to assess what your students know about the behavior of good readers and writers. Use their responses as an instructional guide to what they need. As students' knowledge grows, keep adding to the chart (your evidence of student learning).<br><br>Check that students know how to choose books they can actually read. *"What does a good reader do?"*<br>Probe students' thinking (so you know what they know and what you need to | • Often, students can parrot our language and say what a good reader does without actually doing what they say. (They can "talk the talk.") How can we ensure that students know and apply how to choose appropriate books to read? | • Begin to self-select text to read at *just the right level* (94%–96% accuracy) and independent level (97%–100% accuracy).<br>• Reread for meaning with teacher guidance.<br>• Reread to self-correct.<br>• With teacher guidance, begin to use monitoring strategies to increase comprehension. |

*Video* **SCENES**

**DEEPER UNDERSTANDING: Setting Up the Classroom for Independent Readers and Writers**

<table>
<tr><th>Setting, Notes, and Explicit Teaching Points<br>The What, Why, and How of Teaching</th><th>Ongoing Assessment<br>Informing Our Instruction</th><th>Questions/Reflections<br>For Professional Conversations</th><th>Learning Outcomes<br>What Students Know and Are Able to Do</th></tr>
<tr><td>• Tell students the chart is a draft (first thinking). "This chart is going to change [as students learn more]."<br>• Affirm students' smart thinking (so they and others will incorporate it). "David, that is so smart! Did you hear what he said? He said, 'I look at the first two pages and see if I want to read the rest.' You know, I do the same thing."<br><br>• Extend students' thinking to attempt to get more explicit, thoughtful responses. "David, when you are looking at those first two pages, what are looking for?" "I'm looking for some-thing, like, interesting." "That was really great what you said, because if it's not interesting who wants to read it?"<br>• Restate important points students make (to underscore their importance and to encourage others to use the stated strategy).<br>  • "If you read books that are too hard for you, it doesn't really help you as a reader. If it's easy, it's good. Good for you."<br>  • "You look through the whole box. You don't just take the very first one, right?"<br>  • "You look at the pictures to help you read the book."</td><td>teach). "What do you mean by that?" [After a student responds, "Pick up a book and read it" to "How do you choose a book to read?"]<br>"So you pick up a book and read it. What does that mean? What do you do?"<br>"Read the words."<br>Invite individual students to share strategies they use. "What else do you do when you're choosing a book? Anything else that's not up here [on our chart]? Are we missing anything?"</td><td>• How can the language we use with students encourage them to do their best thinking?<br>• Do we allow enough time for students to think and respond to the questions we pose?<br>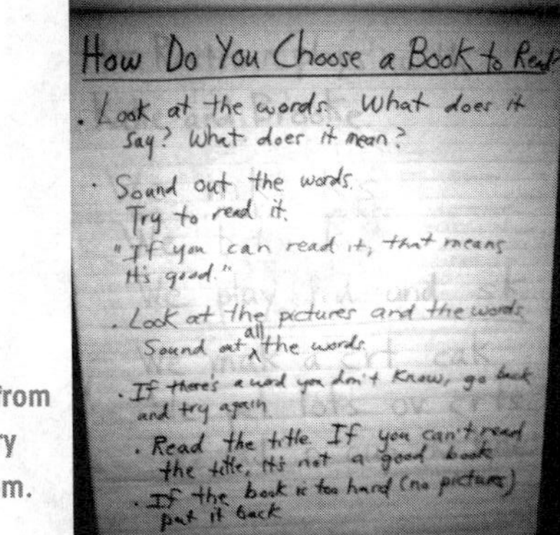<br><br>A chart from a primary classroom.</td><td>• Use oral language to communicate ideas.<br>• Use listening and observation skills to communicate ideas.</td></tr>
<tr><td></td><td>Use language that encourages students to think harder and to clarify their thinking:<br>• "What do you mean by that?"<br>• "Do you mean . . . , or are you talking about . . . ?"<br>• "OK, tell me what you mean when you say. . . . Do you mean . . . or . . . ?"<br>• "Are you thinking of . . . ?"<br>• "How do you decide [what book to pick]? Do you just go over there and pick any book? What do you do? OK. So you look inside? And what're you looking for?"<br>• "What does that mean [that it's easy]?"<br>• "How do you use the pictures to help you?"</td><td>• Struggling readers need more time to read. How can we ensure they do more reading during the school day?<br></td><td>• Use pictures to comprehend the text.</td></tr>
</table>

**Video SCENES**

- Intermediate Grades *(no video)*

**DEEPER UNDERSTANDING: Setting Up the Classroom for Independent Readers and Writers**

| Setting, Notes, and Explicit Teaching Points | Ongoing Assessment | Questions/Reflections | Learning Outcomes |
|---|---|---|---|
| The What, Why, and How of Teaching | Informing Our Instruction | For Professional Conversations | What Students Know and Are Able to Do |
| **NOTES**<br>For grades 2 and above, the process is similar to what you have just seen in grade 1. See below for samples of charts from intermediate grades. | | • What do your students' responses say about the teaching that has occurred?<br>• Why is it important for students to verbalize and to record their thinking?<br>• Why is it important to model and show examples from your life? | • Self-select text for a variety of purposes.<br>• Discuss and share favorite authors, books, and genres with others. Explain reasons for choices.<br>• Begin to understand the use of informational texts such as book reviews.<br>• Self-monitor reading accuracy at the instructional level (94%–96%) and independent reading level (97%–100%).<br>• Apply different reading strategies to self-selected texts.<br>• Apply different reading rates to match text. |

How Do We Choose Books to Read
- Read the blurb.
- Ask a friend
- Read the first chapter
- Read a couple of pages to see if you like it.
- "I look at the cover for details"
- Look at how thick or thin the book
- "It interests me."
- Use the 5 finger rule
- "I go to the section of library that has my level and interest"
- We love the author.
- You can tell someone about it.

Ways We Choose Books
- genre
- author
- interesting cover
- reading the back
- recommend by a friend, parent, teacher
- interesting title
- award winners
- favorite series
- illustrations
- books from movies
- highlighted in book order
- reading 1st page or 2
- good length
- gift
- word choice
- size of print
- just right book
- read part of middle
- read it before

Why We Abandon Books
- not interesting
- not right genre
- too difficult
- too easy
- too slow moving (boring)
- overly descriptive
- too many things going on
- not the right author
- disappointed in author
- too long
- too short
- uninteresting beginning
- poor illustrations
- confusing plot
- Story doesn't flow
- uninteresting theme
- doesn't make sense
- not enough description

How Do We Choose A "Just-Right" Book DRAFT first thinking
- Lauren: Look at back/blurb and see if you like the summary
- Read the first few pages and see if you like it. Is it a genre you like?
- Use a recommendation from a friend
- Read the first few pages; if it's too hard put it down. If there are 3 or 4 words you don't know you don't follow the story
- I look through the book — noticing the size of print and amount of words on the page
- Read through the first few pages; try to retell it to be sure you understand it
- Look at how thick book is
- See if you've read that author before. If you like the author, there's a good chance you'll like the new book.

How Do You Choose A Book
- read 1st pages or sentence
- skim through it
- read book summary in front or back of book
- Author we know & like
- Genres we like
- if it's "just right" for you
- Something you studied or know about
- look at cover
- Someones recommendation
- relates to your intrests
- Read Author's Note
- Interesting title
- A book you've already read or like
- book in a series
- books that are movies
- if you relate to a character
- look at the Pictures!

**DEEPER UNDERSTANDING: Setting Up the Classroom for Independent Readers and Writers**

| *Video* **SCENES** | Setting, Notes, and Explicit Teaching Points<br>The What, Why, and How of Teaching | Ongoing Assessment<br>Informing Our Instruction | Questions/Reflections<br>For Professional Conversations | Learning Outcomes<br>What Students Know and Are Able to Do |
|---|---|---|---|---|
| **Let Assessment Inform You: What Do Good Readers and Writers Do?**<br>(8:56 min.)<br>• What Do Good Readers Do? Grade 1 | **NOTES**<br>It is fall in an urban, diverse, first-grade classroom, and phonics is the main reading strategy that has been taught and practiced. Our goal in a weeklong residency is to get students to also use meaning-based strategies along with phonics.<br>**TEACHING POINTS**<br>• Review and affirm what students know about what good readers do. (We reread the shared writing chart we began the previous day, What a Good Reader Does.)<br>• Elicit what one student did to figure out a word (*like*) so other students will try the strategy when they read. *"Cesar, what was the hard word you figured out* [in guided reading group]*? It's on the word wall here."* Like. *"And how did you figure that out?"* [No response.]<br>• Review what students did that worked in figuring out a word so they will do it again. *"Remember how we kept going through the pages of the book because you* [a group of four] *kept saying 'Danny looks red' but that didn't make sense with the story. And finally when you looked at the word, all of you, and then we looked at the story, we looked at the word, it had to be* like *because* like *was the one that made sense."*<br>• Celebrate one student's word-solving strategy: to *"think." "Wow, and I'm going to put a star here* [on the chart] *because that's what you did. Good readers think. Kids, you're not just sounding out words. You're thinking and it has to make sense."* | Use shared writing to find out what students know about what good readers do and to document their growing knowledge.<br>Check for understanding and build on knowledge. *"So what could we add here that is something else that a good reader does?"*<br>Guide students to say how they know what they know. *"What was going on in your head? You weren't just sounding out the words. You were doing something else. What do we call that? You were working really hard."* (Cesar responds, *"Think."*) | • How can assessing before teaching make teaching more effective and efficient?<br>• What is the value in reviewing a shared text? 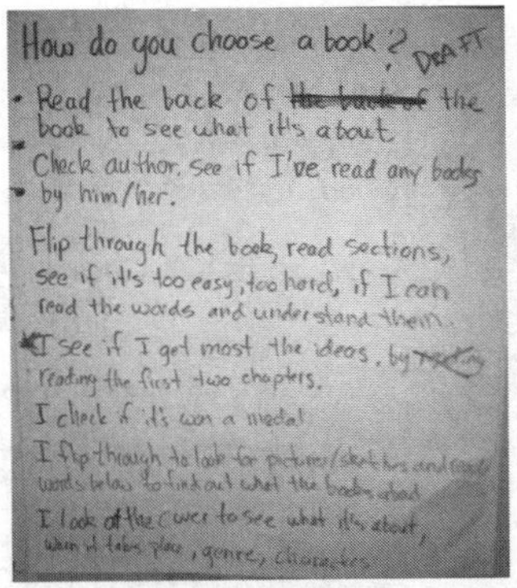 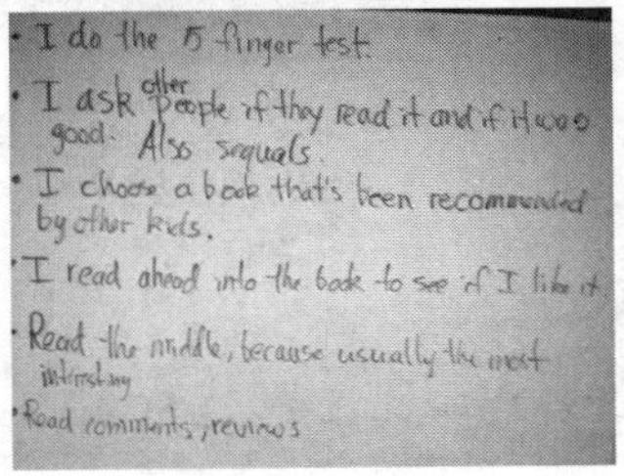 | • Use simple resources (word wall) with teacher guidance.  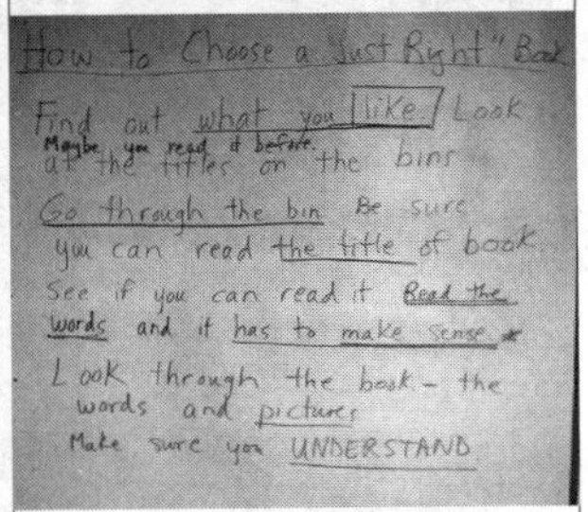<br>**Assessment before teaching and adding on as students learn more.** |
| • What Do Good Writers Do? Grade 1 | **NOTES**<br>In another classroom, students' initial responses on our shared writing chart (before they write) indicate limited knowledge about writing meaningful texts. Until now, writing has concentrated on learning letters and sounds. Notice how children's knowledge grows as they observe teacher demonstration writing, write their own continuous texts with the goal of publishing their stories for the classroom library, and revisit what good writers do by reviewing, with guidance, the teacher's demonstration writing. | | • What do you think the teacher's beliefs are about teaching writing and how do they impact student achievement and students' beliefs about writing? | • Write for an audience and relevant purpose.<br>• Self-select topics for writing continuous text.<br>• Use word choice in writing with teacher guidance.<br>• Develop oral language through listening, speaking, and observation. |

continues

# *Video* SCENES

**DEEPER UNDERSTANDING: Setting Up the Classroom for Independent Readers and Writers**

## Let Assessment Inform You

- What Do Good Writers Do? Grade 1 *continued*

### Setting, Notes, and Explicit Teaching Points
The What, Why, and How of Teaching

Notice the chart at the top right in a second-grade classroom, What Do Smart Writers Do? The students who created that chart were exactly like these first graders a year ago. Notice from the responses on the chart how knowledgeable they are as second graders, a tribute to their teacher's growing knowledge and her shift in beliefs and practices from mostly writing exercises in isolation to authentic daily writing of continuous texts for meaningful audiences and purposes.

**TEACHING POINTS**

- Connect publishing to writing interesting texts. *"If we're publishing, you're doing all the things that good writers do."*
- Encourage students to do what good writers do by restating important student contributions. *"Use the word wall or a chart if you don't know how to spell a word."*
- Affirm and acknowledge students who try out what you've been teaching (so they will do it again and other students will do it). *"Raise your hand if you did that* [reread story before starting to write again, add a title]."

- Revisit and reread demonstration writing to point out what a good writer does that students haven't yet noticed but are ready to learn. *"What do we call this?"* [I reread the title to my demonstration writing story, "Getting to Love Norman"]. After a student responds, *"Title,"* I add *"add a title"* to our chart.
- Record and shape all meaningful student responses. *"They read it again." "I'm going to use a big word here, reread. . . . I'm going to put a star here* [next to the word] *because this is so important."* (See shared writing chart for all recorded responses.)
- Connect a writing action (crossing out) to a meaningful purpose (revision). *"Good writers change their minds."* And, *"I put in a better word.* [I reread from my demonstration writing story and explain why I changed *shiny* to *furry*.] *The word shiny wasn't the right word. It didn't sound right."*
- Set the expectation that giving an oral response requires thinking before speaking. *"Now think before you put your hand up. If your hand is up that means you know."*

### Ongoing Assessment
Informing Our Instruction

Use your shared writing chart to assess what students are learning. (Date entries and write each entry in a different color marker, so you can see the growth.)

- *"What else have you learned?"*
- *"What's something else a good writer does? What are some of the things we did yesterday that you remember?"*
- *"What else did you see me do?"*

Check that students are trying out what you are teaching. (This also sends the message that you expect this behavior.)

- *"How many of you did that yesterday?"* [After student contributes *"use the word wall."*] And, again, later, *"Raise your hand if you put a title in your writing yesterday?"*

Revisit demonstration writing as a scaffold to jump-start students' thinking and to assess what they notice. *"What did I do here?"* [I read and show crossed out line where I changed my mind and revised in the process of writing my draft.] *"Why did I do it?"*

Use what a student has done as a good writer to nudge others to do the same. *"One of you yesterday when you were reading your writing over* [in a public conference] *had left out a word. And what did we do? Who remembers?"*

### Questions/Reflections
For Professional Conversations

- How can you connect assessment with instruction when you do a shared writing with students? Why is this valuable for maximizing instruction and learning?

**These are examples of shared writing to investigate what students know about writing.**

### Learning Outcomes
What Students Know and Are Able to Do

# Video SCENES

**Deeper Understanding: Setting Up the Classroom for Independent Readers and Writers**

| Scene | Setting, Notes, and Explicit Teaching Points | Ongoing Assessment | Questions/Reflections | Learning Outcomes |
|---|---|---|---|---|
| | The What, Why, and How of Teaching | Informing Our Instruction | For Professional Conversations | What Students Know and Are Able to Do |
| | • Demonstrate again when students have not picked up on a demonstration. *"Here's what we did. I'm going to tell you* [because students don't remember]." I write *add a caret* on the chart. *"Do you remember what it looks like? It looks like this* [I make a ^ on chart] *and I saw a few of you try it."* | Assess whether students are learning and utilizing what is being demonstrated.<br>• *"Think. What did we call that when we added something?"* [Referring to putting in a caret when adding a missing word.] | | |
| **Connect Real-World Writing and Reading** (8:08 min.)<br>• Teacher as Writer<br>• Why Do People Write? What Do People Write? | **NOTES**<br>Students see us as readers but rarely as writers. Share the kinds of writing you do in your life—notes, emails, lists, letters to parents, and so on. Bring in samples of your writing, and talk about why you write and what kinds of writing you do.<br><br>**NOTES**<br>To assess if students have connected writing in school with real-world writing and to help them forge that connection, we begin by talking about and recording (through shared writing) the reasons people write and the forms this writing takes. Another equally important purpose is to help students and teachers see many varied, authentic possibilities for writing and to connect that writing with an audience of readers. During this scene, when I share two books with students, I have carefully selected them for cultural relevance, high interest, and literary quality.<br><br>**TEACHING POINTS**<br>• Name some of the types of writing you do and why you do it. *"I was writing those notes to remember. . . . I made a list so I wouldn't forget . . . to thank someone . . . to make someone feel better. . . ."*<br>• Connect writing to life. *"Think about the writing that your mom does, that your dad does. . . . Do you think that writing is just something that people do in school or do people do it at their jobs? Do they do it in their daily life?"*<br>• Show that authors write for readers. *"This one is called* Joe Louis: America's Fighter, *by David Adler* [show book] *and he writes wonderful books for kids. He writes biographies."* | **A "What Do Good Writers Do" chart in progress, indicating students' growing knowledge about the writing–reading connection.**<br><br>After giving demonstrations and examples, check whether students understood enough (in this case, the reasons why people write) to give their own examples:<br>• *"Why else do people write in the world? You're spending . . . a lot of time in school writing. So it must be pretty important. So what are some of the reasons that people write?"*<br>• *"Why do you think Nikki Giovanni wrote* Rosa?*"* [After showing the book and telling about it.]<br>• *"Why do people write journals?"* | **Helping students make the connection between writing and reading: writers write for readers.** | • Share writing with others.<br><br>• Write and communicate with others (notes, cards, letters).<br>• Write to express own ideas.<br>• Identify the intended audience for each piece.<br>• Write to tell (personal) stories. |

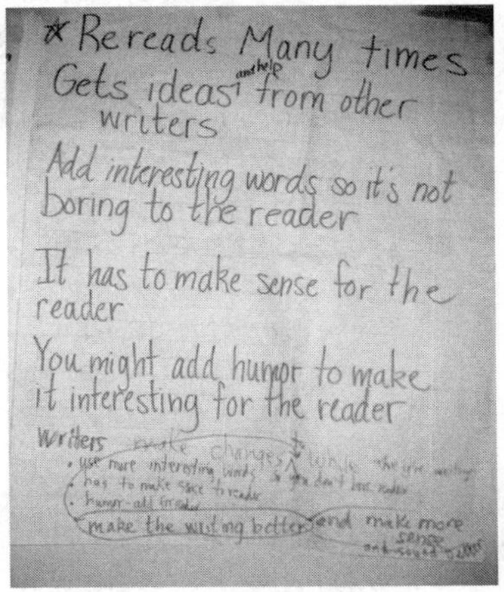

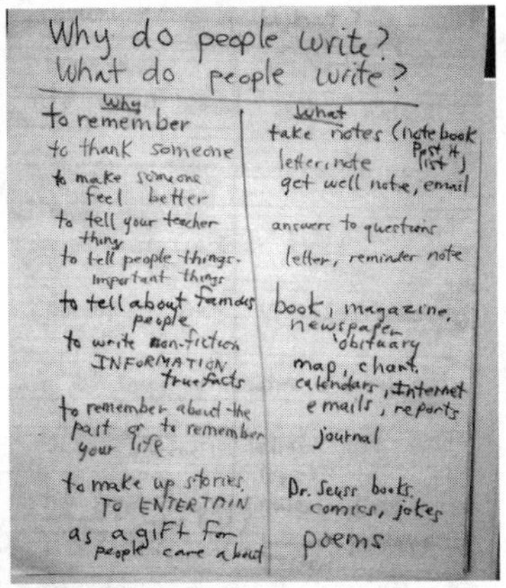

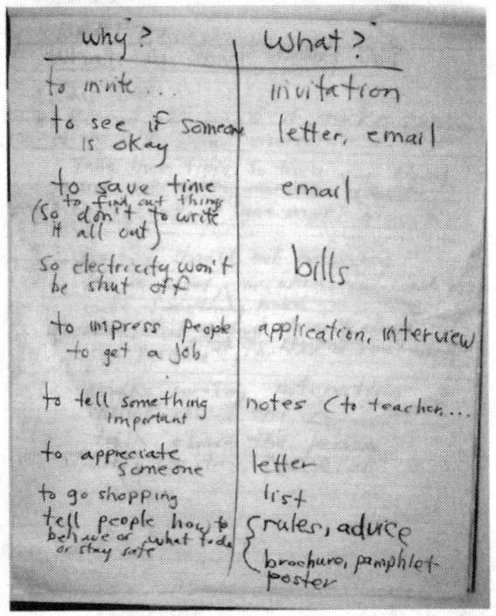

continues

*Video* **SCENES**

**Connect Real-World Writing and Reading *continued***

**Deeper Understanding: Setting Up the Classroom for Independent Readers and Writers**

| Setting, Notes, and Explicit Teaching Points<br>The What, Why, and How of Teaching | Ongoing Assessment<br>Informing Our Instruction | Questions/Reflections<br>For Professional Conversations | Learning Outcomes<br>What Students Know and Are Able to Do |
|---|---|---|---|
| • Explain vocabulary necessary for understanding important concepts. *"What's a biography? It's a story of a person's life."* And, *"People write obituaries when somebody dies. They tell all about that person's life."*<br>• Scaffold and expand students' responses. *"When . . . there are all kinds of facts in the books, true things, what do we call that?"* "Nonfiction." *"Nonfiction, OK, good. And . . . one of the reasons that people write is to give information, to tell you things. . . . Maps give you information . . . charts . . . calendars* [write on chart]."<br>• Provide options for writing choices. *"Why can't they* [the students] *write their own joke books and magazines and information and reports?"* | Attempt to get students to clarify their thoughts (so you can understand their thinking and what, if any, support they need):<br>• *"Give me an example."*<br>• *"Tell me a little more about that."*<br>• *"You're on the right track."*<br>• *"Who can tell me more?"*<br>• *"Where else can you find information? If you wanted to write information for somebody, what, where could it be?"* | | • Write for own purpose (to communicate with friends).<br>• Write in a variety of forms/genres. |
| • Extend writing purposes beyond the classroom. *"I want you to ask your parents tonight, how do they use writing in their life?"* | Assess that students can justify responses (this pushes their thinking):<br>• *"Why is that important?"*<br>• *"Why does that matter?"*<br>• *"Why do people write their life stories down?"*<br>Provide information in your question to help scaffold student's response. *"If you want to read something for entertainment, what might you read?"* | | • Select from a wide range of writing topics.<br>• Maintain focus on a specific writing topic.<br>• Use personal experience and observation to support ideas for writing. |
| • Connect writing parents do to real-world writing. Record and shape responses: invitations, email, bills, applications.<br>• Show authentic examples (written by other students) to connect writing purpose with writing form and audience: rules of life, Welcome to Second Grade, advice to other students, playground rules. | Make sure students know why people write in particular forms/types of writing (so they come to see that people write for a purpose and audience):<br>• *"Why do they send emails? Write applications? Interviews?"*<br>• *"What would be the reason why you might write rules?"*<br>• *"Who do you think their audience was? Who did they write this for?"* | • How does writing for authentic audiences and purposes impact student engagement, effort, and writing quality? | • Publish texts in various ways. |

## Deeper Understanding: Setting Up the Classroom for Independent Readers and Writers

| *Video* SCENES | Setting, Notes, and Explicit Teaching Points<br>The What, Why, and How of Teaching | Ongoing Assessment<br>Informing Our Instruction | Questions/Reflections<br>For Professional Conversations | Learning Outcomes<br>What Students Know and Are Able to Do |
|---|---|---|---|---|
| **Independent Practice: Students Writing and Reading**<br>(0:45 sec.) | **NOTES**<br>When students are invested and know exactly what to do during independent practice, they are completely focused and engaged. This scene shows what that engagement and focus looks like (an expectation for all grade levels) for students as writers (as well as teachers as writers) and readers. | Use this time for formative assessment (roving conferences, taking anecdotal notes, conferring with individual or small groups). | • How can you be sure that students are not just sitting quietly and looking like they are engaged but that they are actually understanding and problem-solving the text? | |
| **Celebration/ Evaluation: Fourth-Grade Writing**<br>(2:01 min.) | **NOTES**<br>This scene takes place after fourth-grade students have written "life story" drafts. Up until now students did not see themselves as writers, did not write for an authentic audience or purpose, and did not write daily. What writing they did was focused on conventions, prompts, and test preparation. Teachers reported that standardized test scores were very low.<br><br>Students were used to connecting good writing mostly with correctness and conventions (handwriting, neatness, skipping lines, getting it "perfect"), which has limited their writing fluency, engagement, and achievement. This was the first time that students had been given topic choice and were asked to focus on the meaning and quality of their writing along with conventions.<br><br>This celebration/evaluation time serves two purposes. First, to help students recognize what they have done well, and second, to see what they value in writing, which we can then use to guide future instruction. Because these students had such low confidence as writers, it was especially important to celebrate and affirm what they had done well. | Assess, affirm, and extend students' learning:<br>• *"How many of you think you did some of your best writing?"*<br>• *"How come you did a good job today?"* Courtney: *"I really thought about it."* *"And also it was a pretty important thing, the story you told."* Michael: *"Because it's not messy."* *"What made you take the time to make it neater? Did you care about what you were writing about? That usually makes the difference."*<br><br>Addressing teachers:<br>*"Sometimes I see handwriting really improve and I don't talk about handwriting because when we care about what we are doing we do a better job."*<br>• *"Why do you think you did a better job?"* Buba: *"I put my mind to it, I ignore people talking to me."* *"Why did you put your mind to it? When I am writing, writing is such hard work that I have to put my mind to it. You said a really smart thing."* | • What do you notice about how an overfocus on conventions has impacted these students as writers? | |

continues

*Video* **SCENES**

**Celebration/ Evaluation: Fourth-Grade Writing *continued***

**DEEPER UNDERSTANDING: Setting Up the Classroom for Independent Readers and Writers**

| Questions/Reflections | Learning Outcomes | |
|---|---|---|
| The What, Why, and How of Teaching and Are Able to Do | Informing Our Instruction | |
| | Buba: *"It was my best thinking."*<br>*"Were you interested in what you were writing about? When I am interested in what I am writing about, I do my best work. I put my mind to it just the way you said that."*<br><br>Clarify student's understanding of revision:<br>• *"That's not a mistake. You were fixing it up to make it clearer for the reader. We call that revising. That's what good writers do."* | What makes the *Reading/Writing Connections* project unique? In addition to showing us how to connect these two literacies, it shows us how to use the Optimal Learning Model (OLM) to help students gain independence. It helps us establish a classroom environment where teachers can release responsibility to students quickly because we've done lots of excellent demonstrating and numerous shared experiences of real-world literacy activities. Students then spend much time practicing, with our guidance, reading and writing meaningful texts instead of doing activities about reading and writing. It is through this extensive practice that students become independent learners; that is, they self-monitor, self-direct, and self-evaluate as they read and write. Setting up a classroom for independent readers and writers establishes a learning environment that facilitates celebration, evaluation, and assessment early on in the school year. Most importantly, it answers that all important question, "What is the rest of the class doing while I am meeting with students one-on-one or in small groups?" |

Students demonstrate their pride as authors.

SESSION 4

# RESPONSENOTES

***Engage, Reflect, Assess, Celebrate!***

SESSION 4

# RESPONSENOTES

*Engage, Reflect, Assess, Celebrate!*

REGIE ROUTMAN in RESIDENCE

Transforming our Teaching through
**Reading/Writing Connections**

# Reading and Writing Lots of Texts

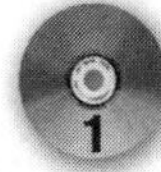

**View Video** (62 min.)

## Reading and Writing Lots of Texts

**PART 1:** READING TO WRITING TO READING

- **Reading Aloud: *Double Pink* by Kate Feiffer**
- **Shared Writing: Class Book on Favorite Colors**
- **Shared Reading: Class Book on Favorite Colors**
- **Reading Aloud as a Springboard for Shared Writing: *We Share Everything* by Robert Munch**
- **Shared Writing: "We Share"**
- **Transition from Reading to Writing**
- **Shared Reading and Writing: Creating Texts About Kindergarten**

**PART 2:** WRITING READABLE TEXTS

- **Demonstration Writing: "My Cat Norman"**
- **Before Writing: Scaffolded Public Conversations**
- **Setting Expectations for Independent Writing**
- **Independent Practice: Writing and Roving Conferences**
- **Public Celebration Conferences**
- **Independent Writing (Continued)**
- **Public Celebration Conferences (Continued)**
- **Independent Writing and Roving Conferences: One Teacher, 23 Students, 10 Minutes**

**RESOURCES**

**In this Session**

- Teaching in Action: Lesson Essentials, Five-Day Plan at a Glance *5-9*
- Melissa's First Writing to Reading in Kindergarten *5-10*
- Ilan's Kindergarten Writing *5-11*

**On the Website**

- Five-Day Lesson Plan, Kindergarten (K–2)
- Children's Writing Samples and Published Books
- Additional Video
    - Scaffolded Conversations
    - Public Celebration Conferences
    - Independent Writing and Roving Conferences (10-minute video)

## 1. Engage, Reflect, Assess

- Review the *Try It/Apply It* activity from Session 4. You were asked to examine your classroom library, assess your learning environment, and use shared writing to find out what students know about how to choose books, what good readers and writers do, and/or why people write and what forms that writing takes. The purpose of all these activities is to set up the classroom for independence, that is, that students are able to read and write on their own when you are working with small groups and one-on-one.
- ***Whole-Group Share:***
    - What did you notice about your classroom library? What changes, if any, did you make or do you plan to make?
    - What did you notice about what students know about authors, genres, reading for understanding, and so on? What simple practices can you incorporate to motivate students to love books and try new genres?
    - What did you learn about what students know (or not) about what good readers and good writers do? How can you use these insights to guide your teaching?
    - What did you learn about how students perceive writing in school as compared to writing in the world? (Why do people write? What do people write?)

## 2. Discuss Professional Reading

- Discuss "Organize an Outstanding Classroom Library" (*Reading Essentials*, pp. 63–77 and downloadable from the website).

## 3. Goals

PART 1:

- Use literature as a springboard for creating shared experiences in reading and writing.
- Show how shared writing can be used to create multiple texts for shared, guided, and independent reading.
- Generate personal responses from students and help them make personal connections with the texts they write and read (texts students create are always the easiest to read).

PART 2:

- Observe how to teach students to tell and write a continuous story over time.
- Observe how to support students in narrowing a topic with elaboration and detail (even if they don't know all their letters and sounds).
- Connect writing with reading by bringing in nonfiction texts for students to read.
- Show how to get ideas for writing nonfiction texts and support students' informational writing.
- Use student-written stories (fiction and nonfiction) for authentic audiences as published texts for reading.

## 4. View Video and Take Notes

- Turn to the Notecatcher to take notes.

## 5. Respond to the Video

- Respond to the video in small-group teams or as a whole group. Perhaps, use the following questions to guide your discussion:
    - How was the teacher able to help all learners be successful?
    - How are students becoming more responsible and independent as learners?
    - What did you observe that you might apply to your own teaching and learning?
    - What part(s) of the Optimal Learning Model did you identify and what did you notice?

## 6. Achieve a Deeper Understanding

- Take a few minutes to read and review the Deeper Understanding charts. These charts are designed to help you apply the essential ideas and strategies to your own teaching.
- Use the Questions/Reflections for Professional Conversations to jumpstart discussion and challenge your thinking. I strongly encourage you to use them to prompt ongoing *schoolwide* conversations between the project sessions. I know how hard it can be to meet and sustain worthwhile dialogue, so I've developed questions here and throughout the project that get to the heart of matters.

## 7. *Try It/Apply It* in the Classroom

PART 1:

- Select a book with high-interest concepts and cultural relevance for your students (or use the one modeled in the video).
- Through shared writing, create a text that becomes a shared reading.

- Use the provided lesson plans (see the website) as a scaffold and/or to create your own 5-day lessons for literacy blocks that include reading, writing, and word study.
- Follow the Optimal Learning Model to plan a series of lessons and activities.

PART 2:

- Tell and write a story from your life that your students will find relevant.
- Try out one or two scaffolded conversations before expecting students to write their own continuing story.
- Conduct roving conferences.
- End with celebration and whole-class sharing (public conferences).

## 8. Wrap-Up

- Before the next session, read "Begin in Kindergarten" *(Writing Essentials* excerpt, pp. 121–127 and downloadable from the website) and be prepared to discuss it during next session.

- Schedule time to meet with your vertical, grade-level, and/or partner teams in between whole-group sessions to revisit the videos on the website, and the Deeper Understanding charts, and/or plan together and try out new learning. You can jot down your ideas and thinking on your Response Notes page for easy reference later.
- Remember to bring any charts, lessons, writing, or student work samples from the *Try It/Apply It* to the next session.

# SESSION 5 NOTECATCHER

| VIDEO SCENES | LENGTH | NOTES & REFLECTION |
|---|---|---|
| **PART 1: READING TO WRITING TO READING** | | |
| **Reading Aloud: *Double Pink* by Kate Feiffer** | 2:22 min. | |
| **Shared Writing: Class Book on Favorite Colors** | 5:05 min. | |
| **Shared Reading: Class Book on Favorite Colors** | 2:37 min. | |
| • Word Work | | |
| **Reading Aloud as a Springboard for Shared Writing: *We Share Everything* by Robert Munch** | 2:27 min. | |
| **Shared Writing: "We Share"** | 3:17 min. | |

# SESSION 5 NOTECATCHER

| VIDEO SCENES | LENGTH | NOTES & REFLECTION |
|---|---|---|
| **Transition from Reading to Writing** | 4:28 min. | |
| • *Down by the Bay* and Reviewing Rhyming Parts | | |
| • Word Work | | |
| **Shared Reading and Writing: Creating Texts About Kindergarten** | 9:00 min. | |
| • Welcome Words | | |
| • *A Child's Day* by Jillian Cutting | | |
| • Generating Ideas | | |
| • Welcome to Kindergarten | | |

SESSION 5

# NOTECATCHER

| VIDEO SCENES | LENGTH | NOTES & REFLECTION |
|---|---|---|
| **PART 2: WRITING READABLE TEXTS** | | |
| **Demonstration Writing: "My Cat Norman"** | 11:19 min. | |
| • Telling the Story First | | |
| • Word Work: Phonemic Awareness | | |
| **Before Writing: Scaffolded Public Conversations** | 2:07 min. | |
| • Scaffolded Conversation with Luis | | |
| **Setting Expectations for Independent Writing** | 3:11 min. | |
| • Assessing Use of Classroom Resources | | |
| • Supporting the Not-So-Ready Writer | | |
| **Independent Practice: Writing and Roving Conferences** | 3:18 min. | |

SESSION **5**

# **NOTE**CATCHER

| VIDEO SCENES | LENGTH | NOTES & REFLECTION |
|---|---|---|
| **Public Celebration Conferences**<br>• Luis<br>• Allison | 4:47 min. | |
| **Independent Writing (Continued)**<br>• Revisiting the Norman Story | 2:09 min. | |
| **Public Celebration Conferences (Continued)**<br>• Ilan | 2:26 min. | |
| **Independent Writing and Roving Conferences: One Teacher, 23 Students, 10 Minutes** | 3:55 min. | |

# Teaching in Action: Lesson Essentials

## *Five-Day Plan at a Glance*

| Optimal Learning Model | Day 1 (40–90 min.) | Day 2 (40–90 min.) | Day 3 (40–90 min.) | Day 4 (40–90 min.) | Day 5 (40–90 min.) |
|---|---|---|---|---|---|
| **DEMONSTRATION** ⟶ **INDEPENDENT PRACTICE** | | | | | |
| | *Strategies:* | *Strategies:* | *Strategies:* | *Strategies:* | *Strategies:* |
| **Demonstration** (5–15 min.)<br>and/or | **Reading Aloud** | **Shared Writing/ Reading** | **Shared Reading, *The Color Book*** | **Shared Reading/ Shared Writing/** | **Shared Reading/ Shared Writing/ Word Work** |
| **Shared Demonstration** (5–15 min.) | **Shared Writing/ Word Work** | **Reading Aloud/ Shared Writing/ Word Work** | **Reading Aloud, *Something Else*** | **Model Independent Journal Writing/ Word Work Scaffolded Conversations** | **Scaffolded Conversations** |
| **Guided & Independent Practice** (20–40 min.) | **Roving One-on-One Conferences**<br>and<br>**Independent Reading Practice** | **Roving One-on-One Conferences**<br>and<br>**Independent Writing Practice** | **Roving One-on-One Conferences**<br>and<br>**Independent Reading Practice** | **Roving One-on-One Conferences**<br>and<br>**Independent Reading/ Writing Practice** | **Supporting Not-So-Ready Readers/Writers**<br>and<br>**Independent Reading/ Writing Practice** |
| **Ongoing Assessment/ Instructional Adjustments** (10–20 min.) | **Celebration (Public Conferences)** | **Celebration (Public Conferences)** | **Celebration (Public Conferences)** | **Celebration (Public Conferences)** | **Celebration (Public Conferences)** |
| Dependence ⟶ Handover of Responsibility ⟶ Independence | | | | | |

# Melissa's First Writing to Reading in Kindergarten (midyear)

### Student Profile: Melissa

Melissa, an English language learner, entered kindergarten with low confidence, almost no letter-sound knowledge, and was one of the lowest performing students in the classroom. When she realized that her written words could tell a story she could read, she was transformed as a learner.

**Melissa's draft.**

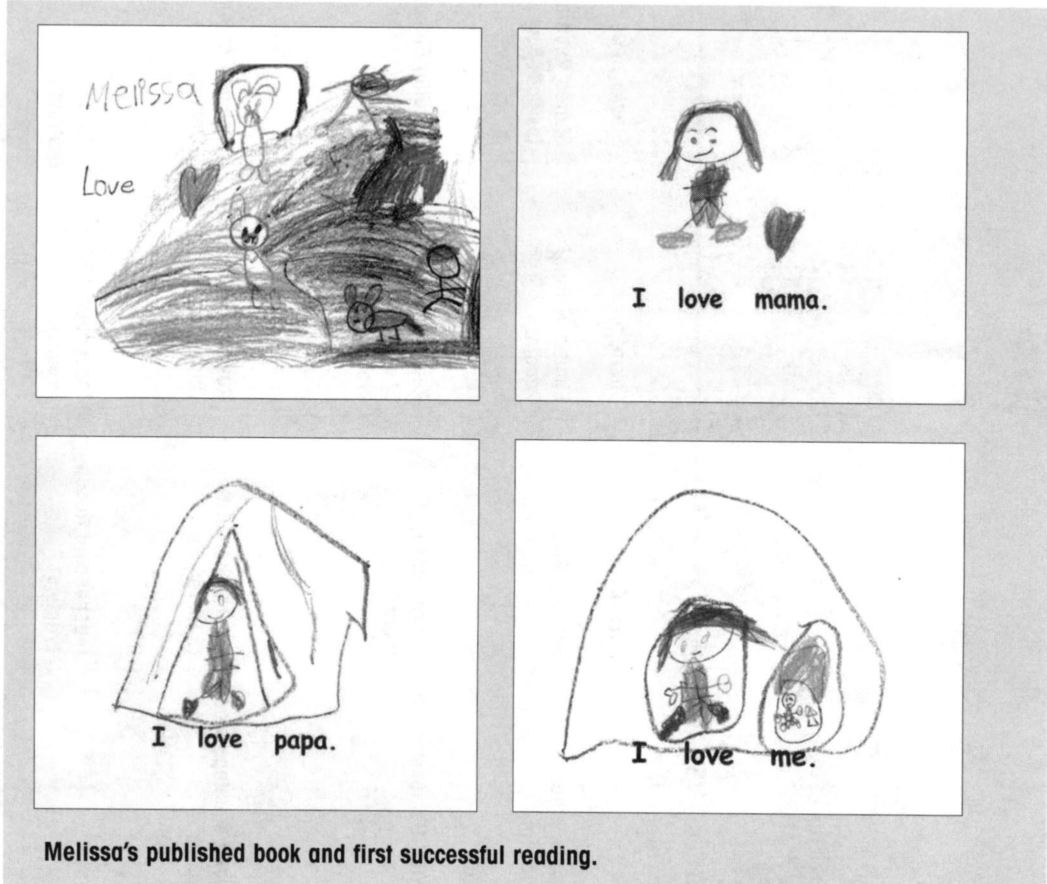



**Melissa's published book and first successful reading.**

*See the website for additional kindergarten writing samples.*

# Ilan's Kindergarten Writing (midyear)

*(See his student profile and public conference on page 5–34.)*

**Ilan's draft.**

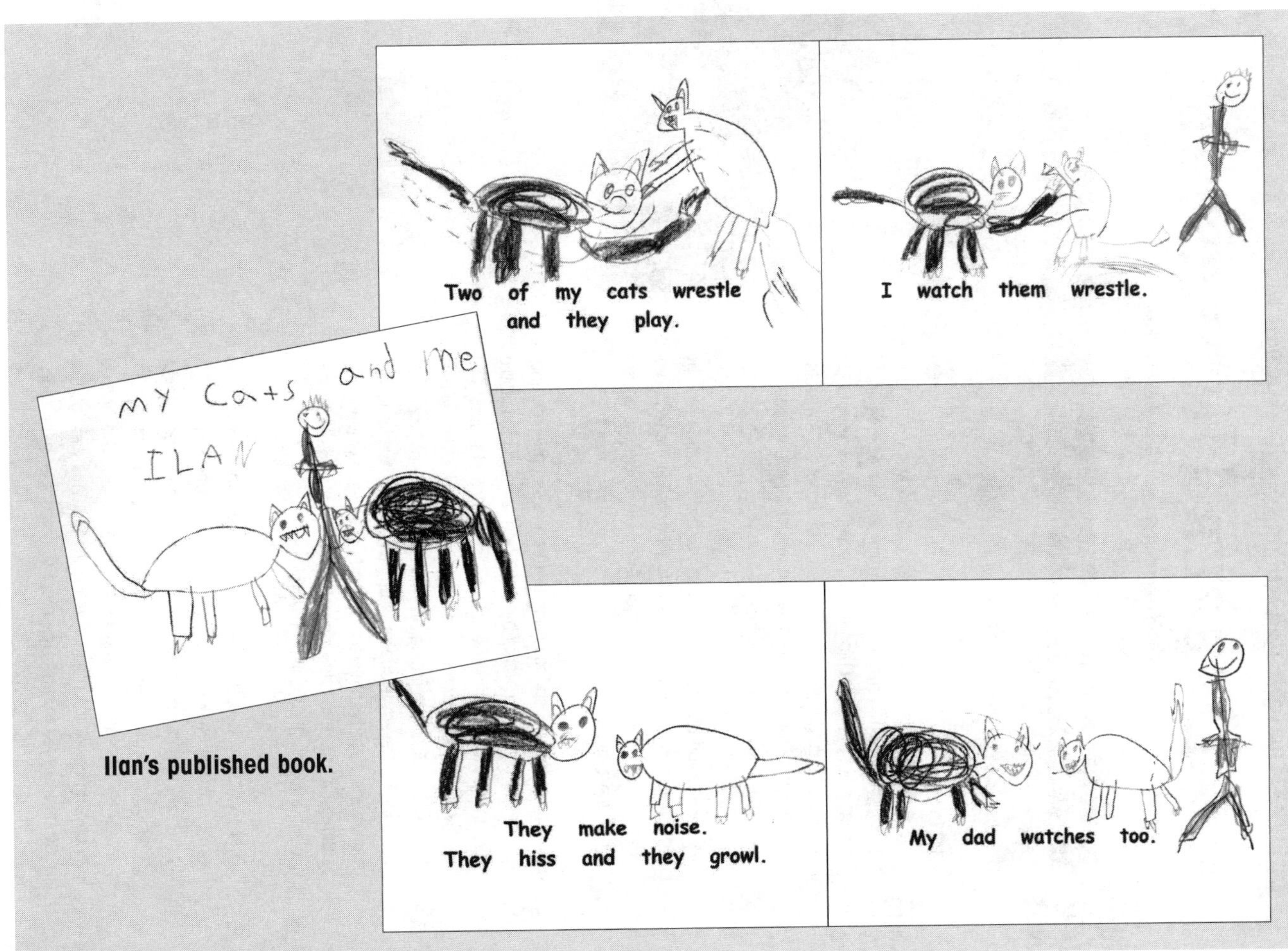

Two of my cats wrestle and they play.
I watch them wrestle.
MY Cats and me
ILAN
They make noise. They hiss and they growl.
My dad watches too.


**Ilan's published book.**

SESSION 5

Reading and Writing Lots of Texts, Part 1

# DEEPER UNDERSTANDING

*The teaching and assessing points reflect the total lesson but not all of these points are on the edited videos you are watching. However, the major points are represented on the edited videos.*

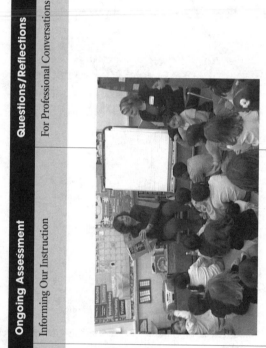

The globe icon indicates that the example is also available when you visit www.regieroutman.com.

*Video* SCENES

**PART 1:**

**READING TO WRITING TO READING**

| Setting, Notes, and Explicit Teaching Points | Ongoing Assessment | Questions/Reflections | Learning Outcomes |
|---|---|---|---|
| The What, Why, and How of Teaching | Informing Our Instruction | For Professional Conversations | What Students Know and Are Able to Do |
| **SETTING**<br>The setting is January (midyear) in Amanda Martinka's kindergarten classroom, Ardmore Elementary, Bellevue, Washington. Amanda has been teaching for six years; this is her third year teaching kindergarten. Her class is made up of 23 students, 40 percent of whom receive free or reduced-price lunches. At least half are English language learners.<br><br>As the session begins, Regie and Amanda are sitting side by side, negotiating text for a class story based on the read-aloud book *Double Pink*, by Kate Feiffer. Twenty teachers are observing in the classroom.<br><br>Until now, the writing focus has been on learning letters and sounds, recognizing words by sight, and reading predictable text. Independent writing has mainly consisted of journal writing. Most of the students were only writing one or two sentences, and Amanda indicated that the writing was not meaningful. Several students struggled to write even one idea with some sounds in words. Students wrote a new journal entry each time and often struggled with new ideas to write about. Individual publishing did not occur.<br><br>Therefore, the focus of the week is to have students read and write as many authentic texts as possible in an effort to increase their reading and writing abilities. The biggest shift in teaching is in using students' individual and class stories in published form as independent reading material. This approach greatly increased the amount of text the students were able to read and wanted to read. The most significant learning that | | • Is it OK to read through a book without stopping to check for comprehension? Discuss.<br><br>• Why is it important to choose highly engaging, relevant picture books as a springboard to writing? | |

# *Video* SCENES

**PART 1:**

**READING TO WRITING TO READING *(continued)***

**DEEPER UNDERSTANDING: Reading and Writing Lots of Texts, Part 1**

| Setting, Notes, and Explicit Teaching Points | Ongoing Assessment | Questions/Reflections | Learning Outcomes |
|---|---|---|---|
| The What, Why, and How of Teaching | Informing Our Instruction | For Professional Conversations | What Students Know and Are Able to Do |

Amanda and other observing teachers take away from the residency is that young children can tell and write a story even if they do not know all their letters and sounds.

End-of-year data from standardized district assessment indicated almost all of these kindergartners were reading at or above grade level. The students' scores at the end of the year were higher than those of kindergartners' in previous years. The classroom teacher and reading specialist attribute the higher reading achievement to the increased attention to writing and to the power of the reading/writing connection. Students who were already reading in January but were still writing in a very stilted way not only improved as readers but were able to write meaningful stories. Nonreaders became readers through writing and the reading/writing connection.

As a result of meaningful daily writing, phonemic awareness greatly increased. The scores on the year-end "Hearing Sounds in Words" (Observation Survey, Clay) were tremendously improved over past years, surpassing even districtwide averages.

**NOTES**

In this session you will observe many reading, shared reading, and shared writing experiences. The purpose of lots of shared experiences in reading and writing is to give students the language, the skills, and the confidence to begin to read and write independently. Note that all word work and skills are embedded (see Part 2 in this session and Session 8). Embedding the word work is not only efficient but also meaningful and purposeful to students. Students often do not understand the purpose of isolated word work and therefore do not always apply what is being taught.

In selecting a text and reading it aloud consider the following factors. Choose read-aloud books carefully for their cultural relevance, their contemporary interest to students, and the quality of the writing and illustrations. When students hear books read aloud, they are able to listen to ideas and vocabulary they may

Kindergartners, heterogeneously grouped, are reading and writing their own stories while the teacher conducts roving conferences.

Melissa, a second language learner, is having a scaffolded conversation about her writing. (See sample writing on p. 5–10.)

Kindergartners work independently and are engaged for an extended period of time.

continues

**DEEPER UNDERSTANDING: Reading and Writing Lots of Texts, Part 1**

| *Video* SCENES | Setting, Notes, and Explicit Teaching Points<br>The What, Why, and How of Teaching | Ongoing Assessment<br>Informing Our Instruction | Questions/Reflections<br>For Professional Conversations | Learning Outcomes<br>What Students Know and Are Able to Do |
|---|---|---|---|---|
| **PART 1:**<br>**READING TO WRITING TO READING *(continued)*** | not yet be able to read on their own and are introduced to new authors and genres. Make connections as you are reading only when they are relevant and add meaning to the text. If possible, show the illustrations as you are reading. The illustrations play an important role in student understanding. Read aloud at a good pace. It is efficient and helps keep the students engaged.<br><br>When going from reading to writing, select a book that will be easy to use as a model for creating a new text with the same structure and/or pattern for writing and reading. | | | |
| **Reading Aloud: *Double Pink* by Kate Feiffer**<br>(2:22 min.) | **TEACHING POINTS**<br>• Engage kids with a familiar concept that every child knows, enjoys, and understands. In this example, it's a favorite color.<br>• Read fluently with expression and enjoyment text that gives all students the opportunity to engage with excellent literature.<br>• Share your thinking as you are reading and encourage children to think along as you read: "*I am thinking. . . . I am wondering. . . . Be thinking in your mind what is going to happen. . . . Think in your head. . . .*" | Make sure students know, understand, and can state the purpose of the instruction and activity:<br>• "*Why are we doing what we're doing?*"<br><br>Write down goals and objectives for and with students.<br>Find out what students know before, during, and after the lesson. | **Regie is reading aloud from *Double Pink* by Kate Feiffer. The children are reacting with a collective "uh-oh!" to what she just read, and she pauses to say "Be thinking in your mind what is going to happen."** | • Use prior knowledge and context in read-aloud and/or shared reading to predict the meaning of unfamiliar words. |
| **Shared Writing: Class Book on Favorite Colors**<br>(5:05 min.) | **NOTES**<br>• Students and teacher write a coherent text collaboratively, the teacher doing the writing and shaping the text while scaffolding children's language and ideas; often these texts become shared reading texts as well as published texts for guided and personal independent reading.<br>• Try not to have your shared writing take more than two days. Invite students to take turns creating their own line of print and encourage all students to help spell words, participate, and listen to one another.<br>• Watch your time and move at a quick pace. Put your energy into composing the content. You won't have time to sound out every word or mention every punctuation mark. Stop after 10 or 15 minutes while engagement and interest are still high. You may need to do two or three sessions to complete the writing. | | • What happens when you are composing writing text with your class and you focus on content and mechanics at the same time?<br><br>• Why is it important to use a predictable pattern or structure for emerging readers and writers? | |

*Video* **SCENES**

**Shared Writing: Class Book on Favorite Colors** ***continued***

**DEEPER UNDERSTANDING: Reading and Writing Lots of Texts, Part 1**

| Setting, Notes, and Explicit Teaching Points<br>The What, Why, and How of Teaching | Ongoing Assessment<br>Informing Our Instruction | Questions/Reflections<br>For Professional Conversations | Learning Outcomes<br>What Students Know and Are Able to Do |
|---|---|---|---|
| • The writing will become a shared reading text for whole-class and independent reading and possibly word work.<br><br>**TEACHING POINTS**<br>• Quickly decide the topic while giving students some choice, and demonstrate your thinking by talking out loud before and as you are writing.<br>• Stretch out the sounds (out loud) in each word as you are writing. | | • Why is it important that we focus on what students know and not try to teach everything at once? | |
| • Ask students to spell words that they know (l-o-v-e-s).<br>• Draw a picture to go along with the message. (Drawing can be a useful scaffold to help young children get ideas for and tell their story.)<br>• Invite children to help spell important words (your name, for example).<br>• Demonstrate the pattern or structure for writing (in this case, model one or two lines of print so that all students are successful and understand the pattern).<br>• Help scaffold and encourage specific and interesting word choice. "*What kind of a pink is it? Is it like . . . ?*"<br>• Put the language they might use in their ear. "*Is it like the pink that you are wearing, a very pale pink? Is it like the pink Susan is wearing? Is it double pink?*"<br>• Accept and affirm students' best efforts.<br>• Set the purpose and audience for writing. "*We are going to put this into a class book.*" | Observe whether students are applying their letter-sound learning to new contexts. For example, "*Help me spell your teacher's name. Everybody what's this word* [l-o-v-e-s]?" | 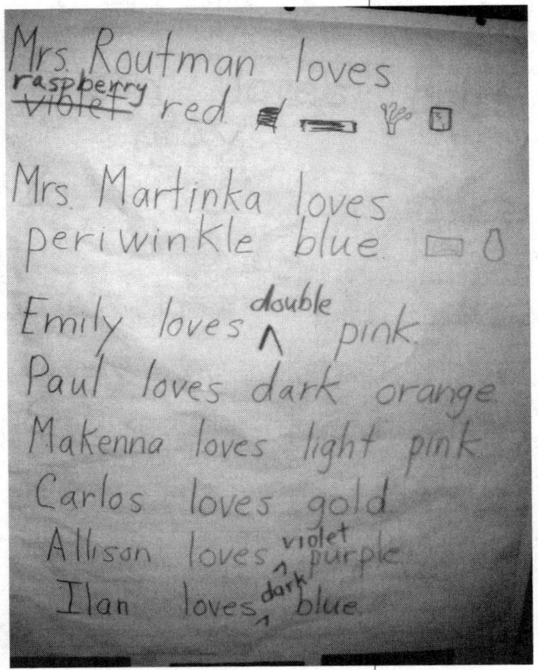 | |
| • Direct students to the word wall for names and high-frequency words so that students will choose to use the word wall as a resource and be able to use these words as they begin to write independently.<br>• Record the correct letters that match words the students are writing (*d_rk*). Add missing letters without commenting (if they knew it they would have done it).<br>• Invite students to illustrate information that they do not put in their text.<br>• Tie in concepts, vocabulary, and ideas, and create a text together that all students will be able to read successfully. | Check to see that students are using resources, such as the word wall, to help their reading and writing. Students show (or don't show) evidence that they can transfer learning and strategies and use resources across the curriculum.<br>• "*Where would you find that word?*" "*Where would you find Emily's name?*" | • Why is it important to teach concepts and vocabulary in a meaningful context? | |

## DEEPER UNDERSTANDING: Reading and Writing Lots of Texts, Part 1

| Video SCENES | Setting, Notes, and Explicit Teaching Points<br>The What, Why, and How of Teaching | Ongoing Assessment<br>Informing Our Instruction | Questions/Reflections<br>For Professional Conversations | Learning Outcomes<br>What Students Know and Are Able to Do |
|---|---|---|---|---|
| **Shared Reading: Class Book on Favorite Colors**<br>(2:37 min.) | **NOTES**<br>Before this session, the teacher has completed the shared writing chart and typed each student's sentence at the bottom of an unlined sheet of paper, making sure the print is large enough and there is adequate space between words. Time during independent writing for each student to illustrate his or her page is limited; they have to write. It is advisable to model how good illustrations support the text. | Notice if students choose to read or write more on the same related topic.<br>Notice if students self-monitor (stop at the point of error or confusion to revise or self-correct) and self-improve the quality of their work. | • In what ways do shared writing texts that become shared reading texts support English language learners? | |
| • Word Work | **TEACHING POINTS**<br>• Note that writers change their minds and use better words.<br>  • Reread.<br>  • Rethink.<br>  • Cross out.<br>  • Add better word.<br>  • Add a caret.<br>• Reread text pointing to each word and checking and thinking about word choice.<br>• Use classroom resources to find correct word spelling (*double*).<br>• Scaffold language and ideas for students through concrete visuals and explicit language.<br>• Model revising a few sentences (in order to keep a fast pace and honor each student's contribution.)<br>• *Then* read through the class chart with the students.<br>• Use a sliding mask to call attention to high-frequency words (*love, pink, red*). | Check for understanding before asking kids to work independently:<br>• *"When I didn't like a word, what did I do?"* (cross out)<br>• *"What is another way that we added a word?"* (caret)<br>• *"There is a word here that occurs over and over again, what is it?"* (use sliding mask)<br><br>Observe if students are learning high-frequency words. Do you see evidence in their reading and writing? | • How can illustrations support emerging readers and writers?<br><br><br><br>**Regie is sharing the "Class Book on Favorite Colors" and all the students are reading along.** | • Understand that writing can be changed.<br>• Begin to understand how to add details to change drawing and writing to better represent ideas.<br>• Listen to and provide personal response to literature.<br>• Get ideas for writing from published authors. Use pictures and talk for thinking about and planning writing.<br>• Label pictures.<br>• Add details to change drawing and writing to better represent ideas.<br>• Call out places where ending punctuation and capitalization are needed during shared writing.<br>• Use oral language structure, letters, and pictures to predict and confirm word meaning, with teacher guidance. |

## Video SCENES

**Deeper Understanding: Reading and Writing Lots of Texts, Part 1**

| Video Scene | Setting, Notes, and Explicit Teaching Points<br>The What, Why, and How of Teaching | Ongoing Assessment<br>Informing Our Instruction | Questions/Reflections<br>For Professional Conversations | Learning Outcomes<br>What Students Know and Are Able to Do |
|---|---|---|---|---|
| **Reading Aloud as a Springboard for Shared Writing: *We Share Everything* by Robert Munch**<br>(2:27 min.) | **NOTES**<br>In this session student's experience a wide variety of shared reading and writing texts, which gives them the confidence to begin to write independently (see Part 2 of this session). It's important that students hear, read, write, view, and talk about many complete and meaningful texts throughout the day. Most of their time, especially that of English language learners and struggling students, must be spent on rich language experiences—not isolated exercises—if they are to make the necessary academic gains. (See also Session 13 within this program.) One of our goals for the week is to begin to create many meaningful texts for reading and writing so students are immersed in reading and writing all day, not just doing reading and writing activities. We are still teaching all the necessary skills kids need but in a whole-part-whole teaching model, which allows for much greater efficiency and enjoyment than a part-to-whole approach.<br><br>**TEACHING POINTS**<br>• Read aloud with expression to convey meaning and enjoyment.<br>• Use the *cloze* technique. *In kindergarten we share ______.*" Have students fill in the missing word to keep the focus on meaning. | 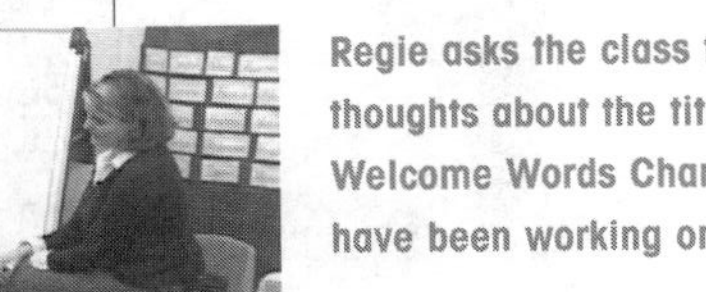<br>**Regie asks the class "Who's got something that's not up here yet?" (to encourage ideas for shared writing).**<br><br>Check for understanding while reading:<br>• "*And illustrated means, that's the person who did the ____?*"<br>Check for knowledge of phonemic awareness and phonics:<br>• "*How does it start? What do you hear?*"<br>• Celebrate, assess, and note students' learning as the whole class reads their newly created text. | • What is the purpose of highlighting and isolating key words in a text? | • Read selected words in text on sight. |
| **Shared Writing: "We Share"**<br>(3:17 min.) | **NOTES**<br>To hold children's attention and move at a fast pace, write without explaining everything. For example, I just give the title ("*We could call it* 'We Share'") and add an exclamation mark at the very end of the text without doing a separate lesson on it. Remember that in shared writing the teacher is holding the pen and doing all the writing and shaping students' thinking. Interactive writing is not our first choice here, because it is not efficient with a whole class of students. It is important to affirm all responses even when a child has repeated what has already been said. For example, I tell |  | **Regie asks the class their thoughts about the title of the Welcome Words Chart they have been working on.** | |

continues

**Deeper Understanding: Reading and Writing Lots of Texts, Part 1**

*Video* **SCENES**

**Shared Writing: "We Share" *continued***

| Setting, Notes, and Explicit Teaching Points | Ongoing Assessment | Questions/Reflections | Learning Outcomes |
|---|---|---|---|
| The What, Why, and How of Teaching | Informing Our Instruction | For Professional Conversations | What Students Know and Are Able to Do |

### Setting, Notes, and Explicit Teaching Points

a student, *"So you are agreeing with. . . ."* I do not say, *"We already have that on the list,"* or, *"You weren't listening."*

**TEACHING POINTS**

- Use a favorite book (*We Share Everything*) as a springboard for writing a "We Share" list about what kids share.
- Solicit students' ideas and thoughts and take their ideas as stated (this is a draft and you can fix it up later).
- Check spellings of important words such as *We Share* with the book, *We Share Everything.* (This is one way to begin to teach students to self-assess words they are writing.)
- Invite students to give the sounds they hear in important words. (For example, "*In* share *how does that start?*")
- State the importance of adding illustrations to words in isolation to aid reading the chart.
- Stretch out the sounds in words as you write them and have your voice match the letters you are writing.
- Provide many opportunities to reread the text:
    - Reread with students to check for meaning and completeness.
    - Invite one or two of the students to point and read the newly written text in front of the class.
- Add an ending. "*How should we end it? Let's check the spelling on that.*"
- Add punctuation (quickly) that lets the reader know how the text should sound (*We Share Everything!*).
- State the reason rereading is important. *"Reread the text to build fluency and confidence in reading the text independently."*
- Show how and why bullets are used in a list. *"Sometimes when you are making a list, kids, you just put a dot before the word."*

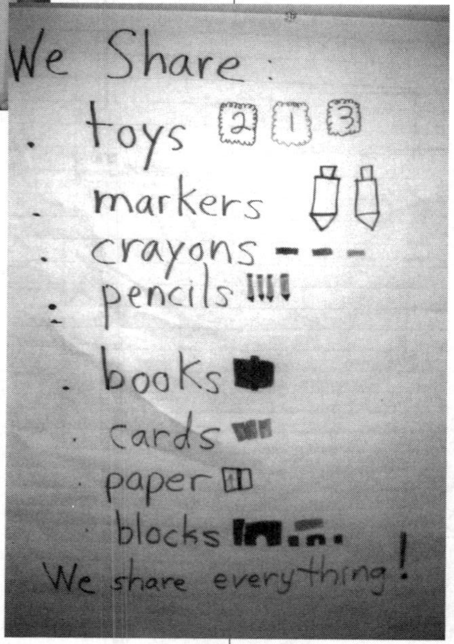

### Ongoing Assessment

Have students reread text to check their reading and where support is needed:

- *"Who thinks they can read the whole thing?"*
- *"What did we say started with a /p/?"* [I make the beginning sound /p/.]

*Video* **SCENES**

**DEEPER UNDERSTANDING: Reading and Writing Lots of Texts, Part 1**

| Video Scenes | Setting, Notes, and Explicit Teaching Points<br>The What, Why, and How of Teaching | Ongoing Assessment<br>Informing Our Instruction | Questions/Reflections<br>For Professional Conversations | Learning Outcomes<br>What Students Know and Are Able to Do |
|---|---|---|---|---|
| **Transition from Reading to Writing** (4:28 min.) | **NOTES**<br>Before this session the classroom teacher has collated the illustrated student pages to make one class book on favorite colors and has made copies of the book for each student. Today's lesson starts with rereading class-authored texts to practice reading, build confidence and fluency, and do important word work. Notice the efficiency and enjoyment of using and applying the whole-part-whole learning approach.<br><br>Notice the importance of asking kids how they know what a word says (metacognitive awareness: knowing how you know). Because our goal is for kids to be independent, they have to be able to bring what they know to consciousness. In kindergarten the most powerful word walls often contain student names with accompanying photos. Because student names are so important, they are an efficient, enjoyable, and sensible way to teach phonemic awareness and phonics. |  | **Mrs. Martinka asks Susan "How did you know that said 'markers'?"** | |
| • *Down by the Bay* and Reviewing Rhyming Parts | **TEACHING POINTS FROM *DOWN BY THE BAY***<br>Using songs, poems, or chants to teach word work or as textual models is an efficient way to engage students with print. In this session, we use a familiar text, *Down by the Bay*, to focus on pairs of rhyming words. Songs and chants invite participation and help build phonemic awareness and comprehension; these participatory texts are a crucial teaching scaffold for English language learners. | Notice and observe students' ability to generate rhyming words that follow the pattern in the familiar text. Adjust instruction accordingly. | • How can you use familiar songs, poems, or chants to capitalize on students' understanding of phonemic awareness?<br><br>• Why is it important to teach and advocate for lots of familiar text to reinforce and teach skills and strategies? | |
| • Word Work<br><br>*(See Session 8 for word work in the primary grades.)* | **TEACHING POINTS FROM WORD WORK**<br>• Use pictures along with the first letter of the word to help developing readers.<br>• Reread the class chart as you point to each word to help kids make the one-to-one match between spoken and written words.<br>• Highlight important words such as *we* using a sliding mask. *"What does* marker *start with?"*<br>• Use a sliding mask to identify and highlight the beginning letters of known and unknown words as well as to gradually reveal a word from beginning to end. | Ask students to explain how they know something and scaffold their thinking. The goal is for students to problem solve independently:<br>• *"What does that word say?"*<br>• *"How did you know that (said markers)?"*<br>• *"If we didn't know, could we use the picture to help us?"*<br>• *"If you don't know, how could you figure that out, what else could you do?"* | • Why is it important to use a predictable pattern or structure for emerging readers and writers? | • Identify front cover, back cover, and title of a book.<br>• Participate in shared reading of a big book.<br>• Use visuals (photographs) to get ideas for writing. |

continues

## DEEPER UNDERSTANDING: Reading and Writing Lots of Texts, Part 1

| Video SCENES | Setting, Notes, and Explicit Teaching Points<br>The What, Why, and How of Teaching | Ongoing Assessment<br>Informing Our Instruction | Questions/Reflections<br>For Professional Conversations | Learning Outcomes<br>What Students Know and Are Able to Do |
|---|---|---|---|---|
| **Transition from Reading to Writing *continued*** | • Ask students to say how they know a word (this reveals their thinking, how they are or are not figuring things out, and their level of print awareness).<br>• Reinforce different ways to figure out words (the word wall with student names and attached photos, written class texts, class charts, name tags, looking at parts of a word, and thinking about what makes sense). | • *"What's this first letter? What's that? Whose name starts with 'D'? Let's check. . . ."*<br>**An example of a name word wall.** | • What do you notice about the word wall you see in the classroom? Is it just a teacher artifact or is it a useful resource that students access?<br>• How is your word wall a useful resource for your students? Or why isn't it? What can you do to ensure it's a workable resource for your students? | |
| **Shared Reading and Writing: Creating Texts About Kindergarten** (9:00 min.)<br><br>• Welcome Words | **NOTES**<br>We have been using three different books (*Something Else, Kindergarten Kids, A Child's Day*) to generate ideas for shared writing that have a meaningful purpose and audience. We quickly create the Welcome Words class chart after the children have heard the book *Something Else* read aloud. It is the story about a creature that was different and made to feel unwelcome. We use the book as a springboard to talk about and write words and phrases to make everyone feel welcome in the classroom. The chart remains posted in the classroom and is used daily. This short video scene takes place the day after the story has been read and the chart has been started.<br><br>**TEACHING POINTS FROM WELCOME WORDS**<br>• Set an authentic purpose and audience for writing.<br>• Reread class chart for the purpose of adding and affirming student suggestions to make others feel welcome.<br><br>**NOTES**<br>Two different picture books about kindergarten are being used to motivate and engage students in creating their own kindergarten photo text (*"What's your day like in kindergarten?"*). You will want to invite students to share their ideas. Get ideas down quickly, accept everything you can, and negotiate what the text will include. Remember that in shared writing the teacher is holding the pen, making the final decisions, and being respectful of students' responses. In the video scene we are generating ideas for an 8-page book with a photo of an important kindergarten activity on each page. (See photographs on pp. 5–21 and 5–22.) | Ask students: *"Why are we making this chart?"* Check to see that they understand the purpose.<br><br>Check to find out what is important to students and what they value in kindergarten. | **The students are suggesting words for the Welcome Words chart.**<br><br>**The final Welcome Words chart is posted and used in the classroom throughout the school year.** | |

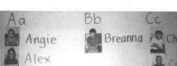

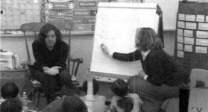

**Video SCENES**

**Deeper Understanding:** Reading and Writing Lots of Texts, Part 1

| Video Scenes | Setting, Notes, and Explicit Teaching Points<br>The What, Why, and How of Teaching | Ongoing Assessment<br>Informing Our Instruction | Questions/Reflections<br>For Professional Conversations | Learning Outcomes<br>What Students Know and Are Able to Do |
|---|---|---|---|---|
| • *A Child's Day* by Jillian Cutting | **TEACHING POINTS FROM *A CHILD'S DAY***<br>• State purpose and audience for writing (new student, parents, next year's students).<br>• Connect words to pictures as students attempt to read the text with you. | | | |
| • Generating Ideas | • Use text to stimulate writing ideas. *"As you go through the kindergarten day, what are the things we would want to have in our book to let other readers know, 'Here is what it is like in our kindergarten classroom'?"*<br>• Accept and help shape student responses. (After a student offers the word *everything* for one page the teacher says, *"We could even say we love everything about kindergarten. That could be our last line."*) | | • Why is it important to give students choice and to negotiate text when creating text from a shared writing?<br>• How do texts about ordinary daily experiences support all learners as readers and writers? | |
| • Welcome to Kindergarten | **NOTES**<br>Before this scene, the purpose and audience for the shared writing of the class photo book *Welcome to Kindergarten* had been discussed. Photographs had been taken of 8 important things kindergarten students do, from a list that had been created earlier in the week. Another class shared writing, a "Welcome Words" poster, was also completed before this scene took place. The poster remained in the classroom and was reread and used for the remainder of the school year.<br><br>**TEACHING POINTS FROM *WELCOME TO KINDERGARTEN***<br>• Point out that all books are written by specific authors.<br>• Highlight features of text, illustrations, and decisions authors make on what to include and where to include it.<br>• Summarize the purpose and framework of the book.<br><br>**TEACHING POINTS**<br>• Decide the title quickly and write it (can also be done with student input).<br>• Write the book together. *"What do we want our first page to say? What should we say about (each photo)? What's the last page going to say?"* | | • Why is reading and writing lots of familiar texts with familiar concepts so meaningful and important for English language learners? | |

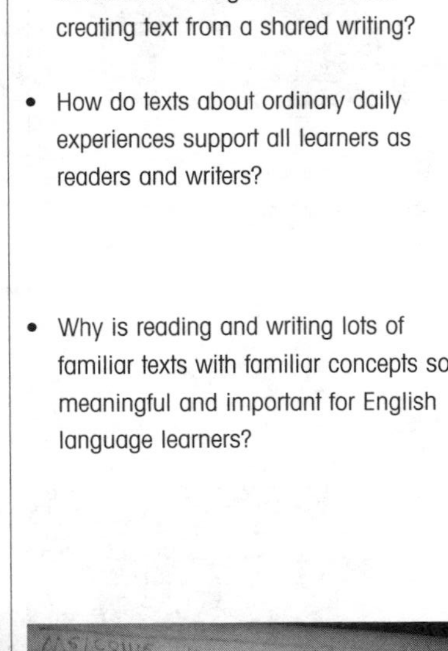

We draft our class photo book.

continues

# Video SCENES

**Shared Reading and Writing: Creating Texts About Kindergarten *continued***

## Deeper Understanding: Reading and Writing Lots of Texts, Part 1

### Setting, Notes, and Explicit Teaching Points

The What, Why, and How of Teaching

- Keep up a steady pace, and complete the writing within 10 minutes. (We completed this text in 6 minutes.)
- Say the words as you write them and stretch out the sounds as you write (models what we want emerging writers to do).
- Keep the pattern of the book predictable so all students can read it. (In this photo book, each page begins with *We* and contains one short sentence of two to five words.)
- Reread the text so far. *"Good writers check their text before going on."*
- Point to each word as you read text aloud (keeps kids engaged and focused on the print).
- Invite students to read along (shared reading).
- Have students help spell high-frequency words.
- Add the last line at the end of the book. *"How do we want our book to end? 'We like kindergarten!'"*
- Extend reading and writing possibilities beyond the original class text by making individual copies for each student—with words for guided and independent reading, as a blank photo text for differentiated instruction in which students use their own language and ideas to create new text as best they can.

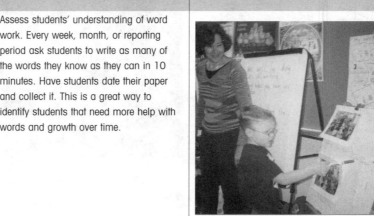

The teacher reviews the class-authored photo-text.

### Ongoing Assessment

Informing Our Instruction

Assess students' understanding of word work. Every week, month, or reporting period ask students to write as many of the words they know as they can in 10 minutes. Have students date their paper and collect it. This is a great way to identify students that need more help with words and growth over time.

Welcome to Kindergarten!

by

Mrs. Martinka's Kindergarten Class

See the website for the complete published book.

### Questions/Reflections

For Professional Conversations

A student in another class reads their class-authored photo text on kindergarten.

We made copies of the book for each student so that they could read the book during independent reading practice.

We learn from the teacher.

We read books.

### Learning Outcomes

What Students Know and Are Able to Do

- Use detail and color in drawings.
- Use words from environmental print.
- Use classroom resources such as the word wall and class charts.
- Participate in reading classroom published text aloud.
- Observe and discuss using ending punctuation in shared writing.

Reading and Writing Lots of Texts, Part 2

# DEEPER UNDERSTANDING

*The teaching and assessing points reflect the total lesson but not all of these points are on the edited videos you are watching. However, the major points are represented on the edited videos.*

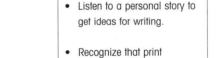

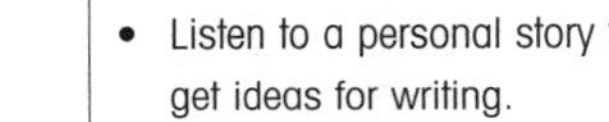
The globe icon indicates that the example is also available when you visit www.regieroutman.com.

*Video* **SCENES**

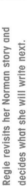

| | Setting, Notes, and Explicit Teaching Points | Ongoing Assessment | Questions/Reflections | Learning Outcomes |
|---|---|---|---|---|
| | The What, Why, and How of Teaching | Informing Our Instruction | For Professional Conversations | What Students Know and Are Able to Do |
| **PART 2:** **WRITING READABLE TEXTS** | **NOTES** **The oral storytelling, demonstration writing, scaffolded public conversations, independent sustained writing, and conferences shown here took place over two days and are a model for daily writing.** If we want students to write interesting, coherent texts, we have to demonstrate telling and writing such stories ourselves. We cannot expect students to come up with a new topic every day, and then get authentic writing. We need to help students find those few topics they deeply care about and can write about and read about over time. All students have worthwhile experiences to write about even those students who have not had lots of experiences with print. |  **Regie revisits her Norman story and decides what she will write next.** | | |
| 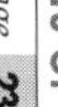 **Demonstration Writing: "My Cat Norman"** (11:19 min.) | Write about an ordinary experience with which all your students will be able to connect, perhaps one you remember when you were their age. Identify possible topics and subtopics in advance, but do your writing and thinking in front of the children so they see your real process and struggle, not a perfect, finished piece written at home. Tell your story with enthusiasm and lots of interesting facts. Use your oral storytelling to help you decide the story you most want to write.<br><br>Complete your demonstration in 10 or 15 minutes. Don't ask for student suggestions: they slow down the process, can be distracting, and divert attention from the meaning of your story. You are in charge! Moreover, students need at least 15 or 20 minutes in which to write and the energy to do so (see *Conversations excerpt*, "Journal Writing," pp. 233–282). Save some student writing examples as models for next year's students. | **Regie tells the class that they don't have to stop at just one page. We have stapled several pages together to give students the message to continue their narrative writing.** |  | • Listen to a personal story to get ideas for writing.<br>• Recognize that print represents spoken language. |

*continues*

**DEEPER UNDERSTANDING: Reading and Writing Lots of Texts, Part 2**

*Video* **SCENES**

**Demonstration Writing: "My Cat Norman"** ***continued***

• Telling the Story First

## Setting, Notes, and Explicit Teaching Points
The What, Why, and How of Teaching

**TEACHING POINTS**

- Begin with the end in mind: Set the expectation for writing that will lead to publication.
- Show children examples of student-authored books so they understand the expectations, purpose, and audience for their writing and are motivated to write:
  - Title, author.
  - Three pages.
  - One line of text or more per page.
  - Illustrations that support and extend text.
  - Ideas that come from what's most important to them.
- Make the connection that their writing will become a published book. *"You're going to get to publish it into a real book just like this, and we can have a special part of the classroom library for our published books."*
- State that the writing, on the same (self-chosen) topic, will occur over several days.
- Demonstrate through your storytelling that what you can talk about you can write about. Use rich language when you tell your story. (These two factors are critical for English language learners.)
- Think out loud as you are deciding on your possible topic and how to begin. *"I think I'll write about . . . ."*
- Say your words before and as you write them so students make the voice–print match, which will aid in their reading and keep them focused.
- Add the title at any time. *"You don't have to decide your title right at the beginning."*
- Show how to access and use the word wall as a resource for spelling. *"Where could we find* we [We feed Norman tuna fish]?"
- Demonstrate possible ways beginning writers can write so all students feel they can be successful. Write using:
  - Beginning consonant sounds by writing the first letter of the word, random letters, dashes, or a line to indicate a letter is missing.
  - Beginning and ending consonant sounds.
  - Hearing additional sounds in words.

## Ongoing Assessment
Informing Our Instruction

Be sure you tell students why you are demonstrating writing. Have students say back to you the key reasons:

- *"Why am I doing this storytelling and writing?"*
- *"How can what I am doing help you as a writer?"*

If students are unable to say why you are demonstrating writing, explain again, and reassess their responses.

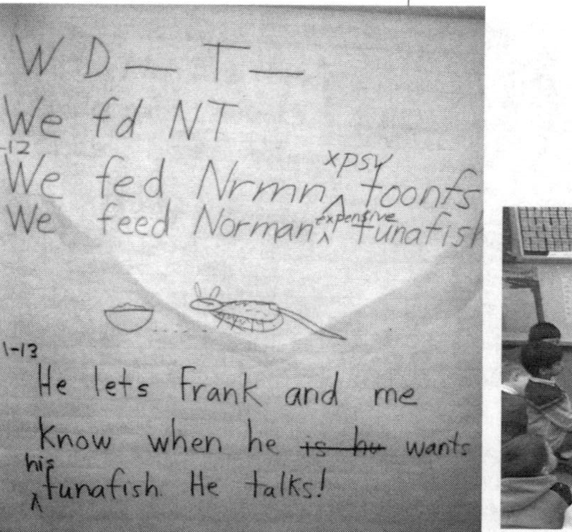


**My demonstration writing over two days.**

## Questions/Reflections
For Professional Conversations

- What are some ways to ensure that your demonstration does not go on too long?
- How can you ensure student engagement when you tell your story and write it?

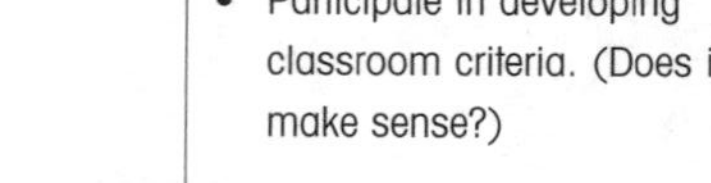

## Learning Outcomes
What Students Know and Are Able to Do

- Use drawing and talk for thinking about and planning writing.
- Use literature to stimulate ideas for writing.
- Draw and write for self, family, friends, and teacher.
- Identify the intended audience for a picture or written piece.
- Draw and write to communicate with others.
- Draw and write to retell, inform, and entertain.
- Participate in developing classroom criteria. (Does it make sense?)
- Identify common consonant sounds, beginning and ending sounds, short vowel sounds.

*Video* **SCENES**

**DEEPER UNDERSTANDING: Reading and Writing Lots of Texts, Part 2**

| | Setting, Notes, and Explicit Teaching Points<br>The What, Why, and How of Teaching | Ongoing Assessment<br>Informing Our Instruction | Questions/Reflections<br>For Professional Conversations | Learning Outcomes<br>What Students Know and Are Able to Do |
|---|---|---|---|---|
| • Word Work: Phonemic Awareness | • Point to each word as you read your writing so students can follow along and read with you (silently or aloud).<br>• Check your writing by rereading out loud, as needed, to decide what to say next and to make sure the story makes sense and sounds the way you want it to sound. Think aloud about the decisions you make and remain focused on content.<br>• Space between words. (*"So other people can read it."*)<br>• Show conventional spelling underneath invented spellings that children have supplied and focus on and confirm what they already know so that students will have confidence to try on their own. *"Watch how close you were in* feed, *you knew the beginning, middle, and the end."*<br>• Draw your picture first if it helps you tell your story.<br>• Add a missing word to add important detail to your story. This is an example of teach it first and label it later. We are not saying, *"I need to add details* (because it is on the standards)." We say, *"I am adding a word that makes the story more explicit and richer."*<br>• Talk about where your story will go next (so students are thinking like writers and are expecting their story to continue). | Occasionally, invite children to help you spell to determine what they know about letters and sounds and words. Use their approximations to assess what they know, are ready to learn, and what you need to teach next. | • What happens when you try to demonstrate everything at once? (Content plus explaining conventions as you make them.)<br>• Why is it important at this time to keep your focus and verbal comments on the meaning of the story, not on the conventions, even though you are including conventions as you write?<br>• How does writing support reading? | • Understand and apply phonological awareness and phonemic awareness so they can:<br>  • Manipulate and segment words orally by onset and rime.<br>  • Segment and blend two and three phoneme words orally. |
| **Before Writing: Scaffolded Public Conversations**<br>(2:07 min.) | **NOTES**<br>Supporting students through in-depth conversation and natural questioning makes it possible for all students to write successfully. Having a conversation with one student with the rest of the class looking on and listening (a scaffolded public conversation) ensures better writing. Aim for 3 to 5 minutes per conversation. (When students hear one or more peers talk through their writing ideas and tell their stories—and understand the purpose of the scaffolded public conversation—all students have an opportunity to write a richer story.) Students are then able to write independently for an extended amount of time. |   | **Amanda Martinka uses responsive questioning and conversation to support a students' storytelling before writing.** | • Use oral language, structure, letters, and pictures to predict and confirm word meanings (with teacher guidance). |

*continues*

# Video SCENES

**Before Writing: Scaffolded Public Conversations *continued***

- Scaffolded Conversation with Luis

WWW *(See additional scaffolded conversations video on the website for specific language and ideas for helping students tell their stories.)*

## DEEPER UNDERSTANDING: Reading and Writing Lots of Texts, Part 2

### Setting, Notes, and Explicit Teaching Points
The What, Why, and How of Teaching

Writing down students' ideas on sticky notes helps capture their thinking. In this demonstration, student ideas are written on chart paper so that the teachers who are observing can see them. Normally you would write a few key words on a sticky note and give it to the student to remind them about their ideas and what they plan to write about. The notes will also remind you about key ideas from the public conversation with the student.

**TEACHING POINTS**

- Verbalize ideas for possible writing topics (*pet, sister grandma, mom, dad, bicycle, friends, brother*) before inviting one student to share their story in front of the class. *"Luis come on up. What do you really like to do with your brother?"*
- Tell and show the difference between boring writing and interesting writing. *"If you just say, 'My brother is nice,' it is kind of boring. Other people are going to be reading your books. What do you like to do with your brother?"*
- Ask questions that will encourage and ensure elaboration and details in a natural way. *"How do you play with your brother? Do you chase your brother? So what do you do?"* [Asked after Luis mentioned two Spiderman masks.]
- Ask clarifying questions to help students verbalize their own story and give them the language to help them make their story meaningful to the reader. *"You play Spiderman with him? So you and your brother have Spiderman masks?"*
- Restate the child's thinking in correct English language structure. *"Let's get that down."* [Addressing observing teachers: *"Luis is going to be writing about his brother, and we write his thoughts down so that we don't lose his language.*] *'Me and my brother play Spiderman mask. We chase each other and we fall down.'"* (We are modeling a critical scaffold for our English language learners, the transfer from oral language to written text.)

### Ongoing Assessment
Informing Our Instruction

Have students say back to you the purpose of the scaffolded conversations and why it's important to listen carefully.

Check that students are clear on expectations for what they are to do. Have a student or two say back to you what students are expected to do:

- *"What did you see me do when I was writing my story?"*
- *"Raise your hand if you know what you are going to write about."*
- *"How many of you do not know what you are going to write about?"*

Assess student understanding of classroom resources. Use your observation notes to inform and adjust your instruction.

Check for student understanding and set expectations for using classroom resources when writing independently:

- *"You know how writers write and you know that they leave spaces between your words."*
- *"What can you do if you don't know a word?"*

*"What do good writers do when they are done?"* (If the word wall does not come up in the discussion, it is probably not being well utilized by students.)

### Questions/Reflections
For Professional Conversations

**Luis having a scaffolded conversation with Regie. (See his student profile on p. 5–30.)**

- What do you notice about the questioning, pacing, and interaction with the student in the scaffolded conference?
- How do scaffolded conversations help set students up for writing success?
- Once you have spent lots of time modeling and having public scaffolded conversations, how can students learn to do this with and for each other (turn-and-talk, partner talk, quick-writes)?
- Why are public scaffolded conversations essential for the literacy success for English language learners and all struggling learners?
- How can you ensure that your struggling students are immediately successful when writing independently?

### Learning Outcomes
What Students Know and Are Able to Do

**Chart showing notes from scaffolded conversations with students before they write. (The notes were taken on a chart so the observing teachers could see them. Most often, I use sticky notes with key words to remind the writer and me what s/he said.)**

# Video SCENES

**Deeper Understanding: Reading and Writing Lots of Texts, Part 2**

| Video Scene | Setting, Notes, and Explicit Teaching Points | Ongoing Assessment | Questions/Reflections | Learning Outcomes |
|---|---|---|---|---|
| | The What, Why, and How of Teaching | Informing Our Instruction | For Professional Conversations | What Students Know and Are Able to Do |
| **Setting Expectations for Independent Writing** (3:11 min.) | **NOTES**<br>Set clear expectations for learning and focus students' attention on the meaning and purpose for what they will be doing and why. *"The reason we are doing this* [refer to your demonstration writing] *is so that you get ideas for writing, so you need to pay attention so that you will know what you are going to write about."*<br>• Drawing pictures allows students to tell their story with great detail and focus on the meaning of their story over several days. *"How many of you like to draw pictures first?"*<br>• Let students know that they are expected to write and make use of all of the support they have received. Review your demonstration writing as a way to support students' understanding and set writing expectations. *"I am going to expect everybody to have something that looks like this* [refer to demonstration writing], *and after you are done writing, we will celebrate your writing. We are going to say what a great job you did."* | Note and build additional support and supplementary materials/scaffolds for struggling learners and English language learners.<br><br>Confer with at least one or two students per day. Collect anecdotal notes and dated samples of student writing. | <br>Regie tells the class they can draw their picture first, since that helps some writers. | |
| • Assessing Use of Classroom Resources | **TEACHING POINTS**<br>• Choose appropriate paper. These students were used to writing on one sheet of paper that had one line of print and a space for illustrations. Giving them three pieces of unlined paper stapled together lets them know they were expected to write a story—more than one sentence, over a period of days. They wrote much more than teachers expected they could.<br>• Show students writing expectations related to directionality, spaces between words, what to do when they get stuck. *"You know how writers write across the page, leave spaces between their words. What do you do if you don't know how to spell something?"* | Check to see whether students know how to problem solve and use classroom resources when they don't know how to write a word:<br>• *"What are you going to do if you don't know how to spell something?"*<br>*"Put a magic line." "Sound it out."*<br>*"Ask the teacher."*<br>*"No, the teacher is going to be busy, what else can you do? What can you do to help yourself? Where can you look in the room to help you write a word?"*<br>(word wall, chart, student work?)<br>Assessing student's problem-solving abilities before they write and teaching them what they need to know ensures greater success for all students. | • If your students are not independently using the word wall as a resource for reading and writing, what does that tell you and what can you do to change that? | • Use simple resources with teacher guidance (for example, alphabet, picture dictionaries, word walls). |

continues

**Video SCENES**

**DEEPER UNDERSTANDING: Reading and Writing Lots of Texts, Part 2**

| | Setting, Notes, and Explicit Teaching Points<br>The What, Why, and How of Teaching | Ongoing Assessment<br>Informing Our Instruction | Questions/Reflections<br>For Professional Conversations | Learning Outcomes<br>What Students Know and Are Able to Do |
|---|---|---|---|---|
| **Setting Expectations for Independent Writing *continued*** | | Check to see whether students know to reread their writing (*"That's how I found out I left out a word"*). This is an example of teaching revising in kindergarten.<br><br>Assess student understanding of task and readiness to write. *"If you don't know what you are going to write about stay with me."* | • What happened before students began to write independently that ensured they would be successful? | |
| • Supporting the Not-So-Ready Writer | **NOTES**<br>Provide additional support for students who are not ready to write. *"If you have no idea what you are going to write about, stay with me. Stay with me and I will help you get started."* In a small group help students generate ideas for writing by asking them about things that are near and dear to them. Move at a fast pace so that students have energy to write. When you ensure students have a topic they want to write about and the language to do so, they are more likely to begin writing immediately.<br><br>**TEACHING POINTS**<br>• Suggest specific ideas for writing. *"You might want to write about your pet, sister or brother, grandma, dog, special doll or person in your life, glasses, best friend, sport, soccer, what do you like to do? You have an idea that you want to write about?"*<br>• Affirm any possible topic the student is excited about. [After Ilan says, *"Two of my cats fight."*] *"That's great! Go! He's got a great start. Look at the smile on his face."* (See student writing sample below and on p. 5–11.) | While students are independently writing, confer one-on-one with one or more students and note writing behaviors and transfer of new learning; talk with them and observe their writing and thinking.<br>• *"What do you play with your sister?"*<br>• *"What do you do when you play outside?"*<br>• *"Do you want to write more today?"*<br>• *"Read me what you have, Niko. Who is going on a trip? Your family?"*<br>• *"Where are you going? When are you going?"*<br>Note that student independent writing and the roving one-on-one conferences are an effective and efficient way to affirm, assess, provide appropriate individual support, differentiate instruction, and focus on new learning. | **A small group remains behind to get help starting on their stories.** | |

# *Video* SCENES

**Independent Practice: Writing and Roving Conferences**

(3:18 min.)

**DEEPER UNDERSTANDING: Reading and Writing Lots of Texts, Part 2**

| Setting, Notes, and Explicit Teaching Points | Ongoing Assessment | Questions/Reflections | Learning Outcomes |
|---|---|---|---|
| The What, Why, and How of Teaching | Informing Our Instruction | For Professional Conversations | What Students Know and Are Able to Do |

**NOTES**

Remember that until now the writing focus in this classroom has been on learning letters and sounds; the children's ability to read and write continuous text has been very limited. **The most significant learning that observing teachers take away from the residency is that young children can tell and write a story even if they do not know all their letters and sounds.** These video scenes show the first story writing these children have done in school. **The continuation of students' daily story writing (and reading those stories) resulted in a classroom of readers and writers and demonstrated the power of the writing/reading connection.** (During this first day of sustained writing conferences, some observing teachers also try out brief roving conferences.)

As students are writing, move about the classroom and have brief "roving" conferences. Observe writing behaviors that approximate your modeling and writing expectations. As you walk around, take brief notes about your students' writing and select one or more students to celebrate at the end of independent writing. (On this first day I did not take notes because I was focused on getting to know as many students as possible.) Remember that independent writing practice needs to follow immediately after the whole-class teacher demonstration in order for our littlest writers to practice and transfer new writing skills and strategies.

The reason we don't want students to erase their writing is to have a record of their thinking. Show and tell students how to cross out with one clean line.

**TEACHING POINTS**

- Affirm student's efforts. *"That's a great start for your story. What do you do when you play...?"*
- Only write on a student's paper with permission—shows respect for the writer. *"If you don't want that* [word written legibly] *there, I won't put it there; would you like me to take it away?"*

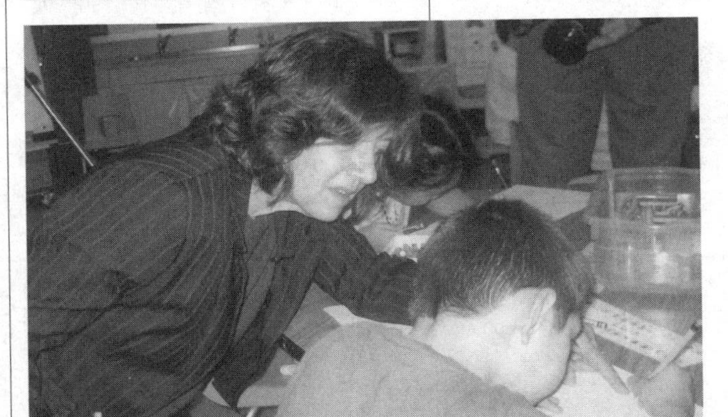

**Roving conferences and students independently writing.**

- What are the advantages of quick roving conferences?
- Some teachers write comments on young children's writing in pen or red pencil. What message does this send to students? What are alternative ways to comment on students' writing?

continues

**Deeper Understanding:** Reading and Writing Lots of Texts, Part 2

| *Video* SCENES | Setting, Notes, and Explicit Teaching Points<br>The What, Why, and How of Teaching | Ongoing Assessment<br>Informing Our Instruction | Questions/Reflections<br>For Professional Conversations | Learning Outcomes<br>What Students Know and Are Able to Do |
|---|---|---|---|---|
| **Independent Practice: Writing and Roving Conferences *continued*** | • Have student point to each word as s/he reads (to be sure the student matches each written and spoken word). Rereading their own texts supports their reading abilities.<br>• Affirm student's language. "'*We chase each other.' That's wonderful. You already have a whole story there.*"<br>• Write the words you can't read on the student's paper and let them know why you are writing on their paper. Write lightly in pencil—is respectful to the student and allows the child's writing to predominate. "*Is it OK if I write very lightly on here so I can read it later?*"<br>• Focus on helping the student reread and tell his story so it makes sense.<br>• Make sure the child holds the pencil and does the writing so that the responsibility is on the child and the child is respected as the writer.<br>• Have the child reread his writing using his reading finger (to make sure the story makes sense and to check if any words need to be added or revised).<br>• Encourage students to say the words slowly as they are writing them (stretch out the sounds in the words they are writing so they write all the sounds that they hear). "*I like the way you are stretching out those sounds.*"<br>• Affirm what the student knows so he will use what he knows again. "*You know a lot of letters and sounds.*"<br>• Reread again to make sure the story makes sense and to reinforce and demonstrate one-to-one matching while reading. "*Use your reading finger and read the whole thing to me.*" | **Student Profiles:**<br><br>**Serena:** Serena entered kindergarten with much literacy knowledge. Although she was a reader, she was underperforming as a writer. According to her teacher, her stories were "very generic" and often the same from day to day. Once she was shown how to write about other topics she cared about and to include interesting information, she took off as a writer.<br><br>**Niko:** Niko, an English language learner and very quiet child, demonstrated limited literacy knowledge at the beginning of kindergarten. At midyear his writing consisted of just a few words, such as "I love my family." After the residency, his teacher commented: "Writing helped get him out of his shell, and then he just took off." He became very motivated, chose to write in every free moment, and was reading at grade level at the end of kindergarten. At the beginning of first grade, on his own, he wrote an 18-page story about his family with "incredible details."<br><br>**Prachantauny:** Prachantauny entered kindergarten with no letter-sound knowledge and little experience with books. She was "an inquisitive learner who had a hard time focusing." Writing became her bridge to reading. The first texts she was able to read were her own, and by the end of kindergarten she was reading at grade level.<br><br>**Luis:** Luis is an English language learner who entered kindergarten with low literacy knowledge. According to his teacher, "Luis knew a few letters and sounds, was very quiet and very shy, and unable to write. He cried with frustration that he couldn't write." Writing opened up the window to reading. Once he could write, he talked more, became more outgoing in class, and ended up the school year reading at grade level. | | |
| **Public Celebration Conferences**<br>(4:47 min.) | **NOTES**<br>After sustained writing time, have students leave their pencils at their tables so they can focus their attention on the conferences. Try to celebrate all students when you are first introducing public conferences even if it means having several celebrations during the day to fit them all in. Noting all students' strengths helps give them the energy and will to write. | | | |

*Video* **SCENES**

**DEEPER UNDERSTANDING: Reading and Writing Lots of Texts, Part 2**

| Video Scenes | Setting, Notes, and Explicit Teaching Points<br>The What, Why, and How of Teaching | Ongoing Assessment<br>Informing Our Instruction | Questions/Reflections<br>For Professional Conversations | Learning Outcomes<br>What Students Know and Are Able to Do |
|---|---|---|---|---|
| • Luis | **TEACHING POINTS**<br>• Have the child do the first reading while holding the paper facing out so that all students can see the text. (In this scene, Luis transfers the brief practice he had doing one-to-one matching in the roving conference to the public conference.) See Luis' student profile on the previous page.<br>• State the reasons for these conferences (so that children will listen, learn, and get ideas for their own writing):<br>  • *"Luis is up here for two reasons, the first thing is to celebrate great writing; second, so that you get ideas for your writing."*<br>• Reinforce how the writer's job is to be sure the story makes sense.<br>• Say everything the child has done well (so he will do it again, he is affirmed, he feels like a writer, he wants to go on writing, and other students see and hear writing possibilities for themselves). *"I want to tell you all the things he (Luis) has done. I asked Luis, 'Does that sound like a story?' He was really smart and Luis made changes to make the story make sense. He stretched out words, he knew how to write* me, *and he knew how to write* play.*"*<br>• Teach what the child is ready to learn and what is necessary for the writing to be coherent and readable. *"Luis, the one thing that was a little bit hard for me to read—because you want everyone to read your words—you want to space between the words. You did such a good job on your picture. You have your picture to go with your drawing. What are you going to write about tomorrow? Because you want everyone to be able to read your story, you want to space between the words. Try that tomorrow. Great job on the pictures that match your words."* | <br>**Luis proudly reads his story.** | • How can you decide what is most important to focus on in the conference?<br><br>• Why is it helpful to do the second reading of the child's writing? | |
| • Allison | • Reread the story after the child has read it to point out all the writing strengths.<br>• Identify and focus on what the student did well. *"What I love about your story is that you said 'I bake cookies with my mom.'"*<br>• Encourage elaboration and detail (without using those terms). *"What kind of cookies do you bake with your mom? Look at her picture. What kind of cookies do you make? What do you do and what does your mom do?"* | 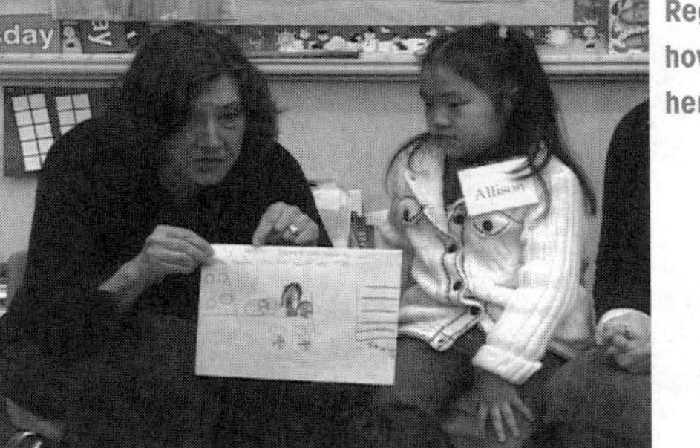 | **Regie tells the class, "Look how carefully Allison spaced her words."** | |

continues

**DEEPER UNDERSTANDING: Reading and Writing Lots of Texts, Part 2**

| *Video* SCENES | Setting, Notes, and Explicit Teaching Points<br>The What, Why, and How of Teaching | Ongoing Assessment<br>Informing Our Instruction | Questions/Reflections<br>For Professional Conversations | Learning Outcomes<br>What Students Know and Are Able to Do |
|---|---|---|---|---|
| • Allison *continued* | • Restate the child's language (to give the child a sense of the whole story, to reinforce the right sequencing, and to make it more likely that the language will appear in the writing). *"So you could say, 'We make gingerbread cookies, I print out the shape of the cookies, we decorate them.'"*<br>• Keep your first comments focused on the content of the child's story before moving to conventions (so students focus on meaning and not just correctness).<br>• Affirm the use of conventions. *"Look at how carefully she spaced her words, and look at how Allison can write down all her sounds and words she knows."* | | | |
| **Independent Writing (Continued)**<br>(2:09 min.)<br><br>• Revisiting the Norman Story | **TEACHING POINTS**<br>• Show students, through explanation and demonstrations, what you expect of them and what they will do to continue writing their story. *"The first thing you're going to do is reread your story."*<br>• Show how to keep going with writing a story by demonstrating how to move on to a new page.<br>• Connect students' story writing to publishing "a real book" for a real audience. (Show and read a previously published student's book.) *"Everyone's going to get to read it (family, other kids)."*<br>• Think before you write. *"That's the first thing you do before you write."*<br>• Date your demonstration writing (on chart paper) by skipping a line where you left off yesterday and putting today's date on the next line. (Dating the paper is a way to assess student growth over time and where the writing started and ended over several days.)<br>• Reread yesterday's writing, pointing to the words as you do. Think out loud. *"What do I want to say today?"*<br>• Think about and say what you want to write next (so that students understand that this is what good writers do and what they will be expected to do on their own).<br>• Add to the story you started the day before by first telling the next part out loud. | | | |

**In the first line, Regie uses her own story of her cat to demonstrate how a kindergartner might write, even if he doesn't know all his letters and sounds.**

**With the second and third lines, Regie captures what students say, which gives her insight into what they know about letters and sounds (assessment embedded in teaching). In the last line, she writes the conventional spellings and celebrates what students know.**

# *Video* SCENES

**DEEPER UNDERSTANDING: Reading and Writing Lots of Texts, Part 2**

| | Setting, Notes, and Explicit Teaching Points<br>The What, Why, and How of Teaching | Ongoing Assessment<br>Informing Our Instruction | Questions/Reflections<br>For Professional Conversations | Learning Outcomes<br>What Students Know and Are Able to Do |
|---|---|---|---|---|
| | • Write the next part of your story, speaking your thoughts and stretching out the sounds of the words as you say them and write them.<br>• Use your finger to space between words as you write.<br>• Show how writers change their minds (revise as you go along):<br>  • Cross out, add better words, and continue to write.<br>  • Then, reread from the beginning to make sure the text makes sense.<br>• Tell the next part of your story (to show it will take several days to tell the whole interesting story). | Check that students are with you and paying attention as you write:<br>• *"What do you hear at the end (of this word)?"*<br>• *"Me."*<br>• *"Everybody?"* [Everyone spells *me*.] | • What is the message we give writers when the writing focus is on mechanics (letters and sounds)? How can focusing on meaningful content, along with letters and sounds, accelerate students' writing abilities and their interest in writing?<br>• What's the message we give to students when we expect them to write on a new topic every day?<br>• How does publishing "books" support students' reading and writing? | |
| <br>**Public Celebration Conferences (Continued)**<br>(2:26 min.) | **NOTES**<br>Because independent story writing is new for these kindergartners, we want to be sure everyone is celebrated and knows what to do next when they write independently. (Yesterday there wasn't time to get through the whole class.) Even though it takes a long time to celebrate everyone, there is a huge payoff. All children will want to write independently and are able to do so.<br>Designate an "author's chair" next to you where student authors can sit and read their writing while pointing to each word. Celebrate student writing by inviting writers to the author's chair, one by one, to share their stories. Highlight especially wonderful work, set the purpose for sharing the writing, set writing expectations for independent writing, and help students decide what to say next. Focus on the meaning of the stories and have students reread the story so that everyone can hear. *"You have a great story. We want you to tell us more."*<br>Give students lots of time to read over, think, and continue writing the story they previously started. Giving students time to write independently allows you time to confer with many students. Take notes on student learning and use the notes to follow student growth over time. Celebrate student writing. Encourage and support all writers as they come up with ideas and focus their writing on what was demonstrated, discussed, and practiced. *"When Zavier went on to write, he actually looked back to find the* m *for* my. *That was such a smart thing to do."* | As you are roaming about the room during sustained writing time, notice how and if students are using rereading to check what they have written so far and to help them decide what to say next. Note students who are doing such rereading, and celebrate those efforts during public celebration conferences (this encourages them and other students to repeat this behavior). | 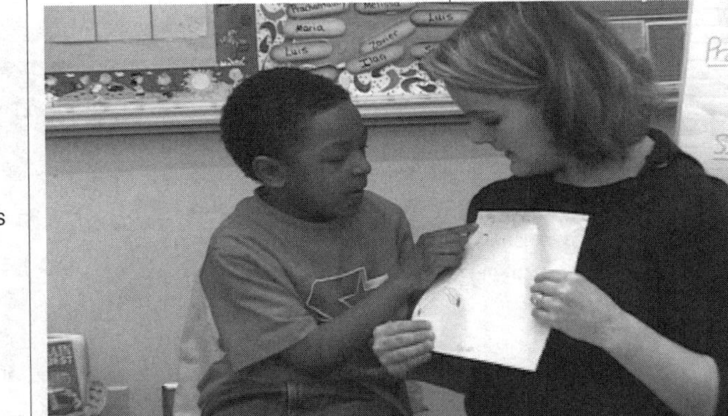<br>**Zavier sits in the author's chair and uses his reading finger to read his story in a public conference with his teacher, Amanda Martinka.** | |

continues

## DEEPER UNDERSTANDING: Reading and Writing Lots of Texts, Part 2

*Video* **SCENES**

**Public Celebration Conferences (Continued)**

• Ilan

*(See the website for more conference videos featuring helpful language to promote independent writing.)*

| Setting, Notes, and Explicit Teaching Points | Ongoing Assessment | Questions/Reflections | Learning Outcomes |
|---|---|---|---|
| The What, Why, and How of Teaching | Informing Our Instruction | For Professional Conversations | What Students Know and Are Able to Do |

**TEACHING POINTS**

These are points for Ilan's public conference:

- State why it is important for students to listen to a peer's conference. *"You're going to be working on your own without help, so you really need to listen. You'll be able to do it because you're such smart kindergarten kids."* And later in another conference, *"You're going to get ideas for your own writing."*
- State what the student did well; include the actual words the student used. *"You did something especially wonderful."* And a little later, *"You know what we loved about his writing—'Two of my cats wrestle and they play'—He used that great word* wrestle. *He didn't just say, 'My cats play.' And we got a picture in our minds. What a great thing that you did."*
- Scaffold conversation to help the student know what to say next in his story. *"Tell us what that wrestling looks like. What happens when they wrestle? What does that look like? When they wrestle what are you doing?"* (This is not the same as saying, *"Add more details."* Young writers don't know what we mean if we say, *"Add details."* They add words to please us, but those words often don't enrich the story. I am asking, *"What does that look like?"* because I am interested and want to know.)
- Put the language of the story we want the student to write in the student's ear. (When Ilan states he is watching, I follow with, *"I watch."*)
- Continue questioning to bring out the student's story. *"And what do you see? When they're wrestling, what do you see them doing? It's a great story. We want to hear more."*

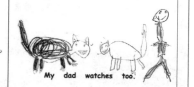

**Regie asks Ilan to read his story to the class.**

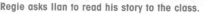

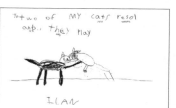

**Student Profile: Ilan**

Ilan entered kindergarten with typical literacy knowledge, knowing some letters and sounds but no words. At midyear he was writing a few words or a short structured sentence. During the residency in late January, he took off and began adding elaboration and detail to his self-chosen writing topics. By the end of the school year, he was reading and writing above grade level.

**Ilan's draft.**

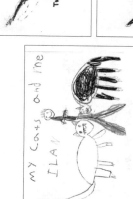

**Ilan's published book with his handwritten cover.**

They make noise.
They hiss and they growl.

## *Video* SCENES

**Independent Writing and Roving Conferences: One Teacher, 23 Students, 10 Minutes**

(3:55 min.)

*(See the website for full 10-minute video.)*

**DEEPER UNDERSTANDING: Reading and Writing Lots of Texts, Part 2**

| Setting, Notes, and Explicit Teaching Points<br>The What, Why, and How of Teaching | Ongoing Assessment<br>Informing Our Instruction | Questions/Reflections<br>For Professional Conversations | Learning Outcomes<br>What Students Know and Are Able to Do |
|---|---|---|---|
| **NOTES**<br>Observing teachers have challenged me to be the only one during roving conferences today, a fair challenge, so I want to be sure students are well prepared to write. (We had already celebrated and had a public conference with every child.) Teachers told me later they were "shocked" by how much writing kindergartners could do on their own and how easily and quickly roving conferences go (because of all the frontloading we have done.) | | | |
| **TEACHING POINTS**<br>• Set expectations before students begin to write: working independently, spacing, sounding out words, writing "*the very best story that you can,*" moving on to a new page.<br>• Affirm students' efforts and encourage them. "*Keep going. Now this sounds like a story. You did so much writing. Good for you.*"<br>• Teach and scaffold what students need to get started and keep going. "*What do you need to put here? What do you want to say now? Do you want to say…?*"<br>• Ask questions that help students move their story along. "*What can you do?*"<br>• Show students how to find and use room resources. (With Makenna: "*Do you know where you could find* pink*…? Let me show you.* [We go together to the class chart on colors.] *Can you find it right here?*"<br>• Encourage best spelling of sounds heard in words. "*What do you hear? I thought you knew that. You know so many sounds. Good for you.*"<br>• Help students continue their story. "*Read me what you have so far. Don't forget this word. Put it in. Leave a space. Do you want to say anything else about that?*"<br>• Move students from illustrating to writing (so that the entire time is not spent illustrating). But if a student has done no writing to continue his story from yesterday, encourage him to move to illustrating: "*Danny, you don't have anything down yet today, so can you do your picture for this? 'My sister* | Although you do not observe here (because I wanted to get to all 23 students quickly), I usually take brief, anecdotal notes during roving conferences (see *Writing Essentials,* p. 217, for an example). I also jot down on a sticky note students I notice doing something well, trying something new, or attempting what has been demonstrated. I call on those students first to share in celebration/whole-class share—to affirm them and so that other students may try out what a peer is doing. | • Why are scaffolded conversations essential for supporting writers in telling their stories before they write them?<br><br>• Note how much support a student needs as you scaffold conversation to help the student tell his story. When students write independently, get to your struggling writers first to ensure they get off to a successful start. | |

*continues*

**Deeper Understanding: Reading and Writing Lots of Texts, Part 2**

*Video* **SCENES**

**Independent Writing and Roving Conferences: One Teacher, 23 Students, 10 Minutes *continued***

| Setting, Notes, and Explicit Teaching Points<br>The What, Why, and How of Teaching | Ongoing Assessment<br>Informing Our Instruction | Questions/Reflections<br>For Professional Conversations | Learning Outcomes<br>What Students Know and Are Able to Do |
|---|---|---|---|
| *Sylvia reads to me.' Can you show us what that looks like? Zavier, you don't have any writing down today. It's time to get some words down. What do you play with your uncle? Put it down. Let's do it together. Don't forget to space. You did something so smart. You went back to check (a spelling of a previously written word)."*<br>• Encourage students to write the story they have told out loud. *"Emily, we want to see here that wonderful story you told us, 'We hold him. . . .' Tell us what you do with your baby brother. You said, 'We hold him in our arms.' Write it here. You can do it. Keep going."*<br>• Clarify what the student is trying to say. *"You might want to start your story with, 'My dad plays games with me.' That lets the reader know what the whole thing is about."*<br>• Near the end of writing time, pause at a student's writing space and celebrate her or his writing. *"Look at what Serena did."* And: *"This young man over here did something really smart as a writer. I want to show you what Zavier did. It's going to give you some ideas. He looked back to find* my *and copied it.* And: *Luis told more of his story today about the Spiderman masks.* And: *Did anybody else do the best writing you've ever done?"* | | • What made it possible for kindergartners to work independently as writers?<br>• Why is it important to touch base with so many young writers, even briefly, during sustained writing? | |

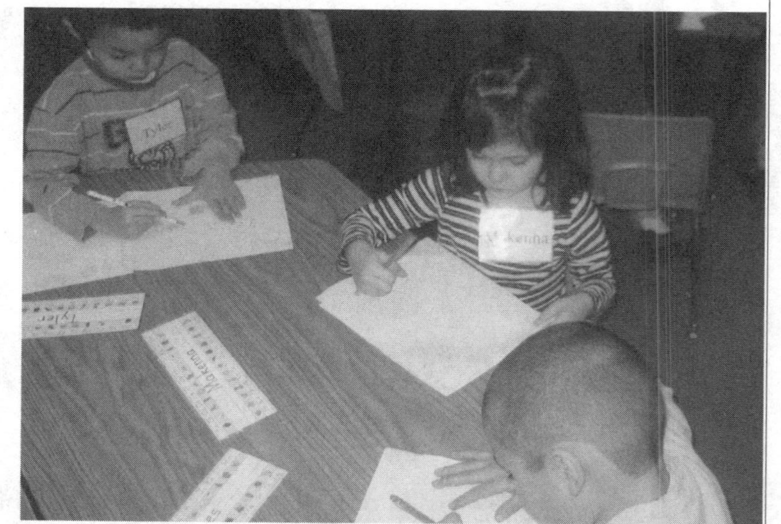

**Kindergarten students are highly motivated and engaged during independent writing practice.**

SESSION 5

# RESPONSENOTES

***Engage, Reflect, Assess, Celebrate!***

SESSION 5

# RESPONSENOTES

***Engage, Reflect, Assess, Celebrate!***

**Transforming** our **Teaching** through

**Reading/Writing Connections**

# Reading to Writing: *Creating Relevant Texts*

**View Video** (31 min.)

**Reading to Writing: Creating Relevant Texts**

**DAY 1**
- **Interactive Read-Aloud: *I Love Saturdays y domingos***
- **Moving from Reading to Shared Writing: "I Love Saturdays"**

**DAY 2**
- **Moving from Shared Writing to Shared Reading to Word Work**

**DAY 3**
- **Extending Shared Writing Through Independent Practice**

## *Agenda*

### Engage, Reflect, Assess

- Review the *Try It/Apply It* activity from Session 5.
  - ***Small-Group Share***

    PART 1:
    - Select a book with conceptual and cultural relevance for your students.
    - Through shared writing, create a text for shared reading.
    - Use the suggested lesson plan in Session 5 as a scaffold and/or create your own five-day lesson plan.
    - Follow the Optimal Learning Model; remember that a literacy block includes reading, writing, and word study.

**RESOURCES**

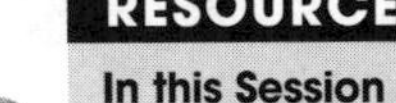

**In this Session**

- Student Writing Samples: Grade 1 *6–5*

**On the Website**

- Reading to Writing to Reading: K–2 Five-Day Lesson Plan
- Example of Bilingual Text(s)

PART 2:

- Write a story of your own that is relevant to your students.
- Try one or two scaffolded conversations before expecting students to write their own stories.
- Conduct roving conferences.
- End with celebration and a whole-class share (public conferences).

## 2. Discuss Professional Reading

- Discuss "Begin in Kindergarten" (*Writing Essentials* excerpt, pp. 121–127 and downloadable from the website).

## 3. Goals

- Understand the purpose and power of reading-to-writing and writing-to-reading experiences for accelerating literacy for *all* students.
- Understand how creating a bilingual text makes it possible for all English language learners to be successful.
- Learn how you can differentiate independent work for all students using one class-authored text.
- Appreciate how application of the Optimal Learning Model can foster independence, confidence, and quality writing—even with our youngest writers.

## 4. View Video and Take Notes

- Turn to the Notecatcher and write down anything you want to explore later in discussion or anything you have questions about.

## 5. Respond to the Video

- Share your thinking with your vertical team. Perhaps, use the following questions to guide your discussion:
    - What were students able to do (or not do) as a result of the reading/writing experiences?
    - What did you see the teacher doing to help all students be successful readers and writers?
    - How was the teacher able to differentiate independent work for all students using one class-authored text?

## 6. Achieve a Deeper Understanding

- Take a few minutes to read through the Deeper Understanding charts. Notice the Teaching Points and interconnected assessment.
- During the group discussion, think more deeply about the purpose of connecting reading to writing.

## 7. *Try It/Apply It* in the Classroom

The *Try It/Apply It* assignment:

- Select a reading text (bilingual, if appropriate) and create a shared writing text inspired by it.
- Expect each student to add to the text (a simple way to achieve differentiated instruction).
- Be prepared to share your work with your vertical team and/or the whole group during the next session.

## 8. Wrap-Up

- Before next session, read "Bring in Stories" (*Reading Essentials* excerpt, pp. 17–20 and downloadable from the website) and be prepared to discuss it during the next session.

- Schedule time to meet with your vertical, grade-level, and/or partner teams in between whole-group sessions to revisit the videos on the website and the Deeper Understanding charts and/or plan together and try out new learning.
- Remember to bring any charts, lessons, writing, or student work samples from the *Try It/Apply It* to the next session.

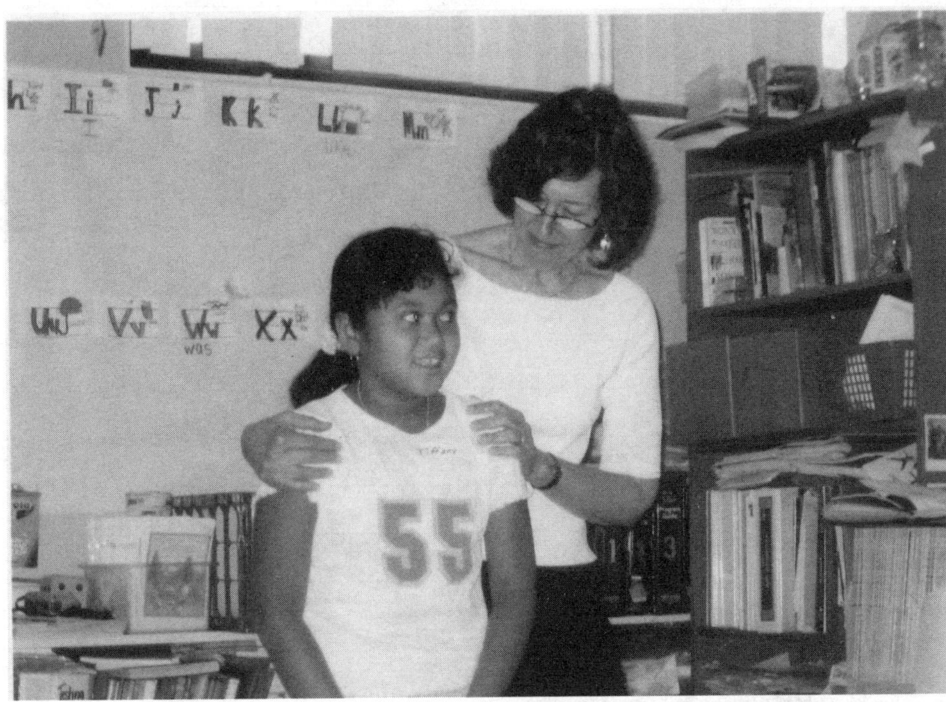

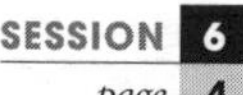

# SESSION 6 NOTECATCHER

| VIDEO SCENES | LENGTH | NOTES & REFLECTION |
|---|---|---|
| **DAY 1**<br>**Interactive Read-Aloud: *I Love Saturdays y domingos*** | 6:01 min. | |
| **Moving from Reading to Shared Writing: "I Love Saturdays"** | 9:56 min. | |
| **DAY 2**<br>**Moving from Shared Writing to Shared Reading to Word Work**<br>• Making the Text Bilingual<br>• Using the Word Walls to Read Students' Names and Important Words | 5:41 min. | |
| **DAY 3**<br>**Extending Shared Writing Through Independent Practice**<br>• Celebrating<br>• Setting Expectations for Extended Writing<br>• Supporting Students Who Need Help with Ideas<br>• Roving Conferences | 10:19 min. | |

# Student Writing Samples: Grade 1

## *Extending Shared Writing Through Independent Practice*

10/21

David gets his allowance.

(His allowance is 1 dollar every saturday. He gives his brother 1 penny every Saturday. My brother Scott has a dog piggy bank. He has about 80 cents in his piggy bank.)

**Instead of using commercially produced worksheets, differentiate instruction using sentences students have written for a class-authored book. After modeling how to elaborate on the teacher-written sentence (see chart on p. 6–15), have several scaffolded conversations with individual students before students go off to write on their own. The sticky note below helps the writer remember and apply key parts of the conversations.**

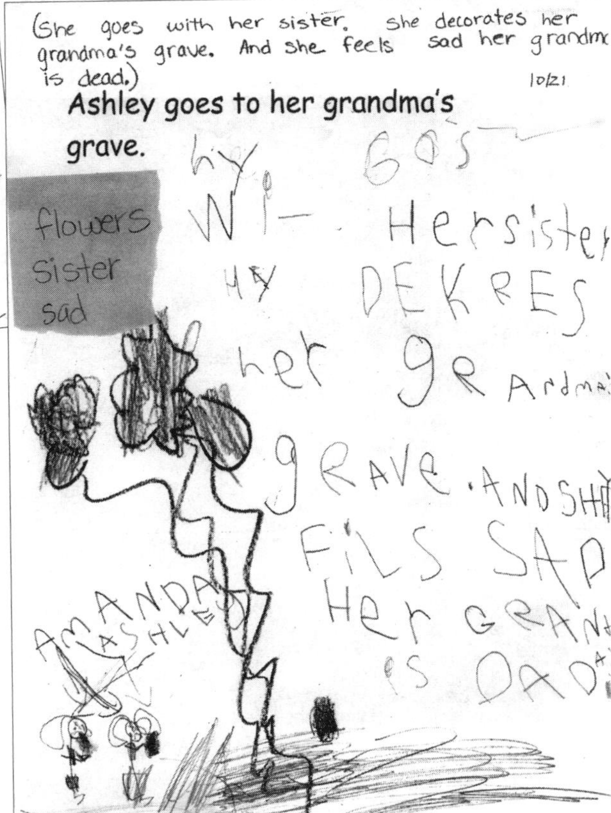

(She goes with her sister. She decorates her grandma's grave. And she feels sad her grandma is dead.)
10/21
Ashley goes to her grandma's grave.
flowers
sister
sad


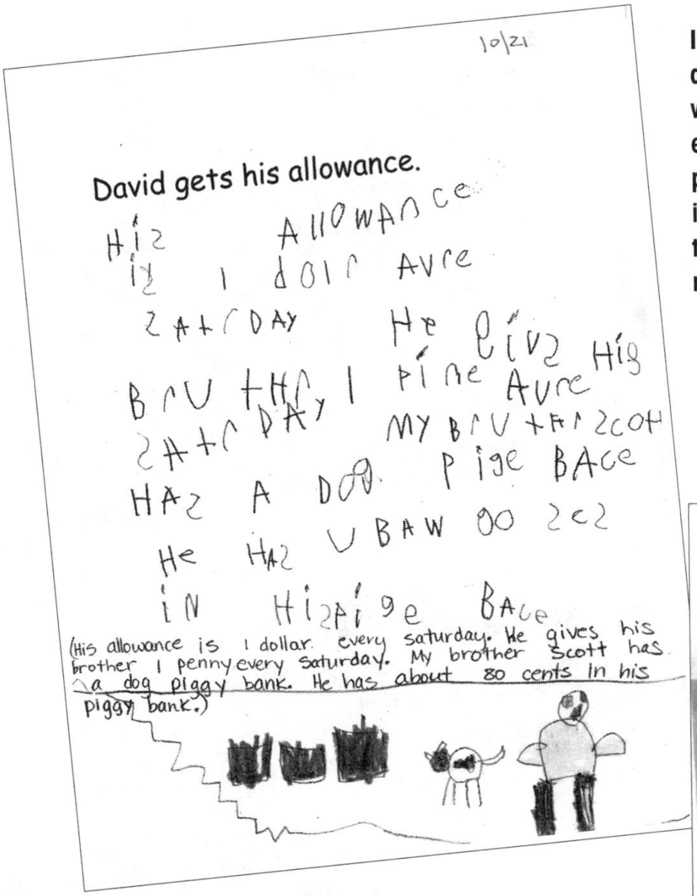

**Notice that students are telling a story in order and writing with elaboration and detail.**

# Student Writing Samples: Grade 1

## *Extending Shared Writing Through Independent Practice*

10/21
Isaac rides his bike.
He rides his bike in The
ale and He rides his
(alley)
bike To The Prci
(park)


**Notice that even our youngest writers can compose a continuing story.**

10/21

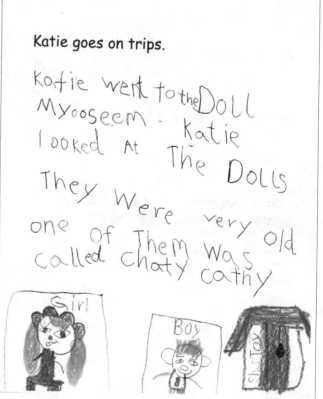

Katie goes on trips.

Katie went to the Doll
Myooseem. Katie
looked At The Dolls
They Were very old
one of Them was
called Chaty cathy

Girl
Boy
ShuToy

**Katie improves on her general statement by narrowing her topic.**

SESSION 6

Reading to Writing: Creating Relevant Texts

# DEEPER UNDERSTANDING

*The teaching and assessing points reflect the total lesson but not all of these points are on the edited videos you are watching. However, the major points are represented on the edited videos.*

The globe icon indicates that the example is also available when you visit www.regieroutman.com.

## *Video* SCENES

| | Setting, Notes, and Explicit Teaching Points<br>The What, Why, and How of Teaching | Ongoing Assessment<br>Informing Our Instruction | Questions/Reflections<br>For Professional Conversations | Learning Outcomes<br>What Students Know and Are Able to Do |
|---|---|---|---|---|
| | **SETTING**<br>The setting for these scenes is Mary Yuhas' first-grade classroom of 22 students at Ardmore Elementary School, Bellevue, WA, on the 32nd day of school. All of the English language learners and special education students, most of whom receive daily pullout services during some part of the reading/writing literacy block, have been included. As is typical for this school, approximately 30 percent of the students in the classroom speak Spanish as a first language. There are also five other languages spoken in the class. Between 40 and 50 percent of the children receive a free or reduced-price lunch.<br><br>Mary Yuhas has been teaching for four years, three years in first grade. I had worked with Mary the previous school year in a one-week residency focused on demonstration teaching and coaching. (Session 3 captures Mary's shifts in beliefs and practices.) Here we are working collaboratively, teaching together after planning and setting the focus for instruction based on her students' needs. Our purpose is to connect reading with writing to maximize enjoyment, engagement, and learning. We begin with a read-aloud to be used as a springboard for writing. | | | |
| 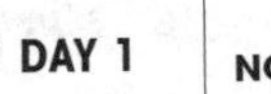 **DAY 1**<br>**Interactive Read-Aloud: *I Love Saturdays y domingos***<br>(6:01 min.) | **NOTES**<br>In an interactive read-aloud, students discuss and comprehend an engaging text as the teacher reads and thinks aloud. All students have the opportunity to hear and talk about ideas and vocabulary they may not yet be able to read and understand on their own. Interactive read-aloud is a great way to introduce students to new authors, genres, and content. | <br>**Regie pauses while reading aloud to ask, "So what's going on in the story so far?"** | | |

*continues*

**Deeper Understanding: Reading to Writing: Creating Relevant Texts**

*Video* **SCENES**

**Interactive Read-Aloud: *I Love Saturdays y domingos continued***

| Setting, Notes, and Explicit Teaching Points<br>The What, Why, and How of Teaching | Ongoing Assessment<br>Informing Our Instruction | Questions/Reflections<br>For Professional Conversations | Learning Outcomes<br>What Students Know and Are Able to Do |
|---|---|---|---|
| *I Love Saturdays y domingos,* by Alma Flor Ada, was selected for its cultural and personal relevance, typical family happenings, age appropriateness, appeal, and as a model for upcoming writing. In the story, a child visits her grandparents each weekend. On Saturdays (on the left-hand side of each page), the child visits her English-speaking grandparents and on Sundays (on the right-hand side of each page with some key words in Spanish), she visits her Spanish-speaking ones. | | | |
| **TEACHING POINTS**<br>• Point to each word in the title as you read it aloud.<br>• Note the author and illustrator: *"This is the author* (say name and point to it)." Do same for the illustrator.<br>• Set a listening purpose: *"This book is a bit different in the way it's set up. I want to see what you notice. See what you notice about this page. See if you notice anything different."*<br>• Affirm/accept what students know that is relevant to the story (Jesus, a potentially disruptive student, corrected my Spanish pronunciation): *"Thank you, Jesus. You knew right away that my Spanish is not so good. Thank you so much. So will you help me with my Spanish all the way through? OK, great."* (Jesus continues to help me with pronunciation throughout the read-aloud.)<br>• Explain how the read-aloud will be used to "write our own story" (sets an additional purpose for careful listening): *"Now, here's what I want you to listen for. After we finish, we're going to be writing our own story, "I Love Saturdays y domingos," and I'm going to be asking you to choose either Saturday or Sunday. So I want you to be thinking about what you love about Saturday and Sunday, because we're going to be writing our own book. Won't that be great?"* | Occasionally, as you are reading aloud, stop and ask students, *"What did you notice?"* Use their responses to gauge their understanding and to guide your teaching, questioning, demonstrating, and opportunities for talk:<br>• *"I want to see what you know."*<br>• *"So what's going on in the story?"*<br>• *"Did you notice something else?"*<br>• *"Here is what I want you to listen for. . . ."* | • What is the purpose of interactive read-aloud?<br>• How is it the same/different from other reading aloud you do with your students?<br>• What did you notice that helps support all students in the classroom regardless of language or reading level? | • Use oral and reading vocabulary gained by listening to and reading narrative text.<br>• Use language (native/ethnic) during class discussions.<br>• With teacher guidance, make inferences before, during, and after hearing a culturally relevant story using prior knowledge, story structure, and prediction. |
| • Use oral cloze [students fill in missing word(s)] to have all students participate and to confirm their understanding (or lack of it): *"So on Saturday, the grandma that they visit speaks—everybody?"*<br>Class: *"Spanish."* (Answer is "English.")<br>*"On Saturday, Grandma speaks . . ."* | Check for understanding:<br>• *"So what's going on so far in the story?"*<br>Angela: *"Well, that picture when her grandma's not hugging her, well, they're speaking English. And* | | • Listen to literature and generate a personal and/or text-based response. |

**DEEPER UNDERSTANDING: Reading to Writing: Creating Relevant Texts**

*Video* **SCENES**

**Interactive Read-Aloud: *I Love Saturdays y domingos* continued**

| Setting, Notes, and Explicit Teaching Points | Ongoing Assessment | Questions/Reflections | Learning Outcomes |
|---|---|---|---|
| The What, Why, and How of Teaching | Informing Our Instruction | For Professional Conversations | What Students Know and Are Able to Do |
| Class: *"English."* *"And on Sunday—is this the same grandma on Sunday, or is it their other set of grandparents?"*<br>Class: *"Other set."*<br>• Connect the story to children's lives: *"The other set of grandparents speak Spanish. Now how many of your grandparents speak Spanish?* (Some raise their hands.) *And how many speak English?* (More hands.) *So both! OK, great! So you know what—your family is probably very similar."*<br>• Summarize important points as you go along: *"So they get to do different things with their grandparents, don't they? Very different things."* And, later: *"So, even though one family speaks English and one speaks Spanish, they're not that different. Everybody likes to tell stories. Everybody likes to have a good time."*<br>• Make personal connections that enhance the understanding of the story (as well as serve as a model to help students think about and make their own relevant connections): *"As I'm reading this book, I'm thinking, this is just like my family, because on Saturday, this Saturday, I'm the grandma to Katie and Brooke, and we're going out to dinner with them on Saturday. On Sunday, they're going to their other grandparents' house, just like this family. Doing something different. They're having a birthday party at the other grandparents' house. And you're going to have a chance to tell us what you do with your grandparents."*<br>• Explain that if you can read almost all the words, you can make meaning. *"And you know what, kids? Even though I can't read every word, because I'm a good reader, I can still understand what's going on. You don't have to be able to read every word to kind of figure out in your head what's happening. I can read almost all the words."*<br>• Think aloud and be explicit about how readers think and make relevant connections (ones that enhance the meaning of the story): *"And you know what I'm thinking? Even though that's the family that speaks Spanish, Katie just turned six, and at her birthday party on Saturday, they had a piñata . . . and it was filled with candy. When you're reading, sometimes you're* | *on that page, they're speaking Spanish."*<br>Restate/summarize important points (to ensure all students' understanding is supported):<br>• *"Exactly! And I want to make sure you all heard that. She said a very smart thing. On this page they're all speaking English. And on this page, they're speaking Spanish. And that's the pattern for the book."*<br><br>Move students closer to you, when necessary, to ensure better attention and engagement:<br>• *"OK, we need this young man, I need you—can we move him? Let's. . . ."*<br>Mrs. Yuhas: *"KC, why don't you come* | • What levels of support did you notice?<br>• Why is it so important to select a read-aloud book that children can identify with?<br>• What do you notice about the children's level of engagement? Why do you think this is true? | |

*continues*

**Video SCENES**

**Interactive Read-Aloud: *I Love Saturdays y domingos* continued**

**DEEPER UNDERSTANDING: Reading to Writing: Creating Relevant Texts**

| Setting, Notes, and Explicit Teaching Points<br>The What, Why, and How of Teaching | Teacher Self-Assessment<br>Informing Our Instruction | Questions/Reflections<br>For Professional Conversations | Learning Outcomes<br>What Students Know and Are Able to Do |
|---|---|---|---|
| *thinking and making connections too. You're thinking about things, 'Well, that's just like what happens in my life.'"* | *sit right here? I'm sad that you're missing the story. So I want you just to move right here. Because when we do our writing, KC, this is how you're going to know just exactly what to do."*<br>Affirm better listening attention, when merited (to ensure desired behavior continues):<br>*"Good listening now, KC, good for you."* | | |
| • Teach vocabulary necessary to understand the story (use "responsive teaching," not "telling teaching," for lasting understanding): *"What do you think it* [a piñata] *is? Look at that picture! . . . What do you think a piñata is from this picture?* [Reading from book.] *'Abuelita is holding the rope to make the piñata go up and down. We gather together to break the piñata that my mom has filled with candy and gifts.' This is just what Katie did at her birthday. So what do you think a piñata is, David?"*<br>*". . . it's something you have and you put candy in it. You buy it at the store. And you smash it."*<br>*"And you smash it, and then what happens?"*<br>*"And you smash it with a baseball bat, and the candy falls out."*<br>• Confirm vocabulary meaning: *"All the stuff comes out. See the piñata there?* [pointing to picture in book]*."*<br>• Tell/give vocabulary meaning necessary to the story that students are not likely to figure out or encounter often. *"'Los Manianitas' is a traditional Mexican song. That means it's a song that they sing all the time at parties."*<br>• Connect the read-aloud book to writing our own book. *"How many of you have grandparents that you visit? Here's what we were thinking, that we would make our own book, either 'I Love Saturdays' or 'I Love Sundays.'"* | Check to be sure students know vocabulary essential to understanding the story:<br>• *"Raise your hand if you know what a piñata is?"* (Some raise hands.)<br>• *"And if you don't know what it is, what do you think it is?"* | | • Use new vocabulary from the text, including text from a variety of cultures and communities in both oral and written communication. |

*Video* **SCENES**

**Moving from Reading to Shared Writing: "I Love Saturdays"**

(9:56 min.)

**DEEPER UNDERSTANDING: Reading to Writing: Creating Relevant Texts**

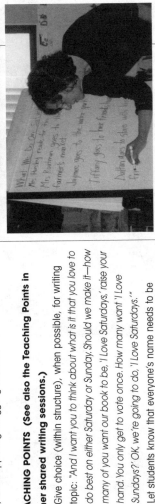

| Setting, Notes, and Explicit Teaching Points<br>The What, Why, and How of Teaching | Ongoing Assessment<br>Informing Our Instruction | Questions/Reflections<br>For Professional Conversations | Learning Outcomes<br>What Students Know and Are Able to Do |
|---|---|---|---|
| **NOTES**<br>Notice how seamless the move is from reading to writing as we begin to compose a text collaboratively. In the shared writing, we help scaffold students' language, thinking, and ideas. When completed, by midweek, each student will get a copy of the illustrated class book (published as a bilingual text), which is then used for shared, guided, and independent reading. The published class book and student-authored pages will also be used for word work, extending writing beyond one line, and supporting struggling learners. |  | **Collaborative text: Mrs. Yuhas is writing what she does on Saturdays.** | |
| **TEACHING POINTS (See also the Teaching Points in other shared writing sessions.)**<br>• Give choice (within structure), when possible, for writing topic: *"And I want you to think about what is it that you love to do best on either Saturday or Sunday. Should we make it—how many of you want our book to be, 'I Love Saturdays,' raise your hand. You only get to vote once. How many want 'I Love Sundays?' OK, we're going to do, 'I Love Saturdays.'"*<br>• Let students know that everyone's name needs to be pronounced correctly (shows respect to all learners): *"My first name, Regie, people mispronounce all the time as Reggie. And I don't let them get away with it. Names are very important. I always say, 'No, that's not the right way to say my first name.' So make sure that I say your name correctly."* | 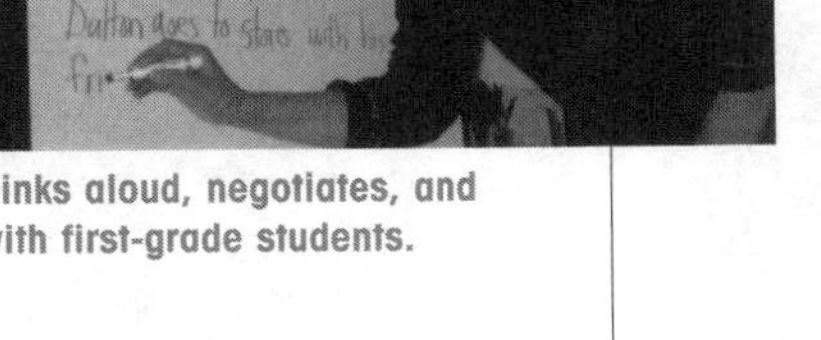**Regie thinks aloud, negotiates, and writes with first-grade students.** | | • Generate personal text or make connections to teacher prompt using information from a culturally relevant read-aloud.<br>• Brainstorm ideas for writing. |
| • Direct students' attention to the chart/surface you are writing on (because we want students to be able to read what we are writing and learn what we are demonstrating): *"So watch me write. . . . Make sure that my spelling is right, kids."*<br>• Show how to use room resources (charts, word wall, books) to find correct spelling of important words. After noting *Saturday* on the calendar wall: *"Could you all spell it* [Saturday] *for me, then?"*<br>Students: *"S-A-T-U-R-D-A-Y"* [write it as they spell it].<br>• Think out loud and tell a personal, meaningful story that engages your audience (so they will think about doing the same before they write): *"Every Saturday, this is what I do. . . .* | Assess whether students know how and where to find and use resources for writing and spelling:<br>• *"And if I wanted to know how to spell* Saturday, *where could I find it?"* | • How does shared writing support all students as learners?<br>• How can you address phonemic awareness and phonics skills in the process of shared writing? | • Use classroom resources.<br>• Recognize that print represents spoken language.<br>• Write for an intended audience. |

continues

**Video SCENES**

**Moving from Reading to Shared Writing: "I Love Saturdays" *continued***

**DEEPER UNDERSTANDING: Reading to Writing: Creating Relevant Texts**

### Setting, Notes, and Explicit Teaching Points
The What, Why, and How of Teaching

*This is a picture of my dad. He's 88 years old. . . . And he had a stroke about three years ago. . . . And every Saturday I visit him, and I try to cheer him up. When I visit him on Saturday, I'm going to tell him about you!"*

- Restate purpose of shared writing and importance of all eyes focused on the chart: *"Because we're going to be taking the story that we write and turning it into a book. It's going to be fabulous! And you're all going to get a copy. So I want to be sure that you can read it, and we want to be sure we have a good story."*
- Write in front of students, saying words and stretching out sounds as you write: *"Mrs. Routman visits, v-v-visits her dad."* And again when the classroom teacher, Mary Yuhas, demonstrates.
- Shape a beginning by suggesting possible language (when it is not forthcoming from students): *"You know what I'm thinking? We need a beginning to our story. . . . We need to let everybody know that we're going to be writing about Saturdays. We love Saturdays. We might say something like, 'We all do different things.' What do you think? . . . So how could we start our book, so it's going to sound like a story. . . ."* Mrs. Yuhas: *"Well, I'm thinking if it's 'We Love Saturdays,' we could say something like, 'We all have fun on Saturdays' or 'We all do different things on Saturdays.'"*
- Take a "good enough" response, write it, and move on. *"I like that."* [Add: *"We all have fun on Saturdays"* as the beginning for the book.]
- Move text around (lasso added second line) so story is in sequence with beginning line first. *"Writers can move things around, and I'm going to put an arrow here and that's going to let the reader, that's us, know that this is our beginning."*
- Read the text from the beginning (to check whether we need to change anything, to hear how the language sounds): *"So read it with me now. Let's see how it sounds so far."*

### Ongoing Assessment
Informing Our Instruction

Make sure students' eyes are on the chart as you write. When learning breaks down (in this case, noticing some students not attending), stop, evaluate, and adjust instruction:

- *"Can you see, Mantry?"*
- *"You know kids, the reason that—and I didn't tell you this—this is really important, this was my fault—the reason that it's important for you to be able to see the chart is this is how you're going to get to be a good reader and writer. I want your eyes up here."*

Occasionally, invite students to help you spell as a way to:

- Keep them engaged.
- Check what they know.
- Let them know what you expect them to spell on their own.

### Questions/Reflections
For Professional Conversations

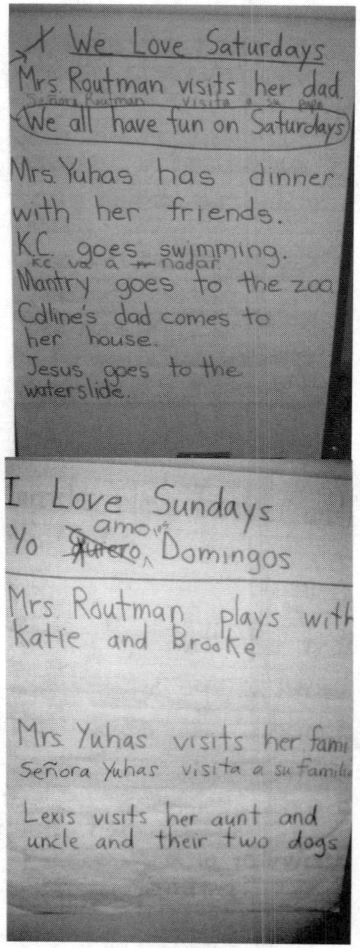

**Two examples of bilingual texts in process based on *I Love Saturdays y domingos.***

### Learning Outcomes
What Students Know and Are Able to Do

- Read selected words on sight with automaticity.

**Deeper Understanding: Reading to Writing: Creating Relevant Texts**

# *Video* SCENES

| | Setting, Notes, and Explicit Teaching Points<br>The What, Why, and How of Teaching | Ongoing Assessment<br>Informing Our Instruction | Questions/Reflections<br>For Professional Conversations | Learning Outcomes<br>What Students Know and Are Able to Do |
|---|---|---|---|---|
| | • Model the language pattern and support students in applying it: Mrs. Yuhas: *"Okay, so if our book went, 'We all have fun on Saturdays. Mrs. Routman visits her dad. Mrs. Yuhas has dinner with her friends. I go swimming,' would that sound right? Or do we need to say your name?"*<br>KC: *"KC goes swimming."*<br><br>• And again later, Mrs. Yuhas: *"Should I write, 'I go to the zoo'? Mantry?"* | See what you need to teach.<br>For example:<br>• *"Everybody spell -ing* [at end of swimming]."<br>• After writing *w-i* for beginning of *with*: *"How do you spell* [make the /th/ sound]? *What is it?"*<br>Student: *"T-H."*<br>Mrs. Yuhas: *"T-H. That's kind of a tricky one."*<br>Check that students understand the language pattern of our book:<br>• *"Who has an idea for something you do on Saturday that you think is pretty terrific?"* [KC raises his hand.]<br>Mrs. Yuhas: *"KC? And start with your name, KC. KC, what do you do on Saturday?"*<br>KC: *"I go swimming."*<br>• *"No. . . . Mantry goes to the zoo."* | | • Use common inflectional endings *(-ing)*. |
| **DAY 2**<br>**Moving from Shared Writing to Shared Reading to Word Work**<br>(5:41 min.) | **NOTES**<br>Shared reading of familiar text is one of the best ways to engage all students in enjoyable reading, reach English language learners and struggling learners, practice fluency, and embed meaningful word work. Prior to this scene, the children worked in small groups with Mrs. Yuhas to complete the class-authored text. So in rereading the text with Mrs. Yuhas, some of the students are seeing the whole text for the first time. In this scene, we also begin to add a line in Spanish (for each one in English) to make our student-authored class text bilingual. Creating a bilingual text shows respect for the large number of Spanish-speaking students, makes the text easier to read for those students, and teaches some Spanish to the English-speaking students. Notice how we use the name wall to help children learn to read one another's names so they will be able to read "We Love Saturdays" independently. | We Love Saturdays<br>~~Nosotros~~<br>Nos encantan los sábados<br>Mrs Routman plays with Katie and Brooke<br>La Sra. Routman juega con Katie y Brooke.<br>Ms. Hoff walks on the beach.<br>La Sra Hoff camina en la playa. | | |

continues

## Deeper Understanding: Reading to Writing: Creating Relevant Texts

| *Video* SCENES | Setting, Notes, and Explicit Teaching Points<br>The What, Why, and How of Teaching | Ongoing Assessment<br>Informing Our Instruction | Questions/Reflections<br>For Professional Conversations | Learning Outcomes<br>What Students Know and Are Able to Do |
|---|---|---|---|---|
| **Moving from Shared Writing to Shared Reading to Word Work *continued*** | **TEACHING POINTS**<br>• Follow the text with your eyes when you read: "*I need everybody to help me read. Get your eyes on my pointer. . . .*"<br>• Set the purpose for rereading: "*We want to make sure everyone can read this, because getting good at this book is going to make you a much better reader.* [And at end of shared reading]: *This is going to help people get to know our class better.*"<br>• Read the book all the way through as a whole (without stopping for word work, so focus is on meaning and enjoyment). | **Mrs. Yuhas places the students' names on their photographs to make the names easier to read.** | | • Use directionality and one-to-one matching. |
| • Making the Text Bilingual | • Show what a bilingual book looks like (to build interest and engagement for creating one): "*And* [showing book from last year's class] *the other thing that we did last year that we haven't done yet this year is we also wrote our book in Spanish so the title of our book was 'I Love Sundays, Yo Amo los domingos.'*" And: "*So you're going to have a chance to make your sentence in English and Spanish and to illustrate it.*" | | | • Participate in shared reading/writing of texts. |
| • Using the Word Walls to Read Students' Names and Important Words | • Connect the published book to the audience (so students will do illustrations carefully): "*Isn't this a beautiful book? They* [last years' students] *did such careful illustrations because they knew that this book was going to be in the library and in our classroom and they were going to get to take a copy home.*"<br>• Show examples of illustrations by students and/or explain why illustrations need to be detailed and carefully done: "*Even though you've only written one sentence in your story, the illustrations are a great place to put lots of detail, lots of other stuff maybe that's not in your story.*"<br>• Write sentences in Spanish (under the English) and pronounce the words as you write them: "*That's called a bilingual book. It's in English and it's in Spanish. Isn't that fabulous?*"<br>• Connect students' names to their photographs (to make names easy to find and read): "*We're going to move the name next to the picture and that's going to make it so easy for you, then, to read everybody's name in the classroom.*" | 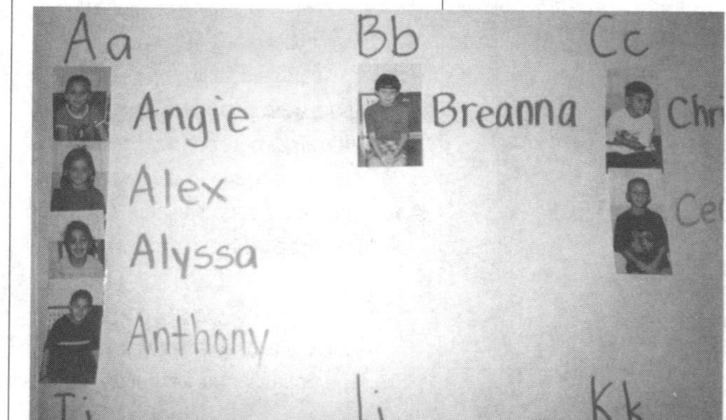**Another example of a name word wall.** | | • Spell first grade high-frequency words.<br>• Use beginning, middle, and ending sounds. |

# *Video* SCENES

**DEEPER UNDERSTANDING: Reading to Writing: Creating Relevant Texts**

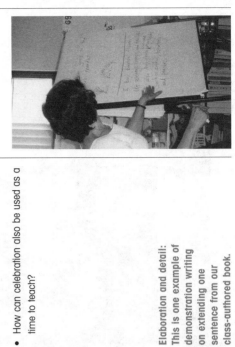

| | Setting, Notes, and Explicit Teaching Points<br>The What, Why, and How of Teaching | Ongoing Assessment<br>Informing Our Instruction | Questions/Reflections<br>For Professional Conversations | Learning Outcomes<br>What Students Know and Are Able to Do |
|---|---|---|---|---|
| | • Highlight and talk about important words from the class text that all students are expected to read and write (here we use the word wall, sliding mask, and choral spelling for *her* and *we*): *"They're important words for everybody to know how to read because they're in almost every book."*<br>• State expectations for correct spelling: *"So when you're writing in your journal, we're going to expect that, if you need the word* we, *you know how to spell it now. . . . If you're writing the word* her, *you don't have to make up the spelling for it. . . . Here it is. We expect you to get it right."* | | • How could you use shared writing to support older students who struggle as readers and writers? | |
| **DAY 3**<br>**Extending Shared Writing Through Independent Practice**<br>(10:19 min.) | **NOTES**<br>Before extending our shared writing (independent practice), we do another shared reading of "We Love Saturdays" and include additional word work: reviewing *her* and *we*, adding *like* to the word wall, and highlighting *-ike* to designate it as a rime. (This is not shown on the video here.) | | **Mrs. Yuhas asks Austin how he knew how to spell "practice."** | • Write using grade-level-appropriate spelling patterns. |
| • Celebrating | Next, we celebrate the high-quality, detailed illustrations students have done on their pages for "I Love Saturdays." Having copied each student's sentence at the top of a blank sheet of paper, we demonstrate and give directions for extending that sentence. By having all students do the same activity as best they can, at their own level, we are differentiating instruction without having to create different sets of materials for students. Also in this scene, students receive needed support and affirmation through quick conferences before and during writing. | 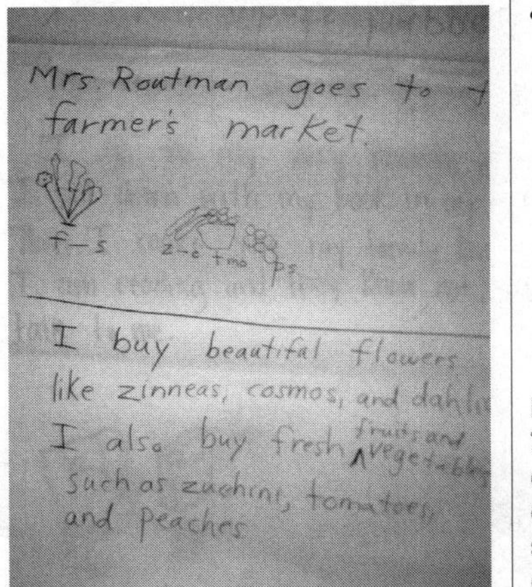<br> | • How can celebration also be used as a time to teach?<br><br>**Elaboration and detail: This is one example of demonstration writing on extending one sentence from our class-authored book.** | 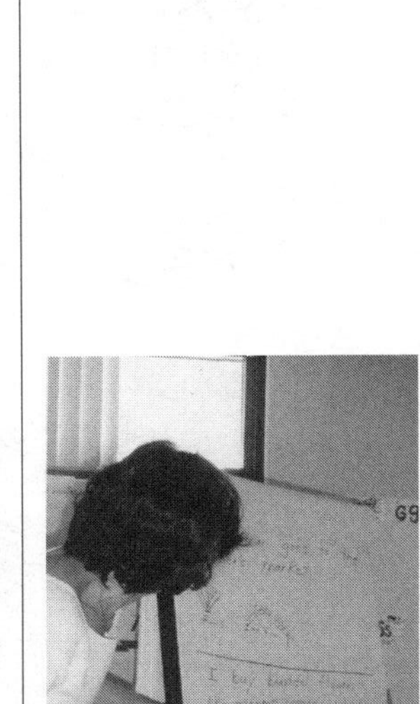 |

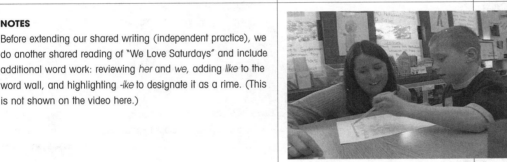

continues

# Video SCENES

**DEEPER UNDERSTANDING: Reading to Writing: Creating Relevant Texts**

| | Setting, Notes, and Explicit Teaching Points<br>The What, Why, and How of Teaching | Ongoing Assessment<br>Informing Our Instruction | Questions/Reflections<br>For Professional Conversations | Learning Outcomes<br>What Students Know and Are Able to Do |
|---|---|---|---|---|
| **Extending Shared Writing Through Independent Practice *continued*** | **TEACHING POINTS**<br>• Affirm excellent illustration efforts with detail (as a model for future illustrations and to connect illustrations with supporting the reader): *"I can tell people are really going to want to read this book because you did such a nice job illustrating it. . . . Mark wrote: 'Mark goes to the football stadium with his friends.' Here's all the football players. He made their blue and orange uniforms. . . . It doesn't say, 'The players wear blue and orange uniforms.' And his sentence didn't say, 'I sat in the bleachers.' But by adding all the wonderful detail to his picture, he gave the reader so much more information."* | | <br><br> | • Elaborate on ideas using descriptive language, words, and phrases. |
| • Setting Expectations for Extended Writing | **TEACHING POINTS**<br>• Give the reasons for the activity (adding on to the writing): *"You get your own page, kids, because some of you yesterday wanted to write more."*<br>• Think out loud prior to doing a writing demonstration: *"Here's what I was thinking about. The first thing I do when I go in to visit my dad is I give him a big kiss. . . . I read some of the news and the sports to him."*<br>• Model exactly what you want students to do (in this case, adding on to their one line): *"So maybe I'll say—I'm thinking, writers always think before they write—'Mrs. Routman visits her dad. She gives him a big kiss. She reads him the news. He smiles.'"*<br>• Expect the best invented spelling and writing work: *"I'm taking my time and really stretching out my sounds. I'm spacing my words so the reader can read it."*<br>• Write conventional spelling under invented spelling: *"Watch this. I want to show you how close you are* [to affirm what they know and so they will do it again]. *You knew the* **s** *at the end* [of *gives*]. Him. *You heard the beginning and ending sound."*<br>• Reread writing: *"Now I'm going to check it to be sure it's the way I want it."*<br>• Check the name wall: *". . . if you have somebody in your class and you want to put their name in the story. . . ."*<br>• Add details to your sentence: *". . . tell your partner. What are you going to add to your sentence to make your story more interesting?"* | Have students help you spell (to assess what they know, to teach them strategies, to confirm what they know, and to raise expectations for their spelling):<br>• *"Help me write this. Then I'm going to show you how I would write it."* [I take their invented spelling of my language and put the conventional spelling underneath.]<br>• *"How does that start?"* (Sh-e)<br>• *"What do you hear at the end?"* | | • Develop ideas for writing orally and visually (discuss, draw, and/or write to develop ideas). |

## DEEPER UNDERSTANDING: Reading to Writing: Creating Relevant Texts

| *Video* SCENES | Setting, Notes, and Explicit Teaching Points<br>The What, Why, and How of Teaching | Ongoing Assessment<br>Informing Our Instruction | Questions/Reflections<br>For Professional Conversations | Learning Outcomes<br>What Students Know and Are Able to Do |
|---|---|---|---|---|
| • Supporting Students Who Need Help with Ideas | • Support through guided questions (from students and from you) those students who need help adding to their sentence: *"If you have your idea and are ready to go, just come up and get your paper. If you're not sure yet, stay and I'll help you."* After students who are ready go off to write: *"People who are still here, let's make a little group."*<br>• Suggest language that seems appropriate. *"OK, do you want to put sad? Is that a good word to describe how you feel?"* [Referring to Ashley's visiting her grandma's grave.] | Check that all students have writing ideas: *"Before you go off to do your writing, I want to be sure you all have your idea . . . turn and tell your partner. . . ."*<br>• Turn-and-talk is a great way to make sure everyone gets a chance to share their ideas. It can also be a useful assessment. Listen in, and see who's talking, what they're saying, what they're understanding, or who's confused.<br>• When handing out papers, do a quick check: *"KC, are you ready to add some more detail? Excellent."* | • Why is it important to have students hold the pencil and read their own writing when you have a conference? | • Share writing with others. |
| • Roving Conferences | • Affirm what's done well; ask questions to help move the writing forward: *"Can you read me your story so far? Why does he . . . ? . . . I love the way you're leaving spaces between your words. It makes it so much easier to read. . . . I see the sounds you heard. That's excellent. . . . What else do you want to say? . . . I have a really clear picture in my mind of what it's like when you and your dad and your sister are playing. . . . You told us a lot of great details."*<br>• Celebration is an important part of each and every lesson. It encompasses closure, evaluation of what went well, the extent of student learning, and next teaching steps.<br><br>At the end of the residency, Mary Yuhas noted that her biggest changes were organizing the structure of her writing conferences and using celebration to praise and teach: "What you praise is what they will repeat and peers will emulate." | Ask questions that give you a window into students' thinking and problem solving:<br>• *"How did you know . . . ?"*<br>• *"How did you figure out . . . ?"*<br>Ask questions that let students know you expect them to take an action:<br>• *"What do you need at the end of your sentence?"*<br>• *"What are you going to look for to figure out . . . ?"*<br>• Take notes and reflect on what students were able to do as a result of your modeling. Identify one or two teaching points for the next reading/writing block.<br>• Collect one or two samples of students' writing to measure growth over time. | • How do roving conferences help students work more independently?<br><br>**The students work independently on their writing.** | • Illustrate work.<br>• Edit text with teacher guidance.<br>• Write for self, family, friends, or teacher. |

SESSION 6

# RESPONSENOTES

*Engage, Reflect, Assess, Celebrate!*

**Transforming** our **Teaching** through
**Reading/Writing Connections**

# Shared Writing to Reading

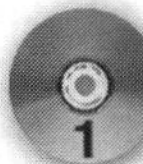

**View Video** (26 min.)

**Shared Writing to Reading**

**DAY 1** ■ **Establishing the Purpose for Shared Writing**
**DAY 2** ■ **Small-Group Revision**
**DAY 3** ■ **Whole-Group Revision**

## 1. Engage, Reflect, Assess

- Review the *Try It/Apply It* Activity:
  - *Whole-Group Share*
    - *How's it going?*
  - *Small-Group Share*
    - *What reading text did you select? Why?*
    - *How did it go to write a shared writing text inspired by it?*
    - *What worked well? What didn't go so smoothly?*
    - *Were your students engaged?*
    - *What did you learn?*
    - *How did you differentiate instruction?*

## 2. Discuss Professional Reading

- In your vertical teams, discuss "Bring in Stories" (*Reading Essentials* excerpt, pp. 17–20 and downloadable from the website).

**RESOURCES**

**In this Session**



WWW **On the Website**

- Shared Writing to Reading in the Intermediate Grades (3–6): Three-Day Lesson Plan
- Tried and True Ideas for Shared Writing

## 3. Goals

- Show the power and possibilities shared writing has when used with older students.
- Use shared writing to establish how to work and behave with peers in the classroom.
- Demonstrate how small-group work can be used to:
  - Hear all students' voices.
  - Help students become independent (by revising shared writing).
  - Provide a written record that can be used as an assessment.
  - Guide and structure teaching and learning across the curriculum.

## 4. View Video and Take Notes

- Turn to the Notecatcher to take notes during the video.

## 5. Respond to the Video

- Share your thinking with your vertical team. Respond to the following discussion questions:
  - What were students able (or not able) to do as a result of the shared writing demonstration?
  - How can you use shared writing to establish classroom management and organizational procedures?
  - What did you notice about how small-group work (guided practice) helped students become independent?
  - How can you use a similar small-group structure in all subject areas?

## 6. Achieve a Deeper Understanding

- Read and review the Deeper Understanding charts. Use the Questions/ Reflections for Professional Conversations to guide a discussion.

## 7. *Try It/Apply It* in the Classroom

- Before the next session:
  - Present the lesson you just viewed on the video (or a similar one) to your students.
  - Structure and present a similar lesson; especially include the small-group collaboration in language arts, math, science, social studies, or any special area (music, art, physical education, and so on).
  - Use the written responses as an assessment of students' participation, thinking, and efforts.
  - Perhaps use the familiar text from a shared writing you did with a small group of struggling readers as a reading text for these students.

## 8. Wrap-Up

- Before next session read "Shared Writing" (*Invitations* excerpt, pp. 59–66 and downloadable from the website) and be prepared to discuss it next session.
- Schedule time to meet with your vertical, grade-level, and/or partner teams in between whole-group sessions to revisit the videos on the website and the Deeper Understanding charts and/or plan together and try out new learning.
- Remember to bring any charts, lessons, writing, or student work samples from the *Try It/Apply It* to the next session.

**This small group is working productively on their reading and writing with teacher guidance.**

SESSION 7

# NOTECATCHER

| VIDEO SCENES | LENGTH | NOTES & REFLECTION |
|---|---|---|
| **DAY 1** **Establishing the Purpose for Shared Writing** | 10:43 min. | |
| • Reading Aloud: "Mending Our Broken Hearts" | | |
| • Selecting a Topic for Writing: "How to Be a Team Member" | | |
| • Setting Goals for Revision | | |

SESSION 7

# NOTECATCHER

| VIDEO SCENES | LENGTH | NOTES & REFLECTION |
|---|---|---|
| **DAY 2**<br>**Small-Group Revision** | 4:24 min. | |
| **DAY 3**<br>**Whole-Group Revision**<br>• Celebrating | 11:10 min. | |

# Samples of Small-Group Revision

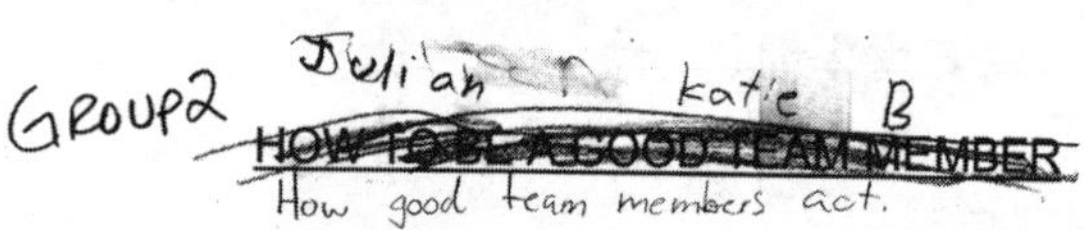


~~HOW TO BE A GOOD TEAM MEMBER~~ How good team members act.

- Be kind to everyone if he or she ~~has an accident.~~ makes a mistake
- ~~Don't call teammates names.~~ Be a loyal friend
- Work together. Help each other out, with kindness
- Respect each other with the words you use.
- Have a positive attitude in how you act and ~~what you say no matter~~ who you are working with. (don't be mean to others no madder who they are.)
- Be encouraging with the words you use and by your actions.
- Don't ~~be a bully~~ pick on people.
- Be a good sport, and cheer people on.
- ~~If you have something bad to say, don't say it.~~ If you don't have anything nice to say don't say anything at all.

After whole-class shared writing, make copies of the text that has been generated and have all students give input into making the text better—clearer, more complete, accurate, interesting. In this case, one of the challenges is to word the text in a more positive manner. After each student does his/her own revision (because we wanted a record of everyone's thinking), students revise together in small groups with one student serving as scribe for the group effort.

Group 3 being a good team mate ~~HOW TO BE A GOOD TEAM MEMBER~~ Angie, Billy, Carlos

- ~~Be kind to~~ Help everyone if he or she has an accident.
- ~~Don't~~ call teammates by the name they like ~~names~~.
- Work together as a teammember and help each other out.
- Respect ~~each other~~ everyone with the words you use.
- Have a positive attitude in how you act and what you say no matter who you are working with.
- Be encouraging with the words you use and by your actions.
- ~~Don't~~ Be a bully, to nobody
- Be a good sport.
- If you have something bad to say, don't say it, instead say something good

~ Mrs Vale's fourth grade team

**Small-group revision lets us hear all our students' voices, promotes collaborative thinking, and gives us an assessment of students' work. Once students have had lots of practice with shared revision, you can rely more on individual, independent practice and use that as a student assessment.**

#  Samples of Small-Group Revision

**Think about promoting collaborative thinking like this across the curriculum—in social studies, science, and problem solving in math.**

Group 6

HOW TO BE A GOOD TEAM MEMBER

- Be kind to everyone ~~if he or she has an accident.~~ no matter what
- ~~Don't call teammates names.~~ your teammates already have a name
- Work together. Help each other out.
- Respect each other with the words you use. and actshoons.
- It's good to Have a positive attitude in how you act and what you say no matter who you are working with.
- Be encouraging with the words you use and by your actions.
- ~~Don't be a bully.~~
- you should always Be a good sport.
- If you have something bad to say, don't say it.
  never bee rud for no uparent reson
  think befor yoa say

Group 5

HOW TO BE A GOOD TEAM ~~MEMBER~~ mate

- Naver blam people of somting you did
- Be kind ~~to everyone if he or she has an accident.~~ to your teme mates no matter what
- Don't call teammates names.
- Work together. Help each other out.
- Respect each other with the words you use.
- think about how the person your efending feels.
- Have a positive attitude in how you act and what you say no matter who you are working with.
- If its not yar bissnis dont lissen
- Be encouraging with the words you use and by your actions.
- all ways be kine
- ~~Don't be a bully.~~
- Be a good sport.
- If you have something bad to say, don't say it.
- dont treat people badle if you dont what to be treted that way

**See p. 7–11 for the final chart that was posted and utilized in the classroom throughout the school year.**

# More Ideas for Shared Writing

## *(Generated by Participants in a Workshop)*

- **Guide for parents**
- **I didn't understand. . . . Now I know**
- **How-to poems**
- **Survival guide for teenage siblings**
- **Morning procedures for substitutes**
- **Lunch procedures**
- **Tourist guide**
- **Trail guide**
- **Surviving winter guide**
- **Advice to teachers**
- **Playground advice**
- **Appreciation letters**
- **How to use the playground equipment**
- **Winter playground rules**
- **Advice to next year's class**
- **Lunchroom etiquette**
- **How to be "cool"**
- **Fifth-grade memories of elementary school**
- **Job description for:**
  - **Hall monitor**
  - **Flag raisers**
  - **School post office workers**
  - **Conflict mediators**
  - **Other classroom jobs**
- **School book about each grade's field trips**
- **Bulletin boards at entry to the school: "What you need to know about our school"**
- **The best school lunches**
- **What you need to know about our teacher (for next year's class)**
- **Fun things to do at recess**

**—Regie Routman**

# Deeper Understanding

*The teaching and assessing points reflect the total lesson but not all of these points are on the edited videos you are watching. However, the major points are represented on the edited videos.*

The globe icon indicates that the example is also available when you visit www.regieroutman.com.

## *Video* SCENES

| | Setting, Notes, and Explicit Teaching Points | Ongoing Assessment | Questions/Reflections | Learning Outcomes |
|---|---|---|---|---|
| | The What, Why, and How of Teaching | Informing Our Instruction | For Professional Conversations | What Students Know and Are Able to Do |
| | **SETTING**<br>This session takes place over three days in Ginny Vale's fourth-grade classroom at the end of the second month of school. There are 22 students in the classroom; 11 receive free or reduced-price lunch and 9 are English language learners. Ginny has been teaching for three years. She and I worked together in a residency the previous year, and she began to shift her beliefs and practices, especially in giving more responsibility to students and in more closely monitoring students' reading comprehension. (See Session 3 for the interview with Ginny about those shifts.)<br><br>Ginny later took what she learned about whole-class shared writing and applied the approach with a small group of her most struggling readers. The results were dramatic. Students who had previously showed little interest or ability in reading began to read not only the group-authored texts but also books in the classroom library. She credits the shared-writing-to-reading process for turning her most reluctant readers into willing and able readers. | | | |
| **DAY 1**<br>**Establishing the Purpose for Shared Writing**<br>(10:43 min.) | **NOTES**<br>Wanting to set up a classroom in which students manage their own behaviors and know what the expectations are, we negotiate these expected behaviors through shared writing. Usually I give students some topic choice, but here, Ginny and I have decided the topic in advance because it is vital to our goal. However, the students have a lot of choice regarding content. (The students did not understand that creating a list is, in fact, real writing. They thought of writing as essays or poems.) | | | |

**Students work collaboratively to revise the whole-class shared writing. Regie uses roving conferences to check on and guide each group.**

**This small group is participating in our final whole-group revision.**

continues

**Deeper Understanding: Shared Writing to Reading**

## *Video* SCENES

| Video Scenes | Setting, Notes, and Explicit Teaching Points<br>The What, Why, and How of Teaching | Ongoing Assessment<br>Informing Our Instruction | Questions/Reflections<br>For Professional Conversations | Learning Outcomes<br>What Students Know and Are Able to Do |
|---|---|---|---|---|
| **Establishing the Purpose for Shared Writing *continued*** | **TEACHING POINTS**<br>• Connect writing to reading and to the students. *"I want you to think about what we're going to write as something other people are going to read. Here's what we were thinking about. You've been talking about how your classroom works, how you treat each other. . . ."* (Later, we also discussed that the principal would want to share this writing with other students, and that got the kids' attention.) | | | |
| • Reading Aloud: "Mending Our Broken Hearts" | • Engage students with an important topic or story that captures their interest. (Here, I tell the story of another classroom where kids weren't getting along, and I read their class-authored poem, "Mending Our Broken Hearts" [see Session 11 on writing poetry].) *"I wanted to share this with you because the kids were close to your age and it just happened last week. It was about how we treat each other as people."* | Assess the language your students use when they speak with one another.<br><br>Listen and observe students' oral language development through student responses and discussion. | • How do we make students aware that the language and words they use need to be stated positively?<br>• Why is the choice of topic so important to the writing outcome?<br>• Why is it important to ask open-ended questions (no right or wrong answers)? | • Understand how to use a student-published text to generate ideas for writing.<br><br>• Generate ideas for writing.<br><br>• Plan for writing. |
| • Selecting a Topic for Writing: "How to Be a Team Member" | • Select the topic and give the reasons you selected it and state the audience you're writing for. Regie: *"Maybe Ms. Poole may want to share our writing with other students in the school. You've been talking in your classroom about behavior."*<br>Ginny: *"We've been talking about how we're all on a team, and team members support each other."*<br>Regie: *"That's great. How about if we write that, what it means to be a team member."*<br>• Choose a title. *"What do you want to call it?"*<br>Carlos: *"Call it, 'How to Be a Team Member'."*<br>• Accept students' responses. *"Let's go with that."*<br>• Connect the writing to the audience (to generate interest). *"This would probably be someplace prominent and important in your room so that if you forget what it means to be a team member, there it is, and it might be something even to share with other classes . . . or to use with next year's students."*<br>• Offer choice within structure (choice with guidance). *"How many of you would like to see a list? . . . If you're a good team member, here are the things that you do."* | Note your observations. | | |

**Regie is suggesting some ideas for how to write "How to Be a Team Member."**

# *Video* SCENES

**Deeper Understanding: Shared Writing to Reading**

| | Setting, Notes, and Explicit Teaching Points<br>The What, Why, and How of Teaching | Ongoing Assessment<br>Informing Our Instruction | Questions/Reflections<br>For Professional Conversations | Learning Outcomes<br>What Students Know and Are Able to Do |
|---|---|---|---|---|
| **Establishing the Purpose for Shared Writing *continued*** | • Affirm, clarify, and help shape student responses. (The following are some examples while drafting the class list.)<br>• *"Who has a beginning sentence?"*<br>Lauren: *"Do something kind for a friend."*<br>*"Or do you want to say, 'Be kind to your friend,' or, 'Do something kind'?"*<br>Loren: *"Be kind."* [I write it on the chart.]<br>• *"Work together."*<br>*"Daniel what does that mean when you say 'work together'?"*<br>Daniel: *"Help each other out."*<br>• *"Respect the teachers and . . . How about if we just say respect each other?"*<br>• Extend thinking. *"So you're talking about respecting each other with the words you use, right? How else do you show your respect? Anybody want to add to that? Kiana?. . . Let me read what we have so far."*<br>• Emphasize the importance of word choice. [Henry adds *anyone* to *Be kind.*] *"How about everyone? Good. That's what good writers do. They're very picky about their words. Good for you, because maybe that person isn't a friend. You still want to be kind to them. Good for you for being so picky."*<br>• State desired behaviors for the class list in a positive tone. *"Maddie, how could we say that? Instead of 'Don't call teammates names' how could we turn that around so it's a positive?. . . Who can help her out with that?"* | Assess student thinking as you write together:<br>• *"How else do you show respect?"*<br>• *"How could you say that?"* | • How and what is the teacher doing to set learning behaviors and expectations? | |
| • Setting Goals for Revision | • Set goals for revision. *"OK, here's what we're going to do. Now that took us about 10 minutes. We're going to type this up and then tomorrow, when I come back, we're going to put you in small groups and you're going to fix it up so it's even better. Like one of the things I want you to think about is taking away the negative language, like how can we change 'Don't call teammates names; don't be a bully'?"* | | | • Understand how to work on more than one draft on a single topic over several days. |

Draft How to Be a Good Team Member

. Be kind to ~~a friend~~ everyone if he or she has an accident.
. Don't call teammates names.
. Work together. Help each other out.
. Respect each other with the words you use
. Have a positive attitude in how you act & what you say no matter who you are working with.
. Be encouraging with the words you use and ~~with~~ your actions
. Don't be a bully.
. Be a good sport
. If you have something bad to say, don't say it.

**Draft**

HOW TO BE A GOOD TEAMMATE

Be kind and respectful to your teammates, no matter what.

Think before you speak.

Call teammates by a name they like.

Work together. Help each other out with kindness and respect.

Think about how the other person feels.

Respect everyone with the words you use.

Have a positive attitude in how you act and what you say no matter who you are working with.

Always be a good sport.

Treat people the way you would want to be treated.

Be encouraging with the words you use and with your actions.

By Ms. Vale's Fourth Grade Team

**Final Copy**

**The class has finished their list and Regie is telling them that they'll type up the list and tomorrow they will make it better.**

**Video SCENES**

**DAY 2**

**Small-Group Revision**

(4:24 min.)

**DEEPER UNDERSTANDING: Shared Writing to Reading**

| Setting, Notes, and Explicit Teaching Points<br>The What, Why, and How of Teaching | Ongoing Assessment<br>Informing Our Instruction | Questions/Reflections<br>For Professional Conversations | Learning Outcomes<br>What Students Know and Are Able to Do |
|---|---|---|---|
| **NOTES**<br>This is the first time these students have worked collaboratively in a small group to make revisions. While the whole-class shared writing allowed some students to contribute their ideas, the small-group work allows all students' voices to be heard. By designating a scribe in each group and having all the group members sign the page, you have a record of the group work and thinking. | | **Regie has roving conferences with the small groups working on revising the "Team Member" list.** | |
| As students are getting started, I am having roving conferences, checking in on each group to give needed guidance. Once students become familiar with this process, a teacher can join just one or two groups and provide substantial guidance. This small-group structure can be used for any subject: solving math problems, taking notes on a social studies text, and so on. | Monitor and observe that all students understand the group process. Adjust support based on your observations. | • What did you notice about how student roles were assigned? Who did all the work? | |
| **TEACHING POINTS**<br>• Connect the purpose for revision to the audience for the writing. "*Ms. Poole* [the principal] *said if it's good enough, she's going to use it with other principals when they're talking about bullying in the district or how to be a good team member. . . . Your parents will get a copy so it's a pretty important piece of writing . . . if we're publishing it, other people are reading it, it's got to be the best and the clearest and the most positive it can be.*"<br>• Establish procedures for group work. (Some of this was done before this scene. Also, right before this scene, each student worked individually on revising the shared writing on a typed copy.)<br>  • Set a time limit. (Ten minutes for this task.)<br>  • Each member of the group signs his or her name at the top of the group sheet (a typed copy of the whole-class shared writing draft from Day 1).<br>  • Everyone contributes ideas.<br>  • One person serves as scribe (makes the revisions on the page).<br>  • The group agrees on the best ideas, and the scribe records them (makes revisions—changes, additions, deletions). | We should be able to assess everything we expect students to do. Small-group work where responses are recorded gives us a window into student effort and thinking even if we are not present. At this point, we are still in the "shared experiences" of the Optimal Learning Model. So, even though students are first expected to complete their own revisions on individual sheets (that is just to be sure each student does some thinking and to give me a window into that thinking), I would not "grade" or evaluate those individual papers as the process is so new to students. Later in the year, when students have had lots of guided practice, I would. | • What do you notice about students' engagement during their first small-group collaboration? Think about the opportunities for "hearing all the voices," give and take of ideas, and recording group thinking. | • Revisit text by adding, deleting, substituting, and moving words or sentences.<br><br>• Revise class-authored writing (as a whole group, in small groups, one-on-one). |

# *Video* SCENES

**DEEPER UNDERSTANDING: Shared Writing to Reading**

| | Setting, Notes, and Explicit Teaching Points<br>The What, Why, and How of Teaching | Ongoing Assessment<br>Informing Our Instruction | Questions/Reflections<br>For Professional Conversations | Learning Outcomes<br>What Students Know and Are Able to Do |
|---|---|---|---|---|
| | • Provide guidance and affirmation to each group in brief roving conferences. (Nudge, but don't tell. Ask questions that support and guide students to do the work.)<br>• *"Who's going to be your scribe? Have you decided? Better pick a scribe."*<br>• *"I like the way you rearranged yourselves so that you can see each other."*<br>• *"So, each of you, hold your own papers and start having a conversation now. So do you want to change the title or do you want to keep it?"*<br>• *"Anyone want to change the wording of it? You need to talk with each other."*<br>• *"Is that worded in a positive way?"* [A student later says to his teammates: *"What do you mean it's a negative anyway? How could it be a negative? Oh, yeah, because of the* don't.*"*] | Having each student work on revision gives us a record of every student's work. The group sheet gives us a record of the group thinking. Both are assessment tools to guide instruction. | | |
| **DAY 3**<br>**Whole-Group Revision**<br>(11:10 min.) | **NOTES**<br>Begin by acknowledging the work of each group. *"We're going to go table by table and we're going to go right down the list of anything that you think we want to change to make this better."* Accept multiple responses and honor all the voices. At the same time, move quickly to maintain interest and engagement. One example (restating and accepting one group's change to the title): *"And we can change this again but for right now: Being a good teammate. Okay. Let's move on."* Remember, in shared writing, the teacher holds the pen and is in charge. At the end of session: *"I'm going to read it, and then Mrs. Vale and I will go over it, and that will be the final."* But the teaching is responsive—that is, there is a back-and-forth exchange to push students' thinking. | Monitor the language you use with students. Check (for yourself or have a colleague you trust observe you) that your language:<br>• Accepts students' responses.<br>• Nudges while being respectful.<br>• Puts the responsibility on students.<br>• Helps shape and extend students' responses. |  **Regie is getting responses from each group to revise the "Team Member" document.** | |

continues

*Video* **SCENES**

**Whole-Group Revision** ***continued***

**DEEPER UNDERSTANDING: Shared Writing to Reading**

| Setting, Notes, and Explicit Teaching Points | Ongoing Assessment | Questions/Reflections | Learning Outcomes |
|---|---|---|---|
| The What, Why, and How of Teaching | Informing Our Instruction | For Professional Conversations | What Students Know and Are Able to Do |
| **TEACHING POINTS**<br>• State and expect that responses offered are those the whole group has agreed on. *"I only want your response if you agreed as a team, OK?"*<br>• Accept the various responses students offer; nudge for the clear, meaningful responses; choose the "best" response. Student (speaking for his group): *"Be kind to everyone if he or she has an accident."*<br>*"Who thinks they've improved that if you've worked on that?"*<br>Repeating Bernice: *"Be kind to everyone if they get hurt."*<br>*"Anybody else have something? Julian? Your group? What did your group agree on?"*<br>*"Be kind to everyone if he or she makes a mistake."*<br>*"Anybody have another idea? Carlos?"*<br>Repeating Carlos: *"Help everyone if he or she has an accident."*<br>*"Okay. And Lauren?"*<br>Lauren: *"We actually have two."*<br>*"Give us the one you agreed on as a group."*<br>*"Be kind to your teammates no matter what."*<br>*"I like that."*<br>Mrs. Vale: *"Oh, I like that too."*<br>• Make revisions to the chart (cross out, add in, change language) with students looking on and say the words as you write them.<br>• Help shape responses in positive language by further questioning and probing.<br>*"Who got this in a positive way?"*<br>*"Don't call teammates names."*<br>*"Who was able to turn that around so it sounds positive? Not just you but your group."*<br>Katie: *"Be a loyal friend."* [Restating another group's response:] *"Call your teammates by their own names."*<br>*"Only call your teammates?"*<br>*"No, not only."*<br>*"Call teammates by their real names. Anybody have anything better? Carlos?"*<br>*"Call teammates by a name they like."* | As students respond, be thinking:<br>• Is this response adequate?<br>• How can I encourage a more meaningful response?<br>• What do I need to ask or say so students will work to clarify existing responses?<br><br>Encourage and affirm self-monitoring and self-assessment in responses students give. Two examples from this scene:<br>• *"Did that start in a positive way?"* [Student shakes head no.] *"Okay. Good for you that you caught that. See, if you're using* don't *and* do not, *we're starting with a negative way. We want to keep it positive."*<br>• *"Frank, here's what you said. You said, 'Don't treat people badly.' And why can't we use that? Because it starts with—how?"*<br>Frank: *"Uhm, do treat people?* [I scaffold and affirm his thinking.] *"Do treat people."*<br>*"OK."* | • How does documenting students' work and thinking on revising in writing provide important assessment information? | • Revises text based on feedback.<br>• Records feedback using writing group procedure |

**DEEPER UNDERSTANDING: Shared Writing to Reading**

*Video* **SCENES**

| | Setting, Notes, and Explicit Teaching Points<br>The What, Why, and How of Teaching | Ongoing Assessment<br>Informing Our Instruction | Questions/Reflections<br>For Professional Conversations | Learning Outcomes<br>What Students Know and Are Able to Do |
|---|---|---|---|---|
| **Whole-Group Revision** ***continued*** | *"I like that."* Mrs. Vale: *"I like that too."*<br>And later: *"Don't be mean to others no matter who they are."*<br>*"OK, but it started with a* don't. *Can you turn it around so it's a positive? Who's got a positive? Billy?"*<br>*"Respect everyone with the words you use."*<br>*"Respect everyone with the words you use."*<br>Mrs. Vale: *"I like that one."*<br>• Affirm a "good enough" response. Reading down the list on our chart: *"'Work together. Help each other out.' That sounds pretty good to me. . . . We don't have to improve everything."*<br>• Respect and accept students' additional smart thinking (shows that revision to make text "better" is always possible).<br>Bjorn: *"We wanted to add, 'Work together. Help each other with kindness.'"*<br>*"Help each other out with kindness. I like that. . . . And, kids, I'm going to look these over* [their sheets with revisions]. *If I see we've left out something wonderful that you have on your paper, we'll come back and talk about that tomorrow."*<br>• Let students know they are expected to listen carefully to other responses (so we don't lose time restating information we already have).<br>Student: *"'Always be kind.' . . . We have 'Be kind to your teammates no matter what.' So we've got that. Pay close attention so we're not repeating."*<br>• Combine two thoughts that go together. *"How about if we add that here?"* [insert "and respectful" to line that begins: "Be kind. . . ."]<br>• Reread for clarity and completeness. | *"Do treat people nicely."*<br>*"Sure."* | • How could you use this small-group structure to maximize student participation in all subject areas? | |
| • Celebrating | • Celebrate students' efforts (teaches that good efforts are rewarded so they will make such efforts again). *"I think you've done an excellent job. How many of you think this is a lot better? This is what a group effort does. . . . Well done!"* | | • Why is it important to always celebrate students' efforts? | |

**Students decide what their "best" response is when contributing to whole-group revision.**

SESSION 7

# RESPONSENOTES

*Engage, Reflect, Assess, Celebrate!*

**Transforming** our **Teaching** through
**Reading/Writing Connections**

# Word Work: *Teaching and Assessing Skills in Context*

**View Video** (30 min.)

**Word Work: Teaching and Assessing Skills in Context**

- **Mystery Message**
- **Reading Aloud: *Stand Tall, Molly Lou Melon***
- **Shared Writing: A Letter to Parents**
- **Shared Reading and Illustrating of Class-Authored Text**
- **More Word Work with a Class-Authored Text**
- **Celebration: Tyana**
-  **Additional Word Work and Video Scenes** *(for independent viewing on the website)*

## 1. Engage, Reflect, Assess

- *Small-Group Share:*
    - In last session's video, Regie Routman led shared writing with a group of fourth graders. Between sessions, you were to present that lesson (or a similar one) to your students and to structure and present a similar lesson in the language arts, content areas, or any special area (music, art, physical education, and so on). Share your experiences with a partner, your vertical team, and/or the whole group. Use these questions to prompt discussion and/or chart responses:
        - *How did it go?*
        - *What did you notice?*
        - *How does shared writing support all students as learners?*
        - *How did the small-group collaboration go?*

**RESOURCES**

**On the Website**

- Additional Word Work and Video Scenes *(for independent viewing)*:
    - Mystery Message: Word Work
    - Making the Word Wall Easier to Use
    - Shared Reading of Shared Writing: Connecting to the Word Wall
    - Word Sorts
    - Cut-up Sentences
    - Word Work with Tiles: Applying Rimes to Spelling Words
    - Challenge Message
- Glossary

## 2. Discuss Professional Reading

- With your vertical team, discuss "Shared Writing" (*Invitations* excerpt, pp. 59–66 and downloadable from the website).

## 3. Goals

- Understand how word work can be integral and seamless in the process of teaching reading and writing.
- Learn a variety of ways to teach phonemic awareness, phonics, spelling, word patterns, high-frequency words, vocabulary, and so on in the context of daily, authentic reading and writing experiences.
- Demonstrate how word work can be used as a tool to foster independence in reading and writing through problem solving, self-checking, self-monitoring, and finding and using resources.
- Learn how to teach word-solving strategies.

## 4. View Video and Take Notes

- Turn to the Notecatcher to take notes during the video.

## 5. Respond to the Video

- Share your thinking with your small group and/or whole-group team. Use the following questions to prompt your discussion:
  - What were students able (or not able) to do as a result of the word work in the context of reading and writing?
  - How did you see the teacher using word work as a tool to help all students learn and apply new words independently?
  - How was word work integrated in the reading/writing lessons you observed?

## 6. Achieve a Deeper Understanding

- Review the Deeper Understanding charts. Read and review the Notes, Teaching Points, Ongoing Assessment, and Questions/Reflections for Professional Conversations. The purpose of the Deeper Understanding charts is to help you recall the video and make it easier for you to apply meaningful word work to your own teaching.

## 7. *Try It/Apply It* in the Classroom

- Present one or more of the word work lessons you observed in the session and/or on the website to your students.
- It's fine to "isolate" a word concept to teach it, because you'll still be embedding it in a meaningful context. Say, for example, you notice students

need to learn endings such as *-ed* or *-ing* when they are reading and writing. You will go ahead and teach this concept. This is very different than "teaching skills in isolation," or in a prescribed sequence—there is no research that supports that approach.

## 8. Wrap-Up

- Before next session, read "Teaching Spelling Well" and "Use Word Walls and Other Resources Effectively" (*Writing Essentials* excerpts, pp. 161–165, 165–172 and downloadable from the website) and be prepared to discuss this with the group.
- Schedule time to meet with your vertical, grade-level, and/or partner teams in between whole-group sessions to revisit and view the videos on the website, the Deeper Understanding charts, and/or plan together and try out new learning. You can jot down your ideas and thinking on your Response Notes page for easy reference later.
- Remember to bring any charts, lessons, writing, or student work samples from the *Try It/Apply It* to the next session.

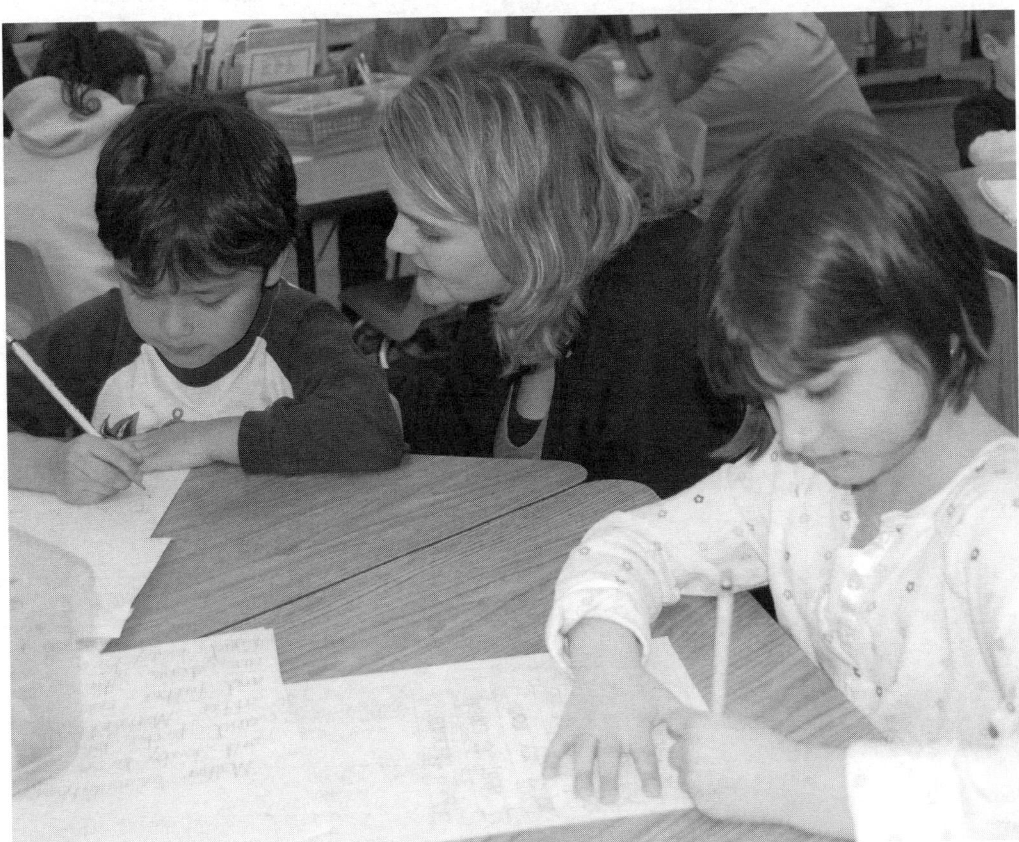

**Mrs. Martinka assists her kindergarten students with their writing.**

SESSION **8**

# **NOTE**CATCHER

| VIDEO SCENES | LENGTH | NOTES & REFLECTION |
|---|---|---|
| **Mystery Message** | 5:42 min. | |
| **Reading Aloud: *Stand Tall, Molly Lou Melon*** | 2:04 min. | |
| **Shared Writing: A Letter to Parents** | 8:39 min. | |
| **Shared Reading and Illustrating of Class-Authored Text** | 2:28 min. | |
| **More Word Work with a Class-Authored Text** | 7:10 min. | |
| • Incorporating Word Work in Independent Practice | | |
| • Guided Reading Overview | | |
| **Celebration: Tyana** | 4:13 min. | |
| **Additional Word Work and Video Scenes** *(for independent viewing on the website)* | | |

SESSION **8**

Word Work: Teaching and Assessing Skills in Context

# Deeper Understanding

*The teaching and assessing points reflect the total lesson but not all of these points are on the edited videos you are watching. However, the major points are represented on the edited videos.*

The globe icon indicates that the example is also available when you visit www.regieroutman.com.

## *Video* SCENES

| | Setting, Notes, and Explicit Teaching Points | Ongoing Assessment | Questions/Reflections | Learning Outcomes |
|---|---|---|---|---|
| | The What, Why, and How of Teaching | Informing Our Instruction | For Professional Conversations | What Students Know and Are Able to Do |
| | **SETTING**<br>These scenes take place, in sequence, in mid-November in a first-grade classroom of 25 students. The classroom teacher, Judy Sipiora, has been teaching for 30 years, most of those years in first grade. These first graders are typical of the general make-up of this large urban K–6 school, in which 87 percent of the students qualify for free or reduced-price lunch and 80 percent of the students speak a language other than English at home (29 languages are represented).<br>Reading is being taught using a basal series and decodable texts. Most of the writing children do follow a highly structured writing program. Phonics is being taught through "direct instruction" in a daily 30-minute block.<br>Test scores in reading at the school, as indicated by the state's high-stakes test, show 40 percent of fourth graders proficient in reading. (Test scores increased after the residency.)<br>The purpose of the weeklong residency is to show many alternate ways to teach phonics and to demonstrate the efficiency, effectiveness, and enjoyment of teaching word work in the meaningful context of authentic reading and writing activities. These scenes show the writing and reading of multiple texts and the application of meaning-based strategies—along with phonics—in the process of that reading and writing. Note that even when the word work is isolated, it is isolated within the larger context of meaning. | **Connecting word work with writing and reading meaningful text.** | | |
| <br>**Mystery Message**<br>(5:42 min.) | **NOTES**<br>The Mystery Message, a form of morning message (see chart), is a fast, enjoyable way to see what students know and to situate letter, sound, and word work in the context of meaning. Write about something you want students to know, and only | | | |

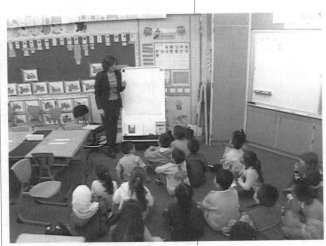

continues

# Video SCENES

**Mystery Message *continued***

## DEEPER UNDERSTANDING: Word Work: Teaching and Assessing Skills in Context

### Setting, Notes, and Explicit Teaching Points
The What, Why, and How of Teaching

write as much as most students write. My message on this first day of meeting these students is: *"Today we will be doing lots of reading and writing. And I have a present for you."* To make sure all students have opportunities to participate and be successful decoding the message, ask something like *"Show me something you know"* (rather than "Who can find a word they know?," which eliminates students who may only know a few letters). Highlight the parts of the message students decode, and continue to reread the message aloud, silently pointing to the words not yet highlighted. Continue to ask (to send the message that reading is about making meaning), *"Does it make sense yet?"*

**TEACHING POINTS**

- State the purpose of the activity and what students are expected to do. *"You're going to be detectives. I'm going to write a message, and when I write it, I want you to try to read the message in your mind. So it's kind of like a game. If you can read it, don't tell anybody. But I want everybody to try. Now watch me write it."*
- Expect students to be watching you write (so they can hear and see your voice/print match). *"I like the way all eyes are here."* Celebrate their efforts to read the message. *"You're working hard."*
- Connect applying reading strategies to writing. *"And I want you to be using everything you know about reading to see if you figure out what I'm writing. But don't say anything! See if you can figure it out."* And a few seconds later: *"Now what I have to do as a good writer is I have to check my writing to see if it makes sense. Don't say anything. See if I've got what I want to say."* [I silently check the sentence while pointing to the words.]
- Ask for a response that goes beyond the right answer, that requires thinking. *"What do you see that you know?"* [Jimmy points to *today*.] *"How did you know that?"*
- Continue to probe students' thinking. *"Who sees something else they know? Come on up and show us."*
  Monique: *"We."*

### Ongoing Assessment
Informing Our Instruction

Today we will be doing lots of reading and writing And, I have a present for you
When you read, check to be sure the words and story make sense

Throughout this scene, I ask the children, *"How did you know that?"* Notice that the students don't know how they know and/or cannot say. I want them to think about their thinking (metacognition) so they can use and apply strategies and resources to problem solve (in this case, word solve). If students cannot articulate how they "know," they are less likely to transfer learning to new contexts.

Ask students to attempt to word solve—that is, read the sentences. Use students' responses to assess what they know about letters, sounds, words, applying strategies, and reading. Use invitational language:

- *"Who sees something that they know?"*
- *"It could be a word, it could be a part of a word, it could be a letter, it could be a sound."*

Check that students can confirm what they say they know.

- *"Come on up and show me. Point to it."* [Jimmy points to the word.]

### Questions/Reflections
For Professional Conversations

**Use a morning message or mystery message to assess what students understand about letters, sounds, and words.**

- Why is it so important for students to explain their thinking (in all academic areas) and how they arrived at their response(s)?

### Learning Outcomes
What Students Know and Are Able to Do

- Apply comprehension-monitoring strategies to increase comprehension, including word-recognition strategies, rereading, and looking forward in the written text.
- Listen to text to learn new information, answer questions, or solve problems with teacher guidance.
- Recognize that print represents spoken language.
- Recognize the difference between words and sentences.
- Recognize that sounds are represented by different single letters or combinations of letters.
- Use knowledge of phonics to read unfamiliar words in isolation.

**Deeper Understanding: Word Work: Teaching and Assessing Skills in Context**

*Video* **SCENES**

**Mystery Message *continued***

| Setting, Notes, and Explicit Teaching Points<br>The What, Why, and How of Teaching | Ongoing Assessment<br>Informing Our Instruction | Questions/Reflections<br>For Professional Conversations | Learning Outcomes<br>What Students Know and Are Able to Do |
|---|---|---|---|
| *"How did you know that?" "I sounded it out."*<br>*"Amir, what do you see?" "Present."*<br>*"How did you know that?"*<br>*"Because first I thought it would be* prison, *but then when I saw the* e, *I said, 'present.'"*<br>• Affirm students' thoughtful responses (so they and others "do it again"). *"Good for you. So you're using all that you know . . . all that fabulous work that your teacher is doing."*<br>• Scaffold students' thinking. "Solomon, what do you see that you know?"<br>*"For—for you."*<br>*"For you. How did you know* for?*"*<br>*"Because it's for you."*<br>*"OK, I'm looking to see if or is on our word wall. Not yet."* Mrs. Sipiora: *"It's actually up here."* Or. *"Where is it? Oh, there it is with Oreo."*<br>• Note words that cannot be "sounded out." *"It's a word (you) you just have to know. And kids here it is on your word wall."* And, again, later: *"Of is a really hard one that you can't sound out."*<br>• Read for meaning. *"Let's see if this makes sense yet."* Reread sentences, pointing and saying aloud the words figured out and highlighted while silently pointing to the words not yet decoded: *"'Today we . . . present for you.' It doesn't make sense yet. And when we're reading it always has to make sense."*<br>• Show how to use the word wall to help figure out or confirm a word. For example: *"Look up here kids, if I wanted to check it* [have], *it's right here on the word wall."*<br>• Frame (using a sliding mask) high-frequency words you want students to know (to draw students' attention to those words. [I frame *of* after the student reads it and it's highlighted.]<br>• Demonstrate that if you know most of the words, you can figure out the message. I read aloud only part of message that is highlighted. *"It almost makes sense."* And after more words are uncovered: *"I think we can do the whole message now. I'm not going to say anything but I think you can read it."* Class reads message: *"Today we will be doing lots of reading and writing. And I have a present for you."* | • *"What does that say?"*<br>[*"Today."*]<br><br>Evaluate student's thinking:<br>• *"How did you know that said* today, will, have, *and so on?"*<br>And, again, later:<br>• *"Is that how you knew it?"* [From the word wall.]<br>• *"So did you sound it out?"*<br>• *"Did any of you look at the word wall?"*<br><br>Focus on meaning first (comprehension). For example, through your questioning, be sure to include meaning cues along with phonics. *"Let's see if this makes sense yet."*<br><br>Assess if students understand the difference between letters and words by using a sliding mask to isolate and locate known and unknown words. | <br>**Regie asks Jimmy, "What do you see that you know?" Jimmy points to "today."** | • Understand how to use classroom resources with teacher guidance. |

*Video* **SCENES**

**Reading Aloud: *Stand Tall, Molly Lou Melon***

(2:04 min.)

**DEEPER UNDERSTANDING: Word Work: Teaching and Assessing Skills in Context**

| Setting, Notes, and Explicit Teaching Points<br>The What, Why, and How of Teaching | Ongoing Assessment<br>Informing Our Instruction | Questions/Reflections<br>For Professional Conversations | Learning Outcomes<br>What Students Know and Are Able to Do |
|---|---|---|---|
| **NOTES**<br>In wanting to bond with the children and build their I-can-do-it spirit, I have selected a book as a gift for these children, *Stand Tall, Molly Lou Melon,* a story of a feisty first grader who stands up for herself when teased.<br><br>**TEACHING POINTS**<br>• Connect words in the book's title with learning to read. In this case, I point to the word *tall* in the title while reading it, holding the book so students can see cover. *"Yesterday we were talking about* all. *Could we highlight that one now? It's on the word wall."*<br>• Teach and highlight rimes (phonics by analogy, see Glossary). *"And we were talking about that if you know* all *you could figure out a whole lot of other words."*<br>• Explain what you are doing on the word wall as you do it, so students see why and how they might use the word wall. [As Mrs. Sipiora goes over to word wall and places colored transparent tape on all to designate it as a rime.] *"That is a clue to you that if you know* all, *you can figure out a whole bunch of other words."*<br>• Explain vocabulary that's necessary to understanding the story. *"And they're not just talking about, like, stand tall, stand up. This is stand tall, and it means like 'stand up for yourself.'. . . Don't let anyone push you around. Be all that you can be."*<br>• Give a framework for what the book is about before reading it aloud. *"It's a wonderful book, and it's about not letting anybody push you around."*<br>• Summarize the main idea of the book. *"Did you hear what she* [Ladaisha] *said? She said, 'Stand up for yourself.' So if anybody's pushing you around, kids, even though you're only in first grade, stand up for yourself. Stand tall!"*<br>• Set the expectation that many students can read this book. *"So this is a present to you, and a lot of you will be able to read this on your own without any trouble."* | <br>**Regie gives a framework for what the book is about before reading it aloud. "It's a wonderful book, and it's about not letting anyone push you around."**<br><br>Check for understanding of whole text.<br>• *"Who can put in their own words what Grandma tells her about how she* [Molly Lou] *should act?"*<br>Ladaisha: *"She should stand up for herself."* (A turn-and-talk, which we didn't do, is a terrific way to allow everyone to respond.) | • How might you use a read-aloud to clarify your thinking process when figuring out an unfamiliar word? | |

# *Video* SCENES

**Shared Writing: A Letter to Parents**
(8:39 min.)

## Deeper Understanding: Word Work: Teaching and Assessing Skills in Context

| Setting, Notes, and Explicit Teaching Points<br>The What, Why, and How of Teaching | Ongoing Assessment<br>Informing Our Instruction | Questions/Reflections<br>For Professional Conversations | Learning Outcomes<br>What Students Know and Are Able to Do |
|---|---|---|---|
| **NOTES**<br>Create at least one shared writing each week as an efficient, enjoyable way to experience real-world writing and reading, enhance reading and writing abilities, teach lots of skills, and publish texts to share with parents and others. (See "Shared Writing to Reading in the Intermediate Grades (3–6): Three-Day Lesson Plan" for Session 7 on the website. Keep your focus on what's most important: the content. If you comment on every time you add punctuation, for example, you will go on too long and you will lose your main focus.) Stop after about 10 minutes (to maintain interest and engagement). Complete the shared writing on a second day, if necessary. | | | |
| **TEACHING POINTS**<br>• Connect writing with reading. *"Your teacher and I had a really great idea . . . we're going to go* [from] *writing into reading."*<br>• Set the purpose and audience for the shared writing. *"You have conferences coming up next week, right? So we thought it would be so great if we wrote a letter to your parents inviting them to the conference. Just one letter."*<br>• Explain the process. *"So I'm going to be doing the writing. You're going to do the thinking."*<br>• Date the letter (*"We're really going to send this"*) and direct students' attention to your writing. *"So today is the 15th. Okay, so watch me write November 15, 2005."*<br>• Direct students to think about how to start the letter. *"We're writing to our parents. How should we start it? Amir?"* *"Capital."*<br>• Affirm response and redirect thinking to focus on the audience for the writing. *"Capital, you're right. We're going to start with a capital letter. But what do we want to say to our parents?"* Siuleo: *"Dear Parents."*<br>• Expect and invite best spelling of letters and sounds students know. *"How's it going to start?* [I sound the first letter out, /d/.] *Dear. How's* dear *going to end?"*<br>• Stretch out sounds in the word as you write the letters. *"P-P-P-Parents* [I enunciate the word as I write the letters.] *What comes next?* R.*"* | Assess what students know about beginning a friendly letter to someone.<br>• *"How should we start it? We're writing to our parents."* (Amir's response, *"Capital,"* indicates he is focusing is on mechanics.)<br><br>Check that students have learned what's been taught (in this case, finding a word on the word wall). *"And I think you know you now. You know where to find it. Everybody look on the word wall."*<br>Students: *"Y-O-U."* | • What do you notice about the children's engagement at the start of this shared letter writing and at the end? What has made the difference? | |

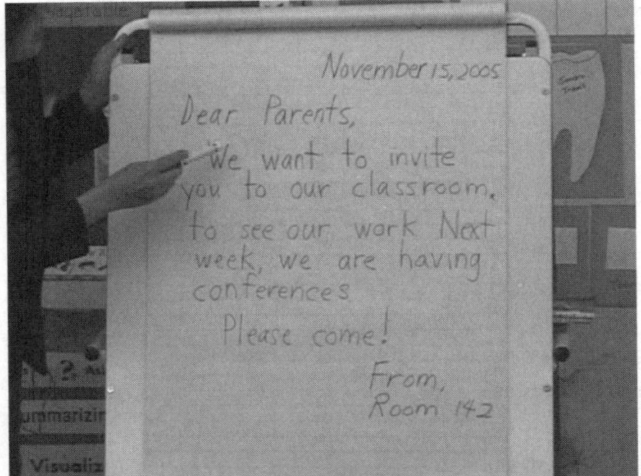


**We reread our completed letter as a shared reading.**

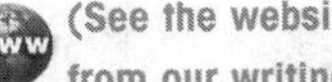 **(See the website for an example of how to do word work from our writing using cut-up sentences.)**

*continues*

*Video* **SCENES**

**Shared Writing: A Letter to Parents *continued***

**DEEPER UNDERSTANDING: Word Work: Teaching and Assessing Skills in Context**

| Setting, Notes, and Explicit Teaching Points | Ongoing Assessment | Questions/Reflections | Learning Outcomes |
|---|---|---|---|
| The What, Why, and How of Teaching | Informing Our Instruction | For Professional Conversations | What Students Know and Are Able to Do |
| • Write the letters students know (affirms what they know) as you write the words.<br>• Give ideas by putting the language in their ears. *"Dear Parents. We want to invite you to conferences next week? What do we want to say? Solomon?"*<br>• Scaffold students' ideas and help shape thinking.<br>Solomon: *"We want to invite you to the school."* *"We want to invite you to our school, or our classroom? What do you want to say?"*<br>Students: *"Classroom."*<br>*"We want to invite you to our classroom."*<br>• Ask students to spell high-frequency words aloud (this lets them know you expect them to spell that word, keeps them focused through participation, and affirms what they know). *"OK. Everybody.* We." [As we begin first sentence of our letter.]<br>Students: *"W-E."* And, again: "To, *everybody."*<br>Students: *"T-O."*<br>And: "In [first syllable in invite]. *You know* in."<br>Students: *"I-N."*<br>• Note spacing between words, and finger-point to spaces as you write. *"Watch how I'm spacing."*<br>• Reread to check writing so far. *"One of the things a good writer does is always check their writing. Oops, and you know what? I left out a letter in November. I didn't do that on purpose.... That's why I have to go back and check."*<br>• Reread draft (*"Dear Parents, We want to invite you to our classroom"*) to help decide what to say next. *"And why do we want to invite them? What do we want to say next? Who has an idea?"*<br>• Offer suggestions (to help students take an idea and make it their own). *"We want to say something about, 'We want to invite you to our classroom to see our work, to have a conference with....' What should we say?"* Sandra: *"To see our work."*<br>• Find and check the spelling of a word *(our)* by referring and pointing to the same word on the previous line. *"Here's* our." | Invite students to spell important letter sounds as you are writing as a way to see what they know and to keep them engaged.<br>• "Classroom, *how does that start?"*<br>Jimmy: *"C-L."*<br>*"Everybody"* [expecting next letter].<br>Students: *"A."* And, again, later, while writing *have*:<br>*"What's the vowel? Everybody."*<br>Students: *"A."* | **Regie writes as the class spells the word(s):**<br>**Regie: "To, *everybody.*"**<br>**Students: "T-O"**<br><br>• Think about how you can routinely use shared writing across the curriculum as an instructional approach to improve writing and reading. (See *Writing Essentials,* pp. 83–118, for many writing ideas for authentic purposes and audiences.) | • Participate in shared reading/writing of texts.<br>• Brainstorm ideas for writing.<br><br>• Write for an intended audience. |

**Video SCENES**

**DEEPER UNDERSTANDING: Word Work: Teaching and Assessing Skills in Context**

| | Setting, Notes, and Explicit Teaching Points | Ongoing Assessment | Questions/Reflections | Learning Outcomes |
|---|---|---|---|---|
| | The What, Why, and How of Teaching | Informing Our Instruction | For Professional Conversations | What Students Know and Are Able to Do |
| | • Shape and guide the writing. *"How about this? 'Next week we are having conferences.'"*<br>• Draft an ending. *"OK, let's just add one more sentence and close our letter. . . . Be thinking about how we should end our letter."* [I reread it, pointing to words while reading.]<br>Mrs. Sipiora: *"'Please come.' That sounds great."*<br>• Add an exclamation mark. *"How about if we do this? We put an exclamation mark. We really want you to come!"*<br>• Add a closing. *"And how should we sign it? . . . 'From Room 142.'"*<br>• Reread again as a final check. *"OK let's read it and see if there's anything we want to change."*<br>• State the purpose for rereading the completed letter as a class, as a shared reading. (In this case, it's to become a better reader and writer.) *"You know, one of the reasons that I want you reading this with me is because this will help you become a good reader. I forgot to tell you that. So it's really important that your eyes are up here. So when you come across some of these words in a book, or when you're writing your own story, you'll know how to spell them; you'll know how to read them. OK, so let's start again."* [I start again, distinctly pointing to each word and sliding across the word while saying it; students read along.]<br>• Connect writing with reading. *"OK, we'll type that up so that everybody has it* [as a text to read and share with parents]. *And, also, we're going to be doing some word work with this tomorrow."* | Assess students' attention and engagement. When it's absent, stop and regroup. Explain why it's important for them as a reader/writer/thinker to be doing what you ask them to do. | • What can you do to embed more word study work in your teaching? | |
| **Shared Reading and Illustrating of Class-Authored Text**<br>(2:28 min.) | **NOTES**<br>To bond with students, increase their confidence, create an authentic text to read, and to teach skills in a meaningful way, we have begun a shared writing ("What We're Great At") the previous day. As Mrs. Sipiora and I demonstrate, each student tells one thing they are "great at." (Mrs. Sipiora completed the shared writing that afternoon.) In this brief scene, we are reviewing our text through a shared reading. Next, we tell them why we want each student to illustrate his/her own page (now | | **A student circles a high-frequency word from our "What We're Great At" text.** | |

continues

**DEEPER UNDERSTANDING: Word Work: Teaching and Assessing Skills in Context**

## Video SCENES

**Shared Reading and Illustrating of Class-Authored Text *continued***

| Setting, Notes, and Explicit Teaching Points | Ongoing Assessment | Questions/Reflections | Learning Outcomes |
|---|---|---|---|
| The What, Why, and How of Teaching | Informing Our Instruction | For Professional Conversations | What Students Know and Are Able to Do |
| typed) and give directions for doing it. The class shared writing will become:<br>• A book for the classroom library.<br>• A reading text—each student will receive a copy to read at school and at home.<br>• An independent writing activity (differentiated instruction during guided reading) in which students elaborate on their one line of text.<br>• A tool for teaching word work and skills in a meaningful context.<br><br>**TEACHING POINTS**<br>• Use shared reading of a class-authored text to practice reading and fluency.<br>• Point out features of words. *"You know what I noticed here. I noticed that just like in* having, *you were looking for that* e. *Look what happens when we add* i-n-g *(pointing to word* making*). The* e *disappears."*<br>• Frame important vocabulary in the context of its use. *"You're each going to get your own page that you wrote yesterday. And you're going to illustrate it. . . . You're going to draw. No, you're not going to copy."*<br>• Set expectations for illustrating:<br>  • Drawing is carefully done.<br>  • Complete drawing in 10 minutes.<br>  • Picture goes with the writing.<br>  • Picture helps the reader read the writing.<br>• Show what carefully done illustrations look like. (In this case, I show illustrations from a similar book other first graders have done.)<br>• Explain why illustrating time is limited. *"Coloring does not help you become a better reader."*<br>• State why illustrations must match the written text. *"Because Amir says, 'Amir is great at basketball.' But what if somebody can't read the word* basketball*? His picture should be so good that that picture will help the reader read it."* | Assess, note, and record what students know and understand about letters, sounds, and words.<br><br>Check that students understand important vocabulary.<br>*"Illustrate it. What does that mean?"*<br>Student: *"Copy."* | • Why is it essential to show exactly what you expect when students illustrate their writing? | |

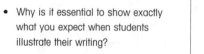

**A student in another first-grade class leads the shared reading of the class text. The teacher can use this time to check that all students are following along.**

Michaela is great at imagining.

**An illustrated page from "What We're Great At."**

*Video* **SCENES**

**More Word Work with a Class-Authored Text**

(7:10 min.)

**DEEPER UNDERSTANDING: Word Work: Teaching and Assessing Skills in Context**

| Setting, Notes, and Explicit Teaching Points<br>The What, Why, and How of Teaching | Ongoing Assessment<br>Informing Our Instruction | Questions/Reflections<br>For Professional Conversations | Learning Outcomes<br>What Students Know and Are Able to Do |
|---|---|---|---|
| **NOTES**<br>Here we project the shared writing text "What We're Great At" on the screen and lead the whole class in a shared reading. We are using two sheets of paper (you can also use 5 x 7-inch index cards) to track the text and expose the text word by word and line by line, and we highlight specific words with a sliding mask. Word work on familiar text makes it easier for English language learners and struggling learners to engage with and successfully apply word-solving strategies. | | | |
| **TEACHING POINTS**<br>• Use the beginning letter(s) of a word in familiar, meaningful text to help figure out a word. [I show *dr* while masking rest of word, *dr-awing.*]<br>• Apply meaning-based cues along with phonics to word solving. [For *drawing*:] *"If we just saw the beginning of that, we could probably figure it out once we see his picture, and also because you remember what he said yesterday ('Umi is great at drawing')."* | Ask students to locate important words in familiar text. (Rapid and accurate word recognition and fluency is an excellent predictor of reading comprehension—as long as students know the meaning of the vocabulary in the text.) Use their responses to adjust instruction. | | • Read selected words on sight.<br>• Identify words by using beginning sounds. |
| • Highlight multisyllable words using a sliding mask. *"You know your sounds so well, even if you didn't know it* [saying and exposing one syllable at a time]: *'com-pu-ters.'"* [Again, later, with *basketball.*] | • Students read: *"Tyana is great at coloring pumpkins."* [Text says *carving.* I wait briefly to see if they self-correct.] *"Let's look at it carefully."* [I use a sliding mask to expose *carv,* then sound out the whole word as it is exposed.] *"Car-/v/-carving. You said* coloring*; there'd have to be an L in there, wouldn't there?"* | • Think about the ways that word work can be intentional and explicit without isolated drills. | • Identify multisyllable words. |
| • Make sure illustrations are clear and explicit. *"You're going to have to make your picture so good that even if somebody can't read that word, the picture will help them."*<br>• State the importance of looking at and reading the text. *"OK, I want all eyes here, because this is going to help you become a great reader."* | • *"Who can find the word* basketball*? Come on up and circle it."* | • For older students, how might you weave in explicit teaching of word parts, Greek and Latin roots, common prefixes and suffixes? | • Use illustrations to confirm word meaning with teacher guidance. |
| • Locate specific words in the text. [Cesar circles *basketball* on the screen after I ask for a volunteer.] *"Now check him. Be sure he's getting it right."*<br>• Clap the syllables in a word. *"Basketball. And that word has three syllables, doesn't it. . . . Let's clap it. Clap it with me."*<br>• Teach phonics daily as part of everyday reading and writing. *"Now what I want you to see, teachers, is that phonics is in everything that we do when we're . . . doing real reading and writing."* | | | • Identify syllables in words. |

*continues*

**DEEPER UNDERSTANDING: Word Work: Teaching and Assessing Skills in Context**

*Video* **SCENES**

| Video Scenes | Setting, Notes, and Explicit Teaching Points<br>The What, Why, and How of Teaching | Ongoing Assessment<br>Informing Our Instruction | Questions/Reflections<br>For Professional Conversations | Learning Outcomes<br>What Students Know and Are Able to Do |
|---|---|---|---|---|
| **More Word Work with a Class-Authored Text *continued*** | **NOTES**<br>I will be meeting with small guided-reading groups for the first time, and I am explaining the work the students who are not in a group will be doing quietly—illustrating their page for the class book and doing word work with rimes. Usually, the first expectation for independent practice is reading, assigned and self-selected reading (see *Reading Essentials,* pp. 160–162, not shown in this scene), but there has not been time to set this up. | | | |
| • Incorporating Word Work in Independent Practice | **TEACHING POINTS**<br>• Take known rimes *at* and *all* and generate new words. Write as many words as you can. *"If you know* all, *you know* ball."<br>• Demonstrate how to find words that fit the rime pattern. "*Where could you find* basketball? *There it is . . . on our chart. 'Solomon is great at basketball.'* And, again, later: "*Who knows another word that has* all *in it?"*<br>Umi: *"Tall." "That was a word we talked about this morning in the book,* Stand Tall, Molly Lou Malone." | Check that students know how to help themselves figure out words that have *at* and *all* in them.<br>• *"If you wanted to know how to spell* basketball, *where could you find it?"* | • Why is it essential that most independent practice be actual reading of authentic texts and not activities about reading?<br>• How does your classroom library influence the success (or failure) of independent reading? | • Use rimes/word families to decode words in isolation and in context. |
| • Guided Reading Overview<br><br>*(See Reading to Understand PD Program for Guided Reading Lessons, Groups 1 and 2.)* | **NOTES**<br>I meet with two reading groups (10 minutes per group) to be sure they understand what they are reading. [Addressing observing teachers] *"What I want to do is I want to be sure that these are good readers, that they're understanding what they read. So that when they go back to their seats and they're working on independent reading—because this is where they're going to become the best readers is through this massive amount of reading that they do—so I want to be sure when they're reading on their own, they're not just sounding out words. But that they're really understanding what they're reading."* | | **Regie meets with a reading group and addresses the observing teachers: "I want to be sure that these are good readers—that they are understanding what they read . . ."** | • Read text to learn new information, answer questions, or solve problems with teacher guidance. |
| **Celebration: Tyana**<br>(4:13 min.) | **NOTES**<br>Bring celebration into all teaching. Honest celebration of students' strengths is not a frill; celebration is essential for students to develop the competence and confidence to do challenging work. In this scene, students are being celebrated for independent practice—adding to their one sentence for our class book "What We're Great At." | Review learning goals and discuss with students what they were able to know and do after the lesson.<br><br>Together, set learning goals for the next literacy block. | • What do you notice about how celebration and teaching interconnect in a conference? | |

**Notice how Tyana, a student who appears to have low self-esteem, visibly changes from one day to the next because of the power of celebration in a scaffolded conversation.**

**DEEPER UNDERSTANDING:** Word Work: Teaching and Assessing Skills in Context

## Video SCENES

**Additional Word Work and Video Scenes**

*(for independent viewing on the website)*

| Setting, Notes, and Explicit Teaching Points | Ongoing Assessment | Questions/Reflections | Learning Outcomes |
|---|---|---|---|
| The What, Why, and How of Teaching | Informing Our Instruction | For Professional Conversations | What Students Know and Are Able to Do |
| **NOTES**<br>Integrate word work all day and every day into reading, writing, and content areas. The following skills and strategies were modeled through reading aloud, shared reading, shared writing, and guided reading throughout the week:<br><br>**GLOSSARY**<br>*(See the Glossary on the website for definitions)*<br>**Graphic awareness**<br>**Phonemic awareness**<br>**Phonics**<br>**Invented spelling**<br>**Word sort**<br>**Word wall** | On a regular basis (weekly, monthly, or every grading period):<br>• Ask kids to write the words they know for a 10-minute period. Have students date their papers, collect samples, and save.<br><br>and/or<br><br>• Take a familiar sentence from the shared reading chart. Ask kids to write down the sounds they hear and/or spell specific words. Date papers and save.<br><br>You will have evidence of spellings, high-frequency words, and vocabulary your students have learned over time. | • How were spelling, vocabulary, high-frequency words, and content-area words taught within the context of shared reading and writing? | • Use word-recognition skills and strategies to read and comprehend text. |

## SELECTED ACTIVITIES FROM DAYS 2 AND 3 (FOLLOW UP OF DAY 1) FOR INDEPENDENT VIEWING

*Go to the website for these independent viewing selections.*

### Additional Word Work Activities for Independent Viewing

- Mystery Message: Word Work
- Making the Word Wall Easier to Use
- Shared Reading of Shared Writing: Connecting to the Word Wall
- Word Sorts
- Cut-up Sentences
- Word Work with Tiles: Applying Rimes to Spelling Words
- Challenge Message

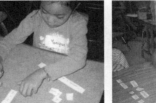

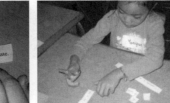

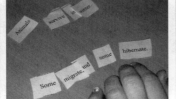

Word work with tiles (see *Writing Essentials*, p. 97)

Word wall

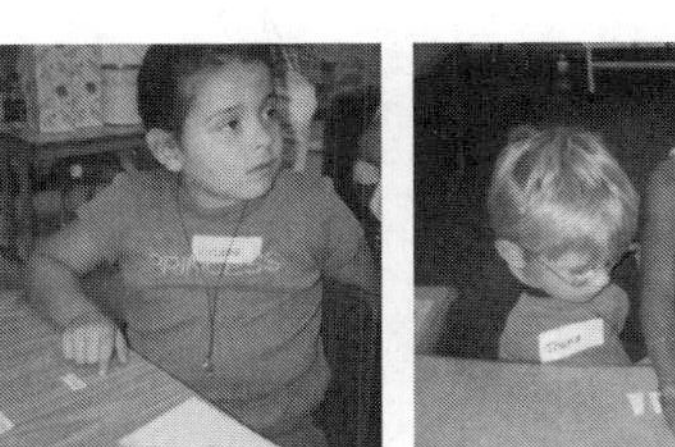

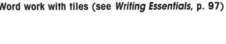

Cut-up sentences (see *Writing Essentials*, pp. 95–96)

SESSION 8

# **RESPONSE**NOTES

***Engage, Reflect, Assess, Celebrate!***

REGIE ROUTMAN in RESIDENCE



**Transforming** our **Teaching** through

## Reading/Writing Connections

# Writers Become Readers Through Daily Writing

**View Video** (31 min.)

**Writers Become Readers Through Daily Writing**

- **What Do Smart Writers Do? Responsive Teaching**
- **Telling the Story Before Writing It: Finding the Topic**
- **Demonstrating Brainstorming and Writing**
- **Small-Group Support**
- **Public Conferences: Celebrating and Moving the Writing Forward**

Agenda

### 1. Engage, Reflect, Assess

- *Small-Group Share*
    - In your small group, talk about one or more word work lessons you tried with your students:
        - *How did it go?*
        - *What did you learn?*
        - *What did you notice about efficiency, enjoyment, effectiveness, what students were able to do?*
        - *What are the advantages of embedding word work into meaningful reading and writing activities? Disadvantages?*

**RESOURCES**

**In this Session**

- Holly's Brainstorming and Start of Her Draft: Second Grade *9–7*
- Andrew's Brainstorming and Start of His Draft: Second Grade *9–8*
- Brandon's Brainstorming and Start of His Draft: Second Grade *9–10*
- Raquel's Brainstorming and Start of Her Draft: Second Grade *9–12*

**On the Website**

- Students' Writing (Holly, Andrew, Brandon, Raquel)
- Class Charts

## 2. Discuss Professional Reading

- Discuss (with a partner, with your vertical team, or as a whole group) "Teaching Spelling Well" and "Use Word Walls and Other Resources Effectively" (*Writing Essentials* excerpts, pp. 161–165, 165–172 and downloadable from the website).

## 3. Goals

- Explore ways to reveal yourself as a writer and a reader.
- Assess what students know about what "smart" writers do.
- Notice what authors do as writers to engage readers.
- Write with a specific purpose, keeping the reader in mind.
- Demonstrate a planning process for brainstorming, narrowing, and organizing a topic while keeping the reader in mind.
- Learn what a scaffolded conversation before writing might look and sound like.
- Begin to have students write with elaboration and detail.
- Understand that reading and writing are reciprocal processes (strong readers develop through writing and reading).

## 4. View Video and Take Notes

- Turn to the Notecatcher to take notes. Notice how much young writers and readers are able to write with elaboration and detail when they have sufficient demonstrations and "handholding." Also notice how being aware of what authors do positively impacts both their writing and reading.

## 5. Respond to Video

- Share your thinking with your small group and whole-group team. Respond to the following discussion questions:
  - How can you reveal yourself (to your students) as a writer and a reader?
  - What did you learn through observing the processes of brainstorming, narrowing, and organizing a topic while keeping the reader in mind?
  - What did you notice about the role of scaffolded conversations with students?
  - How can students become better readers through meaningful daily writing?

## 6. Achieve a Deeper Understanding

- Read and discuss the Deeper Understanding charts. The Notes/Teaching Points, Ongoing Assessments, and Questions/Reflections are designed to help you think more deeply about the video and apply what you have seen and discussed to your teaching. These pages are also meant to help you personalize your learning and to understand the powerful influence effective writing instruction can have on students as writers and readers and to bring those connections into your own teaching. Use these pages to inform your ongoing weekly schoolwide conversations between whole-group sessions.

## 7. *Try It/Apply It* in the Classroom

- Build on your work from Session 4:
  - Show your current writing life to your students. Perhaps bring in samples of recent writing, such as emails, letters, post cards, or parent newsletters.
  - Assess and record (chart) what your students know about what good writers do: "What Do Smart Writers Do?"
- Select a topic that resonates with you and that your students will enjoy hearing about.
- Preplan the stories or subtopics you may choose to talk about and then write about. (Do not write out your story ahead of time, but do jot down the topics and perhaps some key ideas.)
- Begin to tell some of your stories to your students.
- Demonstrate your own thinking/writing process as you tell your story aloud.
- Think aloud while you write with elaboration and detail on one of your topics. (Use your oral storytelling to help you narrow the topic.)
- Incorporate the writing process you have observed into your daily writing program:
  - Demonstrate.
  - Conduct one or more scaffolded conversations before students write.
  - Provide sustained time for writing.
  - Hold roving conferences.
  - Hold one-on-one conferences.
  - Conduct whole-class shares (public conferences) to celebrate and augment learning.
  - Publish for an authentic audience.
- Prepare to share your reading/writing lessons, samples of your students' work, and your own demonstration writing with your team during the next session. If possible, bring in a video clip of what you have done with your students.

## 8. Wrap-Up

- Before next session, read "Capturing a Moment: Learning to Write with Description and Detail" (*Conversations* excerpt, pp. 346–349 and downloadable from the website) and prepare to discuss it at the next session.

- Schedule time to meet with your vertical, grade-level, and/or partner teams in between whole-group sessions to revisit the videos on the website and the Deeper Understanding charts and/or plan together and try out new learning.
- Remember to bring any charts, lessons, writing, or student work samples from the *Try It/Apply It* to the next session.

SESSION 9

# NOTECATCHER

| VIDEO SCENES | LENGTH | NOTES & REFLECTION |
|---|---|---|
| **What Do Smart Writers Do? Responsive Teaching**<br>• Day 1<br>• Day 2 | 5:26 min. | |
| **Telling the Story Before Writing it: Finding the Topic**<br>• Choosing the Topic: Keeping the Reader in Mind | 5:04 min. | |

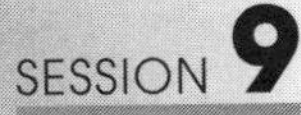

# SESSION 9 NOTECATCHER

| VIDEO SCENES | LENGTH | NOTES & REFLECTION |
|---|---|---|
| **Demonstrating Brainstorming and Writing** | 8:16 min. | |
| • Modeling Brainstorming Through Scaffolded Conversations: Holly | | |
| • Celebrating and Assessing Learning | | |

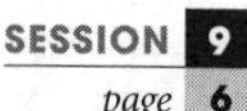

SESSION 9

# NOTECATCHER

| VIDEO SCENES (2) | LENGTH | NOTES & REFLECTION |
|---|---|---|
| **Small-Group Support** | 2:07 min. | |
| **Public Conferences: Celebrating and Moving the Writing Forward**<br>• Destiny | 9:51 min. | |

# Holly's Brainstorming and Start of Her Draft: *Second Grade*

(See student profile, p. 9–21.)

Holly LiZZie life

- An annoying brother
- ✓ brakeing arm
- Mom loves her
- her dog
- *✓ diary loosing
- Soft ball trying out

- brother took
- mom grounding
- LiZZ loughing
- Automik wegie
- ~~leaning~~ learning to love

Holly 12-7

~~I~~ ~~I~~ Once there was a girl name LiZZie. She had an annoying brother. One day he thought he could steale her diary. He snuke into her ~~Roomm~~ and qietley serched the room. At last he found it but it was locked. So he took it to ~~her~~ his room and went to the kitchen. He got some siscors and went back up stairs to his room. But once he got up their LiZZie was home

p. 1

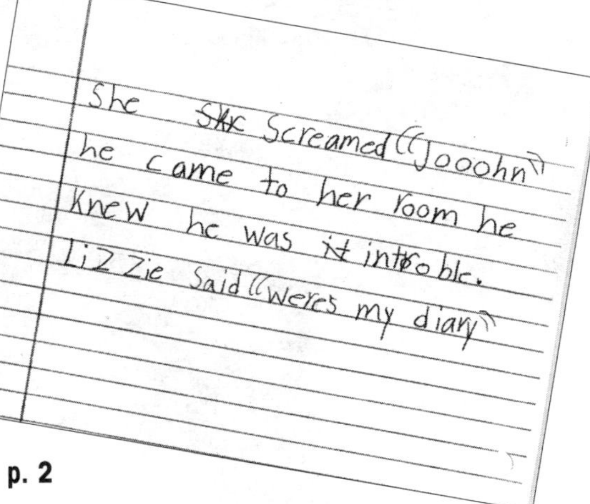

She ~~She~~ Screamed "Jooohn" he came to her room he knew he was ~~it~~ introble. LiZZie Said "weres my diary"

p. 2

Although Holly's public brainstorming addressed a different topic (see pages 9-21–9-23 ), notice how she takes what she learned from the public conference and applies it to slow down her writing and tell this new story in order.

# Andrew's Brainstorming and Start of His Draft: *Second Grade*

(See student profile, p. 9–24.)

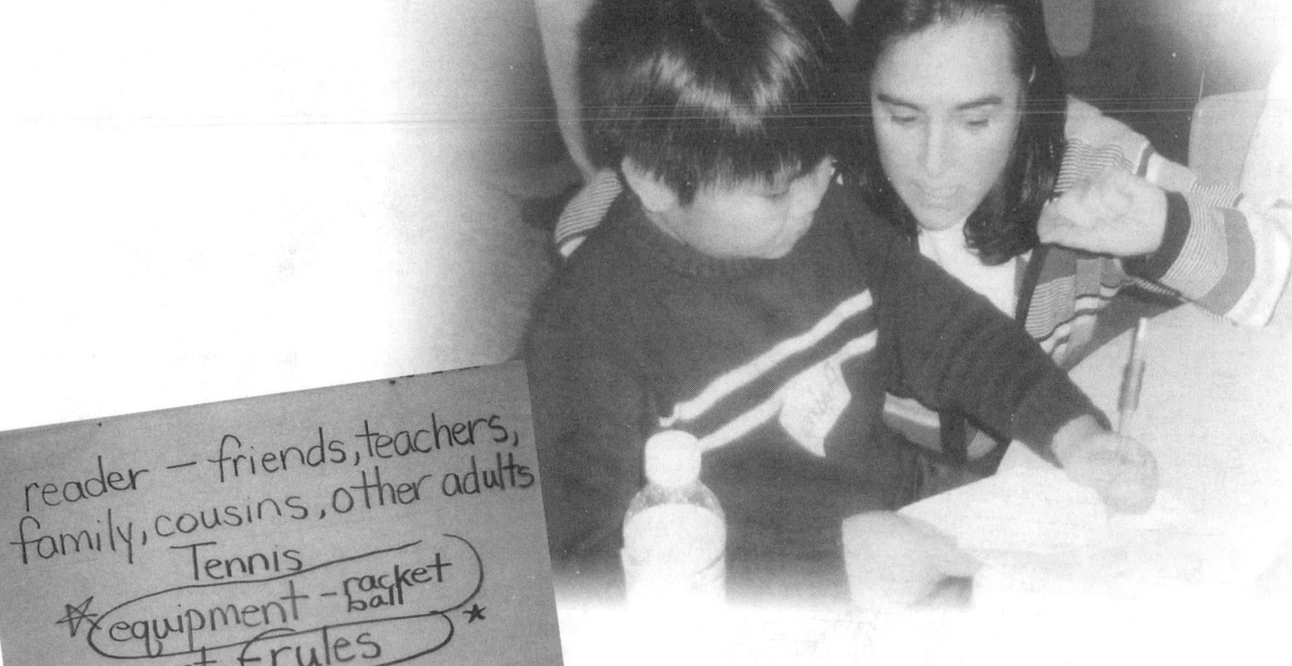


Andrew's teacher checks in on him in a roving conference after our public brainstorming conference.

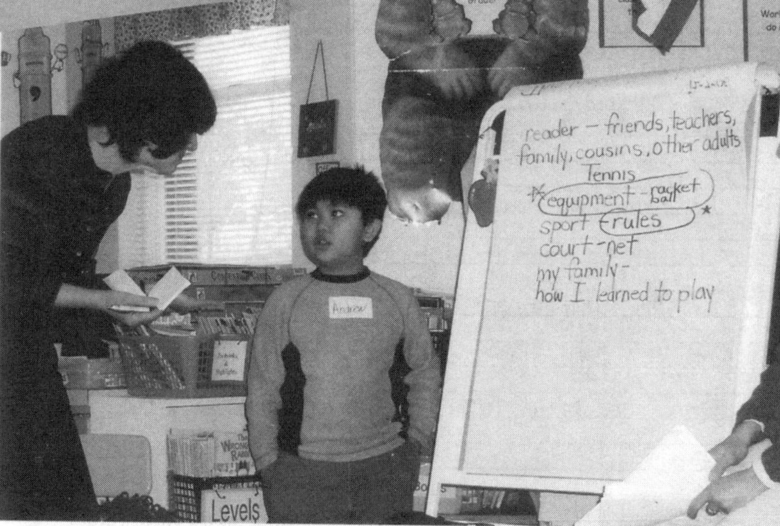

# Andrew, *continued*

**Notice Andrew's writing on December 6 (right) before our brainstorming (see p. 9-8). It is not as well focused or detailed. Now take a look at what he wrote (below) with the aid of brainstorming. His writing is well organized; he has added rich details to elaborate on his story; and he shows evidence of rereading and rethinking through voluntary revisions.**

Tennis
Andrew South 12-6
The equimit you ~~yc~~ use is a racit and a tennis ~~d~~ ball.
~~rate~~
My family plays tennis together.
Tennis is a sport to play.
When we play tennis we have to play at a cort. ~~12-7-05~~
~~12-7-05~~
I am ~~alwas~~ always instsid about tennis.

Andrew South 12-7
Tennis
capter 1 equipment
The equipment you have to use is racket, and a green ball. The ball ~~looke~~ looks ~~gr~~ green and with white ~~striper~~ stripes. The racket is rough, has ~~a~~ hard strings, has a ~~handle, bla~~ ~~ke~~ black handle. capter ~~2~~ rules. 12-8-05 The rules are if you hit the net it is called ~~a a~~ falt ~~false~~. A ~~false~~ falt is when you ~~make~~ make a mistake. That is all the rules I know because it was a long time ago.
capter 3 the court

I ~~am~~ am going to ~~desri~~ desorid the net. About the net. The net is almost bigger then me. It is up to my chest. I

**p. 1** **p. 2**

# Brandon's Brainstorming and Start of His Draft: *Second Grade*

**(See student profile, p. 9-27.) See the website for Brandon's writing progress over two years.**

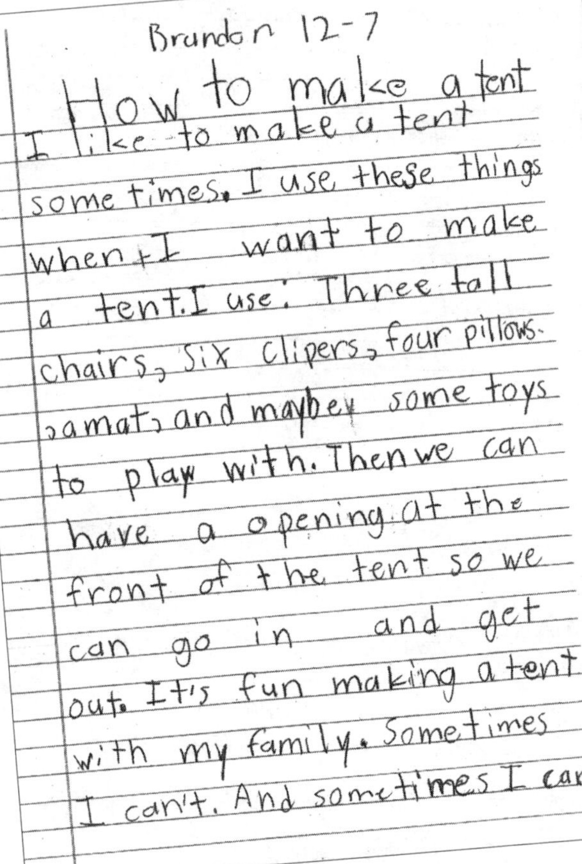

Brandon 12-7

How to make a tent

I like to make a tent
some times. I use these things
when I want to make
a tent. I use: Three tall
chairs, Six clipers, four pillows.
, a mat, and maybey some toys
to play with. Then we can
have a opening at the
front of the tent so we
can go in and get
out. It's fun making a tent
with my family. Sometimes
I can't. And sometimes I can

**p. 1**

**Brandon takes what he learned from listening to two public brainstorming conferences and applies it to his "How to Make a Tent" story. Notice what a fluent writer he is. He writes two full pages in about 15 minutes.**

Brandon 12-7

How to make a tent

It's fun to have fun in my
12-7-05 12-8-05
tent. Because I like having my
own little house at
home. I like playing with
my brother and sister. When
I make a tent my sister
makes a picnic for
us. Even we make food
for the picnic. The cover
will sometimes fall I have
to get out and put
the cover back. Sometimes
the chair will fall we have

**p. 2**

# Brandon, *continued*

Brandon 12-8
How to make a tent
to push it up and strech
the cover again. But when
I play my brother and sister
may get mad. "But I want
to bring my doll's." She
says. "You can't you can
only bring boy toys." my
brother says. But before they
start yelling I run out
the QD for Quick
Door and hide in my
closet or my bed. Then
Then after my sister

p. 3

12-8
How to make a tent
and brother stop yelling
and fighting I come back.
They will be putting the
tent back. Any way that
was thein punishment. But
Any way thein's all ways
a nother day and a nother
dirugument. Some time
at night I think are they
nuts? They aren't they just
get mad at echather. Even
when I make a tent my
brother wants to get everything.
out of my room to and
have fun with everything.

p. 4

**Brandon writes with a sense of audience in mind. He injects conversation, humor, and the personalities of his siblings into his story.**

# Raquel's Brainstorming and Start of Her Draft: *Second Grade*

**(See student profile, p. 9-26.) See the website for Raquel's writing over two years (from beginning of first grade through beginning of third grade).**

Raquel Acuña
12-6

Family
✓1. my brothers
✓2. my sister
3. my mom and Dad
4. my grandma and grandpa
5. my cousins
6. my aunts and uncles
7. my other half of family in Cost Rica.

My sister
. 14 years old
. her name
. my only sis
. being nice
. sharing rooms
helping me out
. playing soccer
☆ geting mad at me
. what grade

I was at our room
destroing the room

**Notice how, on her own, after the public brainstorming demonstrations, Raquel is able to list her main topic and subtopics and then, choose one subtopic and do further brainstorming. What was very powerful in this classroom was that once students understood how to use brainstorming, they independently used it in all their writing across the curriculum. As a result, all their writing was organized, sequential, and written with much description and salient detail.**

# Raquel, *continued*

Raquel 12-7
My family is very nice. ~~I~~
I have a lot of family
but I'm going to start with
my sister. ~~My sister is nice.~~
Sometimes in our room
I invite friends over
and make a huge mess.
When my sister finds
out she gets real mad.
After my sister is mad
she starts to fight and
tells but I'm not worried
at all because my dad
had never got mad or

p. 1

hit me or something.
but when she tells
my mom I ~~he~~ hide.
My mom would put
her ~~stefsse~~ sleves up
with a angry face and
say my whole ~~n~~ name.
You don't wish to see
it, but my dad calms
her down a gets
me untill she does.
After that I go
to my sister's face and

p. 2

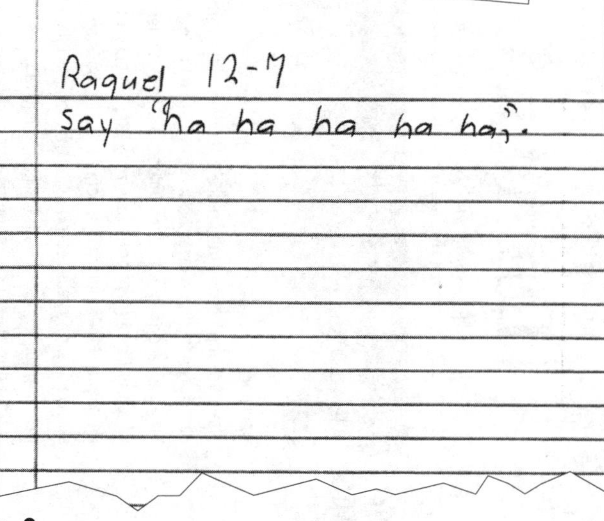
Raquel 12-7
Say "ha ha ha ha ha".

p. 3

**After Raquel reads her piece and is celebrated in a public conference, I encourage her to cross out, "My sister is nice," because it's repetitive and doesn't add to the quality of her writing. (On her own, later, she goes back and deletes that line.) What is especially memorable here is how she describes her mom's anger: "My mom would put her sleeves up with an angry face and say my whole name. You don't wish to see it. . . ." When students craft language in a unique manner, use it as an opportunity to teach other students by saying something like, "Kids, listen to how Raquel described her mom. She didn't just say, 'My mom got angry.' She showed us that anger with her carefully chosen words."**

SESSION 9

Writers Become Readers Through Daily Writing

# DEEPER UNDERSTANDING

*The teaching and assessing points reflect the total lesson but not all of these points are on the edited videos you are watching. However, the major points are represented on the edited videos.*

WWW The globe icon indicates that the example is also available when you visit www.regieroutman.com.

## Video SCENES

| Setting, Notes, and Explicit Teaching Points | Ongoing Assessment | Questions/Reflections | Learning Outcomes |
|---|---|---|---|
| The What, Why, and How of Teaching | Informing Our Instruction | For Professional Conversations | What Students Know and Are Able to Do |
| **SETTING**<br>The following scenes take place in Marlene Ellis' grade 2 classroom in an urban school of 840 students in Nashville, TN. The second-grade class reflects the total student body which is 65 percent non-white of which 50 percent are African American. More than 60 percent of the school's students receive free and reduced-price lunch. Marlene Ellis has been teaching for 17 years and she is looping with this class, that is, she has taken her first-grade class onto second grade. There are 20 students in the classroom, the K–3 district limit.<br><br>Marlene and I worked together in a weeklong writing residency at the beginning of the previous school year. At that time, she was teaching writing mostly through isolated skills and worksheets with a focus on correctness. Our weeklong focus was on bringing joy back into writing and having students write about topics they cared about. The demonstration teaching and coaching in the residency served as a catalyst for Marlene to make major shifts in her beliefs and practices. At the end of first grade, most of her students were reading well above grade level, which she largely credits to the amount of nonfiction writing and reading her students did. Marlene also credits the strong reading-to-writing and writing-to-reading connection, but especially the daily writing emphasis.<br><br>In this second residency, in late fall, her students are fluent readers and writers. We are working on finding and narrowing a self-chosen topic of high interest, brainstorming before writing, organizing writing, and writing with detail. | Teacher Marlene Ellis stops to confer with Andrew during roving conferences. | | |

# *Video* SCENES

**DEEPER UNDERSTANDING: Writers Become Readers Through Daily Writing**

| | Setting, Notes, and Explicit Teaching Points<br>The What, Why, and How of Teaching | Ongoing Assessment<br>Informing Our Instruction | Questions/Reflections<br>For Professional Conversations | Learning Outcomes<br>What Students Know and Are Able to Do |
|---|---|---|---|---|
| | Students continue to become better readers through writing because their writing is meaningful, authentic, and for a purpose. Through writing, students slow down the reading process and understand that writers write with a reader in mind. Standardized test results in the Fall of third grade indicated that most students were reading one or two years above grade level. | | | |
| **What Do Smart Writers Do? Responsive Teaching (Day 1)**<br>(5:26 min.) | **TEACHING POINTS**<br>• State the purpose of the lesson: *"The reason I'm doing this is this will help me teach you. It's also going to show everybody how smart you are and what you know."*<br>• Accept and affirm all reasonable responses.<br>Students: *"Skip lines." "Reread." "Take their time."*<br>(See chart on this page for shared writing list in process.)<br>• Clarify thinking. *"What do you mean when you say 'They want to think so they don't write random stuff.'"*<br>Andrew: *"Don't write other stuff."*<br>• Expand thinking. *"When else do you cross out? Not just when you 'make a mistake.'"* And, later, *"When do you put a caret in?"*<br>• Encourage positive wording. *"How could you word that so it's positive?"* Instead of saying, *"Writing should not be sloppy. . . ."*<br>• Accept first thinking as part of a draft (as it affirms students' efforts, encourages them to respond, and lets them know we can make changes later). *"Let's just leave it the way we have it."* And, again, *"And there's no wrong answers. I just want your best thinking."*<br>• Restate the importance of student choice in writing.<br>Holly: *"Smart writers write something they want to write about."*<br>*"We want to add more choice to your writing, and then you're going to do a better job."*<br>• Help shape language.<br>Kylan: *"You could put periods. . . . You could put punctuation." "Why don't we just say, 'Put periods and other punctuation at the ends of sentences'?"*<br>• Reread shared writing chart (to check the writing so far). | Use a shared writing to assess what students know, and chart their growing knowledge from day to day.<br>Check if students can explain their thinking (to be sure they understand and are not just saying the words):<br>• *"Tell me a little bit about that. Why does a good writer reread?"*<br>• *"What do you mean by that?"*<br>Confirm understanding:<br>• *"So, staying on the topic* (in response to Andrew explaining *'They don't write random stuff'*). *OK, good for you. You do understand."*<br><br>Note that the draft is in process and not complete (without telling students what's missing so you set the expectation for revisiting the draft, figure out what to teach next, and then assess to check if students "got it").<br>• *"Now there's a very big thing missing here that we want to work on."*<br>• *"There's a couple of big things we'll be adding. . . ."* | • How can you use shared writing as an assessment to guide your teaching?<br><br>DRAFT<br>What Do Smart Writers Do?<br>. Skip lines<br>*. Reread- to see if it makes sense, or to add some more.<br>. Take their time so they can think and not write random stuff<br>. Cross out if you make a mistake<br>. Writing should not be sloppy<br>. Put a caret ^ in when you want to add something more.<br>*. Write what you want to write about.<br>. Put periods and other punctuation at the end of sentences.<br>. make writing interesting<br>*. think about the reader<br>. talk about the person tell the story, DESCRIBE | • Brainstorm and generate ideas and plan for writing.<br>• Talk to others to generate ideas.<br>• Write a draft that includes more than one sentence.<br>• Reread own work.<br>• Share writing with others.<br><br><br>**The class reads "What Do Smart Writers Do?" with Regie.** |

*continues*

## Video SCENES

**DEEPER UNDERSTANDING: Writers Become Readers Through Daily Writing**

| | Setting, Notes, and Explicit Teaching Points<br>The What, Why, and How of Teaching | Ongoing Assessment<br>Informing Our Instruction | Questions/Reflections<br>For Professional Conversations | Learning Outcomes<br>What Students Know and Are Able to Do |
|---|---|---|---|---|
| **What Do Smart Writers Do? Responsive Teaching (Day 2)** | • Connect students' writing with a published author. (In this case, it's Nikki Giovanni, author of *Rosa*. Our first day of shared writing indicated missing pieces in what smart writers do. I use *Rosa*, the book they have just heard read aloud to prod them to expand their thinking.)<br>• Be explicit about what good writers do (make writing interesting, write for a reader, use interesting words). *"Describe. You got a picture in your mind."*<br>• Reread text *(Rosa)* and add on to what students notice that the author has done well. (Students' responses indicate they need to hear the story again and notice, with teacher guidance, what Nikki Giovanni has done to "make the writing interesting.")<br>• Notice the language authors use. Addressing observing teachers: "*You want it to come from them . . . what we know from the research is telling teaching doesn't work very well. What kids remember is where we're interactive and we're responsive. I'd read it again because I want them to notice the language. So some of that kind of language will start appearing in their own writing.*"<br>• Continue to add on to the chart and document students' thinking. "*I use a different-color pen so we can actually see how the thinking is growing.*" | Evaluate if students are connecting what well-known authors do with what they can do as writers:<br>• "*What are some things you noticed that she* (Nikki Giovanni) *did as a writer that a smart writer does?*" Student: *"She made the writing interesting"* [adds to chart].<br>Probe student's thinking:<br>• "*Why do they do that? Why do they make the writing interesting? . . .*" Student: *"They think about the reader."*<br><br>Affirm thinking:<br>• "*They think about the reader . . . if your writing is really boring, people are just going to put it down. We are not going to publish anything that's really boring.*"<br>Dig deeper:<br>• "*She made the writing interesting. How did she do that?*"<br>*Brandon: "She talked about the person and what she did."*<br>• "*How did she talk about the person?*" | • How can connecting excellent literature with writing impact students' thinking, reading, and writing abilities?<br><br>• How does modeling rereading help students become fluent and strategic readers and writers?<br><br>• Why is rereading literature and familiar stories frequently so important when teaching something new? | • Use multicultural literature to stimulate ideas for writing.<br><br>**Regie asks, "What did she (Nikki Giovanni) do as a writer that a smart writer does that made this book wonderful?"** |
| **Telling the Story Before Writing It: Finding the Topic**<br>(5:04 min.) | **NOTES**<br>We apply the Optimal Learning Model to move students' writing forward through oral and written demonstrations, planning through brainstorming, scaffolded conversations before writing, guided and independent writing practice, conferences, and celebration. As we did with these students when they were first graders, we continue to emphasize the reading/writing connection and to provide texts (with the help of the classroom teacher and librarian) to support students' interests and quest for knowledge. | Students' inability to respond (to how Nikki Giovanni made the writing interesting) leads to the recommendation that the classroom teacher reread *Rosa* more than once and help students notice what the author does to make the writing interesting (with the goal of application to their own writing). | • Why is it essential that students read and write daily?<br><br>• What do you do daily to help students see and apply the reading-to-writing connection? | |

# *Video* SCENES

## Telling the Story Before Writing It: Finding the Topic *continued*

**DEEPER UNDERSTANDING: Writers Become Readers Through Daily Writing**

### Setting, Notes, and Explicit Teaching Points
The What, Why, and How of Teaching

In these scenes, we teach the students to narrow their important topic into relevant subtopics and write with elaboration and detail (without labeling those traits until students fully understand them through immersion, demonstration, and their own writing). Students also become better readers through writing, rereading, and revisiting texts.

**TEACHING POINTS**

- Use a sticky note to plan before you tell your story.
- Do not practice-write your story by writing it at home first (makes the writing you do in front of students more authentic and more like what we expect from kids).
- Write on the spot. *"If I'm asking kids to write right on the spot, then we have to write right on the spot."*
- Decide the audience for the writing. *"I thought I could write a book for them* (my granddaughters) *and call it* The Norman Stories (writes title on chart) *because I have some fascinating stories about Norman* (our cat) *. . . and when they come over Norman hides. . . . They say, 'Tell us about Norman. What is she doing?'"*
- List possible writing topics. *"I'm just going to make a list of the things that I could write about Norman."*
- Connect appealing, coherent writing with caring about the audience. *"The reason that I want these stories to be really clear and interesting is because I'm going to give them to Katie and Brooke so that they can read them. . . ."*
- State possible audiences for writing. *"Most of the time we are writing for a reader. Sometimes that reader is you. Sometimes it's your teacher. But very often it's somebody else."*
- Tell your stories with gusto (talking to observing teachers): *"You want to pull out all the stops. Everything you want your kids to do with elaboration and detail and verbs and imagery and topic sentence, it's going to be in there. It's not going to be in there if you tell a bare-bones story."*

### Ongoing Assessment
Informing Our Instruction

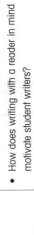

Regie talks about Norman being out all night.

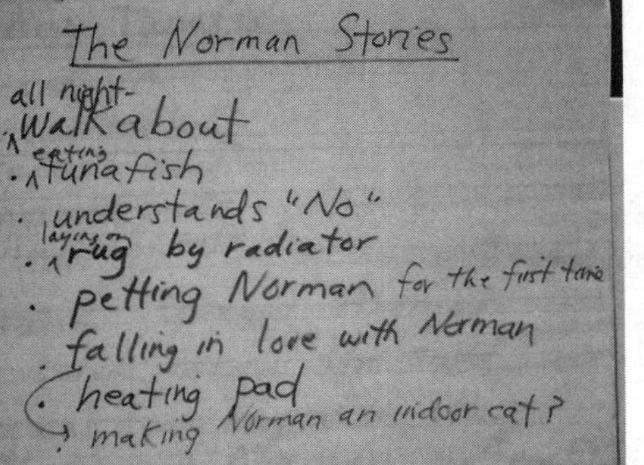


Possible writing topics.

### Questions/Reflections
For Professional Conversations

- How does writing with a reader in mind motivate student writers?

### Learning Outcomes
What Students Know and Are Able to Do

- Plan before writing.
- Write fluently.
- Brainstorm and formulate ideas for writing.
- Write for family, friends, and others.
- Identify intended audience for written piece.

continues

## Deeper Understanding: Writers Become Readers Through Daily Writing

*Video* **SCENES**

| Video Scenes | Setting, Notes, and Explicit Teaching Points<br>The What, Why, and How of Teaching | Ongoing Assessment<br>Informing Our Instruction | Questions/Reflections<br>For Professional Conversations | Learning Outcomes<br>What Students Know and Are Able to Do |
|---|---|---|---|---|
| **Telling the Story Before Writing It: Finding the Topic *continued*** | • Use your oral storytelling to find your topic. *"Listen to what happened…"* (writes each possible story topic on chart before telling the story); begins with the story of Norman's all night walk-about; also tells story about feeding Norman tuna fish; Norman understanding the word *no;* laying by the rug by the radiator; petting Norman for the first time; falling in love with Norman; making a warm outdoor house for Norman. | | | |
| • Choosing the Topic: Keeping the Reader in Mind | • Think about which subtopic resonates for you. (Reads and reviews topics listed on chart on p. 9–17; see preceding bullet.) *"Now I have to decide…."*<br>• Restate real-world purpose for writing. *"I'm going to write these down and put them into a book and give it to Katie and Brooke."*<br>• Connect school writing to our chart, "Why Do People Write? What Do People Write?" (see chart and video, Session 4). *"If I don't write them down, I'm not going to remember…that was one of the reasons that people write…another reason…I want to entertain them 'cause some of these stories are pretty funny…"*<br>• Give students time to come up with their own important topics and audience. *"Tonight I want you to think about…something you're really interested in and who you might want to write this for, because writers always write for a reader."*<br>• Expand school audience for writing beyond the teacher. (Addressing teachers) *"Most often, it* (the audience) *is someone else, and I think that's part of the reason why the kids are having difficulty coming up with topics…"*<br>• Suggest possible topics and audience to think about (to spur students' thinking): *"So you might want to write about something that's very important to you that's also important to your grandma or grandpa, and you could write it and give it to them so they'll always remember that."*<br>• Confirm expectation for coming up with a topic before tomorrow's writing time. *"I have to decide which one of the Norman stories I am going to start with, and I don't know yet. I have to think about it."* | Check if students are coming up with a topic important to them:<br>• *"Who knows what they're going to write about?…* (Addressing teachers:) *Now if they get started tomorrow with their writing and they're done in two sentences, what does that tell us?"*<br>Teacher: *"They're not interested." "They're not invested…."* | • Does writing with the reader in mind improve writing? What evidence do you have?<br>• Why is having a choice in writing topic crucial to students' investment in writing? | • Develop ideas for topics orally and visually.<br>• Develop and choose from a list of general topics for writing. |

**DEEPER UNDERSTANDING:** Writers Become Readers Through Daily Writing

| *Video* **SCENES** | Setting, Notes, and Explicit Teaching Points<br>The What, Why, and How of Teaching | Ongoing Assessment<br>Informing Our Instruction | Questions/Reflections<br>For Professional Conversations | Learning Outcomes<br>What Students Know and Are Able to Do |
|---|---|---|---|---|
| • Choosing the Topic: Keeping the Reader in Mind *continued* | • Stress importance of self-selecting the "right" topic (impacts effort and quality). *"If it's the right topic, it's not going to be easy but it's going to be pretty fluent . . . they're going to be willing to invest some energy into it."*<br>• Think aloud about topic choice. *"Writing helps me think and figure things out. So I might write this one* [pointing to chart of possible topics about Norman.] *"I have to see. I don't know. I have to see which one kind of pulls at my heart. . . ."*<br>• State the plan for the week (prompted by student's question). *"We're going to be continuing the writing we're doing. I'm going to be writing my Norman stories all week. . . . a lot of kids are having trouble with what to write about and then sort of staying on topic and staying with their topic."*<br>• Confirm overall writing purpose. *"So that's what we're going to be writing about—how do you stay with your topic and keep it interesting, kind of all week?"*<br>• Enjoy writing. *"Mostly, I want you to have a really good time with writing. I'm really thinking about entertaining Katie and Brooke. What are they going to like to read and hear about. . . ."* | Determine if students are clear about what was demonstrated and what is expected:<br>• *"Any questions that you have? Anything you want to ask . . . about writing . . . before we stop today?"*<br>Student: *"What are we going to do on Wednesday?"*<br><br>Help students understand what and why you are together. Assessment starts by showing students why and what they will be doing and how they will know they have learned something new. | | • Learn to narrow their topic for writing. |
| **Demonstrating Brainstorming and Writing**<br>(8:16 min.) | **NOTES**<br>Brainstorming a list before writing not only helps students focus and narrow their topic but in this classroom, many students use their list of subtopics to naturally move into writing nonfiction chapter books. Also, after some practice, brainstorming such a list becomes an organizing tool students begin to use independently for all writing as early as second grade.<br><br>My main topic is my cat, Norman. I have told many stories about Norman (subtopics) and listed them with a phrase or title (see chart, p. 9–17). Now I choose one of these (subtopics) and narrow that topic down further through additional brainstorming (see chart, p. 9–20). | My mom and brother moving to Florida.<br>Lonc<br>·moving<br>·helPing to move<br>·what they do<br>·maps<br>·the map to get therc<br>·the moving van<br>·helping unloud it<br>·Puting it therc<br>·Puting it in the house<br>·Sorting it<br>·Puting it in the cbnets.<br>·Puting it in drors<br>·Friends unlouding<br><br>One student's brainstorming before writing (after teacher demonstration). | | |

*Video* **SCENES**

**Demonstrating Brainstorming and Writing *continued***

**DEEPER UNDERSTANDING: Writers Become Readers Through Daily Writing**

## Setting, Notes, and Explicit Teaching Points

The What, Why, and How of Teaching

What I am showing students is writing with elaboration and detail without using those labels. This is an example of, "Teach it first; label it later." Once students understand through immersion, demonstration, and their own writing what elaboration and detail mean, I can say, *"What you have been doing, slowing down your writing, describing what happened, going moment by moment—you have been writing with elaboration and detail, which gives the reader a complete picture."*

**TEACHING POINTS**

- Make a list of possible writing topics. This helps me organize my thinking. *"And, I'm going to ask you to make a list today before you write . . .* (rereads list made yesterday). *"I decided I'm going to write about the tuna fish."*
- Narrow your topic. *"Make your big list, and then choose one thing on that list . . . and put a check on it. That's the first one I'm going to write. Just that one. And I'm really going to describe that."*
- Prepare your subtopics before you write (but not what you're going to write about them). *"Here's what I wrote down"* (points to sticky note). Writes "Loving Tuna Fish" on chart as story title and copies subtopics for "Loving Tuna Fish" from sticky note onto chart:
    - brand—oil
    - fixing the tuna
    - special bowl
    - Norman talks
    - how she eats it
- Think aloud before you write and as you write (to help organize your thinking and decide what to say). *"Let me think how I'm going to start. . . ."*
- Say the words as you write them (to maintain students' attention).
- State purpose for demonstration writing. *"Now, I want you to watch my writing, kids, because even though it's not your story, you're going to get ideas."*

## Ongoing Assessment

Informing Our Instruction

Loving Tunafish
brand-oil
fixing the tuna
special bowl
Norman talks
how she eats it

Frank thought Norman was bored eating the same dry cat food day after day.
"Let's get Norman a treat," he said.
"Norman is just fine," I said.
Frank went right out and bought Norman gourmet, packed-in-oil, imported Italian tunafish. Not just one can, half a dozen cans. to make sure we had plenty

Check to see if students understand that writers deliberately add humor:

- *"They're laughing. Am I doing that on purpose?"*

## Questions/Reflections

For Professional Conversations

- Why is it critical for all students, but especially struggling readers and writers, to show and not tell?
- How can the type of planning (or prewriting) we ask students to do support, or limit, their writing efforts?

## Learning Outcomes

What Students Know and Are Able to Do

- Generate writing topics from a list.
- Brainstorm ideas for writing orally.
- Use detail in writing.
- Build a rich vocabulary through listening, talking, and writing for an audience and meaningful purpose.
- Elaborate on ideas using descriptive words and phrases.
- Select titles for a piece of writing.

**DEEPER UNDERSTANDING: Writers Become Readers Through Daily Writing**

*Video* **SCENES**

| | Setting, Notes, and Explicit Teaching Points<br>The What, Why, and How of Teaching | Ongoing Assessment<br>Informing Our Instruction | Questions/Reflections<br>For Professional Conversations | Learning Outcomes<br>What Students Know and Are Able to Do |
|---|---|---|---|---|
| | • Include lots of detail (without naming it "detail") as you tell and write your story.<br>• Write with the reader in mind. *"They're* (the teachers) *laughing.* [After I say and write] *"Frank went right out and bought Norman gourmet, packed in oil, imported Italian tuna fish. I'm feeling great that they're laughing. Are they bored with my story?"* Students: *"No."*<br>• Write your story in 10 minutes (so kids have time and energy to write. Reread and continue writing tomorrow.).<br>• Reread [to check your writing]. *"Let me read it again and see if it's the way I like it. . . . And this is why you have to reread it, to see if it sounds right, do you want to change anything, add anything."* | | • How can rereading writing help make students better readers and writers? | |

• Modeling Brainstorming Through Scaffolded Conversations: Holly

**NOTES**

Supporting kids to tell their stories before they write them, and doing so publicly with one or more students, pays huge dividends. Stories and detail emerge that would not ordinarily show up. Students get ideas, not just about topic choice but also how to write with memorable detail, by listening to peers' responses. Take the time to do one or two in-depth scaffolded conversations rather than having many quick, superficial ones.

My scaffolded conversation is with Holly. Holly began first grade as a limited writer but quickly progressed in writing and reading with her teacher, Marlene Ellis, who—after the writing residency in grade 1—devoted 1 hour each day to writing. (See the website for samples of Holly's writing over 2 years.)

**TEACHING POINTS**

- Use brainstorming of ideas to help students slow down their writing.
- Have a face-to-face conversation with a student *"What are you writing about today?"*
  Holly: *"A Girl Named Lizzie."*
  *"'A Girl Named Lizzie' is a great title. Now, what are your stories about Lizzie?"* (See chart at right.)

**Holly: Student Profile**

**Holly was a mostly typically performing student who became high-performing through her writing-to-reading connection.**

**Holly benefited from the scaffolded conversations. Rather than writing just a simple sentence, Holly was guided in how to expand on an idea—how to add meaningful details to make her writing come alive. She developed into a confident writer with a strong voice and an excellent reader.**

Make sure students know why it is important for them to listen to a peer's storytelling. (Otherwise, they may not pay attention and won't have the benefit of getting ideas for their own writing.)

- *"Aaron, could you tell him* (another student who appears not to be paying attention) *why it's important that you're watching what we're doing with Holly? Maybe this is my fault for not making it clear. I'm helping Holly but who else are we helping? Everybody. Because as soon as we're done with Holly, and maybe one other person, you're going to go back and do this. And I don't want anybody saying,*

- Why are scaffolded conversations supportive to the oral language development of English language learners?
- How can slowing down the writing help students become better readers?

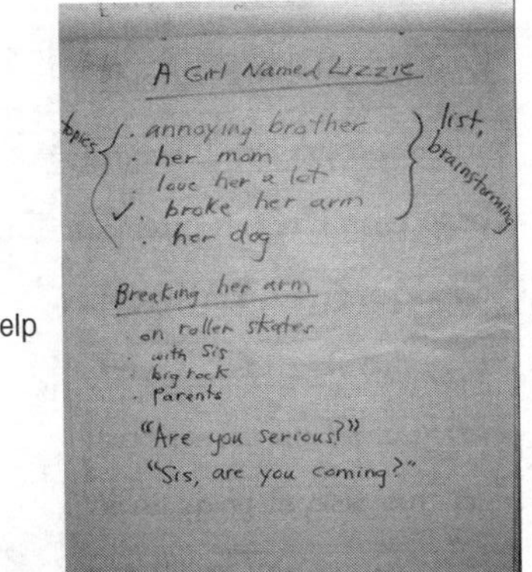

Charting Holly's brainstorming.

continues

## DEEPER UNDERSTANDING: Writers Become Readers Through Daily Writing

*Video* **SCENES**

- Modeling Brainstorming Through Scaffolded Conversations: Holly *continued*

### Setting, Notes, and Explicit Teaching Points

The What, Why, and How of Teaching

- Help student list her topics. *"What are your different stories about Lizzie?"*

  Holly: ***"Her little brother is really annoying."***

  *"And don't tell us the story yet."* (Lists "annoying brother" on chart.)
- List each topic with just a few words. *"Do we have to write 'Lizzie has an annoying brother?' No. Just a few words to help make your brain remember. This is really important because this will save you time as a writer. . . . So 'annoying brother' is one story. What else?"*

  Holly: ***"Her mom."*** (Writes it on chart and continues to probe [*"What else?"*] and adds topics to the list in process.)
- Connect student's list to teacher's list. (Go back to that chart and show student.) *"When I made my list about Norman . . . just a couple of words . . . to jog your memory."*
- Choose a topic to begin writing. *"Which story do you want to start with, do you think?"*

  Holly: ***"Her breaking her arm."***

  *"OK, so I'm going to put a check here."* (Checks off topic on the chart and writes this topic below the brainstormed list.)
- Through responsive questioning, guide the student to tell her story with description and detail and move the story along. *"Remember everything you can. Now tell us what happened when she broke her arm."* (Writes key words from her telling the story on chart.)
  - *"OK, so now what happened?"*
  - *"What did they* (the roller skates) *look like? Is it like a shoe roller skate?"*

    Holly: ***"Looks like a tennis shoe except it has wheels on it."***
  - *"OK, now I have a picture in my mind."*
  - *"What else? What's going on?"*
  - *"Where is it? Is it summertime? Is she wearing her shorts? Is it a hot day?"*
  - *"So how do you know this story?"*
  - *"OK, so then what happened?"*

### Ongoing Assessment

Informing Our Instruction

*'Huh? What am I supposed to do?' If you pay attention now, you're going to know exactly what to do."*

Through responsive questioning, try and find out if the story the student is telling is true. Encourage stories based on fact when students are first writing with elaboration and detail. In Holly's case, as I was questioning her, I was never sure if she was telling me a true story or making it up. I suspect she made it up because the story she actually wrote was not the one she told but was about her first topic, her annoying brother. Or, it may have been that after telling the story about Lizzie breaking her arm roller skating, she was no longer interested in the story. It's a good idea to let students know that it's okay for a writer to change her mind.

Notice in Lizzie's story, "Annoying Brother," she does write with great elaboration and detail, demonstrating that she has understood the writing expectations and benefited from the scaffolded conversation.

### Questions/Reflections

For Professional Conversations

- Why is it critical that we model for students how to listen to each other?

Holly Lizzie life
- An annoying brother
- ✓ brakeing arm
- Mom loves her
- her dog
- ✓* diary loosing
- Soft ball trying out
- brother took
- mom grounding
- Lizz laughing
- Automik weap
- ~~leaving~~ learning to love

- Why is modeling responsive questioning a strategy that empowers struggling readers?

### Learning Outcomes

What Students Know and Are Able to Do

Holly 12-7

Once there was a girl name Lizzie. She had an annoying brother. One day he thought he could steal her diary. He snuke into her room and qietley serched the room. At last he found it but it was locked. So he took it to his room and went to the kitchen. He got some siscors and went back up stairs to his room. But once he got up their Lizzie was home

She ~~She~~ Screamed "Jooohn" he came to her room he knew he was introble. Lizzie said "weres my diary"

**Video SCENES**

## DEEPER UNDERSTANDING: Writers Become Readers Through Daily Writing

| | Setting, Notes, and Explicit Teaching Points<br>The What, Why, and How of Teaching | Ongoing Assessment<br>Informing Our Instruction | Questions/Reflections<br>For Professional Conversations | Learning Outcomes<br>What Students Know and Are Able to Do |
|---|---|---|---|---|
| • Celebrating and Assessing Learning | • Put students' memorable comments on a sticky note (lets student know you think comment is important, jogs their memory, encourages student to use the idea, is a reminder note to the teacher of what was said). *"I'm going to put that on a Post-it for you. . . . And that's so when you say something really smart, I'm going to write it down so it will show up in your writing. It will remind you. . . . I'm just going to put down 'tennis shoe, wheels.' That will be enough for you to remember"* (in response to *"What did the roller skates look like?"*).<br>• Have student state first sentence, and suggest possible language, as necessary, to get students going and off to a successful start. *"How are you going to start this?"*<br>• Celebrate what the student has done well. *"OK, she did something really wonderful. Do you notice how she is really slowing down her story?. . . Doesn't this sound like something you would read in a book?"* (Restate descriptive language student has used.) | <br>**Regie: "When you say something smart, I'm going to write it down so it will show up in your writing. It will remind you . . . ."** | • Reflect upon/discuss the benefits of public, scaffolded conversations.<br>• Why is it so important for students, especially English language learners, to tell their story before writing it?<br>• Why is celebration of student learning an important part of the closure to reading and writing time? | • Generate ideas for writing.<br>• Use nonfiction texts to research and generate ideas for writing. |
| **Small-Group Support** (2:07 min.) | **NOTES**<br>No matter how much modeling we do, there are almost always some students who don't know what to write about when it's time to write. Keep those students with you to make sure all students have ideas before they go off to write. This helps ensure that they get off to a meaningful start.<br>**TEACHING POINTS**<br>• Affirm students for recognizing they need help choosing a topic. *"I'm glad you were smart enough to think, 'I don't have an idea so I'm going to stay up here and get some more help.' Good for you."*<br>• Suggest a range of topics. *"Think about something you're really fascinated by. Whether it might be sports, somebody in your family, a favorite person."* | Identify individual students' needs and who needs the most support. Students need to self-monitor their own learning and ask for help when needed:<br>• *"I'm glad you were smart enough to think, 'I don't have an idea so I'm going to stay up here and get some more help.' Good for you."* | <br>**Regie meets with a small group of students who need additional support.** | • Elaborate on ideas using descriptive words and phrases. |

continues

# *Video* SCENES

**Small-Group Support *continued***

## DEEPER UNDERSTANDING: Writers Become Readers Through Daily Writing

### Setting, Notes, and Explicit Teaching Points
The What, Why, and How of Teaching

- Scaffold ideas with the student.
  Andrew (raises his hand indicating he has an idea):
  *"Sports." "Which one?" "Tennis."*
  *"OK, so you might want to make your list of tennis, and what are all the things that go with tennis."*
  *"Like, you can hit the ball back and forth."*
  *"Perfect. So the ball is coming. What else? What about equipment? Do you know about equipment in tennis?"*
  *"A tennis ball. A racquet."*
- Let the student know he's ready to write. *"Perfect! Go back and make your list. You're all set."*
- Help students find additional information when they don't know enough about their chosen topic.
  Jocelyn: *"When I grow up, I want to be a vet."*
  *"You want to be a vet! OK, do you know a lot about being a vet?* (Jocelyn: shakes her head no.) *OK, so will you be able to do a story about that? I'll tell you what we should do. . . . We need to get you some books about being a vet and what a vet does. What does a vet do?"*
  *"A vet takes care of animals."*
  *"And what else do they do?"*
  *"They're like doctors."*
  [Addressing classroom teacher] *"I'm wondering if we can help her get some books."* Teacher says, *"That's not a problem."*
- Connect writing with reading. Use texts (from library) to gain information on topic. *"So, write down what you know about being a vet. And then we'll get some books . . . to help you. . . ."*
- Review purpose of brainstorming lists (and collect them to assess how students did). *"I think you're going to find, like when I wrote my story today, if I didn't have that list about the tuna fish, I wouldn't have remembered everything that I wanted to put in there . . . . And that's how a list helps you. So I know that's something new for you, but you're ready for it. And that's going to make your writing even better."*

### Ongoing Assessment
Informing Our Instruction

**Andrew: Student Profile**
Andrew was a focused child with a strong work ethic. English was not the only language spoken in his home. Scaffolded conversations before writing helped him verbalize the information he knew and gave him the confidence to express his many ideas. Those conversations also helped him realize that his writing didn't have to be "perfect."

Notice how this very short conference and just a few suggestions get Andrew off and writing.

Tennis
Andrew South 12-6
The equimit you use use
is a racit and a tennis ball.
My Family plays tennis togethr.
Tennis is a sport to play.
When we play tennis we have
to play at a cort.
I am always insid
about tennis.

Andrew South 12-7
Tennis
capter 1 equipment
The equipment you have to
use is racket and a green
ball. The ball looks
green and with white stripes.
The racket is rough, has a
hard strings, has a handle, the
use black handle. The rules
are if you hit the net
it is called a fault.
is when you make
make a mistake. That is all
the rules I know because
it was a long time
ago. capter 3 the court

I am going to descrie the net
The net is almost bigger
er then me. It is up to
my chest.

### Questions/Reflections
For Professional Conversations

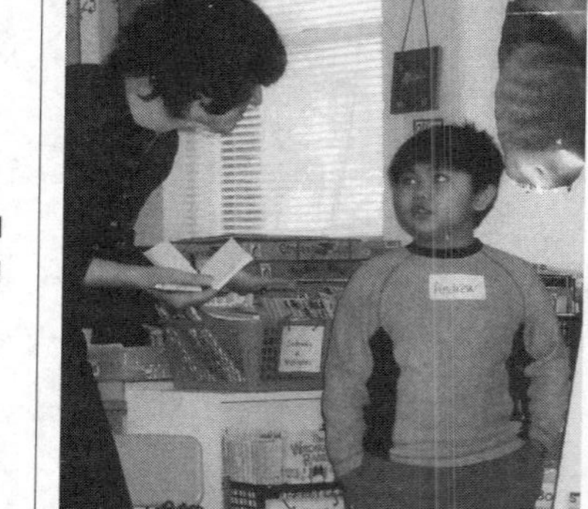


**Public scaffolded conversation with Andrew.**

- How can you find more authentic ways to connect reading and writing, especially nonfiction? What are the benefits of that connection on both writing and reading comprehension?

### Learning Outcomes
What Students Know and Are Able to Do

- Generate ideas or writing.
- Use nonfiction texts to research and generate ideas for writing.
- Use reading and features of nonfiction texts for writing own text.
- Talk and listen to get ideas from others.
- Share writing with others.

# *Video* SCENES

**Public Conferences: Celebrating and Moving the Writing Forward**

(9:51 min.)

## DEEPER UNDERSTANDING: Writers Become Readers Through Daily Writing

### Setting, Notes, and Explicit Teaching Points
The What, Why, and How of Teaching

**NOTES**

The celebrations in these video scenes take place the day after the children have completed their brainstorming lists, had only about 15 minutes to begin to write on their self-chosen topics, and then had some celebrations through public conferences. In those conferences students read their pieces aloud to get a sense of the whole. Then I read it a second time to make celebration and teaching points. (This modeling of response needs to take place before students can give helpful feedback to peers.)

After writing time, I read all the students' writing: to see how they have done, note what I need to teach, and select student papers to read that would serve as good models for other students. The conferences in these scenes take place the following day, before students continue their writing.

**TEACHING POINTS**

- Celebrate, and be specific, what students have done well (so they and others will do it). *"Andrew did some amazing things. He has 'Chapter One. Equipment' He's got a heading just like you have in a real nonfiction book. So what does that mean for you as a writer? If you're thinking about writing all about space, all about dinosaurs, some of you are writing about football. You might have a heading too."*
- Use ideas from other writers. *"I get ideas from other writers all the time. . . . It's too hard to think up everything yourself."*
- Explain and confirm changes in usual procedures. (Here, it is the teacher doing the first reading of students' writing.) *"Usually, kids, like we did yesterday, you read your paper, then I read it, and we spend a lot of time, but I know you were upset that we didn't have a lot of time writing, so is it OK if I speed things up and read it for you? Would that be all right?"* (Students agree.)
- Read aloud student writing (Christina) to affirm writing (*"This is a beautiful piece of writing"*) and make suggestions. *"You could actually use that for your title. 'My Broken Heart.'"*

### Ongoing Assessment
Informing Our Instruction

Check that students are making the connection between what a peer does well as a writer with what they might do:

- *"So we're not just celebrating what Andrew did . . . but how could that help you as a writer when you see something that one of your friends did?"*

  Beni: *"Think about what he wrote, and then you might write something of your own. . . ."*

Confirm and extend student's response:

*"You can piggyback. You can get ideas from other writers."*

### Questions/Reflections
For Professional Conversations

**Marlene Ellis has a conference with Andrew during sustained writing time.**

- Why is it important to celebrate and assess student learning at the end of each Literacy Block?

**Regie talks about using ideas from other writers: "How could that help you as a writer when you see what one of your friends did?"**

### Learning Outcomes
What Students Know and Are Able to Do

- Read own writing for audience.
- Understand that reading and writing are connected to the real world.

*continues*

**Deeper Understanding: Writers Become Readers Through Daily Writing**

# *Video* SCENES

**Public Conferences: Celebrating and Moving the Writing Forward *continued***

## Setting, Notes, and Explicit Teaching Points

The What, Why, and How of Teaching

- Connect writing to audience. *". . . if you gave this to your dad as a present, it's going to make him happy and sad at the same time, but he's always going to remember it."*
- Ask permission to read student's (Raquel's) writing aloud. *"Can I read yours? Is it OK?"*
- Connect student's quality writing to her brainstormed list. *". . . she had all the members of her family, and then she decided to write about her sister and she checked off 'getting mad at me.'"*
- Comment on everything the writer has done well. *"You've slowed down your writing and you have really made the reader feel like they're right there. We were all laughing. Mrs. Ellis came and showed us this yesterday. And she said, 'Oh, you have to read this.'"*
- Connect good student writing to books we read. *"That's just like I am when I read a good book and I tell teachers, 'You've got to read this book.'"*
- Acknowledge voice in writing (but it's not necessary to label it). *"It sounds like you're the only person who could say it that way"* (referring to *"My mom would put her sleeves up with an angry face and say my whole name. You don't wish to see it."*).
- Offer specific suggestions (after celebration so writer will be more likely to consider these). *"The only suggestion I have for you. . . . Maybe you want to cross that out. . . . What do you think?"*
  Raquel: *"Cross that out."*
  *"Just cross out 'My sister is nice,' because you don't say anything about that. And right here? 'My family is very nice.' My suggestion to you, and I think we can be direct, cross that out too. 'I have a lot of family, but I'm going to start with my sister.' That's a great beginning, isn't it? Because you want the reader to be really interested."*
- Expand suggestion to one student to others. *"Is anybody else writing a book about their family? Because you might want to just start, 'My Wonderful Family' or 'My Family' and then Chapter 1 or Part 1."*

## Ongoing Assessment

Informing Our Instruction

**Raquel: Student Profile**

Raquel entered school as a limited English speaker and a shy, timid child. According to her teacher, Marlene Ellis, it was the ongoing class-authored shared writing and seeing and hearing words spoken and written down that played a major role in Raquel's developing language skills and confidence. Raquel then began to tackle language in her own daily writing—with the support of scaffolded conversations and conferring. It was through writing that Raquel found her way into reading. By the end of first grade, and through the intermediate grades, she continued to read "well above grade level."

Raquel Acuña 12-6
Family
1. my brothers
2. my sister
3. my mom and Dad
4. my grandma and grandpa
5. my cousins
6. my aunts and uncles
7. my other half of family in Cost Rica.
My sister
. 14 years old
. her name
. my only sis
. being nice
. sharing rooms
helping me out
. playing soccer
. geting mad at me
. what grade
I was at our room
destroing the room

**Raquel's brainstorming (see beginning of her draft, p. 9–13).**

## Questions/Reflections

For Professional Conversations

- Why is it essential to comment fully on everything the writer has done well and to begin with content, not conventions?
- What message does it send to the writer(s) when we celebrate conventions first?
- How and why must we hold students accountable for basic, agreed-upon conventions and spelling words, even in a draft?

## Learning Outcomes

What Students Know and Are Able to Do

- Understand that writing has voice.
- Use revision to elaborate and add detail to writing.
- Share writing with others.
- Listen to other's ideas to revise own writing.

# *Video* SCENES

**Public Conferences: Celebrating and Moving the Writing Forward *continued***

- Destiny

**Deeper Understanding: Writers Become Readers Through Daily Writing**

## Setting, Notes, and Explicit Teaching Points
The What, Why, and How of Teaching

- Point out a writing form and conventions one student (Brandon) has used (so other students may think about doing the same). *"Brandon did something wonderful. Look at how Brandon is starting. How-to books, kids, in second grade are fabulous . . . How to Walk a Dog, How to Take Care of My Sister. . . . He's got a colon and then he's got a list: three tall chairs comma, six clippers comma, four pillows. . . . Many of you know how to use commas, which is amazing."*
- Use one-on-one conferences to help the writer (Destiny) clear up confusions (after celebrating her strengths). *"This was so wonderful because I got a picture in my mind of what your dog was doing . . . and I love the fact that you slowed the writing down and you just stayed with 'when my dog gets sprayed'. . . . Can I write this word here? I couldn't read it. . . . Here's what I was wondering. I'm the reader and I have no idea why. . . . So tell us a little more about. . . ."*
- Teach what the writer needs. "What are you going to put there so the reader knows?"
  Destiny: *"Caret."*
  *"Let me see you do that. 'For his itching' Put that in there."* (Have the child do the writing.)
- Ask questions to clarify the writing. *"I'm thinking your dog has fleas. So why is he itching?"*
  Destiny: *"Because he has dry skin."*
- State purpose for clarifying the writing. *"So, you have to be thinking, Destiny, is the reader going to know what I'm talking about? Because you are such a good writer, you don't want your reader to be confused."*
- Support, but leave final decision to writer. *"I'm just going to write down* [dry skin] *on a Post-it . . . and you're going to have to decide, as the writer, where you want to put that in. . . ."*
- Begin to teach grammar (without labeling) through how language sounds to the reader.
  *"What is 'it'?"*
  Destiny: *"The spray."*
  *"Can you cross out 'it' and put 'the spray'? That's so much easier for the reader."*

## Ongoing Assessment
Informing Our Instruction

## Questions/Reflections
For Professional Conversations

**Brandon: Student Profile**

Brandon entered first grade as a strong reader. As a writer, he was completing one and two sentences with correct spelling. Once he was given choice of topic and lots of demonstrations, he took off as a writer.

In particular, his interest in nonfiction fueled his writing. Through effective conferences, Brandon was directed to reading material that broadened his knowledge of his chosen subject matter. His writing became increasingly informative and thoughtful and his reading comprehension soared.

**Brandon reads his writing and is celebrated in a public conference.** **(See the beginning of his draft on pages 9–10 and 9–11.)**

- Why is it important for the student to hold the pencil and make the changes?
- Think about the language you use in a public conference. Focus on the writer first and having a conversation, not an interrogation, about what the writer is trying to say.

## Learning Outcomes
What Students Know and Are Able to Do

- Reread writing to revise and edit own writing.
- Reread and use meaning and structure to revise writing.

*continues*

# *Video* SCENES

**Public Conferences: Celebrating and Moving the Writing Forward *continued***

**DEEPER UNDERSTANDING: Writers Become Readers Through Daily Writing**

| Setting, Notes, and Explicit Teaching Points | Ongoing Assessment | Questions/Reflections | Learning Outcomes |
|---|---|---|---|
| The What, Why, and How of Teaching | Informing Our Instruction | For Professional Conversations | What Students Know and Are Able to Do |
| • Teach detail (without naming it yet) through responsive questioning. *"How do you hold him down to spray him?* [Addressing teachers] *I'm not asking these questions because I want 'more details.' OK? And I would be very cautious when kids say what good writers do, 'They add details.' That's not child language.* [Child language might be] *They make their writing interesting. They tell more so the reader will know more about what's going on."* | | • What is the advantage for student depth of understanding for "teach it first; label it later"? | • Add details to writing. |
| • Help student organize the writing. *"You might want to think about adding a heading . . . your title. What is this whole thing about?"*<br>Destiny: *"When he gets sprayed."*<br>*"Perfect. That's your heading right there."* | | • How did these writers become better readers through their own writing? | • Organize writing. |

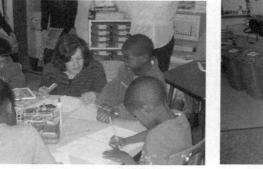

**Through conferences, coaching, and independent practice, the writers in this classroom really took off. Two years later, as fourth graders, they are superior writers and readers. Marlene Ellis notes, "All the frontloading in grades 1 and 2 was critical. These kids are doing phenomenally!"**

SESSION 9

# RESPONSENOTES

***Engage, Reflect, Assess, Celebrate!***

SESSION 9

# RESPONSENOTES

*Engage,*
*Reflect,*
*Assess,*
*Celebrate!*

**Transforming** our **Teaching** through
**Reading/Writing Connections**

# Reading and Writing Book Reviews

**View Video** (31 min.)

**Reading and Writing Book Reviews**

DAY 1
- Sharing Your Writing and Reading Life
- Reading Aloud Book Reviews
- Shared Writing: What Do We Know About Book Reviews?
- Shared Writing: Writing a Review of a Familiar Text

DAY 2
- Shared Writing: Establishing Our Criteria
- Shared Writing: Preparing to Write Book Reviews
- Ensuring All Students Are Ready to Write
- Independent Writing/Roving Conferences
- A Teacher's Changing Beliefs and Practices: An Interview with Nicole Akerson

## 1. Engage, Reflect, Assess

- *Whole-Group Share*
  - Share your experiences demonstrating your own writing to your students. Ask:
    - *How did it go?*
    - *What did you notice?*
    - *How will you support your student writers as a result of your learning?*

**RESOURCES**

**In this Session**

- Teaching Students How to Write Book Reviews: Moving to a Whole-Part-Whole Focus *10–7*
- Sample Student Book Reviews: Drafts *10–8*
- Illustrated Book Reviews *10–9*
- Rubrics for Book Reviews: Shared Writing *10–10*

**On the Website**

- Additional Samples of Student Book Reviews
- Sources for Publishing Book Reviews
- Book Reviews from Shared Writing

- Share your insights and experiences with the following aspects of teaching writing:
    - Demonstrating how writers work.
    - Conducting scaffolded conversations before writing.
    - Providing sustained time for writing.
    - Holding roving conferences.
    - Holding one-on-one conferences.
    - Conducting whole-class shares (public conferences) to celebrate and augment learning.
    - Publishing for an authentic audience.

- ***Small-Group Share***
    - Share your lessons and samples of student work with your team.

## 2. Discuss Professional Reading

- Discuss with your group "Capturing a Moment: Learning to Write with Description and Detail" (*Conversations* excerpt, pp. 346–349 and downloadable from the website).

## 3. Goals

- Connect reading with writing in the way reading and writing connect in the world—that is, readers select books to read based on book reviews (as opposed to a book report, which is a contrived form that only exists in school).
- Understand that when students write book reviews for other readers (peers, other classes, next year's students, libraries, bookstores, websites) it immediately casts both reading and writing in a real-world context.
- Discover that peer recommendations are far more persuasive and motivating than teacher recommendations—just as adult readers are compelled to read a book when a friend raves about it.
- Use book reviews as a way to begin to teach summary writing.
- Learn how writing book reviews with students helped a teacher to rethink her beliefs and practices.

## 4. View Video and Take Notes

- Turn to the Notecatcher to take notes. Write down anything you find important or meaningful.
    - *What did you notice and wonder about?*
    - *What did you observe being taught? Assessed?*
    - *What were students able to do?*
    - *What surprised you?*

## 5. Respond to the Video

- Share your thinking with your small-group and/or whole-group team. Perhaps use the following discussion questions:
  - What were students able (or not able) to do as a result of all the shared experiences *before* they wrote their book reviews independently?
  - How can you connect book reviews with the reading and writing life of your classroom?
  - What did you take away from the interview with Nicole?

## 6. Achieve a Deeper Understanding

- Read, review, and discuss the Deeper Understanding charts. Recall that the notes and questions are designed to accelerate your learning, challenge your thinking, and guide your weekly schoolwide conversations between whole-group sessions.
- As a whole group or in small-group teams, examine and discuss "Teaching Students How to Write Book Reviews: Moving to a Whole-Part-Whole Focus." Focus on how one teacher's evolving beliefs changed her practice and what the implications are for your own teaching.

**Planning with Nicole Akerson before teaching book reviews.**

## 7. *Try It/Apply It* in the Classroom

- Assess what students know about book reviews through shared writing.
- Demonstrate, through shared writing, how to write a book review of a favorite class read-aloud.
- Establish criteria for writing a book review by creating, with your students, a rubric based on the shared-writing book review.
- Have your students write book review drafts in small groups, with a partner, and/or independently.
- Bring your shared-writing book review and samples of your students' work to share with your vertical team.
- Continue to think about and assess your changing beliefs and practices.
- Use "Teaching Students How to Write Book Reviews" as a guide to thinking about planning your lesson with the Optimal Learning Model and whole-part-whole teaching emphasis for maximum effectiveness and enjoyment.

## 8. Wrap-Up

- Before the next session, read "Writing Book Reviews" (*Conversations* excerpt, pp. 339–345 and downloadable from the website) and be prepared to discuss it at the next session.
- Schedule time to meet with your vertical, grade-level, and/or partner teams in between whole-group sessions to revisit the videos on the website and the Deeper Understanding charts and/or plan together and try out new learning.
- Remember to bring any charts, lessons, writing, or student work samples from the *Try It/Apply It* to the next session.

**This is the main wall you see when you enter Elliott Bay Book Company, one of Regie Routman's favorite independent bookstores in Seattle, WA. These reviews are handwritten by the staff, and she always reads them for ideas on what to read next. (Used by permission.)**

# SESSION 10 NOTECATCHER

| VIDEO SCENES | LENGTH | NOTES & REFLECTION |
|---|---|---|
| **DAY 1** | | |
| **Sharing Your Writing and Reading Life** | 2:58 min. | |
| **Reading Aloud Book Reviews** | 3:42 min. | |
| **Shared Writing: What Do We Know About Book Reviews?** | 4:04 min. | |
| **Shared Writing: Writing a Review of a Familiar Text** | 6:43 min. | |

# SESSION 10 NOTECATCHER

| VIDEO SCENES | LENGTH | NOTES & REFLECTION |
|---|---|---|
| **DAY 2** | | |
| **Shared Writing: Establishing Our Criteria** | 4:13 min. | |
| **Shared Writing: Preparing to Write Book Reviews** | 2:07 min. | |
| **Ensuring All Students Are Ready to Write** | 0:41 sec. | |
| **Independent Writing/Roving Conferences** | 0:43 sec. | |
| **A Teacher's Changing Beliefs and Practices: An Interview with Nicole Akerson** | 5:48 min. | |

# Teaching Students How to Write Book Reviews

## *Moving to a Whole-Part-Whole Focus*

### BEFORE

Before I participated in Regie Routman's residency, I taught the skills and strategies related to writing book reviews in isolation. In separate lessons I might focus on:

- Generating a rough draft
- Leads
- Editing
- Revision (but my teaching was isolated from the rough draft)
- Main idea
- Publishing
- Title and author
- Conferring

### AFTER

My students' book review writing really took off once I approached teaching in a whole-part-whole manner. I taught book reviews with more depth, through demonstration lessons, teacher modeling, shared writing, conferring, and read alouds. As you can tell from the following list, my teaching became more interactive, I was better at assessing and teaching responsively along the way, and students' thinking and feedback helped shape what we did.

- Immersion in the genre of book reviews
- Authentic audience
- Underlining title and author
- Main idea
- Leads, grabbing the reader
- Thinking aloud
- Constantly revising during first draft: rereading for meaning, getting stuck, adding, deleting, lassoing words to move them
- Word choice: "Every word counts."
- Recommendation for reader
- Conventions and editing (including spelling). Be relentless!
- High expectations: kids writing the "must haves" list (rubric)
- Roving conferences
- Sustained 20–30 minutes of writing, might write several book reviews
- Sharing and celebration
- Creating a book review form
- Creating a system to organize our book reviews
- Publishing

*—By Nicole Akerson, Grade 3 teacher, Westminster, CO, with Regie Routman*

# Sample Student Book Reviews: Drafts

Gulivers Travels

By:Jonathan Swift

Recommended for 1st grade and up
Have you ever heard of men that are six inches tall? Well this bone chilling classic has them! This family favorite book includes a man named Dr. Lemuel Gulliver and tells about his adventures at sea. If you read this book you will find out how he comes so very close to dieing. Recommended for good imaginers 1st grade and up.

Book review by
Andrew M.

---

The Twits
Written by Roald Dahl
illustrated by Quentin Blake
76 pages, $3.99
ages 7-11

"Two thumbs up" for Roald Dahls hilarious book The Twits! Are you always playing tricks on a family member? Well read this book to find out what 2 crazy people do to eachother. For kids that love to play jokes on people. Reccomended for ages 6 and up.

By Rachel
L.

(10)

---

The Phantom
Tollboth
by Norton Juster

This spellbinding classic will hook you like a fish on a fishing rod from the beginning of the story. This story is about a boy who thinks life is one big bore. Until mysteriously a tollboth apears in his room. To get the rest of the story Read it.

(14)

Prefered for daydreamers 3-4

---

Tales of a Fourth Grade Nothing
By: Judy Blune
120 pages, $9.95
For ages 7 and up

Is your life run by a yunge sibling? If so you should read this b… Fudge Peters little brother is monopoliz… his life getting him in troble, an… eating little pets!

Judy Blume has out done herself this time with great laughs, stupid brothers and 1 MAD PETER.

By the way its fiction

By RJ K.

# Illustrated Book Reviews

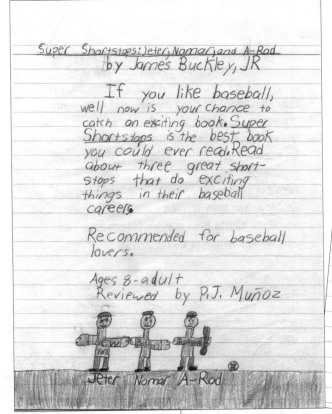

Super Shortstops: Jeter, Nomar, and A-Rod
by James Buckley, JR

If you like baseball, well now is your chance to catch an exciting book. Super Shortstops is the best book you could ever read. Read about three great short-stops that do exciting things in their baseball careers.

Recommended for baseball lovers.

Ages 8-adult
Reviewed by P.J. Muñoz

Jeter Nomar A-Rod

Duck on a Bike
by David Shannon

Two thumbs up for the funniest book by David Shannon! It's about a duck that gets a crazy idea that he can ride a bike. All the other animals say he can't. Read on to find the surprise ending. Recommended for people who like David Shannon. Grades 3 and up.

by Isaac Johnson

meow

The BFG
by Roald Dahl

Oh No! What is that? Really? Have you ever heard of a giant that does not eat humans? Well in this book there is one. If you like books with a lot of adventure and good word choice get the BFG. Recommended for people that are tall and full of imagination.

Grade 3-adult

by Conor McNamara

BFG
Sophie

**Use these reviews and the drafts on p. 10–8 as models until you have your own student examples. (You can download book reviews from the website.)**

# Rubrics for Book Reviews: Shared Writing

BOOK REVIEW
FORMAT

**Headline:**

Title, author, illustrator, publisher, number of pages, price, ages, (child's book)

Catchy lead
Describe main characters / or main character
Tell the problem (if fiction)
Type of book:
(biogaphy, mystery, fantasy, fairy tales, folktales, picture book)
May include illustration from book
Opinion
If recommend or not
Closing

**Name of reviewer:** (why they know or have fame to warrant an opinion)
Example: author of certain book
critic
expert in some area

**Once you have immersed your students in book reviews (reading them aloud, noticing what reviewers do, charting the characteristics), use that knowledge to draft an informal rubric with students. The rubric is a valuable tool that helps set writing expectations for students and can also be used for evaluation. This page shows two examples. Make sure that the language of the rubric is student-friendly, that is, students can easily understand it. (Too often, the language on our class charts is in academic language that only makes sense to us teachers.)**

DRAFT
Book Review
- title and author
- lead: getting the reader excite[d] / hooks the reader
- tell a little bit about the story / not too much or just enough to make the reader read it
- get the reader to read the book
- recommendation: who should read i[t]
  - kind of reader
  - how old they are
- ending that lets the reader know you are done
- no boring words

# DEEPER UNDERSTANDING

*The teaching and assessing points reflect the total lesson but not all of these points are on the edited videos you are watching. However, the major points are represented on the edited videos.*

The globe icon indicates that the example is also available when you visit www.regieroutman.com.

## *Video* SCENES

| | Setting, Notes, and Explicit Teaching Points | Ongoing Assessment | Questions/Reflections | Learning Outcomes |
|---|---|---|---|---|
| | The What, Why, and How of Teaching | Informing Our Instruction | For Professional Conversations | What Students Know and Are Able to Do |
| | **SETTING**<br>These video scenes take place over three days in Nicole Akerson's third-grade classroom of mostly typically performing students in Westminster, CO. Nicole has been teaching for nine years, three years in grade 5 and six years in grade 3. She is a conscientious teacher who relies on a lot of structure and who has focused first on teaching the "parts" in writing and reading. Nicole has requested we focus on summary writing (a district requirement), and I suggest we begin with book reviews as an authentic, engaging lead-in.<br><br>During the week, Nicole begins to understand the difference between "telling" teaching and "responsive" teaching. Her students had previously written summaries, but she had told them exactly what to include. At the end of the week Nicole tells me: "You didn't give the kids the script; they developed the script with your guidance." The last scene is a follow-up interview with Nicole, who is solidly moving to whole-part-whole teaching: teaching more skills, more efficiently, with more enjoyment. | <br>Nicole and Regie plan together. | | |
| DAY 1<br>**Sharing Your Writing and Reading Life**<br>(2:58 min.) | **NOTES**<br>Students need to see us as writers as well as readers and they need to know that writing and reading continually intersect and supplement and support each other.<br><br>**TEACHING POINTS**<br>• Show students what you write and why you write. Demonstrate how you use different types of writing materials and forms (stationery, greeting cards, thank-you cards, emails, letters, notes, poems). | <br>Regie shows the class a greeting card she wrote that she is going to be giving to her husband for Valentine's Day. | • Why is it necessary for our students to see us as readers and writers? | • Decide an author's purpose for writing and support the decision with evidence/details from the text. |

continues

## Video SCENES

**DEEPER UNDERSTANDING: Reading and Writing Book Reviews**

| | Setting, Notes, and Explicit Teaching Points<br>The What, Why, and How of Teaching | Ongoing Assessment<br>Informing Our Instruction | Questions/Reflections<br>For Professional Conversations | Learning Outcomes<br>What Students Know and Are Able to Do |
|---|---|---|---|---|
| **Sharing Your Writing and Reading Life** ***continued*** | • Note that writing is what people do in the world to communicate a variety of messages for authentic audiences and purposes.<br>• Demonstrate yourself as a reader, perhaps by showing how you keep a reading record of all the reading you do. *"You can't be a writer without being a reader."*<br>• Connect favorite books to book reviews.<br>• Describe why you enjoyed a book and why you would recommend it. (Connect recommendations to reviews.) | | | • Develop a list of favorite authors and books, including the reason each was selected, and share the list with others. |
| **Reading Aloud Book Reviews**<br>(3:42 min.) | **NOTES**<br>If we want students to write a book review independently, they first have to know what a good one looks like and sounds like, as well as understand and value the purpose for writing one. In this immersion stage of the Optimal Learning Model, we read and think about what book reviews are and how they work.<br><br>Once you and your students have written book reviews, save some to use as examples for next year's students.<br><br>**TEACHING POINTS**<br>• Show copies of some book reviews (in this case, they're from *The New York Times*). *"It was such an amazing review I went out and bought the book."*<br>• Share several book reviews from various sources (Internet, students, newspapers, journals, bookstores, etc.).<br>• Connect real-life reading with book reviews.<br>• Set the stage and purpose for writing reviews. *"I'm going to read you some book reviews . . . and then I'm going to ask you what you think a book review is because we're going to write one."*<br>• Read aloud several book reviews (so students begin to get the feel for what makes a book review).<br>• Emphasize elements of a book review (careful word choice, voice, engaging beginning, humor, recommendation, closure). *"Isn't that a great last line? These are third graders just like you."* (See examples of book reviews on pp. 10–8, 10–9, and 10–14.) | **Even kindergarten students are not too young to begin to read and write book reviews.**<br><br>See what students know about book reviews. Ask:<br>• *"So, what do you think a book review is?"*<br><br>Set a purpose for careful listening (so students will know what to do when they write):<br>• *"What did you notice about what these kids did?"* | • How can beginning with assessment impact the specificity and efficiency of our instruction?<br><br>• Why is it important to read aloud many book reviews before students attempt to write one? | • Explain connection between themselves and characters, events, and information occurring within a culturally relevant text or among multiple texts.<br>• Listen to, read, and discuss a variety of literature representing different perspectives of family, friendship, culture, and tradition, generating a personal and/or text-based response.<br>• Select, from multiple choices, the main idea of a passage, poem, or selection. |

## Video SCENES

**Shared Writing: What Do We Know About Book Reviews?**

(4:04 min.)

**DEEPER UNDERSTANDING: Reading and Writing Book Reviews**

| Setting, Notes, and Explicit Teaching Points | Ongoing Assessment | Questions/Reflections | Learning Outcomes |
|---|---|---|---|
| The What, Why, and How of Teaching | Informing Our Instruction | For Professional Conversations | What Students Know and Are Able to Do |
| **TEACHING POINTS**<br>• Identify possible audiences for student-written book reviews—bookstore customers, library patrons, other students, teachers, parents. (This was done before this scene takes place.) (See chart on p. 10–18.)<br>• Chart what students have noticed about book reviews.<br>• Shape students' thinking. *"OK, I would say not only just detail words, but interesting words. . . . We heard 'hilarious,' 'two thumbs up.'"* (Putting the language in the students' ears is a necessity, especially for our English language learners.)<br>• Accept all reasonable responses (affirms each child; shared-writing draft can be revised later).<br>• Have the book in hand and refer to it when you write the review (to help you decide what to include). *"When you're writing a book review you do have to go back and reread the book."*<br>• List the title and author first.<br>• Include a recommendation with age/grade of reader, series, genre, and so on.<br>• Capture the reader's attention from the start. *"You can ask the reader a question, 'Do you like mysteries?'" Or, 'Do you like spooky stories?'"*<br>• Use and define the term *draft*. *"It's your first thinking. We're just getting our ideas down. . . ."*<br>• Reread and revise the What Do We Know About Book Reviews? chart as you go along.<br>• Reread the first sentence of several book reviews and call attention to the first line. Clarify that it is not necessarily the topic sentence. *"You're making an effort to bring that reader in . . . you're trying to really get that reader captivated. We're talking about . . . a lead. It's like a hook . . . you're leading your reader into a piece of writing."* | Start with assessment to find out what students already know about book reviews (so you know how much more immersion is needed and what to emphasize).<br>• *"What have you noticed about the book reviews that I read to you?"* Student: *"It tells the main idea of the story."*<br><br>Confirm, nudge, and extend responses:<br>• *"Does it* [book review] *tell everything about the story?"*<br>• *"What else did you notice?"*<br>Student: *"They recommend it for certain ages."*<br>*"Tell a little more about that. . . ."*<br>• *"What else did you notice about the way* [these students] *started? I gave you a lot of really good examples. . . ."*<br>• *"What are these kids doing in their very first sentence?"*<br><br>Check whether students understand key writing terms (so when you use them, you are sure they know what you mean):<br>• *"What is a draft?"*<br>• *"What do you call this, to get the reader's attention?* [a lead]*"* | • How can a valued audience and purpose impact students' willingness to write and their quality of writing?<br><br>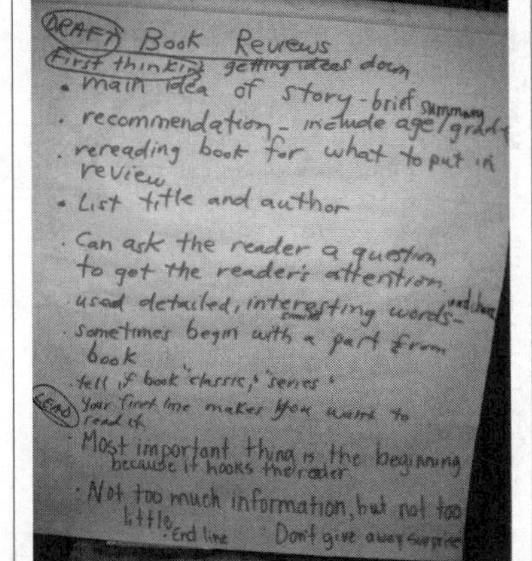<br><br><br>Assessing what students know about book reviews and adding on to the chart as their knowledge grows. | • Write for an audience.<br><br>• Summarize the events, information, or ideas, citing text-based evidence.<br><br>• Explain how certain text features help them understand the selection.<br>• Explain and use grade-level-appropriate text features. |

**DEEPER UNDERSTANDING: Reading and Writing Book Reviews**

**Video SCENES**

**Shared Writing: Writing a Review of a Familiar Text**

(6:43 min.)

| Setting, Notes, and Explicit Teaching Points | Ongoing Assessment | Questions/Reflections | Learning Outcomes |
|---|---|---|---|
| The What, Why, and How of Teaching | Informing Our Instruction | For Professional Conversations | What Students Know and Are Able to Do |
| **TEACHING POINTS**<br>• Set the purpose for shared writing. *"The reason that we're writing one together first is we're going to expect you to write your own tomorrow."*<br>• Establish the audience for the book reviews students will write. *"Other kids are going to be reading them. We're going to be posting them on a website. If they're good enough, we're going to be taking them to the bookstore. . . ."*<br>• Explain what blurbs are and why they are written. Show them the back of the book to assess student understanding. *"This is called a blurb, and it is written to sell the book. Do you think the publisher is going to want to have a bad blurb? Who might write a blurb? A publisher is the person who sells the book."*<br>• Write a book review by thinking aloud, writing aloud, and negotiating the text with students. *"What is the first thing we need to do? How can we start our book review? We need a dynamite opening line . . . a great knock-your-socks-off lead, so I want you to turn-and-talk to your partner."* Write author, title, lead.<br>• Help build on and expand student responses and ideas. *"Who can add to that? 'Have you ever met a nine-year-old girl who didn't know how to read?' What are we going to say? What do we want the reader to know?"*<br>• Emphasize economy of words. *"Every word counts. . . . You're only going to write a little bit so every word's got to be a clincher."*<br>• Remind students we are writing for readers. *"What do we want the reader to know that's going to pull him in or pull her in and make them pick up a book? What could we say? . . . Anything else really important you want to tell the reader?"*<br>• Scaffold conversation to help shape the writing. *"What's this really about?"*<br>Student: *"It's about a girl who does not know how to read and she has a hard life."*<br>Read text-in-process and add, *"She has a hard life."* | Check that students understand the difference between a book review and a blurb (show blurb on back cover).<br>• *"Does anyone know what this is called?"*<br>Student: *"It's like a summary."*<br>Clarify and extend meaning:<br>• *"So who writes the blurb?"*<br>Students: *"The author." "The illustrator." "The publisher."*<br>• *"This [the blurb] will give you an idea of what the book is about, but you can't depend on it because they're always going to tell you it's a great book."*<br><br>Use "turn-and-talk" (students briefly talk with one or two other students) as a way to make sure everyone has an opportunity to give ideas. Assess thinking and understanding; call on students to state what was talked about with their partner or small group. Use responses to guide your instruction. | **Examples of whole-class shared writing of book reviews before students write their own.** | • Write for an audience.<br>• Decide on the author's purpose for writing and support the decision with evidence/details from the text.<br>• Explain the characteristics of a variety of genres.<br><br>• Generate a personal text-based response to text.<br><br>• With teacher guidance, identify simple elements of style (word choice, sentence structure and length, literary devices). |

# *Video* SCENES

**Shared Writing: Writing a Review of a Familiar Text *continued***

**DEEPER UNDERSTANDING: Reading and Writing Book Reviews**

| Setting, Notes, and Explicit Teaching Points | Ongoing Assessment | Questions/Reflections | Learning Outcomes |
|---|---|---|---|
| The What, Why, and How of Teaching | Informing Our Instruction | For Professional Conversations | What Students Know and Are Able to Do |
| • Acknowledge and accept student thinking and, at the same time, move it forward. *"What about if we say* [recommending additional wording], *'You won't believe what she does.' Would that fit?"*<br>Students: *"Yes."*<br>• Organize the writing. *"How about if we move this here?"* Lasso a sentence and indicate a more meaningful placement.<br>• Negotiate the ending. *"'Read on.' What do we want to say?"*<br>Student: *"Read on to figure out the amazing. . . ."*<br>*"Is it a surprise ending?"*<br>Student: *"Yes."*<br>• Using responsive questioning, identify the specific audience for the book review. *"Recommended for what kind of readers?"*<br>Students: *"Recommended for readers and dreamers that like surprises. For grades 3 to adult."*<br>• Complete the draft quickly. [Speaking to observing teachers] *"Just get it down quickly. You can always change it."* (Honors students' responses; keeps students' attention.)<br>• Reread (more than once) the shared writing for clarity, how the text sounds, for any needed changes, and to encourage student thinking and input. *"Anything you want to change? Let's see how it sounds."* | **Regie says to the class, "Let's see if we want to change anything here. Let's hear how it sounds . . . what we've got so far."** | • How can you use shared writing in all content areas? What are the benefits? | • Recognize and use previously learned text organizational structures of simple listing and sequential order to aid comprehension of text. |
| • Set expectation for tomorrow's writing. *"Think of your last favorite book, and you need to have it with you."* (So students can spell title and author correctly, reread, and go back to the book for information.)<br>• Restate the difference between a summary and a book review. (Point out that a book review—a partial summary—has a lead that hooks the reader, a real audience, careful word choice, a specific recommendation.)<br>• Add to the "What Do We Know About Book Reviews?" chart anything else that has come up. (Chart will be a guide for establishing criteria for writing.) | Check that students understand the difference between a summary and a book review. (Students had just completed summaries of a book.)<br>• *"Who can tell me the difference? . . . What does the book review have that the summary doesn't have?"*<br>Student: *"It has better wording. . . ."*<br>*"What else?"*<br>Student: *"The recommendation."* | | • Identify and use grade-level-appropriate text features.<br>• Select, from multiple choices, a sentence that best summarizes the text and support the choice with evidence in the text.<br>• With teacher guidance, state the message in a culturally relevant text and support with text-based evidence. |

**Video SCENES**

**DAY 2**

**Shared Writing: Establishing Our Criteria**

(4:13 min.)

## Deeper Understanding: Reading and Writing Book Reviews

### Setting, Notes, and Explicit Teaching Points
The What, Why, and How of Teaching

**NOTES**

Before this video scene, we word-processed the shared writing we completed with the students and made copies for every student. The students added to and revised the writing individually for a few minutes. Then student groups of three or four worked together to improve the writing. The groups selected a scribe ("the person doing the writing for the group"). We projected the original class-authored shared writing and asked groups to contribute their thinking. We recorded and guided student responses. (Revisit Session 7 to review how this process works. Remember, you are in charge of the writing, and you may finalize the writing when you feel it is good enough. See also *Writing Essentials*, pp. 132–133.)

This lesson establishes simple criteria before students write their book reviews independently. The criteria help ensure that all students include the agreed-on content. Having the criteria as talking points also saves time during conferences. The Book Reviews chart uses the students' language in order to validate their thinking and to make the chart meaningful. Using their language also makes it more likely they will understand and apply the criteria to their writing.

**TEACHING POINTS**

- Reread as a shared reading the class-authored book review written the previous day. (Rereading on a new day makes it easier to "see" needed revisions.) *"Let's see if we want to change anything here. Let's hear how it sounds . . . what we've got so far."*
- Make any needed changes, but accept a "good enough" draft. Student: *"I think it's good the way it is."* *"I kind of think it's OK the way it is for our first try."*
- Review purpose for writing. *"We're going to be writing book reviews today."*
- Reread the What Do We Know About Book Reviews? chart (shared writing from previous day). *"Let's take a look at . . . this was your first thinking about what a book review is."*

### Ongoing Assessment
Informing Our Instruction

**A shared writing of the characteristics of a book review becomes our criteria for writing one.**

### Questions/Reflections
For Professional Conversations

- What are some ways you can give every student a chance to respond and check his or her understanding?
- When is it important and OK to accept "good enough" writing from students and not expect further revision?

### Learning Outcomes
What Students Know and Are Able to Do

- Reread their own writing (orally or silently) for meaning.
- Revise at any stage of the writing process.

*Video* **SCENES**

**Shared Writing: Establishing Our Criteria *continued***

**DEEPER UNDERSTANDING: Reading and Writing Book Reviews**

| Setting, Notes, and Explicit Teaching Points<br>The What, Why, and How of Teaching | Ongoing Assessment<br>Informing Our Instruction | Questions/Reflections<br>For Professional Conversations | Learning Outcomes<br>What Students Know and Are Able to Do |
|---|---|---|---|
| • Add to the chart and agree on the elements of a book review. *"Let's come to some agreement about what's going to be in your book review so that when you write it, you can check yourself."*<br>• Set the purpose for writing down the criteria for book reviews. *"Because tomorrow you're going to be coming up and having conferences. Those conferences are going to go fast, because your book reviews are going to be so good. You're going to know exactly what to put in them. Then we're going to talk about the audience for your book review."*<br>• Connect reading and writing book reviews to real-world reading and writing for an audience. *"We're not just writing it for your teacher and she's going to stick it up here and nobody else is going to see it. We want to talk about that. These are pretty important."* | Build on what students already know:<br>• *"What do we mean by* audience*?"*<br>• *"Who can find the part that talks about the main idea?"*<br>• *"What is the main idea in the story?"* | • What are the advantages of developing the writing criteria with students instead of just telling them what to include? | • Identify purpose for writing.<br>• Write to learn. |
| • Connect the two shared-writing charts (book review of *Just Juice*, p. 10–14, and What Makes a Good Book Review?, p. 10–13) when establishing criteria. *"Who can read the line that gives us the main idea of the story? . . . This whole thing here was our lead."* (Pointing to lead in book review of *Just Juice*.) | Check for understanding:<br>• *"Now let's look at everything that we've written about book reviews* [shared writing chart] *and see if we can agree what we need to have in our book review. . . . So we decided that it was the main idea of the story, the brief summary."* | • How can writing book reviews help students with summary writing in reading and the content areas? | • Evaluate their own writing process. |
| • Guide and support student responses. *"Yes, that's part of the summary. What else is part of the summary of the story? The main idea of the story? That's really where we tell what the whole thing is about, isn't it? What else is the book about?"*<br>• Chart/record in students' language what will be included in student book reviews. Head new chart "Book Review."<br>• Review and identify elements of a book review with students and continue recording on chart in students' language. *"How can we say that?"* (Title, author, lead/hook, tell just enough so the reader wants to read it, recommendation, ending that lets the reader know you are done.) | Make sure students know what a summary includes when writing a book review. Underline parts of review that pertain to "summary":<br>• *"Who can read the line that gives us the main idea of the story?"*<br>• *"What part of this has to do with the main idea of the story or summary?"*<br>• *"What else is part of the summary?"* | | • Compare their own writing with the rubric and the anchor paper.<br>• Identify specific writing strengths. |
| • Scaffold students' thinking and extend it. *"What do we need to add to this?* [Repeating student response] *Tell a little bit about the story, but not too much. Just enough to let the reader know what?"*<br>Matt: ***"Just enough to make the reader want to read it."***<br>*". . . What else are we going to have in our review?"* | Check that students know what goes into a book review and that they understand the terms:<br>• *"What was the very first thing we put in a book review? Let's go in order."*<br>• *"Who knows what we mean by* lead*?"* | | |

*continues*

**Deeper Understanding: Reading and Writing Book Reviews**

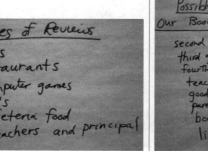

| *Video* SCENES | Setting, Notes, and Explicit Teaching Points<br>The What, Why, and How of Teaching | Ongoing Assessment<br>Informing Our Instruction | Questions/Reflections<br>For Professional Conversations | Learning Outcomes<br>What Students Know and Are Able to Do |
|---|---|---|---|---|
| **Shared Writing: Establishing Our Criteria** ***continued*** | • Reread from book review to remind students of components of a review. *"'Recommended for readers and dreamers that believe that they're smart, grade 3 through adult.' What do we call that?"*<br>• Accept all logical thinking. *"That was perfect, Janae—'Ending that lets the reader know' what?"*<br>Janae: *"That lets the reader know you are done with it?"*<br>*"That's very important."*<br>• Reread chart and revise (check to be sure it's complete, sounds right, and makes sense). *"Let's add that. . . . That's very important."* | Lucas: *"The beginning sentence." "OK, but more than that."*<br>Jake: *"The first few beginning sentences."*<br>• *"What makes it a lead or an interesting lead?"*<br>Jake: *"Getting your reader excited to read it."*<br>*"Good thinking."*<br>• *"What else did we do here? What do you call this?"*<br>• *"What do you include in a recommendation?"*<br>Student: *"Who should read it."* | • How can responsive questioning help students think more deeply about their responses? | |
| **Shared Writing: Preparing to Write Book Reviews**<br>(2:07 min.) | **NOTES**<br>Students need to have selected the book they will review for this part of the session. In this scene, we also connect writing a book review to writing all types of reviews. Remember that the better job you do frontloading (demonstrating and preparing students to write), the better writing you will get and the less reteaching you will need to do.<br><br>**TEACHING POINTS**<br>• Connect the importance of writing a book review for an audience with writing different types of reviews for various audiences. *"Once you get good at this, there are lots of things that you can review. . . . You could review restaurants."*<br>Mrs. Akerson: *"You could review teachers."* And, *"What about computer games?"*<br>• Chart ideas for different types of reviews.<br>• *"You could review movies for other kids in school."*<br>• *"You could review CDs (or DVDs) that are just out and good for third graders."*<br>• *"You could review cafeteria food."*<br>• *"There are lots of things you could review."*<br>• Establish and chart possible authentic audiences for student book reviews. *"Who are possible audiences?"*<br>*Students: "Second graders." "Teachers." "Third, fourth, fifth graders." "Good readers." "Parents."* | <br>**Regie suggests students could write reviews of teachers at the end of the school year.**<br>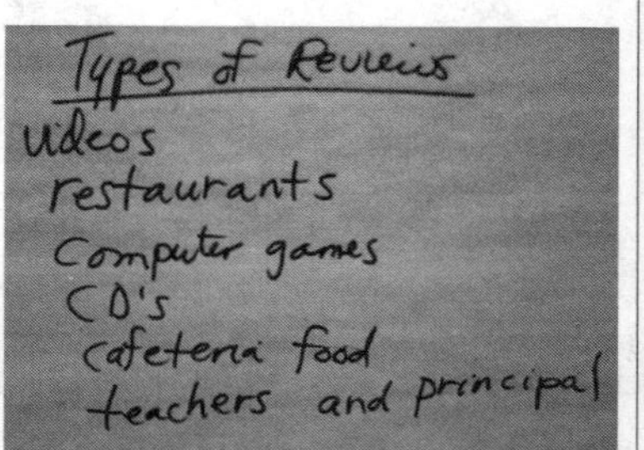<br> |  | • Select form to match purpose (book review).<br><br>• Demonstrate knowledge of specific audience. |

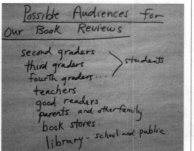

*Video* **SCENES**

**Shared Writing: Preparing to Write Book Reviews *continued***

**DEEPER UNDERSTANDING: Reading and Writing Book Reviews**

| Setting, Notes, and Explicit Teaching Points<br>The What, Why, and How of Teaching | Ongoing Assessment<br>Informing Our Instruction | Questions/Reflections<br>For Professional Conversations | Learning Outcomes<br>What Students Know and Are Able to Do |
|---|---|---|---|
| A teacher: *"I have a son who works at Borders.* [She offers to check with him about having Borders display student reviews] *So that anybody who comes into Borders to look for a good book could read your book review and see if they would like to buy that book. Doesn't that sound awesome?"*<br>• Set expectations for quality. *"That means your review has to be excellent. . . ."* And later: *"We're going to be writing, right now, best book reviews."*<br>• Ask students to consider where they might publish their reviews and for whom. *"Books that we think all the third graders should know about. Public and school library, family, teachers, good readers, bookstores."* | Use a student's question to assess what students think and know:<br>• Lacey: *"If we do write these, will we edit them?"*<br>*"What do you think? Why would editing be important?"*<br>Tanner: *"Because you don't want your spelling and your capitals and periods to be in the wrong spot."* | • How can caring about the audience for the writing impact students' editing efforts? | • Identify purpose for writing.<br>• Write to explain.<br>• Edit as needed at any stage of the process.<br>• Contribute to different parts of the writing process when writing together as a class.<br>• Publish work crediting an author and illustrator, sometimes including a dedication. |
| • Set expectations for independent writing practice.<br>• Refer to criteria. *"If you forgot what it is that you have to do, look up here* [referring to Book Reviews chart]*."*<br>• State today's writing expectation. *"You are going to finish your review today."*<br>• Direct students to reread their drafts more than once. *"How many times did we read this* [shared-writing review] *over to be sure it was the way we wanted it? Three, four, five? We kept reading it over and over. Did I write the whole thing down the page and then read it over, or did I write a little bit and then stopped and read it?"*<br>• Set the time for sustained silent writing and let students know that you will collect the writing.<br>• Encourage students to have a good time writing and have fun writing. | Have students explain their response and reasoning:<br>• *"Why does that matter?"* Tanner: *"Because it won't make sense."*<br>Push students' thinking and expectations for quality:<br>• *"What would happen if we put book reviews at Borders and they were pretty good in terms of the words, but the spelling wasn't very good, the handwriting was sloppy?"* | 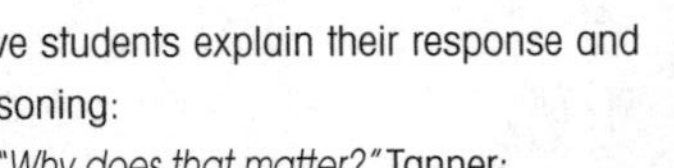The final book reviews, hand written are posted at the local bookstore. (See p. 10–9 for examples.) | • Include text features.<br>• Work on a draft over several days. |
| • Remind students to use their books to write the book review. *"I am going to expect you to spell the title and the author correctly the first time, because you have your book in front of you. No misspelling there."*<br>• Expect word wall words (frequently used words) to be spelled correctly. *"We're going to expect that the words that you know how to spell are spelled correctly."* | Check that students know when and how to improve their writing:<br>• *"Suppose you write a lead and you think, 'Boring.' What could you do? What does a writer do?"*<br>Alfredo: *"Reread it."* | | • Identify and correct errors in grade-level conventions.<br>• Use checklist for editing.<br>• Use references when editing (e.g., word wall, student dictionary, friend).<br>• Use a variety of available technology as part of publication (software, video, etc.). |

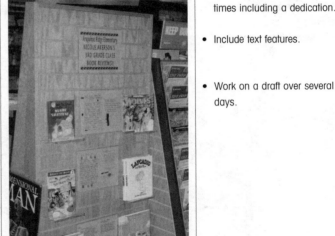

*continues*

## DEEPER UNDERSTANDING: Reading and Writing Book Reviews

| Video SCENES | Setting, Notes, and Explicit Teaching Points<br>The What, Why, and How of Teaching | Ongoing Assessment<br>Informing Our Instruction | Questions/Reflections<br>For Professional Conversations | Learning Outcomes<br>What Students Know and Are Able to Do |
|---|---|---|---|---|
| **Shared Writing: Preparing to Write Book Reviews *continued*** | • Think before you write. *"Think about your lead. Do my sentences hook the reader?"*<br>• Expect students to make changes to make the writing better: cross out, circle, and add to their writing as they read and reread to revise. *"No erasing, because we want to see your thinking. Cross it out. And you cross it out like this, one straight line. No big mess. Just one straight line. We want to see your thinking."*<br>• Include word choice as one aspect of the writing. *"What else are we going to say? Exciting words? No boring words. Good."* | Push students to say more about their thinking:<br>• *"Reread it and then do what?"*<br>Alfredo: *"See if it makes sense."*<br>*"What if it doesn't make sense and it's boring? What would you do then?"*<br>PJ: *"Try to change things."*<br>*"What would I see on the paper?"* | | |
| **Ensuring All Students Are Ready to Write**<br>(0:41 sec.) | **NOTES**<br>There are always a handful of students who, despite our best efforts, need more explanation and support. Your work as a teacher of writing will be easier if these students know what to do when they write independently. In addition to facilitating scaffolded talk before they write, roam about the room as students are writing, concentrating on your writers who struggle first (this ensures a successful beginning, which makes continuous, meaningful text more likely).<br><br>**TEACHING POINTS**<br>• Give encouragement so students quickly begin writing. *"How you should start is really hard. Don't worry so much about it. Just get your first line down and if you don't like it, you can always change it later."*<br>• Ask questions to spur students' thinking. *"What would be an interesting way to bring the reader in? . . . What do you think is kind of unusual about this book that you could just start . . . ?"*<br>• Put the language in their ears; give students suggestions for getting their review started.<br>• *"Can you believe it? There's a guy who actually takes pictures of snowflakes? And then tell a little bit about that."*<br>• *"How could you start it to . . . make it kind of exciting for the reader? What could your first line be? 'There's a boy who's scared of . . . ?'"*<br>• *"You could just start . . . 'If you are a person that likes funny words, made up words, this is a book for you.'"* | Make sure that all students know what to do before they begin writing:<br>• *"Now is there anybody who does not know what to do?"*<br>• *"I need those people to stay here with me."*<br>• *"When you go back and work at your seat, you're going to be working on your own, so I need to be sure you know what to do."*<br>• *"If you don't know what to do stay with me."* | • How can helping students get off to a successful start make it more likely that they will be able to sustain some independent writing?<br>• What can you do to make sure this happens?<br> | • Talk about and generate ideas and rehearse writing (talk with a partner, role-play, talk into a tape recorder).<br>• Make decisions about writing based on feedback.<br><br>**Regie meets with a small group of students who aren't sure what they'll be writing about. She asks, "How could you bring the reader in, because this is a very unusual book?"** |

**Deeper Understanding: Reading and Writing Book Reviews**

# *Video* SCENES

| | Setting, Notes, and Explicit Teaching Points<br>The What, Why, and How of Teaching | Ongoing Assessment<br>Informing Our Instruction | Questions/Reflections<br>For Professional Conversations | Learning Outcomes<br>What Students Know and Are Able to Do |
|---|---|---|---|---|
| **Independent Writing/ Roving Conferences**<br>(0:43 sec.) | **NOTES**<br>When students are writing and know what to do, we can expect them to work quietly and independently. In this scene, observing teachers choose to offer some assistance. However, in the primary and intermediate grades, if we have properly prepared students to write, one teacher can get around to all students through roving conferences. See Session 5, Part 2, for how that worked in kindergarten. *(Videos of days 3 and 4, conferring, and days 5 and 6, publishing, are not shown.)* | | | |
| **A Teacher's Changing Beliefs and Practices: An Interview with Nicole Akerson**<br>(5:48 min.) | **NOTES**<br>Some educators who saw this video thought Nicole and I had practiced it and that she had received the questions in advance. Not so. In fact, I had no prewritten questions, and we had an authentic conversation on the spot. All Nicole knew was that I'd be asking her to talk about how and why her beliefs and practices had changed. The interview seems polished because Nicole did a lot of thinking ahead of time and because she has made great gains in confidence and competence as a teacher of writing.<br>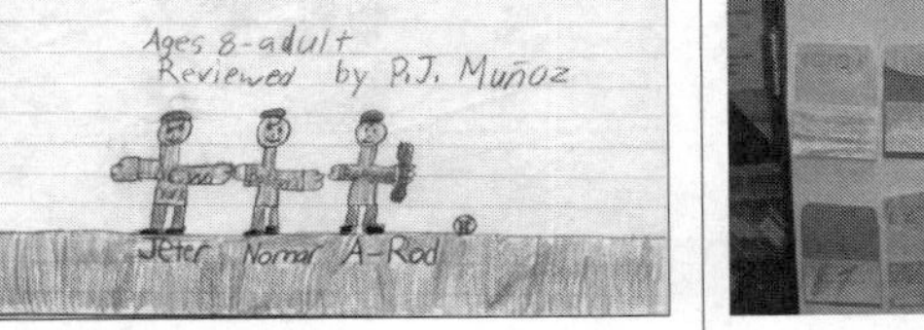<br>**Book reviews from Nicole's class are displayed at a local bookstore.** | Take a look at one area of your teaching. Identify where you are teaching parts in isolation and where you are using the Optimal Learning Model to teach whole-part-whole with ongoing demonstrations, shared experiences, and guided and independent practice. Where are your students meeting the most success? Why?<br>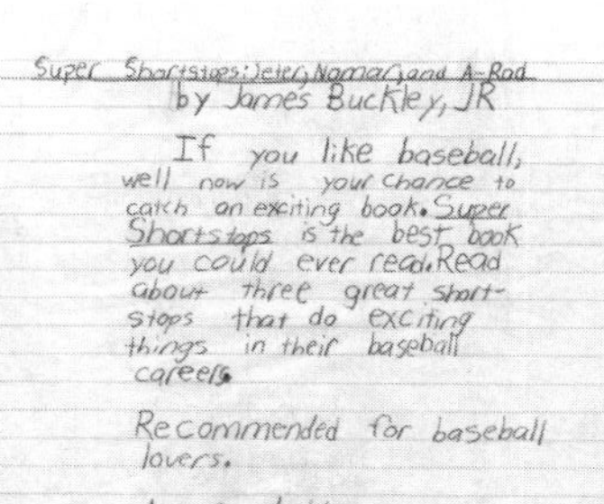<br>Super Shortstops: Jeter, Nomar, and A-Rod by James Buckley, JR<br>If you like baseball, well now is your chance to catch an exciting book. Super Shortstops is the best book you could ever read. Read about three great shortstops that do exciting things in their baseball careers.<br>Recommended for baseball lovers.<br>Ages 8-adult<br>Reviewed by R.J. Muñoz<br>Jeter Nomar A-Rod<br>**A displayed review.** | • How do Nicole's changes in beliefs and practices relate (or not relate) to your own change process? (See also "Teaching Students How to Write Book Reviews: Moving to a Whole-Part-Whole Focus" in this session, p. 10–7.)<br>• How did an authentic audience for writing book reviews impact her beliefs and practices?<br>• Were you surprised by any of her comments? Why or why not?<br><br><br>**A different type of display of reviews created by students.** | |

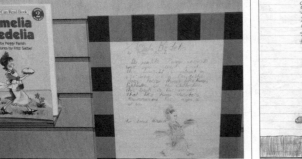

## SESSION 10 RESPONSENOTES

***Engage, Reflect, Assess, Celebrate!***

# Reading and Writing Poetry

**View Video** (31 min.)

**Reading and Writing Poetry**

**DAY 1**
- **Getting Ready to Write Poems: Immersion in Poetry**
- **Demonstrating Poetry Writing**
- **Scaffolding Poetry Writing Before Kids Write: Public Conferences**

**DAY 2**
- **Celebrating Kids' Poems: Public Conferences**
- **Revisiting the "What Do We Know About Poetry?" Chart**

**DAY 3**
- **Celebrating Revision Efforts**
- **Planning for a Poetry Anthology**
- **Shared Poetry Writing: Writing a Poem That Matters**

**RESOURCES**

**In this Session**
- Students' Poem Drafts *11-6*
- Students' Final Poems *11-7*
- Poetry Writing at a Glance *(within Deeper Understanding chart) 11-8*

**On the Website**
- Samples of Students' Free-Verse Poetry
- Poetry Writing at a Glance
- Poetry Rubric
- Some Favorite Poetry Books: Bibliography
- Ideas for Publishing Students' Poetry: Anthologies by Students
- "Everyone Succeeds with Poetry" (*Instructor*, 2002)
- Kids' Poems to Use as Models
- Additional Video:
  - Celebrating Kids' Poems: Public Conferences
  - Celebrating Revision Efforts

## 1. Engage, Reflect, Assess

- *Partner Share*
  - With your partner, share and discuss your shared-writing book review, rubrics/criteria for writing a book review, and samples of student work produced after the previous session.

## 2. Discuss Professional Reading

- Discuss with your partner, vertical group, or as a whole group "Writing Book Reviews" (*Conversations* excerpt, pp. 339–345 and downloadable from the website).

## 3. Goals

- Help all students read and write poetry successfully through free verse (non-rhyming poetry).
- Learn how to think aloud about and write poetry in front of students, modeling how to express ideas in rich language.
- Choose writing topics that resonate with students (life experiences, interests, worries, and so on).
- Write together (shared writing) a poem on a meaningful topic to students.
- Publish and celebrate students' free verse.

## 4. View Video and Take Notes

- Turn to the Notecatcher and take notes during the video. Write down anything you find important or meaningful. Note what all students are able to do and how poetry reading and writing help them meet success.

## 5. Respond to the Video

- Share your thinking with your small-group and/or whole-group team. Perhaps use the following discussion questions:
  - What helped all students meet success writing free-verse poetry?
  - How can writing free verse be a great equalizer in the classroom? What did you notice about Diago and the other students?

## 6. Achieve a Deeper Understanding

- Read, review, and discuss the Deeper Understanding charts. The Notes and Questions are designed to accelerate your learning, challenge your thinking, and guide your weekly schoolwide conversations between whole-group sessions.
- You may also choose to refer to "Heart Poems" (*Writing Essentials*, pp. 305–315 with the accompanying DVD) and "Poetry Writing at a Glance," p. 11–8 when developing your lesson plans.

## 7. *Try It/Apply It* in the Classroom

- Immerse students in reading free-verse poems.
- Demonstrate through shared writing how to draft, revise, and publish a free-verse poem on a topic your students find interesting.
- Think aloud about and write a poem in front of your students on a topic that is important to you and that students will relate to (something that happened to you when you were their age, for example).
- Use public conferences to celebrate students' work and amplify their teaching.
- Publish a classroom poetry anthology.
- Bring samples of lessons and student poems to share during the next session.

## 8. Wrap-Up

- Before next session, read "Poetry Writing" (*Conversations* excerpt, pp. 364–382 and downloadable from the website) and be prepared to discuss for next session.
- Schedule time to meet with your vertical, grade-level, and/or partner teams in between whole-group sessions to revisit and view the videos on the website and the Deeper Understanding charts and/or plan together and try out new learning. Jot down your ideas and thinking on your Response Notes page for easy reference later.
- Remember to bring any charts, lessons, writing, or student work samples from the *Try It/Apply It* to the next session.

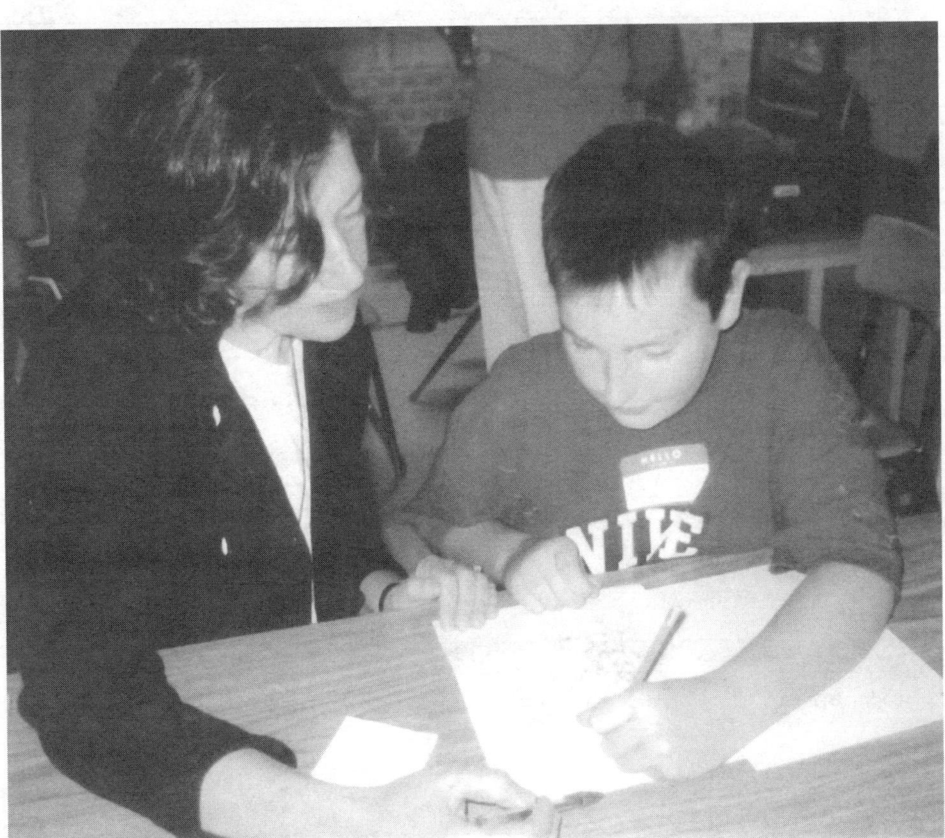

**Conferring with a poet.**

# SESSION 11 NOTECATCHER

| VIDEO SCENES | LENGTH | NOTES & REFLECTION |
|---|---|---|
| **DAY 1** | | |
| **Getting Ready to Write Poems: Immersion in Poetry** | 7:02 min. | |
| **Demonstrating Poetry Writing** | 4:42 min. | |
| **Scaffolding Poetry Writing Before Kids Write: Public Conferences** | 2:55 min. | |
| **DAY 2** | | |
| **Celebrating Kids' Poems: Public Conferences** | 5:45 min. | |

# SESSION 11 NOTECATCHER

| VIDEO SCENES (2) | LENGTH | NOTES & REFLECTION |
|---|---|---|
| Revisiting the "What Do We Know About Poetry?" Chart | 2:26 min. | |
| **DAY 3** | | |
| Celebrating Revision Efforts | 2:56 min. | |
| Planning for a Poetry Anthology | 1:20 min. | |
| Shared Poetry Writing: Writing a Poem That Matters | 3:37 min. | |

# Students' Poem Drafts (first thinking)

(See student profiles on pp. 11-14 and 11-15.)

Michael Leander

Fifth grade anger
In the 5th grade
I had a teacher
who canceled a good recess.

I ~~turned to anger~~ became angry
in a spit second.

I became so ~~mad~~ angry
I literally
tore a few hairs
out of my head.

From then on
I ~~when~~ I think of ~~it~~ the moment
I grind my teeth

football
Diago Vielle

Wine I
Play football.
I Play with
grow-nomps.
Wine I
gint tackald
it fils like
I hint thiwsins
of trees. ~~wth my~~
~~arplane and the~~
trees cunt me
in hafe. ~~so~~
~~Same times I~~
~~Play with grow-nomps~~
~~but~~ I walick
Off the filnd
in pan.

Kenneth Jenks

my dog Duke
It was a tragical Day
my dog
Duke had
DIEd.
my Dad I and cosines
Cried all Day
because Duke
Was a great Dog.
It took us
a couple of years
to get over Duke.
But when we did
Every thing went back
to normal
but ower hearts
where still broken.

(See the complete transcript of the conference with Kenneth, pp. 11-15–11-17.)

# Students' Final Poems

## Football

When I
play football
I play with
grownups.
When I
get tackled
it feels like
I hit thousands
of trees.
Trees cut me
in half.
I walk
off the field
in PAIN!

By: Diago Vielle

**Students are responsible for editing their final poems.**

## Fifth Grade Anger

In the fifth grade
I had a teacher
who canceled
a good recess.

I became angry
in a split second.

I became so angry
I literally
tore a few hairs
out of my head

From then on
when I think of the moment
I grind my teeth

Michael Leander

## My Dog Duke

It was a tragic day
My dog Duke had
DIED.
My Dad, I, and cousins
cried all day
because Duke was a great dog.
It took us
a couple of years
to get over Duke.
But when we did
Everything went back
to normal
but our hearts were still broken.

Kenneth Jenks

SESSION **11**

**Reading and Writing Poetry**

# DEEPER UNDERSTANDING

*The teaching and assessing points reflect the total lesson but not all of these points are on the edited videos you are watching. However, the major points are represented on the edited videos.*

The globe icon indicates that the example is also available when you visit www.regieroutman.com.

*Video* **SCENES**

| Setting, Notes, and Explicit Teaching Points | Ongoing Assessment | Questions/Reflections | Learning Outcomes |
|---|---|---|---|
| The What, Why, and How of Teaching | Informing Our Instruction | For Professional Conversations | What Students Know and Are Able to Do |

**SETTING**

These video scenes take place over three days in early fall in Gwen Sanders' sixth-grade urban classroom of 28 students. As is typical for this school, 80 percent of the students receive a free or reduced-price lunch, and there is high student turnover. Gwen has been teaching for twenty years and sees herself as "a veteran teacher who never quite got hold of a writing philosophy or belief system that helped me make children see themselves as writers." The daily writing program has focused on forms and traits, and most students are not enjoying writing or feeling successful as writers. I've deliberately chosen to teach how to write poetry for its potential to bring the joy back into teaching and writing and to guarantee success for every student. One unintended beneficial effect is that our whole-class shared writing of a poem helps students deal with an ongoing, troubling school issue. Writing poetry also helps many students see themselves as writers for the first time.

## POETRY WRITING AT A GLANCE

1. Share kids' poems, and notice what student poets have done. (10–15 min.)
2. Write a poem or two in front of your students. (5–10 min.)
3. Write a poem together. (5–10 min.)
4. With the class listening in, orally brainstorm with several students about the poem they are about to write. (5–10 min.)
5. Students independently write poems. (20–25 min.)
6. Celebrate students' efforts in a whole-class share. (10–15 min.)

*Note:* Aim for a 2–3 week focus on poetry writing. Based on your time constraints, the continuous cycle above can easily be spaced over multiple days.

## BENEFITS OF POETRY WRITING

- builds immediate success for all students
- focuses on the joy of writing
- sets a positive tone for the classroom
- encourages experimentation with language and form
- de-emphasizes (initially) punctuation and "skills"
- teaches a powerful way to express personal voice
- fosters delight in rhythm, repetition, and word play
- teaches importance of titles, ending lines, word choice
- taps into students' interests and knowledge
- connects writing with reading
- frees kids up to write

*Note:* Once students know how to write free verse, they often choose to write poems when they are given free choice of topic and genre.

**Regie reads from *Baseball, Snakes, and Summer Squash* by Don Graves**

**DAY 1**

**Getting Ready to Write Poems: Immersion in Poetry**

(7:02 min.)

**NOTES**

The lessons you are observing are part of a reading, writing, and word study block. That is, poetry writing is not isolated. It is part of daily reading and writing. It is recommended that you have a poetry section in your classroom library all year long.

Be sure to select and read lots of wonderful free verse to students over several days and weeks in order to help all students understand and internalize the features of this kind of poetry and to help prepare them for what they will be expected to do in guided and independent practice. (See the website for a list of recommended titles as well as for student published anthologies.)

- Where does this lesson fit in the context of a 90-minute literacy block?

- Set purpose for reading.

# *Video* SCENES

**Getting Ready to Write Poems: Immersion in Poetry *continued***

**DEEPER UNDERSTANDING: Reading and Writing Poetry**

| Setting, Notes, and Explicit Teaching Points<br>The What, Why, and How of Teaching | Ongoing Assessment<br>Informing Our Instruction | Questions/Reflections<br>For Professional Conversations | Learning Outcomes<br>What Students Know and Are Able to Do |
|---|---|---|---|
| It is more meaningful, effective, and efficient to teach the features of poetry—such as line breaks, white space, titles, ending lines, and so on—all at once. Students easily pick up what makes a poem a poem when we immerse them in the "whole" and guide them to notice what poets do. Focus on the "parts" as needed once students have had some experience writing whole poems.<br><br>Because we only have three days for these lessons, in this first scene on Day 1, I spend lots of time reading many poems. You will want to spread your immersion over at least several days or, better yet, a few weeks. Plan to read lots of poems (from a collection of free verse you have gathered) to help students enjoy, understand, and internalize features of poetry. Asking "What do you notice?" lets us in on what kids are picking up after hearing a poem read aloud. | Assess whether students understand the relationship between writing for excellent quality and a valued audience:<br>• *"Why would I work that hard* [writing poems for Frank]?"<br>Jordan: *"To make sure that it was neat and that all the spelling was correct."*<br>*"Actually, it had nothing to do with neatness and spelling. But good thinking."*<br>• *"Why would I work that hard?*<br>Gloria: *"Because you love him."*<br>*"That's right. He was my audience. I didn't want to write some mediocre, crummy poem. . . . He has* [the book of poems] *on his desk all the time."* | • Why do we need to immerse students in poetry reading and writing before we expect them to read and write poetry by themselves?<br>• What part of the Optimal Learning Model is the teacher focused on when immersing students? | |
| **TEACHING POINTS**<br>• If applicable, show students how and why you use poetry in your life to connect with people you care about. (I talk about and show poems I've written to my husband Frank and my dad.)<br>• Explain how your audience impacts your writing efforts.<br>• Chart responses to "What Do We Know About Writing Poetry?"<br>• Explain what *free verse* means (after student response, "Poems don't have to rhyme"). *"Most of the poems in the world are* free verse. *Unless you're Shel Silverstein or somebody like that, or some famous poet, it's really hard to write excellent rhyming poetry. What happens is you wind up trying to get the rhyme and then, often the poetry doesn't make sense."* | Assess what students know and understand about poetry and chart responses:<br>• *"What do you know about poetry writing? That will help me teach you better."*<br>Ashley: *"Poems don't have to rhyme."*<br>• *"Does anybody know what you call non-rhyming poems?"* [Explaining what free verse is and writing the term on a chart.]<br>Student: *"They can be heart poems."* | 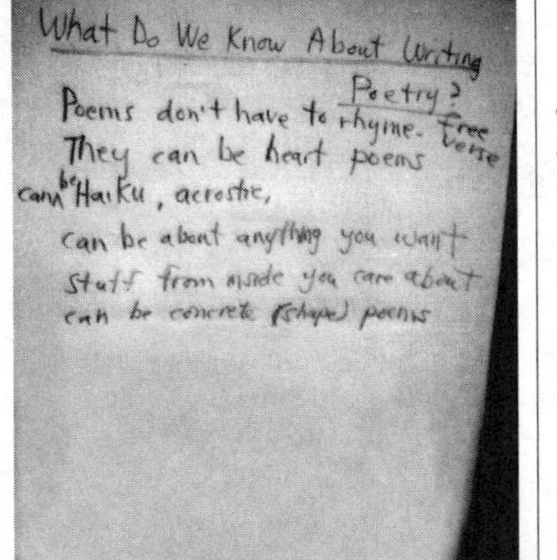<br><br>**"What Do We Know About Writing Poetry?": First response from students.** | • Set goals for reading.<br>• Recommend books to others and explain the reason for the recommendation.<br>• Activate prior knowledge about poetry.<br>• Discuss common reading selections and experiences with others. |
| • Begin to immerse students in poetry by reading lots of poems, including poems by other students (see examples).<br>• Think aloud and talk about how poetry is set up, how the writer gets to decide. *"This is what I love about poetry. She's got it set up in stanzas. Do you know what I mean by* stanza*? See, she's got three lines, space, three lines, space. . . . You can decide exactly how you want* [the poem] *to look on the page. That's what I love about it."* | • *"What else do you know about poetry?"*<br>Student: *"Haiku."*<br>*"What do you mean by* Haiku?*"* | • Reflect on the effectiveness and efficiency of applying a whole-part-whole teaching model to poetry writing. | • Determine the author's target audience(s) and cite examples of details, facts, and/or arguments that appeal to the audience. |

continues

*Video* **SCENES**

**Getting Ready to Write Poems: Immersion in Poetry *continued***

**DEEPER UNDERSTANDING: Reading and Writing Poetry**

| Setting, Notes, and Explicit Teaching Points<br>The What, Why, and How of Teaching | Ongoing Assessment<br>Informing Our Instruction | Questions/Reflections<br>For Professional Conversations | Learning Outcomes<br>What Students Know and Are Able to Do |
|---|---|---|---|
| • Read aloud many poems of your choice and tell students to be thinking about what they might write about as you are reading. *"You have so many choices. . . ."*<br>• Invite students to think about writing a poem about themselves. *"I want you to be thinking about writing a poem that's going to let your classmates get to know you better. Something about you that they might not know, that you're willing for them to know."* | • *"What else could it be?"* Student: *"Can be about anything you want."* Gloria: *"Stuff from inside you care about."*<br>• *"What else do you know about poetry?"* Student: *"You can write concrete poems."*<br><br>Probe thinking:<br>• *"What do you mean by that?"* Cody: *"A concrete poem is like a poem that takes a shape of what you're writing about. And it describes it and stuff about what it is."* | **I<br>LOVE<br>Gymnastics<br><br>I feel<br>So graceful<br>Up on the<br>Balance beam<br><br>Like a bird<br>With wings<br>Outstretched<br>Reaching for the clouds<br><br>On the floor<br>Tumbling<br>And cartwheeling<br>My way to the finish<br><br>Vault<br>Springing like a kangaroo<br>Almost touching<br>The sky<br><br>Feeling<br>So<br>Graceful<br><br>Makayla Chatterton**<br><br>**Some of the poems we read aloud are by former students, saved as exemplars.** | • Explain how author's use of word choice, sentence structure and length, and/or literary devices contributes to imagery, suggests a mood, or otherwise influences an audience. |
| • Give students ideas for writing poetry by reading favorites. Valerie Worth's, *All the Small Poems: "Some of you who maybe don't like to do a lot of writing, you're going to love poetry because you don't have to write a lot.* Nikki Grimes', *Stepping Out with Grandma Mack,* Pat Mora, ed.: *You could certainly write a poem like this.* Donald Graves', *Baseball, Snakes and Summer Squash: He writes about what it was like when he was growing up. 'Love to Mama.'"* (See Bibliography for more recommended titles.)<br>• Show students different aspects of poetry as you read, reread, and think aloud. *"Look at the shape of it. This is set up deliberately. This is when you're going to decide where to end your line. That's called line breaks. . . . He uses lots of detail, really slows down the writing."* | Check that students are noticing aspects of the poems you read aloud:<br>• *"What is she saying here?"*<br>• *"What did you notice about what he does when he writes?"*<br>• *"How does he put humor in there?"*<br>• *"What else do you notice?"* Student: *"He uses a lot of detail."* | | • Identify and explain the author's purpose.<br>• Select, from multiple choices, a statement that best represents the most important conclusion that may be drawn from the text.<br>• Recognize previously taught literary devices (simile, personification, humor, metaphor, idiom, imagery, exaggeration, and dialogue) and explain how they make the poem more interesting and/or convey a message.<br>• Use personal experiences, observations, and research to support opinions and ideas.<br>• Publish in an appropriate form and format. |
| • Connect poems you read with poems students will write. *"This is something you could write about. . . . What did you notice about what* [Graves] *does that possibly you could put into your writing?"* And: *"You have a lot of freedom to do what you want."*<br>• Reread poems (so students figure out what's going on in the poem and notice poems' features). [After rereading "T-Shirt," by Jane Medina, in *My Name Is Jorge on Both Sides of the River,* a book in which the poems are presented in both English and Spanish.] *"Let me read it again. It's about more than that. Poetry has to be heard over and over again."* | Check for deep understanding:<br>• *"What's this* [poem] *about? . . . Yes, but it's about something much deeper than that."* Ben: *"I think it's about* [the teacher] *wants to be called by her real name and so does* [the student, George]." | | |

# Video SCENES

**DEEPER UNDERSTANDING: Reading and Writing Poetry**

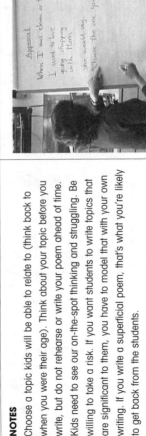

<table>
<tr><th></th><th>Setting, Notes, and Explicit Teaching Points<br>The What, Why, and How of Teaching</th><th>Ongoing Assessment<br>Informing Our Instruction</th><th>Questions/Reflections<br>For Professional Conversations</th><th>Learning Outcomes<br>What Students Know and Are Able to Do</th></tr>
<tr><td>www</td><td>• Read and reread many poems by students. (Until you have your own examples, use the ones provided here, on the website, or in my book series Kids' Poems.)<br>• Encourage publishing an anthology for a real audience. "Some of you, if you really love poetry, you might want to make your own poetry book, just like I did for my husband. A wonderful gift that you could give to someone in your family. This one, and I'm going to leave this here this week, was done by a class of fourth graders." (See "Heart Poems," Writing Essentials, pp. 305–315, with accompanying DVD.)<br>• State that published poems have perfect spelling. "Not only are the words really good, but there are no spelling mistakes. . . . How many times do you think they had to read it over?"<br>• Set expectations for writing and publishing. "What these kids did was they wrote about five or six poems, which is what I'm going to want you to do. Then they chose their favorite. That was the one they published."</td><td>Confirm and extend thinking:<br>• "Exactly. And so, to me what [the poem "T-Shirt"] is about is respect, treating people the way they want to be treated."</td><td>• Why is publication of an anthology by students important? Who are some possible audiences?</td><td>• Use different technologies to produce a finished product.</td></tr>
<tr><td><br>Demonstrating Poetry Writing<br>(4:42 min.)</td><td>NOTES<br>Choose a topic kids will be able to relate to (think back to when you were their age). Think about your topic before you write, but do not rehearse or write your poem ahead of time. Kids need to see our on-the-spot thinking and struggling. Be willing to take a risk. If you want students to write topics that are significant to them, you have to model that with your own writing. If you write a superficial poem, that's what you're likely to get back from the students.<br><br>TEACHING POINTS<br>• Tell your story before writing to show students your thinking about your topic. "One of my favorite things that I liked to do with [my mom] was to go shopping for new clothes, because that didn't happen often. . . . She would say, 'You can choose the one that you like.' But then she would say, 'But that's the one that really looks good on you.' . . . It wasn't till I was almost 30 years old that I could go shopping by myself . . . and not worry about what anyone else thought."</td><td><br><br>Regie writes her poem "Approval" in front of the students.</td><td>• Oral language development is an important aspect of becoming literate. How does modeling your own stories in front of your students help them become better readers and writers?<br>• Setting goals and expectations is part of a complete lesson. What does the teacher do to set goals and expectations for reading and writing?<br><br>• Whatever you pay attention to, students will pay attention to. What are some things that you observed? What are some ways of knowing that students apply what was modeled?</td><td>• Generate ideas prior to organizing and adjust prewriting strategies accordingly (telling the story before writing).</td></tr>
</table>

continues

**Deeper Understanding:** Reading and Writing Poetry

# Video SCENES

## Demonstrating Poetry Writing *continued*

### Setting, Notes, and Explicit Teaching Points
The What, Why, and How of Teaching

- Explain what you're doing and what you are thinking about before writing. *"I'm going to think out loud, kids, while I'm writing so that you get an idea of what's going on in my head. When you're writing, I want you to be doing the same kind of thinking, not just writing straight down on the page."*
- Think aloud as you write in front of students (to show what you want students to do in guided and independent practice). *"Let me see how I want to start this."*
- Reread aloud to demonstrate the importance of making sure the writing sounds right and looks right.
- Demonstrate moving things around, adding new thoughts, words, and ideas to show how writers do their best thinking.
- Reread as many times as necessary to get the poem the way you want it to be. *"Now I have to read it, because I don't know if I like where my line breaks are. I don't know if I want to change some words. I like my title because that's what it was about, 'Approval.'"*
- Think about how you want to end the poem. [Rereading, changing words.] *"Let me see if I like the way that sounds."*
- Keep the writing short and focused so that students have time and energy to write. (Time yourself, if necessary. Try to finish within 10 minutes.)

### Ongoing Assessment
Informing Our Instruction

If you have never thought aloud in front of your students, try it and have a colleague you trust give you feedback:

- Gwen Sanders says, *"When I first tried this part, it was not natural for me to think aloud. You prompted me several times. Then I got a sense of how to do it and how important it was for kids to see it."*

### Questions/Reflections
For Professional Conversations

- Why is teacher demonstration of writing so powerful? How good a writer do you have to be for students to take something away from your writing efforts? [You only need to be a tiny bit better; they will appreciate your efforts and risk taking.]

### Learning Outcomes
What Students Know and Are Able to Do

- Use a variety of prewriting strategies.
- Reread work several times.
- Revise at any stage of the writing process.
- Record feedback using writing group procedure.

Approval

When I was your age
I loved going shopping
Getting new clothes
Was a rare treat.
Until
Mom said,
"Choose the one ~~you~~ YOU like."
But I ^already knew
at that young ~~age~~
~~There was a~~ ~~Schoice~~ RIGHT ~~right choice~~
^a In my mind
I thought
"Which one does ~~she~~ SHE like?"
And
That's the one I ^always picked.
It took me twenty years
To finally choose
What I wanted.

Approval

When I was your age
I loved going shopping
Getting new clothes
Was a real treat.
Until
Mom said,
"Choose the one YOU like."
But I already knew
at that young age
There was a RIGHT choice
In my mind
I thought
"Which one does SHE like?"
And
That's the one I always picked.
It took me twenty years
To finally choose
What I wanted.

**Regie's draft (left) and published poem.**

## Scaffolding Poetry Writing Before Kids Write: Public Conferences

(2:55 min.)

### Setting, Notes, and Explicit Teaching Points

**NOTES**

Especially with poetry, students need to talk through their thoughts out loud and hear how their words and rhythms sound before they write, as they write, and after they write. Have a public conversation with one or two students about their ideas; help shape their thinking to be sure they know what to do and will have immediate success. Write the student's poem out on a chart (or project it so all students can see it) as student says the words (with your guidance). Reread student's words so she or he hears how they sound. At the same time, set the expectation for all other students to listen in and observe—to get ideas for their writing as well as begin to think about important poetry features, such as titles, line breaks, white space, having a good rhythm, ending lines, and so on.

### Ongoing Assessment

Check for readiness to write:

- *"Who has an idea of what they're going to write about?"*
- *"Kenneth, what are you thinking about?"*
- *"Tell us, is this going to be a humorous poem, a serious poem?"*
- *"What are you thinking about?"*
- *"Who else might be an audience for your poetry anthology?"*
- *"Who else might want to see it?"*

### Questions/Reflections

- How do public conferences support your students who struggle the most?

*Video* **SCENES**

**Scaffolding Poetry Writing Before Kids Write: Public Conferences *continued***

**DEEPER UNDERSTANDING: Reading and Writing Poetry**

## Setting, Notes, and Explicit Teaching Points
The What, Why, and How of Teaching

**TEACHING POINTS**

- Use back-and-forth conversation to get students thinking and talking out the poem-in-process. *"How could you start that? You said you wanted to be funny."*
- Put language choices in their ear. *"Do you want to say 'My little brother'? Or, 'Wait till you hear about my brother'? How do you want to start it?"*
  Cary Ann: *"Daniel does lots of funny things."*
- Give options for line breaks, spacing, punctuation. [Writing on a chart.] *"You could do:*
  *Daniel does*
  *lots of funny things"*
- *"Is this how you want it?"*
  Cary Ann: *"Yeah."*
  *"OK, you could capitalize* [the *l* of *lots*] *or not."*
- Suggest language to keep poem flowing. *"Then what could you say? 'One day,' or, 'You won't believe what he said,' or . . . .*
  Cary Ann: *"Just the other day. . . ."*
- Evaluate poem-in-process by reading it aloud. *"See if you like the way it sounds so far."*
- Pay attention to the line breaks and white space when you read poem aloud. *"It doesn't look like a paragraph, does it?"* (See Cary Ann's poem, far right.)
- Point out the importance of the ending. *"Your last line, you want to let the reader know that your poem has ended."*
- Review audience and purpose so that students do their best writing. *"I want you to have fun with your poems. We're going to publish this into an anthology of poems. You will all get a copy. Who else might be an audience for your poetry anthology?"*
  Students: *"Family." "Our teachers." "Friends." "Mr. B* [the principal]. *"*
- Show published anthologies (commercial and student) to offer publication choices. *"Now look at how these kids did their own 'About the Poet' page."*
- Explain that writing is thinking and that getting one's best ideas down on paper is most important.

## Ongoing Assessment
Informing Our Instruction

Be sure all students have a writing idea before sending them off to write:

- *"How many of you think you know what you're going to write about?"*
- *"How many of you have no idea? If you're not sure, stay here with me."*

### About the Poet

Hola Amigos. I'm Gloria Yates, and I'm in sixth grade at Audubon Elementary. My hobby is crocheting; it's pretty artistic. I can make scarves, hats, bags, Afghans, blankets, and stuff like that. I love the country and all the wild animals that live there. My favorite kinds of wild animals are moose, monkeys, frogs, deer, bears, and wolves. My favorite kinds of pets are cats, dogs, horses, and hamsters. I LOVE the water. I love going swimming and tubing. My favorite amphibians are goldfish, betas, sharks, dolphins, and many others. My favorite thing to do is poetry, I love it. My favorite kind of poetry to do is heart poems. Now you know all about my favorite things to do and my favorite subjects.

**After examining anthologies with "About the Poet" pages, students write their own.**

## Questions/Reflections
For Professional Conversations

**Regie and Cary Ann discuss her poem about Cary Ann's brother. Regie says, "Your last line, you want to let the reader know the poem has ended."**

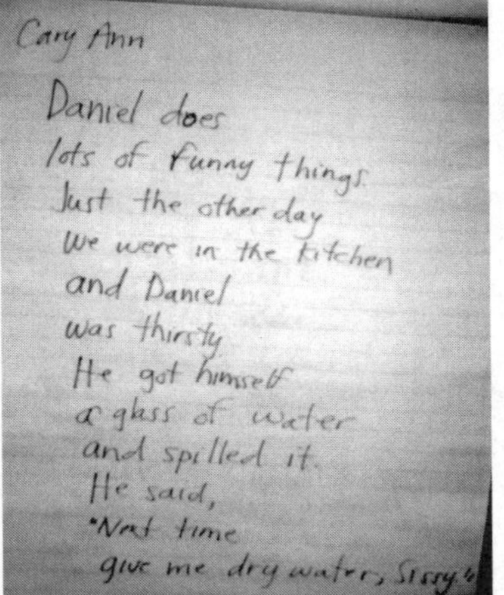


- Reflect on spending more time with one or two students (in depth) before students write versus talking very briefly with many students. What are the advantages and disadvantages of each approach?

## Learning Outcomes
What Students Know and Are Able to Do

- Write with a clearly defined voice appropriate to the audience.
- Search for alternatives to commonly used words, particularly in persuasive writing and poetry.
- Select and use precise language.
- Use rhythm and cadence in sentences and lines to influence meaning in prose and poetry.
- Write a variety of sentence lengths.
- Publish in an appropriate form and format.
- Use different available technologies to produce a finished product.

continues

**Deeper Understanding: Reading and Writing Poetry**

# *Video* SCENES

## Scaffolding Poetry Writing Before Kids Write: Public Conferences *continued*

**Setting, Notes, and Explicit Teaching Points** — The What, Why, and How of Teaching

- Suggest possible topics. *"See if you're willing to be kind of honest about yourself. If you don't want to write anything personal, it could be about like what you did with your brother . . . or somebody in your family, or it could be your pet. Or maybe even that you're really good at some sport or some hobby that the kids don't know about."*
- Tell students not to worry too much about conventions at this time. *"Don't worry too much about your spelling and your editing right now. That comes later. I want you to think about the best word choice. I want you to think about your line breaks, your spacing, really good title, all of these things that we did together."*
- Stress that they should enjoy writing. *"Mostly, I want you to have a good time writing about it."*
- Collect papers at the end of the session. Celebrate students' efforts, assess their work, and adjust tomorrow's instruction accordingly.
- Give additional time and support to students who do not have ideas for writing or who struggle with writing.

**Ongoing Assessment** — Informing Our Instruction

CaryAnn

Reading

When I read,
I am anywhere
and I
can be
anything.
I run
with tigers,
Fly
with bats,
and
Sing
with sparrows.
Read.

**One of many poems Cary Ann chooses to write.**

**Questions/Reflections** — For Professional Conversations

- Why is it important for students to have opportunities to write their first thinking without overconcern for conventions? (Conventions *are* of major importance when publishing.)

**Learning Outcomes** — What Students Know and Are Able to Do

## DAY 2

## Celebrating Kids' Poems: Public Conferences

(5:45 min.)

**NOTES**

The previous day, students had 30 minutes to write a poem. I collected these poems and read them all that night. Starting with celebration affirms writers, gives all students more ideas for writing, and gives students energy to continue writing. Regardless of the age of the students, my preferred arrangement is to have the students seated close to me.

Students share their "first thinking" poems from the author's chair primarily to celebrate but also to get ideas (line breaks, white space, good beginnings, good endings, revisions). First the student reads her or his poem aloud. Then I read the poem aloud, holding the paper facing outward so students can see how the poem looks on the page.

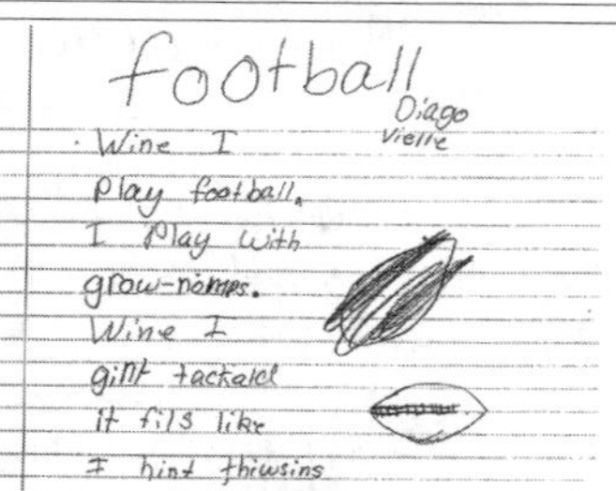
football
Diago Vielle
Wine I
play football,
I play with
grow-nomps.
Wine I
gitt tackeld
it fils like
I hint thiwsins
of frees.
frees cant me
in hafe.
I walick
off the filnd
in pan.

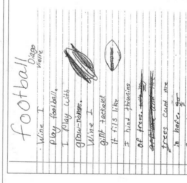

**Revisions by Diago after his celebration conference.**

- Celebration is an important aspect of reading and writing. How can public conferences be used to both celebrate and assess student learning?
- How does sharing and celebrating students' poems by highlighting strengths give other students ideas for new poems?

### Student Profiles: The Impact of Poetry Writing

**Diago:** Diago is a low-performing student with IEPs in reading, written language, and math. He was such a reluctant writer, he often asked for a scribe when he had to do a writing assignment. After the poetry writing residency, he began to see himself as a writer and continued to write poems.

*(continues)*

*Video* **SCENES**

**Deeper Understanding: Reading and Writing Poetry**

## Setting, Notes, and Explicit Teaching Points

The What, Why, and How of Teaching

I had 7 celebration conferences in 26 minutes. You will want to have ready an "author's chair" (for the writer/reader), sticky notes (to jot down comments, language for the writer to use), pencils (for the writers). To show respect for the writer and to make him or her responsible for revisions, I do not write on the paper.

Be sure to celebrate all students (one or two a day, at a minimum) over several days, and to highlight strengths.

**TEACHING POINTS**

- Celebrate students' efforts. *"You did a great job, each and every one of you."*
- State purposes for the public conferences. *"The first thing is to celebrate all the good work that you did. That's most important. The second thing is to give you some ideas. . . ."*
- Connect reading with writing. [Pointing to collection of poetry books] *"How many of you took some time to read some poems?* [Many students raise their hands.] *Perfect."*
- Read the poem at least twice in order to capture the focus and meaning of each poem and celebrate the writer. The student does the first reading. *"I'm going to ask if you'll read it. Then, if it's OK* [with the writer], *I'm going to read it the second time and point out some of the things that he's done. I always like to hear the poem twice, teachers and kids, so that I can really appreciate how it sounds, what the writer's trying to say."*
- State and celebrate everything the writer has done well (title, pattern or rhythm, stanzas, conversation, surprise ending, humor, word choice, putting feelings in poem, moving things around). *"I'm going to read this again, and then I'm going to tell you what I liked about what you did. I could tell you really cared about him . . . because of the way you wrote it. . . . I really liked your ending, it was kind of gentle. Like you're not sure when he died ('He died this year, in April or May'). I could tell from your line breaks that you really thought about how you wanted this to look on the page. What I really like about what you did. . . . The part I really love. . . ."*

## Ongoing Assessment

Informing Our Instruction

Conferring with a poet, Tyler.

Mentally assess the "whole" of the student's poem as she or he reads it aloud. Focus on:

- What is the writer trying to say?
- What has the writer done well?
- What are the most important things to say to this writer, right now, to support his or her efforts?
- How can I ensure that when the conference is done the writer has the skills and confidence to go on writing?

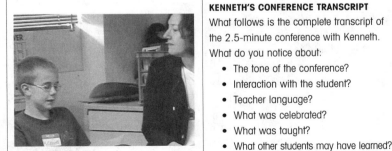

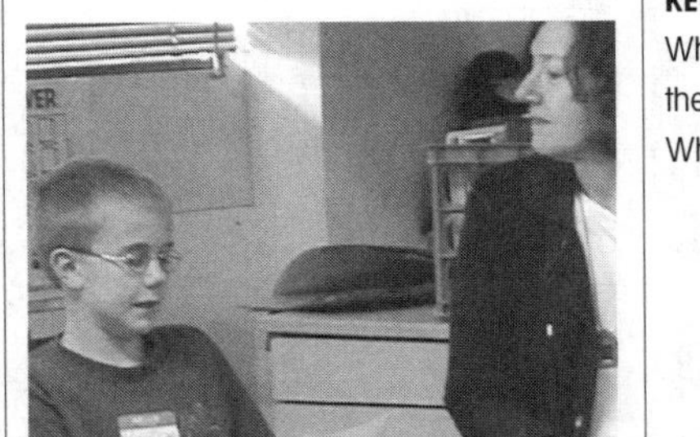

Conferring with Kenneth.

## Questions/Reflections

For Professional Conversations

Michael leander

Fifth grade anger

In the 5th grade
I had a teacher
who canceled a good recess.
I ~~turned to anger~~ became angry
in a spit second.

I became so ~~mad~~ angry
I literally
tore a few hairs
out of my head.

From then on
I ~~when~~ I think of ~~it~~ the moment
I grind my teeth

One of Michael's first poems.

**KENNETH'S CONFERENCE TRANSCRIPT**

What follows is the complete transcript of the 2.5-minute conference with Kenneth. What do you notice about:

- The tone of the conference?
- Interaction with the student?
- Teacher language?
- What was celebrated?
- What was taught?
- What other students may have learned?

What, if any, are the implications for your teaching?

## Learning Outcomes

What Students Know and Are Able to Do

Gwen Sanders reports: *"His narrative and expository writing improved as well. In fact, he wrote a letter to an author of a book he read. It was such a good piece of writing I shared it at a staff meeting. Diago had attended our school since kindergarten, so I wanted the staff to see the progress he had made."*

**Michael:** Michael was a reluctant writer as he began the sixth grade, but with poetry he discovered a place to use his delightful sense of humor. His writing improved in all genres, and he became more confident and enthusiastic.

**Kenneth:** Kenneth is a typically performing student who took off in writing during sixth grade. His passion for writing spread to all of his writing—poetry, narrative, and exposition.

continues

**Deeper Understanding: Reading and Writing Poetry**

# Video SCENES

**Celebrating Kids' Poems: Public Conferences *continued***

## Setting, Notes, and Explicit Teaching Points
The What, Why, and How of Teaching

• Diago

- Repeat the exact language the writer has used. [Talking to Diago about his poem "Football"] *"I love when you said, 'It feels like I hit thousands of trees.' I'm thinking you're in pain. That really hurts. 'Trees cut me in half.' Wow!"*
- Acknowledge the influence of reading on writing (so other students employ that influence in their writing). *"So you got that image from a book you read. That's great. That's what good writers do. You were taking something from literature . . . and getting it in your poem."*
- Offer specific suggestions (only if needed and only after all strengths of poem have been noted). *"I wondered about the ending. It's such a great poem the way you started. Then you go, 'So sometimes I play with grownups.'"*

  Diago: *"That's not a good ending."*

  *"You know what you could do. You could just cross that ending out."*

  Diago: *"Like that?"*

  *"Yeah, hold the pencil, then cross out this whole thing."*
- Place responsibility on the student while guiding him. *"Let me read it again and see what you think, how you might want to end it. 'When I play football / I play with grownups / When I get tackled / it feels like / I hit thousands of trees / Trees cut me in half.'"*

  Diago: *"I think that should be the ending."*

  *"That could be the ending. . . . That actually works better. . . . You might want to read it a couple of more times and see, am I happy with that? do I want to add something else?"*

• Cody

- Teach line breaks, as needed. *"You have all the good words, Cody, and the only thing you need to do is add some line breaks . . . to think about how you want it to sound. You don't have to copy it over. . . . Do you want it to sound like this? 'It was when I was six years old'? Or, 'It was when / I was six years old'? Which one do you like, the first one?"*

  Cody: *"The second one."*

  *"Put a line break right here.* [He does, and we do a few more together.] *When you go back and read this again . . . just put in the line breaks. . . . You've got the words of a poem. Now you just want to make it look like a poem on the page. You can do that."*

## Ongoing Assessment
Informing Our Instruction

Kenneth Jenks

my dog Duke
It was a tragical Day
my dog
Duke had
DIED.
my Dad I and cosines
Cried all Day
because Duke
Was a great Dog.
It took us
a couple of years
to get over Duke.
But when we did
Every thing went back
to normal
but ower hearts
where still broken

**Kenneth uses poetry writing to express his thoughts about his dog's death. (See the transcript of his conference at right.)**

**Cody, a struggling writer, is affirmed for his poem before teaching him line breaks. (See his student profile at far right and his published poem on p. 11-17.)**

## Questions/Reflections
For Professional Conversations

Regie: *"Kenneth, read yours please."*

Kenneth: *"There's one thing about my title. I forgot to put 'My Dog.'"*

Regie: *"You can change it. That's what I love about poetry writing. . . . You don't have to worry about getting it perfect. Change it the way you want it."*

Kenneth [reads his poem aloud]: *"Duke. It was a tragical day. My dog, Duke, had died. My dad and I and cousins cried all day, because Duke was a great dog. It took us a couple of years to get over Duke, but when we did, everything went back to normal. But our hearts were still broken."* [Students applaud.]

Regie: *"Did you hear that silence* [in the room] *at the end? Do you know what that silence at the end was? That you really touched people. They were like—I was thinking, 'Wow.' Let me read it again.* [Does so.] *I actually have never heard the word* tragical *but I love it there. Poets can do that. I think* tragical day *sounds actually better than,* It was a tragic day. *Personally, I would just leave it. . . .*

[Reads the poem again.] *You've done a number of wonderful things here. I can tell that you've read the poem over a number of times, because you changed the white space and line breaks. The only way you can do that is by saying it out loud to yourself. How many times did you read that as you were writing it?"*

Kenneth: *"About twenty times."*

Regie [speaking about organization and line breaks]: *"You worked really hard on that. First he had, 'It was a tragical day. My dog, Duke, had died.' That's how he wrote it. Then,*

## Learning Outcomes
What Students Know and Are Able to Do

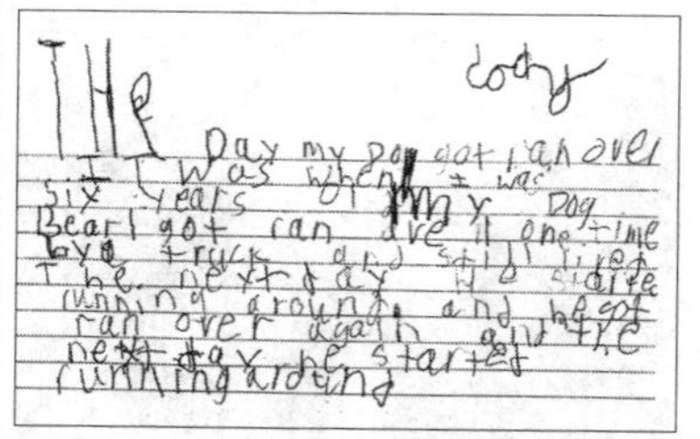

**Cody:** Cody is a low-performing student living in foster care. Public recognition of his skills as a writer did wonders for him and his peer status. Cody continued to write poems throughout the year and showed some progress with his other writing as well. Gwen Sanders comments: *"The day you invited him to the front of the class to discuss his writing and how to use line breaks to make it look more like a poem, he whispered to me as he returned to his seat, 'I'm going to be famous.' That easily could have been the most important day of his school life."*

- Monitor and evaluate progress and adjust goals over time.
- Identify aspects of writer's craft (e.g., sentence variation, voice, word choice).

# *Video* SCENES

**DEEPER UNDERSTANDING: Reading and Writing Poetry**

| | Setting, Notes, and Explicit Teaching Points<br>The What, Why, and How of Teaching | Ongoing Assessment<br>Informing Our Instruction | Questions/Reflections<br>For Professional Conversations | Learning Outcomes<br>What Students Know and Are Able to Do |
|---|---|---|---|---|
| | <br>**Conferring with Diago.** | **The Day My Dog Got Run Over**<br>—by Cody<br><br>It was when<br>I was six years old<br>My dog Bear<br>got run over<br>one time by a truck<br>and still lived.<br>The next day<br>he started<br>running around.<br>And he got<br>run over again<br>and the next day<br>he started<br>running around.<br><br>**Cody's poem, with line breaks.** | *look how he changed it. . . . He really worked on that. . . . He was really thinking about how he wanted the poem to sound. How poems sound, kids, are very, very important."*<br>Regie: *"I have one tiny, tiny suggestion that you can think about.* [Reading] *It took us a couple of years to get over Duke, but when we did, everything went back to normal. But our hearts were still broken. I love your ending. But I was thinking instead of* but, *maybe the word* except. *"Everything went back to normal,* except *our hearts were still broken." It's just a very little thing, but I think it makes the poem make more sense. What do you think?"*<br>Kenneth: *"Uh-huh."*<br>Regie: *"That's just something for you to think about. It's a really lovely poem. Thank you for sharing that."* | |
| **Revisiting the "What Do We Know About Writing Poetry?" Chart**<br><br>(2:26 min.) | **NOTES**<br>At the start of this scene, we review what students have understood about poetry and add to the class chart, "What Do We Know About Writing Poetry?" Students are also reminded to try at least one poem *"that's just about you . . . so that kids in the classroom can get to know you better."* After this scene, students write three or four poems independently, after being reminded that they will select their best or favorite poem for the class anthology. Immersion and reading poetry continue throughout the focus on poetry writing.<br><br>After this review/assessment, Gwen Sanders, the classroom teacher, thinks out loud in front of her students and writes a poem about when she was a shy child their age, nervously entering seventh grade and a new building for the first time and being embarrassed because her mother came with her and nobody else's mother or father did. | Read aloud "What Do We Know About Writing Poetry?" and assess students' growing knowledge:<br>• *"Let's add on to this list. . . . What are some things now you can do as a poet?"* [Writing students' responses on chart.]<br>• *"What's very important that's not on our list?"*<br>Cody: *"Realistic poems."*<br>Cary Ann: *"They may have stanzas."*<br>Student: *"They can be humorous."*<br>• *"What else do you notice?"*<br>Student: *"They can have surprise endings."* [Repeating what a student has said] | • What do students' responses let us know about what they are learning and enjoying about poetry writing?<br><br>What Do We Know About Writing Poetry?<br>Poems don't have to rhyme. free verse<br>They can be heart poems<br>can be Haiku, acrostic,<br>can be about anything you want<br>stuff from inside you care about<br>can be concrete (shape) poems<br>can be realistic<br>" have stanzas<br>" have humor<br>" be sad, angry, happy<br>have surprise endings<br>re-read lots of times | |

continues

## *Video* SCENES

**DEEPER UNDERSTANDING: Reading and Writing Poetry**

| | Setting, Notes, and Explicit Teaching Points<br>The What, Why, and How of Teaching | Ongoing Assessment<br>Informing Our Instruction | Questions/Reflections<br>For Professional Conversations | Learning Outcomes<br>What Students Know and Are Able to Do |
|---|---|---|---|---|
| | **TEACHING POINTS**<br>• Read aloud and review chart, "What Do We Know About Poetry Writing?"<br>• Validate students' growing knowledge by writing their new responses on the chart (use a different-color marker to distinguish from previous responses). | *"They can be sad, angry, you can put your emotions in there."*<br>Student: *"They can be heartbreaking."* Student: *"It can be any way you want it."*<br>*"You can decide where you want to put your punctuation or not."* | | **Teacher Gwen Sanders writes a poem in front of her students about an embarrassing moment when she was their age.** |
| **DAY 3**<br>**Celebrating Revision Efforts**<br>(2:56 min.) | **NOTES**<br>These celebration conferences (six in 12 minutes) take place after students have spent some time revisiting and revising their first poems. I focus on student strengths, highlighting changes students have made to improve their poems. Putting a sticky note on a student's poem reminds the writer of possible ideas to incorporate (and reminds me what was discussed). Out of respect for the writer, I typically do not write on a student's paper without his or her permission. | | • What evidence do you see that students have incorporated suggestions and ideas from public conferences? What does this mean for our teaching? | |
| | **TEACHING POINTS**<br>• I celebrate Diago as a poet and how he independently added a better ending after our last conference (helps other students focus on their endings too). *"You put an ending on it that was way better than what you had before."* I read the whole poem aloud, concluding with the new last line, *"I walk off the field in pain."*<br>• I celebrate Cody because he added a stanza to his writing and wrote a new poem (encourages other students to do the same). *"Remember yesterday . . . good for you, you were paying such close attention. He's got stanzas, look at that, even your handwriting looks better, Cody, but most of all you wrote a really wonderful poem."* I read the new poem, "The Day My Grandma Called Me Shorty," out loud. *"You took such a leap in such a short period of time."*<br>• I celebrate Michael for changes he made to strengthen his poem. *"I was really pleased to see that you took the time to read your poem again, and make some changes. . . . See he's got a lasso here, he's changed his rhythm . . . see the cross-outs?"* I read the poem, "Fifth Grade Anger." *"You took it, we didn't know what it was; you said the moment. Perfect."* | Make sure students understand that what one student does well (highlighted in a public conference) is something they might try to apply:<br>• *"What was the big change that Diago had in his writing that maybe you can think about for your writing?*<br>Student: *"New ending."*<br>Affirm and extend response (to encourage students to take thoughtful action).<br>• *"So when you go back and you're writing a new poem or revisiting an old poem, check your ending. Does it fit? Does it sound right? . . . Sometimes the ending is the hardest part for me."* | • Why are peer models so powerful for other students, and how can we best take advantage of this influence?<br>• How does everything we teach in poetry apply to writing and reading in other genres? | • Write with purpose and audience in mind.<br>• Revise and edit their own writing.<br>• Read and write poetry.<br>• Use multicultural literature to get ideas for writing.<br>• Reread their own work for the craft of writing (e.g., sentence openings, sentence variety).<br>• Produce readable cursive handwriting (e.g., letter size, letter spacing, letter formation, uppercase and lowercase letters).<br>• Select details and elaboration to strengthen writing. |

*Video* **SCENES**

**DEEPER UNDERSTANDING: Reading and Writing Poetry**

| | Setting, Notes, and Explicit Teaching Points<br>The What, Why, and How of Teaching | Ongoing Assessment<br>Informing Our Instruction | Questions/Reflections<br>For Professional Conversations | Learning Outcomes<br>What Students Know and Are Able to Do |
|---|---|---|---|---|
| | • I celebrate Tyler; he has moved from writing only concrete poems to free verse. *"Tyler took a huge leap yesterday. . . . He wrote a poem called 'In the Middle* [about being a middle child].'" I read it. *"What was this like for you when you wrote this?"* | | | • Identify and include information audience needs to know.<br>• Identify audience interests and knowledge of topic to determine emphasis. |
| **Planning for a Poetry Anthology**<br>(1:20 min.) | **NOTES**<br>During these public conferences, I show samples of anthologies to encourage students to publish their own anthology of poems and show them options for doing so. ("Heart Poems," a lesson in *Writing Essentials*, is one example; the website has others.)<br>I also read from a favorite book of poems, *The Dream on Blanca's Wall*, by Jane Medina, about a poor sixth-grade Hispanic girl who dreams of becoming a teacher.<br><br>**TEACHING POINTS**<br>• Suggest that since students love to write poems, they write their own poetry anthology. *"Lots of you are really wonderful writers."*<br>• Discuss procedures and options for putting together a class anthology. *"Choose your best poem, your favorite poem, the one you think you're willing to share, that you think says the most about you, your very best work."*<br>• Define anthology. *"And an anthology is just a collection of poems. It could be a collection of short stories, it could be a collection of one writer's work, but in this case it's going to be a collection of poems from this class."*<br>• Show published anthologies (to give kids choices and ideas on how they want theirs to be). *"This one, kids, has a table of contents, it has an about the author page . . . it has an index."*<br>• Connect writing to reading by reading poems—such as *The Dream on Blanca's Wall* by Jane Medina—that reflect and reinforce what students are writing. *"And what I want you to notice here is, it's like this girl, Blanca, is writing all these poems, and she's a sixth grader. And so she's used poetry as a way to talk about what's happening in her life. Here she's writing about her teacher, she writes about her mother braiding her hair, she writes about kids teasing her, and notice the ending. Look at how she set this up on the page. . . ."* | **Regie talks to the class about planning a class poetry anthology. "Choose your best poem, your favorite poem, the one you think you're willing to share, that you think says the most about you, your very best work."**<br><br>Check that students understand the poems read aloud:<br>• *"What's this poem about?"*<br>• *"What are you learning about this person's life? What's going on in her family? . . . Sometimes we make assumptions about people that are not true."* | • What is the role of publication in writing and why is it essential? What gets published? How much and how often? (You will want to have these discussions at your grade level and as a whole school.)<br>• Why is poetry an excellent vehicle for holding students accountable for editing? | • Identify an intended audience.<br>• Publish with a variety of formats and forms.<br>• Respond to literature written in free verse based on given criteria. |

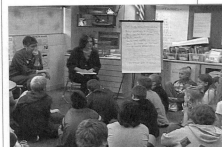

## DEEPER UNDERSTANDING: Reading and Writing Poetry

*Video* **SCENES**

**Shared Poetry Writing: Writing a Poem That Matters**

(3:37 min.)

| Setting, Notes, and Explicit Teaching Points<br>The What, Why, and How of Teaching | Ongoing Assessment<br>Informing Our Instruction | Questions/Reflections<br>For Professional Conversations | Learning Outcomes<br>What Students Know and Are Able to Do |
|---|---|---|---|
| **NOTES**<br>This shared writing developed from a community meeting the students had participated in earlier in the day. The students were concerned about the name calling and bullying they continued to experience at their school. Writing this poem helps the students begin to work through the problem.<br><br>Remember that in shared writing the teacher is holding the pen and shaping the language and the students are sharing their ideas. The writing is quick (10 or 15 minutes). | | | |
| **TEACHING POINTS**<br>• Decide on an authentic writing topic and purpose for the shared writing. *"Every kid goes through school and gets teased, gets bullied, or something. And they shouldn't have to wait until sixth grade to get that worked out. And it could be pretty fabulous if you wrote something. . . ."* Mrs. Sanders: *"I don't want these kids to lose the feeling of what happened to us today, about becoming a group and taking care of each other."* | Make sure students are clear on what we mean by "audience":<br>• *"What do I mean by the audience for what we're going to write?"*<br>Paige: *"The person that will be reading it."* [Affirming her response]<br>*"We have huge possibilities here. . . . The more you care about your audience, the better a job you're going to do on your writing."* [Writing possible audiences for poem on chart.] | • What are the advantages of shared writing to the teacher and to the students? | • Identify and discuss recurring theme (identity, struggle). |
| • Share thinking about possible audiences. Mrs. Sanders: *"It could be something that we keep up in our room so that we can see it every day, and it'll be like our own classroom contract . . . that will help guide us along our path to being better citizens."* | | | • Connect current issues, previous information, and experiences to character, events, and information within and across culturally relevant texts. |
| • Negotiate, with students, the audience for the writing. *"Who do you want the writing to be for?"*<br>Kenneth: *"Just for us."* Lee: *"For the whole school?"*<br>*"How many of you think this is so personal that it should be only for the class?"* [Most want the poem to be for the class.] | | | • Select audience and purpose for writing. |
| • Ask students to suggest a title. *"What do you want to call it?"*<br>Student: *"A Community Classroom."*<br>Another student: *"Sadness at Room 219."*<br>*"Wow, those are both good. I'm going to put them both down; we can come back to that."* | | | |
| • Request a beginning for the poem. *"How do you want to start this, because first lines are important?"* Mrs. Sanders: *"We started our meeting today with me saying, 'Kids, we're falling apart here.' Why don't we start with that* [writing it on chart]*?"* | | | • Collaborate on drafting, revising, and editing. |

*Video* **SCENES**

**Shared Poetry Writing: Writing a Poem That Matters *continued***

**DEEPER UNDERSTANDING: Reading and Writing Poetry**

| Setting, Notes, and Explicit Teaching Points | Ongoing Assessment | Questions/Reflections | Learning Outcomes |
|---|---|---|---|
| The What, Why, and How of Teaching | Informing Our Instruction | For Professional Conversations | What Students Know and Are Able to Do |
| • Write draft on the chart paper and let students know that draft means the very best "first thinking."<br>• Negotiate, lead, and shape the writing of the poem. *"What should come next? . . . Should we add . . . ? . . . How many like it on a separate line by itself? . . . What should come next?"* (See draft.)<br>• Reread poem-in-process. *"Now one of the things with poetry is, you have to keep reading it and reading it and that helps your thinking."*<br>• List all student responses and capture students' language and ideas (affirms and respects every student; changes can be made later).<br>• Reread to make sure it sounds like the students' language and stress importance of rereading. *"Let's hear how it sounds. . . . How many times did we read this poem? . . . Five times."*<br>• Set a purpose for independent writing by asking students to continue rereading, revising, and selecting at least three poems for the class poetry anthology. *"Tomorrow, in the morning, you have time to write. You'll get back the poems you've already written and you'll have time to write one or two if you want and then really decide what your best poem is. You might want to write something like this* [pointing to class poem on chart]."<br>• Affirm the role of poetry in people's lives. *"You can write poems just for yourself."* | **Our shared writing of an important poem. See the published poem at right.** | **Mending Our Broken Hearts**<br><br>"Kids,<br>we're falling<br>apart."<br><br>"Mrs. Sanders<br>Ms. Crisp<br>we've been called<br>too many names."<br><br>Shrimp<br>Shorty<br>Midget<br>Four eyes<br>Blondie<br>Big foot<br>Stupid<br>Overweight<br>Underweight<br>Dumb<br>Can't count<br><br>WE<br>WON'T<br>TOLERATE<br>THIS<br>ANYMORE!<br><br>NO MORE NAMES<br>NO MORE NAMES | • Vary leads and endings.<br><br>• Reread for meaning.<br><br>• Write in an appropriate and consistent voice.<br>• Search for alternatives to commonly used words.<br>• Reread text and continue drafting over time.<br><br>• Write to pursue a personal interest, to explain, or to persuade. |

**FINAL NOTES FOR SHARED POETRY WRITING**

Type up the shared poem and make copies for every student for the following day. Then:

- Ask students to read and revise the poem by themselves.
- Invite students to from small groups and select a scribe for the group.
- Challenge each group, using their individually revised copies and a clean copy, to revise the poem. (Having a scribe record revisions the group agrees on gives you a record of each group's work.)
- Bring the class together by asking each group for their best ideas.
- Lead the final shaping and revising of the class poem.
- Display final version.

Mrs. Sanders reported that the poem became a credo of behavior for the entire school year. Also, after students had several more days to complete their poems, they began work on the class anthology. At Tyler's suggestion, the poem created through shared writing (see above) became the first poem in the anthology.

**Grade 1 teachers celebrate the poetry writing their students have done.**

SESSION 11

# RESPONSE NOTES

*Engage, Reflect, Assess, Celebrate!*

**Transforming** our **Teaching** through
**Reading/Writing Connections**

# Reading and Writing Nonfiction Reports

**View Video** (31 min.)

**Reading and Writing Nonfiction Reports**

- **Coaching the Teacher: Giving Feedback**
- **Valuing Audience and Purpose**
- **Examining Nonfiction Texts**
- **Turning Notes into Paragraphs: Demonstration Writing**
- **Turning Notes into Paragraphs: Shared Writing (Whole Class)**
- **Conferring with Students: Small-Group Public Conferences**

## 1. Engage, Reflect, Assess

- ***Whole-Group Share***
    - Revisit the *Try It/Apply It* activity from the last session. (You were asked to use shared writing to draft, revise, and publish a free-verse poem on a topic of high interest to your students.)
    - Use the following questions to begin a conversation about your experience:
        - *How did your students respond to your poetry writing demonstration? What did they learn from watching you think aloud and write in front of them?*
        - *How did public conferences impact the writing in your classroom?*
        - *Share your poetry anthology. Who was the audience for the poems? What was the purpose? How did having an audience and purpose affect your class as writers?*

**RESOURCES**

**In this Session**

- Nonfiction Organizer (One Group's Example) *12-6*
- Nonfiction Organizer (blank form) *12-7*
- What Makes Nonfiction Writing Interesting? (Shared Writing) *12-8*
- Taking Research Notes (Shared Writing) *12-9*
- Class-Authored Report Writing Rubric *12-10*
- One Teacher's Changes in Beliefs and Practices Over Time *12-11*
- Lesson Plan Summary (Sample from Web-Only Lesson) *12-13*
- Student Samples of Nonfiction Reports (Small-Group Shared Writing) *12-14*
- Nonfiction Report by Fourth-Grade Students *12-16*

**On the Website**

- Learning to Write Nonfiction Reports: Daily Lesson Plans (20 Days, with Notes to the Teacher) and Learning Outcomes Overview
- Class-Authored Published Book, *Colorado Wildlife Book of Facts*

- *Small-Group Share*
  - Share lesson samples and students' poems in your vertical team.

## 2. Discuss Professional Reading

- Discuss "Poetry Writing" (*Conversations* excerpt, pp. 364–382 and downloadable from the website).

## 3. Goals

- Be able to apply the qualities and characteristics of good nonfiction models.
- See how writing demonstrations can effectively teach students how to draft an interesting and accurate report.
- Recognize the importance of explicitly teaching the process of taking notes and turning them into a paragraph.
- Understand that multiple shared-writing experiences (whole class and small student groups) improve the quality of students' writing.
- Learn how to use small-group public conferences to celebrate, revisit, and revise writing.

## 4. View Video and Take Notes

- Turn to the Notecatcher to take notes during the video.

## 5. Respond to the Video

- Share your thoughts about the video with your small group. Perhaps use the following discussion questions:
  - What do you notice about the students in the video? What are their strengths? To what do you attribute their strengths? What strengths do you notice in their writing?
  - What are the benefits of all students participating in shared experiences? What are the benefits to English language learners?
  - What did you notice about the public conferences? How might such conferences support students in their writing?

## 6. Achieve a Deeper Understanding

- Read and review the Deeper Understanding charts.
- *Small-Group Share*
  - Use the Deeper Understanding charts as a basis for discussing the video scenes with your vertical group.
  - Use the Questions/Reflections for Professional Conversations to think more deeply about the video scenes.

  - Please read "Learning to Write Nonfiction Reports: Daily Lesson Plans (20 Days)" (available on the website). In your vertical team, review the lesson plans related to one or more of the following video segments or plan a lesson of your own:

- Valuing Audience and Purpose (Day 1)
- Examining Nonfiction Texts (Day 2)
- Turning Notes into Paragraphs: Demonstration Writing (Day 9)
- Turning Notes into Paragraphs: Shared Writing (Days 10 and 11)
- Conferring with Students: Small-Group Public Conferences (Days 11, 12, 13, and 14)

- Think about how the lesson plans might be modified for primary grades.

## 7. *Try It/Apply It* in the Classroom

- In vertical teams, revisit this session's Deeper Understanding charts, "Optimal Learning Model in a Daily Literacy Block" (Session 2, p. 2–8), and the comprehensive "Learning to Write Nonfiction Reports: Daily Lesson Plans (20 Days)" (on the website) to help you plan and apply report writing lessons in your classroom. You can use the following list, which uses the Optimal Learning Model, as a guide:

**Demonstration**

- Read aloud from and think aloud about a nonfiction text, noticing author's craft and organization.
- Reread and think aloud as you take notes from the text.
- Think and write aloud as you turn the notes into a paragraph.

**Shared Experiences: Whole Group**

- Select and read a nonfiction text and use the organizer (see pp. 12–6, 12–7, and 12–8) to list how to make nonfiction writing interesting.
- Take notes.
- Turn notes into a paragraph.
- Assess what students learned about taking notes. (See "Taking Research Notes" on p. 12–9 for important teaching points.)

**Shared and Guided Practice**

- Repeat the previous process, allowing students, who are working in small heterogeneous groups of three or four, to take the lead in reading, discussing, note taking, and turning notes into a paragraph. Remind students to refer to "Taking Research Notes" (p. 12–9).

**Celebration/Assessment**

- Use public conferences to celebrate, teach, and/or assess.
- Publish (after revisions, formatting, editing, and adding references and illustrations) for a selected audience (other students, school library, or school community).
- Negotiate and create a rubric with your class (use the "Class-Authored Report Writing Rubric" p. 12–10 as a guide) to evaluate reports.

- Use the rubric to evaluate your students' work, and ask them to use it to evaluate their own work.

- You may also find "One Teacher's Changes in Beliefs and Practices Over Time" p. 12–11 very useful in thinking about report writing, both in the classroom and schoolwide.
- Be prepared to share samples of your lesson plans, demonstrations, shared experiences, student work, observations, and ideas with your vertical and/or small-group team during the next session.

## 8. Wrap-Up

- Before next session, read "Reading Nonfiction" and "On Research Writing" (*Conversations* excerpts, pp. 440–448, 482–490 and downloadable from the website).

- Schedule time to meet with your vertical, grade-level, and/or partner teams in between whole-group sessions to revisit the videos on the website and the Deeper Understanding charts and/or plan together and try out new learning. Jot down your ideas and thinking on your Response Notes page for easy reference later.
- Remember to bring any charts, lessons, writing, or student work samples from the *Try It/Apply It* to the next session.

# SESSION 12 NOTECATCHER

| VIDEO SCENES | LENGTH | NOTES & REFLECTION |
|---|---|---|
| **Coaching the Teacher: Giving Feedback** | 5:13 min. | |
| **Valuing Audience and Purpose** | 1:45 min. | |
| **Examining Nonfiction Texts** | 3:34 min. | |
| **Turning Notes into Paragraphs: Demonstration Writing** | 5:06 min. | |
| **Turning Notes into Paragraphs: Shared Writing (Whole Class)**<br>• Reviewing Notes<br>• Beginning the Shared Writing | 6:19 min. | |
| **Conferring with Students: Small-Group Public Conferences** | 8:55 min. | |

# Nonfiction Organizer

## *(One Group's Example)*

| Leads (How does it begin?) | (Conclusion-How does it wrap everything up?) |
| --- | --- |
| · animal in action (dramatic and fright migration acorss A)<br>· doscribing a body prart pigs/are. loudestion form)<br>· Sound (Mewwww.. )<br>· humming bird lives all overworld | · they ended it with how they grow up<br>gives a fact how to Stay Safe. |
| **What kinds of comparisons did the writing use?** | **Clever words or descriptions** |
| · A cloud of desert locusts in the sky<br>· thunderous noies<br>· It seems like night<br>· their brain is potected like a helmet<br>· humming birds can fly backword | · thunderous noies<br>· bright colorado sunshine<br>· hovering beak |

# Nonfiction Organizer

**Leads**
(How does it begin?)

**Conclusion**
(How does it wrap everything up?)

**What kinds of comparisons did the author use?**

**Clever words or descriptions**

# WHAT MAKES NONFICTION WRITING INTERESTING?

## *(Shared Writing)*

- Unique facts (a bat's wing span is six feet).
- Leads the reader into the next topic by tying up the ending to the last topic, then uses a new fact to take the reader into the next section.
- Makes you want to keep reading (flying foxes, for example).
- Uses the word *you* so it sounds like "the writer is talking to me."
- Humor (*thought I was batty*).
- Clever word choice (*sends a shiver down your spine*).
- Comparing (*seems like*, or *as*).
- Pictures are interesting.
- Diagram tells why body part is important.
- Boldface type.
- Use of commas to set off an explanation, (*pachyderm, or elephant*).
- Captions (facts)/headings (clever).
- Questions.
- Pronunciation.
- Interesting words (*delicate, fragile, beautiful*).
- Uses your senses (*thunderous sounds*).
- Changing mood—catches the reader by surprise. (*You may think a butterfly is delicate, but they are strong.*)
- Beginnings:
  - Question lead (still teaches a fact).
  - Dialogue (conversation).
  - Quote from animal. ("*Yes! It's spring.*")
  - Setting.
  - Action.
- Endings:
  - Dialogue.
  - Circular.
  - Fact.
  - Comparisons.

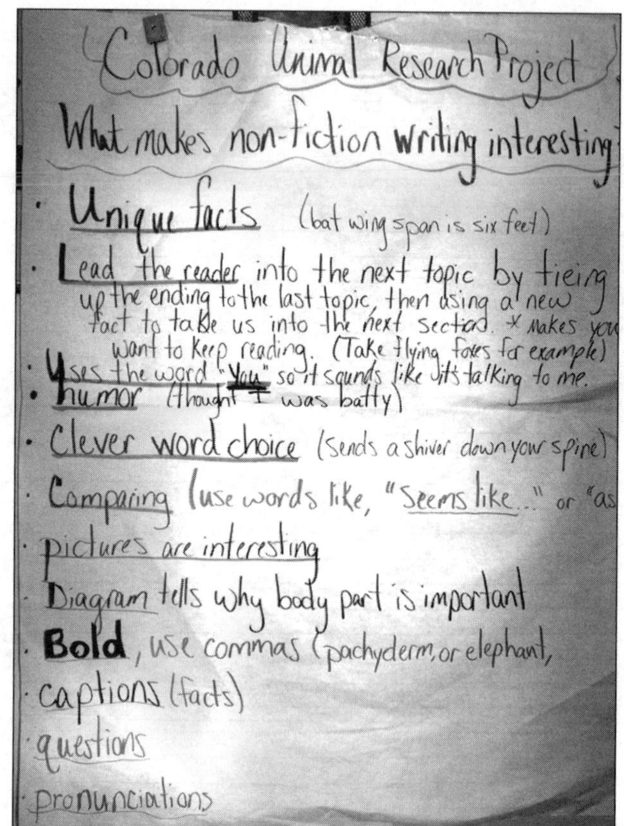

**This chart is a shared writing created by Darcy Ballentine and her class as a resource on how to make nonfiction writing interesting. On Days 3, 4, and 5 of the "Learning to Write Nonfiction Reports: Daily Lesson Plans (20 Days)" students are immersed in good nonfiction text in order to notice how the author's craft is used effectively in nonfiction. The chart represents what the students noticed during read-aloud, shared reading, and reading in collaborative groups. The complete lesson plans are available on the website.**

# 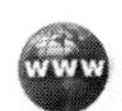 TAKING RESEARCH NOTES

## *(Shared Writing)*

**The chart below was created by Darcy Ballentine and her class following note-taking demonstrations on Days 8 and 9 of the "Learning to Write Nonfiction Reports: Daily Lesson Plans (20 Days)" in response to the question: "What did you see me doing while I was taking my notes?" The chart is then posted in the classroom as a resource for students while they work in groups to**  **take notes for their reports. The complete lesson plans are available on the website.**

- Only write key words (not complete sentences).
- When you read, understand what you read first to learn about the animal.
- Reread three or four times so you can make sure your information is accurate.
- Write notes so you remember your facts (after one or two readings).
- Stick with topic.
- Close the book when you write key words.
- Keep track of books you used (title, author, publishing company, city, and date).

#  Class-Authored Report Writing Rubric

*(Created with Darcy Ballentine's fourth-grade class for their animal research reports)*

| CRITERIA | YES | NO |
|---|---|---|
| **Clever heading that grabs the reader's attention**<br>**Writing stays on topic** | | |
| **Interesting introduction**<br>• Humor<br>• May use the word *you*<br>• Comparisons<br>• Setting<br>• Action<br>• Interesting fact(s)<br>• Quote<br>• Story<br>• Question | | |
| **Plays around with print to make it more exciting and easier to understand for the reader**<br>• Headings<br>• Bold<br>• Parentheses<br>• Punctuation<br>• Bullets | | |
| **Creative word choice**<br>• Strong verbs<br>• Uses words we would use<br>• Uses senses<br>• Repeats words to make a rhythm | | |
| **Report has at least three paragraphs describing topics about a Colorado animal in an interesting way.**<br>Possible topics:<br>• Diet<br>• Physical description<br>• Habitat<br>• Life cycle | | |
| **Writes facts in own words**<br>Facts are interesting:<br>• Compares animal fact to something the reader is familiar with<br>• Humor<br>• Action<br>• Compares animals to reader | | |
| **Uses at least three sources to research facts** | | |
| **Publishes with perfect conventions**<br>• Spelling<br>• Punctuation<br>• Grammar<br>• Paragraphs | | |
| **Includes an organized diagram of animal, with facts** | | |
| **Has a conclusion**<br>• Ends with a fact<br>• Circular ending<br>• Slows writing down | | |
| **Accurate bibliography** | | |

# One Teacher's Changes in Beliefs and Practices Over Time

| | I CHANGED FROM: | I CHANGED TO: |
|---|---|---|
| Report Writing Process | A process that was long and drawn out, very laborious, and painful. Kids were not excited to write, and I hated teaching research. The students' final reports were formulaic and without personality. They were shared with another class and then put away. | A process that is much more enjoyable for me and for the kids. We enjoy reading interesting examples and listening to one another's clever ones. The quality of writing is much better. We're very proud of our work after we've finished. Kids pull out the book and read it during silent reading time. |
| Audience | Having the class and me be the sole audience for the reports. | Extending the audience to include other classrooms and grades, parents, visitors to the library, etc. A wider audience led to higher expectations. |
| Immersion | Immersing students in nonfiction text without charting what students noticed, reading examples only once, and telling them what I noticed. Students not sharing what they noticed, so it was hard to assess their understanding. | Immersing students in nonfiction text by reading and rereading the text, then charting what students noticed once they finished "table talk."<br><br>Using a different color each day to chart what students noticed to assess their development. |
| Making Writing Interesting | Sharing ideas for making writing interesting once before writing. No "table talking" or "turn-and-talk" after reading through examples. | Sharing student examples more often.<br>Reading each example through two times.<br>"Turn-and-talk" often, and share each time we read an example. |
| Skills | Teaching a minilesson—one skill at a time—and then asking kids to work on it in isolation. | Teaching skills within the context of writing and allowing time for scaffolding (*"We do it," "We do it," "We do it"*). |
| Note Taking | Providing a structured note-taking worksheet: breaking down a paragraph to (1) topic sentence box, (2) supporting details boxes, (3) concluding sentences box. This approach resulted in very formulaic, unoriginal writing.<br><br>Modeling how to use the note-taking worksheet, then assigning students the task without establishing expectations. | Using the Optimal Learning Model to teach note taking:<br>• (*"I do it."*) Read aloud a selection of nonfiction text, demonstrate how to use key words to write notes, then write notes as a class.<br>• (*"We do it."*) Read aloud nonfiction text, write notes as a shared writing with the whole class.<br>• (*"We do it."*) Repeat shared writing as needed.<br>• (*"We do it."*) Students, in "table groups," take notes. |

*continues*

# One Teacher's Changes in Beliefs and Practices Over Time, *continued*

| | I CHANGED FROM: | I CHANGED TO: |
|---|---|---|
| **Turning Notes into Paragraphs** | Modeling how to turn notes into a paragraph and moving straight into independent writing without scaffolding or gradual release. | Using the Optimal Learning Model to teach how to turn notes into a paragraph:<br>• ("*I do it.*") Demonstrate how to write a paragraph from notes.<br>• ("*We do it.*") Turn my notes into a paragraph in shared writing.<br>• ("*We do it.*") Students, in table groups, rewrite the paragraph using my notes.<br>• ("*We do it.*") Students, in table groups, write paragraphs using their own notes. |
| **Conferring** | Conferring with individual students, with very little celebration and sharing ideas among students. | Conferring with individual students in public conferences or using whole-class shares to:<br>• Celebrate what students do well.<br>• Assess what students need more of.<br>• Let students share their ideas with their classmates.<br><br>Limiting individual conferences to editing. |
| **Publishing** | Choosing the audience, usually the teacher, without student input.<br><br>Choosing the format—"one size fits all."<br><br>Doing most of the publishing work, including lots of editing. | Choosing the possible real-world audiences with much student input.<br><br>Giving students lots of examples and choices for publishing options and formats.<br><br>Having students do most of the publishing work, including the editing. |

—*Darcy Ballentine*

# Lesson Plan Summary

## (Sample from Web-Only Lesson)

### Learning to Write Nonfiction Reports: Daily Lesson Plans (20 Days)

*Learning Outcomes Overview*

The icon indicates a video scene is linked to that lesson.

| Video SCENES | What Students Will Know and Are Able to Do |
|---|---|
| | The following calendar lists the learning goals of each lesson in the 20-day plan. Please note that this entire lesson sequence is based on the Optimal Learning Model. The lessons are based on demonstration (*"I do it"*) and shared demonstration (*"We do it"*). Therefore, students will know and be able to apply these skills within the context of a shared learning, not necessarily at the independent level. |
|  **DAY 1, Valuing Audience and Purpose** | • Identify the intended audience and set the purpose for writing the report.<br>• Analyze the characteristics of nonfiction text to generate ideas for topics and understand content and organization. |
|  **DAY 2, Examining Nonfiction Texts** | • Continue to explore and list the characteristics of a nonfiction text to generate topic ideas and extend thinking about ways to organize information.<br>• Identify and list information that meets the needs of a diverse audience (e.g., background information on the topic, definition of specialized vocabulary). |
| **DAYS 3, 4, 5, Examining Nonfiction Texts: Author's Craft** | • Analyze and list features from one or more texts to expand awareness of nonfiction text features including illustrations, captions, graphs, charts, and/or maps, etc.<br>• Identify and explain how an author engages the reader by using craft techniques such as humor, simile, metaphor, a variety of leads and conclusions, etc.<br>• Use graphic organizers to record author's craft in the following categories: leads, conclusions, comparisons (simile/metaphor), and clever word choice and descriptive language. |
| **DAYS 6 and 7, Developing Research Questions** | • Formulate central research questions based on the content schema (subtopics) of the topic.<br>• Use texts, students' interests, and background knowledge to formulate research questions.<br>• Locate information in a text using the table of contents, heading, and index in a variety of nonfiction texts.<br>• Determine the importance and accuracy of research questions to answer in the report. |
| **DAY 8, Taking Notes** | • Select text resources with appropriate content and readability.<br>• Define the purpose for reading nonfiction text.<br>• Learn to vary reading rate to locate information and answer research questions (skimming and scanning).<br>• Read and reread to extend content knowledge.<br>• Summarize, paraphrase and record important details (note-taking) central to research questions.<br>• Take notes using key words and phrases.<br>• Extend vocabulary knowledge by learning and using new content-specific words.<br>• Participate in individual and/or group conferences by listening actively and contributing ideas about the content of a paragraph.<br>• Identify and explain how an author engages the reader by using craft techniques such as humor, simile, metaphor, a variety of leads and conclusions, etc. |

# Student Samples of Nonfiction Reports

## (Small-Group Shared Writing)

**Delicious Dinners**

"**Sssssssscrumptious!** Is that a rat I sense?" All rattlesnakes love mice, rats, and other pesky rodents. This amazing reptile uses special senses to find their prey because of their poor eyesight. One of them is called the **Jacobson's Organ**. They stick their forked tongue up two holes in the back of their head. This interesting reptile has many fearsome predators of its own, like the hawk and owl. "**Delisssssh!** What's for dessert?"

This is a rattlesnake hunting for food i
very dry area.

**Daniel and Jorge published this final copy of their rattlesnake paragraph on what rattlesnakes eat. Notice that they added the information about the "Jacobson's Organ," which was discussed during their public conference.**

Daniel Jorge

Sussrumpcous is that a rat I Sense? All rattlesnaks love mice, rats and other pesky rodents. These amazing reptile use spechal senses to find its prey bec-caus of their poor eye site. This forcome predtor has many driedful preditor like the hawk, and owl.

**This is the draft (as seen on the video) that Daniel and Jorge shared during their public conference.**

# Student Samples of Nonfiction Reports, *continued*

## *(Small-Group Shared Writing)*

Otters 1,2,3
Otters' tails are very useful. They steer the otter underwater like a steering wheel.
An otter's balance isn't the greatest thing because its hind legs (back) are bigger than their front legs, which causes them to wobble.
An otter's feet are very sensitive. They are so sensitive they can feel vibrations from another animal.
Otters' thick fur is like a warm winter coat. This is useful because during the winter the water is freezing.
The otter has a to
body to help it sw


**Not only do students study how to write nonfiction, they study nonfiction texts for design and formatting tips. Notice that the students formatted their paragraphs using typical nonfiction styles.**

Dinner Time

"Where's the food around here? I've been waiting here for hours!" Did you know rattlesnakes lie motionless in a bush waiting for a small rodent to pass? When it does the rattlesnake leans forward to attack with fearsome speed and poisonous venom. The victim tries running but the venom acts fast! All of the following animals are edible for a rattlesnake: rats, mice, prairie dog, and other small rodents.

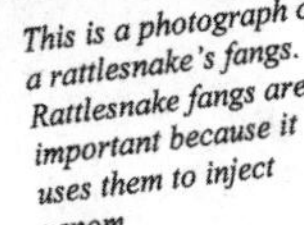

*This is a photograph of a rattlesnake's fangs. Rattlesnake fangs are important because it uses them to inject venom.*

# Nonfiction Report by Fourth-Grade Students

**It is important to save student samples from year to year to use as models.**

How would you like it if your mom had ababy that was a blind fuzz ball? Well, that is ~~expected for lynx~~ expected for lynx babies. They are born with bad hearing and they are blind. Lynx Kittens are barly bigger than house kittens. It is hard to tell the diverce beatween each other. Because they are born alive they look almost the same and drink their mothers milk. They play a mean game of wrestling but I'm not sure they can do the hymlic monver. They play tumble, tusle, and hide and seek.

**Draft**

## Lynx

### Home Sweet Home

What if your dad went up to your room and said, "We're moving far north to a rock cave!" Such an offer for a lynx would be sweet and dreamy. Most of the time lynxes live in shrubs, hollow trees, dens, or under spruce trees. They move to different places if an enemy moves into its territory. So next time you're hiking look for a lynx.

### Fast Food

If the lynx was at a French restaurant, it would not be ordering escargot. It would more likely choose mice, voles, squirrels, grouse, rabbit, deer, caribou, and snowshoe hare would be a rich dessert. So you can tell it's a real carnivore. Like some animals it catches, eats, and barfs up for its young, or dear ol' dad will eat them when mom is out. Lynxes will sneak up on their prey one, two, three they pounce. Someone is not hungry tonight.

### Fuzzy

How would you like it if your mom had a baby that was a blind fuzz ball? Well that is expected for lynx babies. They are born with bad hearing and they are blind. Lynx kittens are barely bigger than house kittens. It is hard to tell the difference between each other because they are born alive, they look almost the same, and they drink their mother's milk. They play a mean game of wrestling but I'm not sure they can do the Heimlich maneuver. They play tumble, tussle, and hide and seek.

Long, tall, and somewhat tan, the lynx is very similar to the bobcat in appearance. It is different in size and color. Lynx can be tan, gray, reddish brown, and black. The lynx weighs 20–45 pounds so it's about the size of a first grader. They have long legs and big feet. Some people call them snowshoe paws. Lynxes have fur from the tip of their short stubby tail to the tip of their long ears. Speak of ears; lynxes have tufts of hair on their ears.

**Cool Stuff to Know**

- It can stand -30 degrees f.
- It lives on four continents: Asia, Africa, Europe, and North America.
- Only in the U.S.A. is it called a lynx. In other places it is called a caracal.
- Lynxes have hairy toes.

**Bibliography**

Switzer, Merebeth. *Nature's Children Lynx.* Connecticut: Grolier, 1986.

**Published report**

**A fourth-grade teacher read this rough draft paragraph on a lynx to her class to initiate a discussion on how to make nonfiction writing interesting. This paragraph (left) was written by a former fourth-grade student working within a small group. See right for the final group-published report. Note that the students did all the editing work.**

# Deeper Understanding

*The teaching and assessing points reflect all of the nonfiction writing lessons, but not all of these points or lessons are on the edited videos you are watching. However, the major points are represented on the edited videos. A major purpose here is for you to view an effective teacher who capitalizes on shared experiences to get great writing results.*

The globe icon indicates that the example is also available when you visit www.regieroutman.com.

## Video SCENES

These video scenes are linked to a series of day-by-day lessons on report writing. The complete lesson plans and Learning Outcomes Overview for "Learning to Write Nonfiction Reports: Daily Lesson Plans (20 Days)," are provided on the website. The scenes and complete lesson plans will help you plan, teach, and assess report writing with your own students.

The video scenes give you a picture of what it sounds like and looks like to:

- Teach and assess simultaneously (responsive teaching).
- Use models of nonfiction writing to teach author's craft.
- Turn notes into a paragraph.
- Revise while drafting.
- Confer with students to celebrate and teach.
- Use shared writing as the main instructional approach for teaching and learning how to write reports.

| Setting, Notes, and Explicit Teaching Points | Ongoing Assessment | Questions/Reflections | Learning Outcomes |
|---|---|---|---|
| The What, Why, and How of Teaching | Informing Our Instruction | For Professional Conversations | What Students Know and Are Able to Do |
| **SETTING**<br>In these scenes, Darcy Ballentine, a fourth-grade teacher at Arapahoe Ridge Elementary in Westminster, Colorado, is teaching her students how to write a report. Darcy has been a classroom teacher for twelve years and currently teaches language arts in the morning and is her school's literacy coach in the afternoon. Her school draws students from an affluent suburban neighborhood, a mobile home park, and a middle-class neighborhood. Her classroom comprises 26 students, 8 of whom have special needs: 4 students have an Individual Education Plan for language arts, 2 students are English language learners, and 2 students have a gifted and talented Individual Education Plan. | | <br>**A member of the small group that has worked together reads their collaborative draft in a public conference.** | |
| Darcy and I have worked together over the past several years, beginning with a residency and continuing with coaching in follow-up years. Her beliefs and practices have shifted. She has raised her expectations, and she's changed from being, in her own words, "a dominating teacher needing to be in control to a teacher who is willing to gradually shift responsibility over to the students."<br><br>Darcy's teaching is an excellent example of applying the Optimal Learning Model effectively. Notice in the following video scenes and in the lesson plans how much frontloading she does and how she effectively uses heterogeneous small groups as a way for students to talk, think, and write together. | When I coached, I was impressed with how Darcy continually used assessment—mostly in the form of thoughtful questioning followed by responsive teaching—to push students' thinking and guide her instruction. Notice how seamless her integration of teaching and assessing are in these scenes. | | |

continues

*Video* **SCENES**

**Coaching the Teacher: Giving Feedback**

(5:13 min.)

(See Days 10 and 11 in "Learning to Write Nonfiction Reports: Daily Lesson Plans")

## DEEPER UNDERSTANDING: Reading and Writing Nonfiction Reports

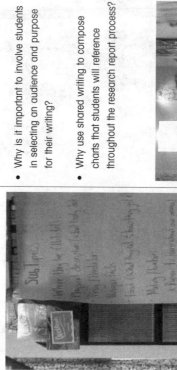

| Setting, Notes, and Explicit Teaching Points | Ongoing Assessment | Questions/Reflections | Learning Outcomes |
|---|---|---|---|
| The What, Why, and How of Teaching | Informing Our Instruction | For Professional Conversations | What Students Know and Are Able to Do |
| **NOTES**<br>In this first scene, Darcy, her colleagues, and I are giving her feedback on a lesson we saw her teach on note taking. First, I refer back to the notes I took while observing and affirm all she has done so well (not shown in this video clip; see Teaching Points, below). My major suggestion is to limit her students to shared experiences, since many do not seem quite ready to write a report on their own. Darcy puts this suggestion into practice. The students continue to receive support from Darcy and their peers as they write collaboratively in groups of four. The final group reports are excellent and reflect the expert, careful teaching and assessing—as well as many shared experiences—that have taken place. | 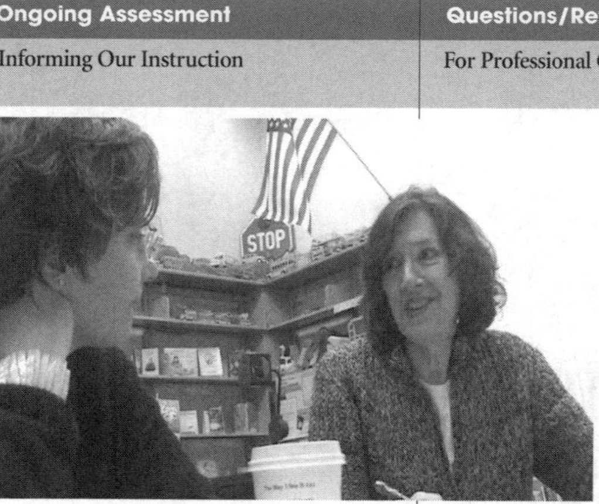<br><br>**Regie tells the group of teachers what Darcy did well, "I thought she was very, very, very skillful."** | | |
| **TEACHING POINTS**<br>• Do lots of "frontloading" (demonstrations, preparation, immersion) to prompt high-quality work from students.<br>• Negotiate with students the purpose and audience for their reports.<br>• Use shared writing to compose charts such as a list of topics and subtopics, elements of author's craft, tips for taking smart notes, etc.<br>• Refer students to charts around the room that will provide support while they take their notes and write their paragraphs.<br>• Examine features of nonfiction by reading lots of nonfiction texts with students (immersion).<br>• Use think-alouds and shared writing as you write notes with the students.<br>• Use "table talk" or "turn-and-talk" to "hear all the voices," engage students, and assess what they know and are thinking about.<br>• Apply the research that favors a responsive classroom over a telling classroom. | 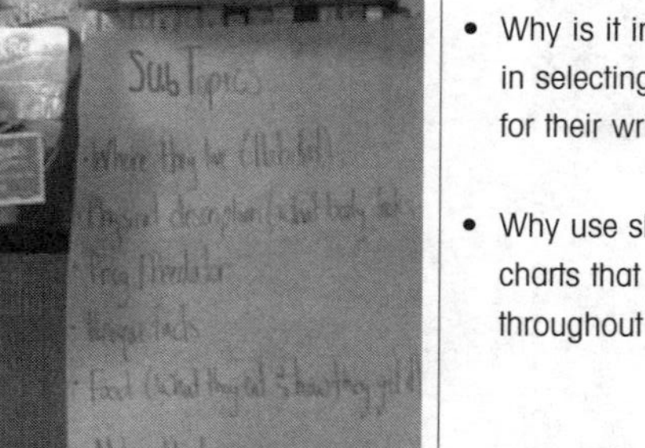<br><br>**List of possible subtopics for animal research reports.** | • Why is it important to involve students in selecting an audience and purpose for their writing?<br>• Why use shared writing to compose charts that students will reference throughout the research report process?<br><br>**A participant in the debriefing talks about how impressed she was by the "table talk" and how it engaged students.** | • Identify intended audience.<br>• Apply more than one strategy for generating ideas and planning report writing. |

# *Video* SCENES

**Deeper Understanding:** Reading and Writing Nonfiction Reports

| Video Scene | Setting, Notes, and Explicit Teaching Points<br>The What, Why, and How of Teaching | Ongoing Assessment<br>Informing Our Instruction | Questions/Reflections<br>For Professional Conversations | Learning Outcomes<br>What Students Know and Are Able to Do |
|---|---|---|---|---|
| **Valuing Audience and Purpose**<br>(1:45 min.)<br> (See Day 1 in "Learning to Write Nonfiction Reports: Daily Lesson Plans") | **NOTES**<br>State and district guidelines require teaching report writing in grade 4 as well as life zones and animals indigenous to Colorado. Darcy uses those requirements to teach writing with a real audience and purpose: students research, learn about, and write about Colorado animals and publish the results to share with other students and their families. (For more on audience and purpose, refer to *Conversations* excerpt, pp. 218–220.)<br><br>**TEACHING POINTS**<br>• Provide time and opportunity for all students to "turn-and-talk," sharing their ideas about audience and purpose for the writing.<br>• Make the writing interesting for the reader. Students mention using comparison and contrast, a good lead, wanting *"to do a good job so your mom and dad will say, 'I love it!'"* Other students say they *"want to make a good impression"* and *"lots of people are going to read it, so you want to do your best."* | Make sure students are clear on the purpose and audience for the report and notes. (Students do their best writing when they know and care about their audience.)<br>• *"Why are we writing these reports?"*<br>• *"Why else are you writing this?"* | <br>**Darcy asks the class, "Who is going to be reading our book?"** | • Analyze ideas, select a narrow topic, and elaborate using specific details or examples.<br>• Identify and include information a diverse audience needs to know (e.g., background information on the topic, definition of specialized vocabulary). |
| **Examining Nonfiction Texts**<br>(3:34 min.)<br>(See Day 2 in "Learning to Write Nonfiction Reports: Daily Lesson Plans") | **NOTES**<br>In the following scene, we continue to immerse students in nonfiction text. Darcy reads an example of nonfiction text written by a former student. Students are asked to say what the paragraph is about and then tell how the author made the paragraph interesting to read. (See author's craft chart at right.)<br><br>**TEACHING POINTS**<br>• Read aloud and project examples of student nonfiction work from previous year (or use any examples of excellent nonfiction writing). For the complete text that Darcy reads, see the draft on p. 12–16. | 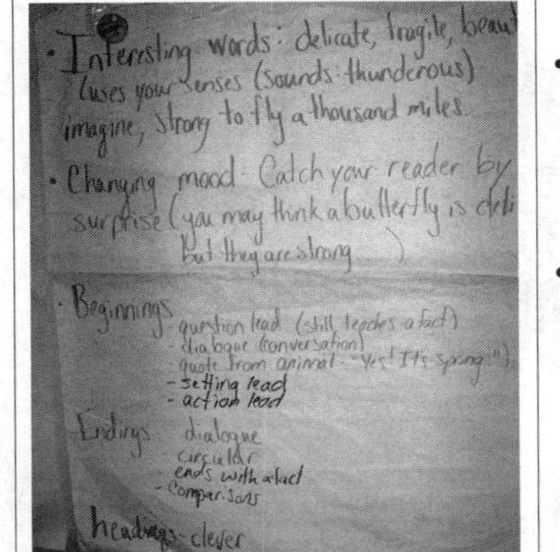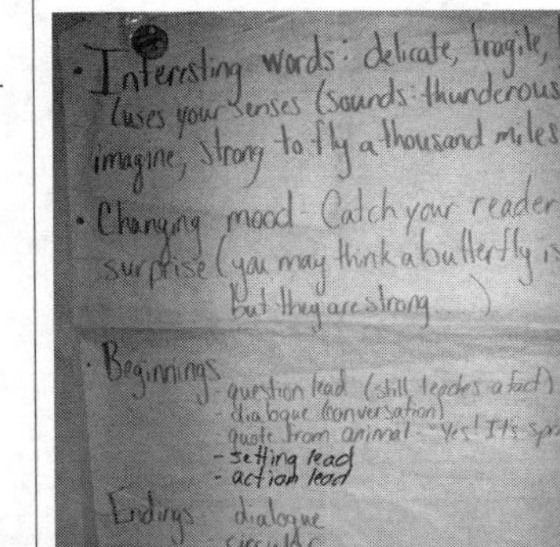<br><br>**Author's craft chart.** | • Why do you think it's beneficial to continue to immerse students in nonfiction text throughout the research process?<br>• What are the benefits of using text written by peers as models of good writing? (See *Conversations* excerpt, pp. 221–222.) | • Identify author's style and technique.<br>• Identify and use grade-level-appropriate text features. |

continues

# *Video* SCENES

**Examining Nonfiction Texts *continued***

## DEEPER UNDERSTANDING: Reading and Writing Nonfiction Reports

| Setting, Notes, and Explicit Teaching Points<br>The What, Why, and How of Teaching | Ongoing Assessment<br>Informing Our Instruction | Questions/Reflections<br>For Professional Conversations | Learning Outcomes<br>What Students Know and Are Able to Do |
|---|---|---|---|
| • Set listening expectations for a second reading of the example. *"I want you to be thinking about what this is about . . . and what makes the writing interesting."*<br>• Take every opportunity to refer students to resource charts around the room (so they will refer to these charts when writing).<br>• At the end of the lesson, ask students to think about how they may use author's craft in their own writing. *"So when you write your reports, you may want to do the same thing."*<br>• Provide time for students to share ideas with the whole group. | | **Darcy talks to the students about how humor makes you want to keep reading.** | • Use more than one resource (charts, notes, books, etc.). |
| • Connect what students notice in the reading with what students will be able to do when they write their own reports.<br><br>**Darcy discusses qualities of nonfiction texts with her students.** | Assess student understanding through questioning:<br>• Read the text first for understanding. *"What's it about?"*<br>• Read a second time. *"What makes the writing interesting?"*<br>• Give students time to discuss and share in small groups. *"What did you notice about the writing?"*<br>• Call on students randomly (to let students know everyone is expected to listen to their peers and be able to respond). *"I'm going to call on anyone because you've all had time to 'turn-and-talk'."*<br>• Acknowledge what students know about what makes the writing interesting (comparison, humor, ending). | • What are we teaching students by reading and rereading text before they "turn-and-talk"?<br>• Why is small-group "turn-and-talk" discussion a worthwhile activity?<br>• Why is it important to group four, five, or six students heterogeneously? | • Read several times adding specific details.<br>• Summarize information or ideas.<br>• Organize summary information in a teacher-selected organizer to enhance comprehension.<br>• Recognize and use previously learned organizational structures of nonfiction text.<br>• Identify where certain information/ideas might be found in nonfiction text.<br>• Explain how certain features of nonfiction text help us understand the content.<br>• Collect and use information from a variety of resources to solve a problem or answer a question. |

*Video* **SCENES**

**Turning Notes into Paragraphs: Demonstration Writing**

(5:06 min.)

(See Day 9 in "Learning to Write Nonfiction Reports: Daily Lesson Plans")

**DEEPER UNDERSTANDING: Reading and Writing Nonfiction Reports**

## Setting, Notes, and Explicit Teaching Points

The What, Why, and How of Teaching

**NOTES**

Darcy has chosen her own topic (beavers) to model the nonfiction writing process in front of her students. The notes she uses in this scene were taken on Day 6 during a lesson to teach students how to read nonfiction for facts and take notes. Here she is showing how to use those notes to write meaningful paragraphs.

**TEACHING POINTS**

- Review notes before writing the paragraph. (Darcy projects them on the screen.)
- Elaborate on notes while reviewing them. Show students how notes "jog" your memory.
- Think aloud and use notes while writing (*"keeping my notes handy"*).
- Begin writing by planning aloud. Writing and thinking aloud in front of students maximizes learning. Prewriting your whole piece at home does not show your students how writers work.
- Use what was noticed from examining models. *"Some of the stories or paragraphs that we read had conversation in them, so maybe I'll start with something the mom is saying."*
- Demonstrate the following as you compose your own writing in front of students (Darcy writes on a projected transparency):
  - Choose most important information from notes.
  - Stay focused on the topic.
  - Show ways to explain vocabulary.
    - *"One thing that I noticed that they do in nonfiction* [is] *. . . use parentheses* [to explain meaning]*."*
    - *". . . sometimes we use a comma after* yearling *to show that it means one-year-old."*

## Ongoing Assessment

Informing Our Instruction

After the demonstration has been completed, assess student learning in small groups to see what they noticed from you turning notes into a paragraph.

Check off all the points students notice from this list (or create your own list):

- Choose most important information.
- Delete information that does not answer a question or fit into the paragraph.
- Check off parts of notes used as you read along.
- Reread to help you decide what to say next.
- Stay focused on the topic.
- Explain vocabulary.
- Ensure facts are accurate and interesting.
- Use humor to teach facts.

## Questions/Reflections

For Professional Conversations

- By reviewing your notes and elaborating as you go, what are you teaching students about comprehension?
- Why is it important to write and think aloud in front of students versus doing the writing behind the scenes and then showing it to them? (Refer to *Writing Essentials*, pp. 157–159, on writing aloud and revising in front of students.)

Darcy modeling writing.

## Learning Outcomes

What Students Know and Are Able to Do

- Generate and answer questions before, during, and after reading.
- Use a variety of nonfiction text, identify and explain how the author's use of word choice, sentence structure, and length affect the reader.
- Make decisions about writing based on feedback.
- Reread work several times.
- Construct a recognizable introduction and ending.
- Write a logically organized paragraph.
- Revise at every stage of the writing process.
- Use a variety of transitional words and phrases.
- Use research to support ideas.
- Elaborate using details relevant to the topic.

continues

*Video* **SCENES**

**Turning Notes into Paragraphs: Demonstration Writing *continued***

**DEEPER UNDERSTANDING: Reading and Writing Nonfiction Reports**

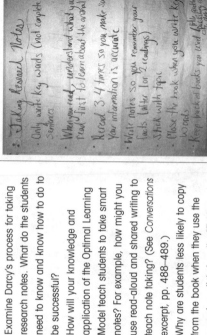

| Setting, Notes, and Explicit Teaching Points | Ongoing Assessment | Questions/Reflections | Learning Outcomes |
|---|---|---|---|
| The What, Why, and How of Teaching | Informing Our Instruction | For Professional Conversations | What Students Know and Are Able to Do |
| • Reread to:<br>  • Decide what to say next (use carets).<br>  • Delete information that does not answer a question or fit into the paragraph (cross out).<br>  • Change words or sentences (lasso and move).<br>  • Make sure draft makes sense.<br>• Use humor to teach facts.<br>  • *"Max used humor . . . I think I'll say 'stork delivery!'"*<br>• Check off parts of notes used as you read along.<br>• Ensure facts are accurate and interesting. *"Does she do this here?"*<br>• Perhaps write a heading or a title at the end to demonstrate that it's not necessary to have a title or a heading before you start your writing.<br>• Make connections with the reading and writing demonstrations to help students make their writing more interesting to the reader. | | • What is the purpose and value of rereading while writing?<br>• How will you teach students to make rereading and revising part of writing a draft?<br>• How has voice been part of this writing lesson even though the word *voice* has not been mentioned? | **Projected notes from the teacher demonstration.** |
| • Following the demonstration, expect students to take their own notes.<br>  • Remind students to take more notes than they will use. Overdo your notes so you can pick and choose.<br>  • Remind students that when they take notes they may find information that might be useful to another group. Suggest that they share that information with the appropriate group.<br>  • Review what students are to do before writing:<br>    • Reread notes several times.<br>    • *"Why do we read the first time through?"*<br>    • *"What do we do the second, third, fourth . . ."*<br>    • Look over "Taking Research Notes" chart. (Darcy rereads chart to students.) | Assess what students have taken away from your thinking-aloud and writing-aloud demonstration.<br>• *"Share with your table* [small group]. *What did you notice me doing when I turned my notes into a paragraph?"*<br>Students' replies include:<br>• *"Narrowing down information."*<br>• *"Checking off notes as you use them."*<br>• *"Focusing on one topic."* | • Examine Darcy's process for taking research notes. What do the students need to know and know how to do to be successful?<br>• How will your knowledge and application of the Optimal Learning Model teach students to take smart notes? For example, how might you use read-aloud and shared writing to teach note taking? (See *Conversations* excerpt, pp. 488–489.)<br>• Why are students less likely to copy from the book when they use the procedures listed on the "Taking Research Notes" chart? | Taking Research Notes<br>· Only write key words (not complete sentences<br>· When you read, understand what you read first to learn about the animal<br>· Reread 3-4 times so you make sure your information is accurate<br>· Write notes so you remember your facts (after 1 or 2 readings)<br>· Stick with topic<br>· Close the book when you write key words<br>· Keep track of books you used (title, author, publishing company, city, date)<br>**Shared writing on what students took away from the demonstration.** |

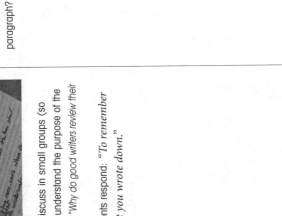

| *Video* SCENES | Setting, Notes, and Explicit Teaching Points<br>The What, Why, and How of Teaching | Ongoing Assessment<br>Informing Our Instruction | Questions/Reflections<br>For Professional Conversations | Learning Outcomes<br>What Students Know and Are Able to Do |
|---|---|---|---|---|
| **Turning Notes into Paragraphs: Shared Writing (Whole Class)**<br>(6:19 min.) | **NOTES**<br>Following up on what Darcy has just modeled in the previous scene, she and her students compose a paragraph together. Each student is first provided a copy of Darcy's notes (written by the class with her guidance) on "predators and prey." Before Darcy and the students write the paragraph, they read and revisit a published nonfiction paragraph on predators and prey (from last year's fourth-grade class) and discuss how the writer made the paragraph interesting to read. | 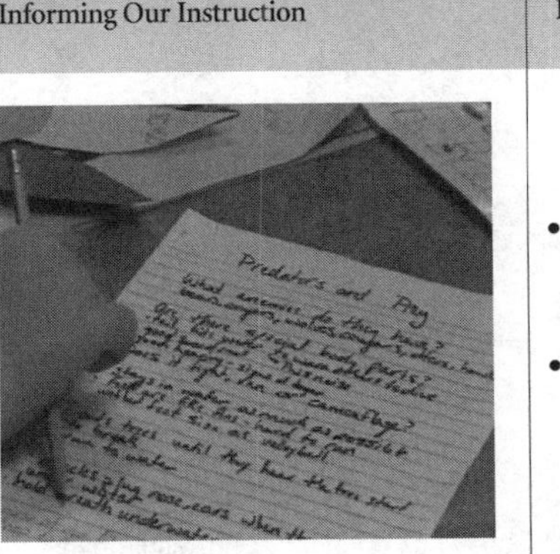 | • Why is it important for students to have a copy of the notes during shared writing?<br>• Why do you think it's a good idea to use notes previously taken in class to demonstrate how to turn notes into a paragraph? | 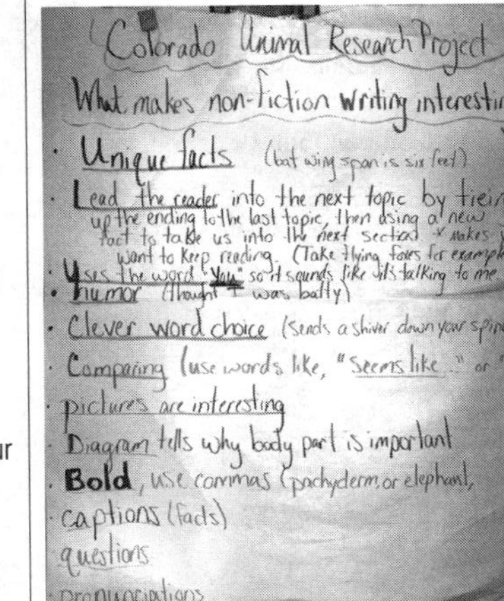<br><br>Shared writing: Taking notes. |
| (See Days 10 and 11 in "Learning to Write Nonfiction Reports: Daily Lesson Plans") | Darcy begins the shared writing with the whole class gathered on the floor at the front of the room. She writes on chart paper as she and her students negotiate text and write a paragraph together. This class paragraph will be about the beaver; focus will be on the subtopic—predators and prey. (Remember that you are demonstrating and setting expectations for what you want your students to do independently—in this case, independently as a small group.) | Review/discuss in small groups (so students understand the purpose of the lesson). *"Why do good writers review their notes?"*<br>• Students respond: *"To remember what you wrote down."* | | |
| • Reviewing Notes | **TEACHING POINTS**<br>• Refer to your notes to compose a paragraph and organize your thinking. *"I'm going to keep these notes with me so we can cross off as we use the information."*<br>• Project and review notes (so that students follow along). | | | Colorado Animal Research Project<br>What makes non-fiction writing interesting<br>• Unique facts<br>• Lead the reader into the next topic by tieing<br>• Humor<br>• Clever word choice<br>• Comparing<br>• pictures are interesting<br>• Diagram tells why body part is important<br>• Bold, use commas<br>• captions (facts)<br>• questions<br>• pronunciations |
| • Beginning the Shared Writing | • Review the "What Makes Our Writing Interesting?" chart (author's craft).<br>• Write with your reader in mind. Refer to making the writing interesting, accurate, or enjoyable, etc., for the audience, or reader, as often as possible: *"One thing I remember about interesting writing is beginnings. We want to make sure we bring our reader in so he wants to keep reading."* | Give students time to talk in small groups before making suggestions during shared writing (to "hear all the voices" and see what they have learned from immersion and your demonstrations).<br>• *"One thing I need you to be thinking about though is how are we going to start our paragraph so it's interesting. How should we begin our paragraph?"* | • How can you apply this shared writing demonstration to your grade-level content area?<br>• What topics would you choose?<br>• How would you modify and adjust your shared writing demonstration to meet the needs of your students? Why? | |

*continues*

*Video* **SCENES**

**Turning Notes into Paragraphs: Shared Writing (Whole Class) *continued***

**DEEPER UNDERSTANDING: Reading and Writing Nonfiction Reports**

<table>
<tr><th>Setting, Notes, and Explicit Teaching Points<br>The What, Why, and How of Teaching</th><th>Ongoing Assessment<br>Informing Our Instruction</th><th>Questions/Reflections<br>For Professional Conversations</th><th>Learning Outcomes<br>What Students Know and Are Able to Do</th></tr>
<tr>
<td>• Use headings as subtitles. Let the students know that it isn't necessary to have a heading before writing.<br>• Shape the writing (remember, you, the teacher, are in charge).<br>• Take all ideas from students (shows respect for the learner).<br>• Refer to notes while drafting (models what you expect students to do).<br>• Acknowledge students for what they are good at doing. "You're so good at those sound words. Wham's an option."<br>• Negotiate and check the text with students before writing it on the chart. "So is that OK with everybody?"<br>• Reread aloud with students as you write to make sure the writing makes sense and sounds good and to decide what to say next. "Let's see what we have so far. [Read it together.] Does that make sense?"<br>• Prompt students to clarify meaning. "What's a word we could use to explain [to our reader why].... Do you want to use ... or ..."?<br>• Periodically, refer to notes to check off entries that have been added to the paragraph.<br>• Here is the completed text based on the notes about beavers' predators/prey:<br><br>Danger! Danger! Whack! It's surprising that a beaver's tail only has to slap against the water to alert other beavers to dive under water. These extremely strong, expert swimmers can hold their breath for 10 minutes. That way otters, hawks, and owls can't snatch them. Is it safe now? Can I swim up to the surface again? The beavers can't stay in water forever. They need to come up sometime so they can breath, eat, and chop down wood to build and repair dams. Although these overgrown rodents are fast in water, they are clumsy on land.</td>
<td>• "What interesting information should we share [on predators and prey]?"<br><br>Probe and push students' thinking through questioning:<br>• "What words did your group come up with?"<br>• "What's a better word? What is the tail [of the beaver] doing? Talk to your partner."<br>• "How can we insert information?"<br>• "Is it just their family they are alerting?"<br>• "So now, I want you to share with your group. Where should we go next?"<br>When you do your own shared writing with your students, observe and listen carefully and use what you notice from students' responses and suggestions:<br>• Assess what they know about author's craft.<br>• What kinds of beginnings do they suggest: start with a question? start with an action word? a quotation?<br>• What do they know? What do you need to teach them?<br>• Assess their interaction with each other (give and take of information, who's doing the work, group dynamics).</td>
<td>• Why is it important to teach students to consider their audience while writing their reports?<br><br>• Why is it important to provide students with time to "turn-and-talk" during shared writing?<br><br>• Perhaps re-view the video while looking at a copy of the draft for specific reading and writing skills that were taught.</td>
<td>• Apply a variety of listening strategies to accommodate the listening situation:<br>  • Adapt listening behaviors to attend to a task.<br>  • Respond to verbal and nonverbal cues associated with the situation.<br>  • Sustain attention during group activities.<br>  • Use strategies for enjoyment, listening, active listening, and critical listening.<br>• Participate in shared reading/writing of texts.<br><br><br>During shared writing Darcy asks for students to give examples of some animals that prey on beavers so they can "sneak in" other facts about animals.</td>
</tr>
</table>

*Video* **SCENES**

**DEEPER UNDERSTANDING: Reading and Writing Nonfiction Reports**

| | Setting, Notes, and Explicit Teaching Points | Ongoing Assessment | Questions/Reflections | Learning Outcomes |
|---|---|---|---|---|
| | The What, Why, and How of Teaching | Informing Our Instruction | For Professional Conversations | What Students Know and Are Able to Do |
| | *Beavers do not run very well with their webbed feet. These feet, the size of a volleyball, put them in harm's way. That's why their hearing is stellar. They listen for bears, cougars, and wolves so they don't become beaver munch for their predators.* | | | |
| • Writing Research Reports: Small-Group Report Writing and Guided Practice<br><br>*(not shown on video)* | **NOTES**<br>Immediately following the whole-class shared writing, the students are given sustained time to work in small groups to write their paragraphs about their Colorado animal. The students choose one topic about their group's chosen animal from the following list and draft their paragraph:<br>• Where they live (habitat).<br>• Physical description.<br>• Prey/predators.<br>• Unique facts.<br>• Mating/babies.<br>• Food. | Darcy has several scaffolded conversations (talking, guiding, and supporting before writing) with groups of students to ensure that they are clear about what and how they are to write and work together.<br><br>While students are working in groups, Darcy has roving conferences with all groups, joins one group to offer more assistance, and makes anecdotal notes to be used for assessment and future instruction. | • What are the advantages of giving students time to talk in their groups before writing their paragraphs?<br><br>• How does this practice support English language learners and struggling readers and writers? | • Contribute to different parts of the writing process when working as a whole class or in small groups.<br>• Collaborate with a partner or a group on a writing project.<br>• Critique a peer's writing and support the opinion using established criteria (see sample rubric, p. 12–10).<br>• Edit as needed at every stage of the writing process.<br>• Work on a draft over several days.<br>• Provide evidence that writing goals have been met.<br>• Explain strengths and weaknesses of one's own writing using criteria (class rubric).<br>• Spell high-frequency words correctly.<br>• Use capitalization and convention rules learned in earlier grades. |

**Keep Away**

The mother raccoon is slowly creeping around in the long grass succeeding on staying away from her enemies. Some of the enemies are the mountain lion, the fox, the coyote and the wolf. If any of these enemies get near, the raccoon will start hissing and show its teeth so the enemy will run away. If the enemy doesn't run away, the raccoon will fight. At the end of the fight one or the other wins.

This raccoon is running away from an enemy.

**This is an example of a paragraph on Predators and Prey (written by a former student) that Darcy read to the class before they turned notes into a paragraph.** **See p. 12–23.**

# Video SCENES

**Conferring with Students: Small-Group Public Conferences**

(8:55 min.)

(See Days 11, 12, 13, and 14 in "Learning to Write Nonfiction Reports: Daily Lesson Plans")

## Deeper Understanding: Reading and Writing Nonfiction Reports

| Setting, Notes, and Explicit Teaching Points<br>The What, Why, and How of Teaching | Ongoing Assessment<br>Informing Our Instruction | Questions/Reflections<br>For Professional Conversations | Learning Outcomes<br>What Students Know and Are Able to Do |
|---|---|---|---|
| **NOTES**<br>In this scene, a small group of writers comes to the front of the class while the rest of the class remains seated on the floor in front of them. Students share their group-authored writing, and both teacher and students give feedback to the writers in a public conference, also called a whole-class share. Notice that Darcy's students are able to give helpful feedback because they have previously been taught how to do so and have had lots of guided practice. | Show group-authored draft.<br>• Make sure students understand the purpose for the whole-class share (so they invest their energies, listen carefully, and get ideas). *"Why else do we share? What are we celebrating?"*<br>• Check for careful listening and appropriate response to peer's writing.<br>  • Have students "turn-and-talk." *"What did you notice about this paragraph?"*<br>  • Randomly call on students (so all know they are expected to participate). *"What did your group notice?"* (Students comment on the beginning and good word choice, such as *scrumptious.*) | • Can you transfer the learning from this video scene to other content areas? Why or why not? Explain your thinking.<br>• What are the advantages of having the student or teacher read the piece a second time? (*Connect to Writing Essentials,* pp. 207–214.) | • Publish a piece of nonfiction writing and explain choice of format, graphics, and illustrations. |
| **TEACHING POINTS**<br>• Honor the writer by having one group member read the draft of the group-authored paragraph.<br>• Read the paragraph aloud again (so students and you have another opportunity to listen to the "whole" and think about how to respond).<br>• Celebrate, teach, reflect on student writing:<br>  • Piggyback on students' responses whenever appropriate. *"That was very clever of you to consider the sound the snake makes."*<br>  • Prompt for specificity. *"Give us an example"* [after a student says, *"They had good word choice"*].<br>  • Make it a point to elaborate students' comments into a teaching point by explaining exactly what the writer did and why it's good or important.<br>  • Ask questions of the writer and encourage other students to do the same. You might ask for clarification or give students something to think about and possibly add to their writing.<br>  • Reinforce student responses/suggestions to the writers. Perhaps, say things like:<br>    • *"I thought that was very clever."*<br>    • *"That was very smart thinking."*<br>    • *"I could tell you went back and reread. . . ."* | • Build on students' responses. *"Right, they're elaborating on. . . . They keep coming back to their big idea, so that was very smart writing. One question I have is. . . ."*<br>• Refer to student responses in public conferences when revising student writing:<br>  • *"What did we learn listening to other people's writing?"*<br>  • *"What are you going to try?"*<br>  • *"Why do we celebrate?"* | • Why do you think it's important to prompt students for an example when they say something like, *"They used good word choice,"* when giving feedback to the group?<br>• How can you emphasize the importance of word choice without isolating it as a separate lesson?<br>• How does immersion in nonfiction text prepare students to give feedback during public conferences? | |

*Video* **SCENES**

**Conferring with Students: Small-Group Public Conferences *continued***

**DEEPER UNDERSTANDING: Reading and Writing Nonfiction Reports**

| Setting, Notes, and Explicit Teaching Points | Ongoing Assessment | Questions/Reflections | Learning Outcomes |
|---|---|---|---|
| The What, Why, and How of Teaching | Informing Our Instruction | For Professional Conversations | What Students Know and Are Able to Do |
| • *"You did a really good job teaching the reader . . . ."*<br>• *"One thing you might want to think about. . . ."*<br>• *"That was very thoughtful. Thank you for mentioning that."*<br>• *"If you add that, it makes it much more accurate."*<br>• *"Something that really surprised me. . . ."*<br>• Make suggestions (don't give directives). *"You may want to add this, but you don't have to," or, "You may want to teach the reader about. . . ," or,* [after a student offers a suggestion] *"That might be something you want to think about."*<br><br>A small-group public conference. | When you conduct your own public conferences in your classroom, take charge of the celebration, teaching, assessing, and reflecting (see *Writing Essentials,* pp. 206–216). Use public conferences to assess what students know and are able to do.<br>• Make comments to students that help them move forward with their writing. (The quality of public conferences depends on the quality of the feedback.)<br><br>Have students share the responsibility for providing feedback during public conferences after they have had lots of opportunities to observe and practice what you have been demonstrating. Students need to learn what helpful feedback sounds like and also be knowledgeable about craft, content, writing forms, etc., and recognize them in examples of good writing.<br>• Use "turn-and-talk" to find out what students learned from the public conference(s) and may possibly apply to their own writing.<br>• Note student responses, process, and samples of group writing to measure growth. | • How can you connect the importance of revision to the audience for the writing?<br>• Why is it important for the writer to have the final decision on most of the suggestions that the teacher gives?<br>• How do we show respect for the writer during public conferences?<br>• What do you notice about Darcy's students during public conferences? | |

# SESSION 12 RESPONSE NOTES

***Engage, Reflect, Assess, Celebrate!***

Transforming our Teaching through
**Reading/Writing Connections**

# Using Writing to Reach and Teach Struggling Learners

**View Video** (32 min.)

### Using Writing to Reach and Teach Struggling Learners

SCENES WITH PRIMARY STUDENTS

- Raising Expectations and Beliefs for a Nonwriter: Akira
- Using Publishing to Motivate a Reluctant Writer: Jacob
- Turning a Child into a Reader Through His Writing: Matt

SCENES WITH INTERMEDIATE STUDENTS

- Setting the Scene for Writing Success
- A Public Scaffolded Conversation Before Writing: Tiara
- Small-Group Support Before Writing
- Writing Independently
- Celebration and Teaching Conference

## 1. Engage, Reflect, Assess

- *Small-Group Share:*
  - Discuss the previous *Try It/Apply It* experience with your vertical team: lesson plans, student work, observations, and ideas.
    - How did it go?
    - What did you notice when you did demonstrations? Shared experiences? Guided practice?
      - Demonstrate, through your own thinking, planning, and drafting, and through a class shared writing, how to write a short nonfiction report.

**RESOURCES**

**In this Session**
- Samples of Matt's Writing 13–6

**On the Website**
- Additional Samples of Student Work
- Publishing Resources
- Interview with Owen (a struggling student who became a writer) (See video resources, *Teaching Essentials* home page)

- Revise the report, dealing with such things as references, format, and illustrations.
- Publish the report for a selected audience (other students, the school library, new families to the school).

## 2. Discuss Professional Reading

- Discuss "Reading Nonfiction" and "On Research Writing" (*Conversations* excerpts, pp. 440–448, 482–490 and downloadable from the website).

## 3. Goals

- Observe how all students, regardless of former struggle or failure, are able to write successfully.
- Show how a public scaffolded conversation with a student, before writing, can ensure writing success and elicit elaboration and detail in a child's oral and written story.
- Support and teach readers who struggle by using their own written texts as reading materials.
- Celebrate all learners' strengths.

## 4. View Video and Take Notes

- Turn to the Notecatcher to take notes during the video.

## 5. Respond to the Video

- Share your thinking with your small-group. Perhaps use the following questions in your discussion:
  - Why were all students able to write successfully?
  - What did you see the teacher do to help these struggling students be successful readers through writing?
  - What did you notice about the impact of first-time writing success on writers who struggle?

## 6. Achieve a Deeper Understanding

- Read and review the Deeper Understanding charts to help recall or think more deeply about the purpose of supporting struggling readers by using writing as an instructional focus.
- The Notes, Teaching Points, Ongoing Assessment, and Questions/Reflections are designed to personalize and accelerate your learning, challenge your thinking, and guide your weekly schoolwide conversations between whole-group sessions.

## 7. *Try It/Apply It* in the Classroom

- Choose one or more of your struggling students and use the examples and demonstrations from this session (as well as previous sessions) to plan and implement a lesson in which students will be immediately successful writing and reading their own student-authored text.
- Have one or more public scaffolded conversations before writing. In a natural back-and-forth conversation, help the student "find" his or her story. Use the video and/or Deeper Understanding charts to help you discover language you might use in soliciting the story from the student.
- Quickly and easily celebrate and publish (if possible) your student's writing, and keep the focus on the student's strengths.

## 8. Wrap-Up

- Before next session read "Working with Struggling Readers" and "Teaching for Strategies" (*Conversations* excerpts, pp. 121–130, 130–136 and downloadable from the website).
- Schedule time to meet with your vertical, grade-level, and/or partner teams in between whole-group sessions to revisit the videos on the website and the Deeper Understanding charts and/or plan together and try out new learning.
- Remember to bring any charts, lessons, writing, or student work samples from the *Try It/Apply It* to the next session.

**Celebrating Antonio's writing.**

# SESSION 13 NOTECATCHER

| VIDEO SCENES | LENGTH | NOTES & REFLECTION |
|---|---|---|
| **SCENES WITH PRIMARY STUDENTS** | | |
| **Raising Expectations and Beliefs for a Nonwriter: Akira (First Grader)** | 1:48 min. | |
| **Using Publishing to Motivate a Reluctant Writer: Jacob (First Grader)** | 11:30 min. | |
| • Day 1: Scaffolded Conversation Before Writing | | |
| • Day 2: Celebration Conference | | |
| • Day 3: From Draft to Published Book | | |
| **Turning a Child into a Reader Through His Writing: Matt (First Grader)** | 4:36 min. | |
| • Day 1: Roving Conference | | |
| • Day 2: Public Conference: Celebrating the Writer | | |
| • Day 3: Using Lines and Spacing to Make Writing Easier to Read | | |

# SESSION 13 NOTECATCHER

| VIDEO SCENES | LENGTH | NOTES & REFLECTION |
|---|---|---|
| **SCENES WITH INTERMEDIATE STUDENTS** | | |
| **Setting the Scene for Writing Success** | 1:09 min. | |
| **A Public Scaffolded Conversation Before Writing: Tiara**<br>• Tiara (Fourth Grader) | 4:41 min. | |
| **Small-Group Support Before Writing**<br>• Courtney (Fourth Grader)<br>• Antonio (Fourth Grader) | 2:13 min. | |
| **Writing Independently** | 0:19 sec. | |
| **Celebration and Teaching Conference**<br>• Antonio | 5:58 min. | |

# Samples of Matt's Writing

Matt's first-grade teacher, Nancy McLean, reports that Matt had a great interest in nonfiction and curiosity about the world around him. While he was struggling to learn letters and sounds in reading, he began to transfer that letter–sound knowledge first to his writing.

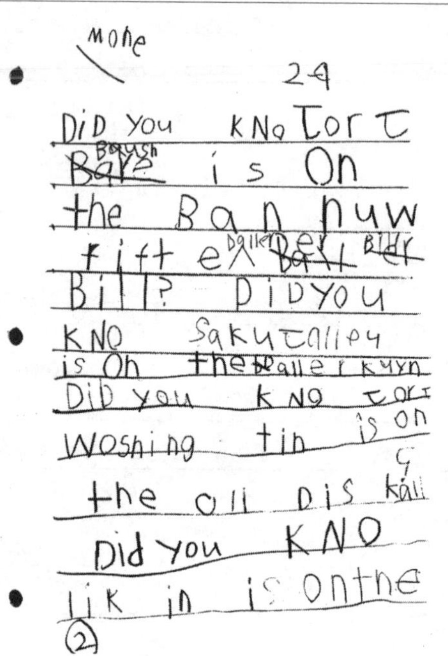

Interesting Facts
The strongest wolf is the leader of the pack. Wolves use their ears to hear animals moving around. A large male wolf can be three feet tall.


**See Matt's writing-to-reading story on pp. 13–14 and 13–15.**

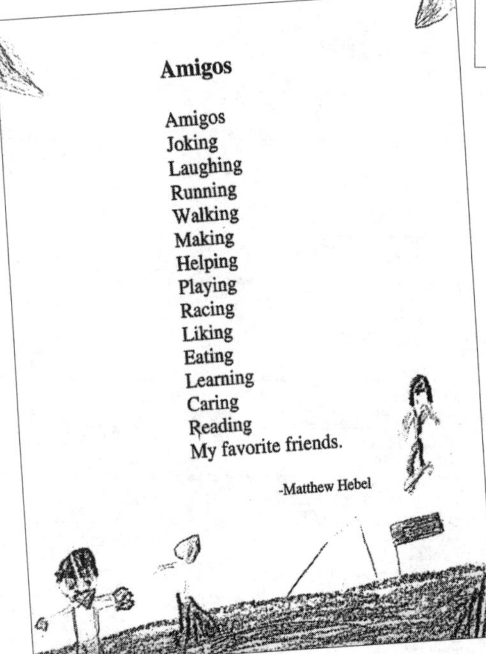
**Amigos**

Amigos
Joking
Laughing
Running
Walking
Making
Helping
Playing
Racing
Liking
Eating
Learning
Caring
Reading
My favorite friends.

-Matthew Hebel

The Dirt Hill

I went to a MASSIVE dirt hill! I climbed up. I fell off the dirt hill on my first try. Then I fell again. Finally I got it. I had fun. I found my friends on top of the hill.

Notice how strong Matt's content is. Once he was celebrated for his writing, it began to be important to him to have readers be able to read his writing, and he worked harder at spacing and applying his growing letter–sound knowledge. His writing became his reading texts. His poem was a result of a poetry focus in his classroom and all the rich language he was hearing. A page from his nonfiction published book about wolves shows his continuing interest in writing nonfiction.

# Samples of Matt's Writing, *continued*

I am working on
my story.


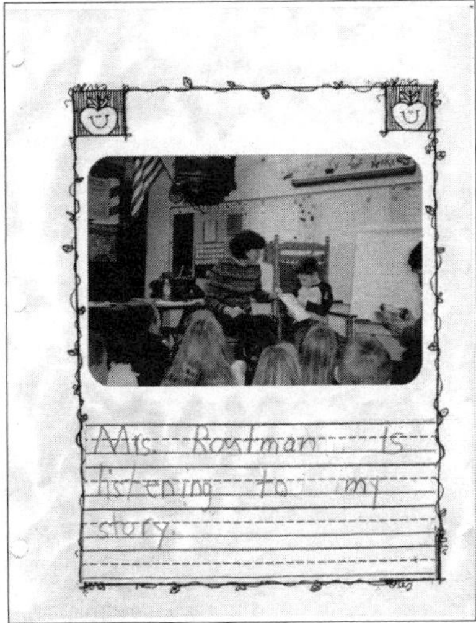

Mrs. Routman is
listening to my
story.


Once a month, Nancy McLean takes photos of students' learning experiences. Here are two pages from Matt's portfolio, which becomes an end-of-the-year memory scrapbook that both kids and parents treasure.

Dear Mrs. Routman,
How are you? I went horse back riting Im Reading the Harry Potter series.
from Matthew Hebel.

Matt's writing turns him into an avid reader! Here is a letter he wrote to me over the summer after grade 1 and my reply (right).

8.23

Dear Matt,

Thanks for your note. I loved getting it. It's amazing what a great reader and writer you are. Congratulations!

I remember when I first met you, back in February. You weren't reading yet, but I knew by your writing (I could read your terrific story about money) that you were ready to take off. And you did. Your own stories became the first stories you read in school. And, now, Harry Potter. Awesome!

Good luck in second grade.

Love,
Mrs. Routman

SESSION **13**

**Using Writing to Reach and Teach Struggling Learners**

# DEEPER UNDERSTANDING

*The teaching and assessing points reflect the total lesson but not all of these points are on the edited videos you are watching. However, the major points are represented on the edited videos.*

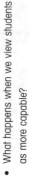

WWW The globe icon indicates that the example is also available when you visit www.regieroutman.com.

| *Video* SCENES | Setting, Notes, and Explicit Teaching Points | Ongoing Assessment | Questions/Reflections | Learning Outcomes |
|---|---|---|---|---|
| | The What, Why, and How of Teaching | Informing Our Instruction | For Professional Conversations | What Students Know and Are Able to Do |
| | **SETTING**<br>These scenes were filmed in schools in three diverse regions—the Northwest, the South, and the Midwest. Two of the schools have large numbers of English language learners and students from families with low incomes. The students in these scenes show what's possible for *all* students when we set aside assumptions, raise our expectations, teach explicitly, and celebrate learning accomplishments. In particular, the powerful influence of writing on reading is demonstrated and celebrated. | Conferences enable us to move the students forward. Notice how a one-on-one conference can take place publicly. Not only does the whole class benefit by getting ideas, but the student who has not been seen by his peers as a "star" gains a new standing in the classroom. Notice, too, the power of publishing a child's writing on his reading and self-esteem. | • What are you doing in your classroom and school to ensure that students who struggle are meeting success? | |
| **SCENES WITH PRIMARY STUDENTS**<br>2<br>**Raising Expectations and Beliefs for a Nonwriter: Akira (First Grader)**<br>(1:48 min.) | **NOTES**<br>Akira is a first grader who arrived in the United States in January, mid–school year. He had only been in school for two weeks when I met him. An English language learner (his first language was Hmong), he appeared to have almost no letter–sound knowledge; that is, he independently wrote only a handful of letters. Therefore, his teacher believed he could not write and did so for him as he dictated. As I sat next to Akira and worked with him one-on-one, the observing teachers and I were surprised to find out that he knew much more than everyone thought.<br><br>Once Akira knew he could write without assistance and that we now held that expectation, he took over and became independent. His writing texts—all about his family—became his first reading texts. His classroom teacher, Nancy McLean, said, "He soared in every way. Quickly, he was on the road to becoming a great reader and writer. He now had confidence and believed he could do it."<br><br>This brief scene is part of a roving conference in process taking place as students are writing independently. | <br>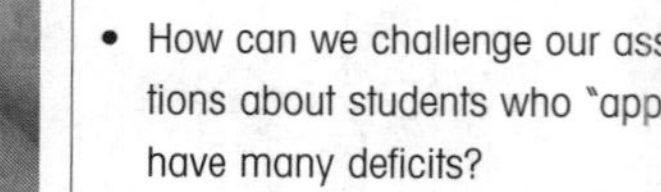<br>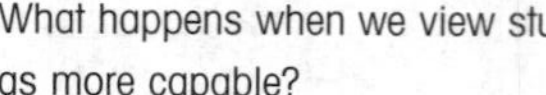<br>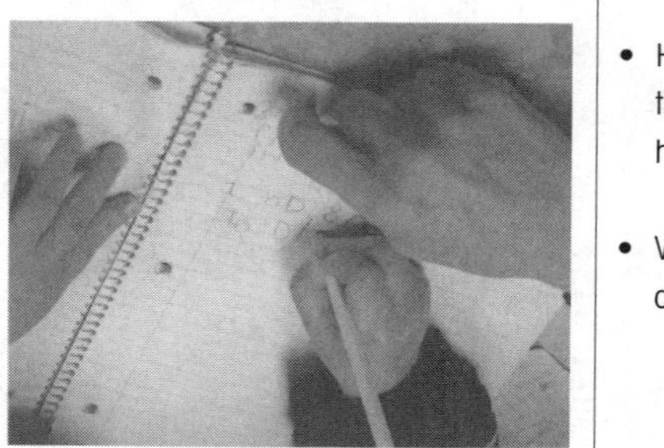<br>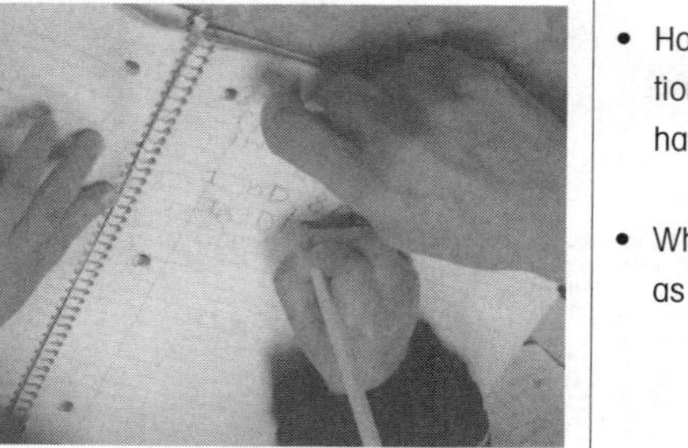<br>**Conferring with Akira.** | • How can we challenge our assumptions about students who "appear" to have many deficits?<br><br>• What happens when we view students as more capable? | |

# Video SCENES

**Deeper Understanding:** Using Writing to Reach and Teach Struggling Learners

| | Setting, Notes, and Explicit Teaching Points<br>The What, Why, and How of Teaching | Ongoing Assessment<br>Informing Our Instruction | Questions/Reflections<br>For Professional Conversations | Learning Outcomes<br>What Students Know and Are Able to Do |
|---|---|---|---|---|
| | **TEACHING POINTS**<br>• Space words when writing (so reader can read the writing). *"Now this is going to get tricky for the reader right here because this looks like one word. You forgot to space here . . . use your finger."*<br>• Teach high-frequency words student needs and is ready to learn (in this case, *my*). *"I want to show you because you're so close and you're going to be writing that word a lot. . . ."*<br>• Show student how to help himself. (I take him over to word wall.)<br>• Set expectation for correct spelling of important word. "My *is a word that you probably know that you're not allowed to misspell in first grade."*<br>• Teach self-checking. *"It is on the word wall. So let's go over to the word all and see if we can find it."* (I walk with Akira to word wall.)<br>• Confirm the word (on the word wall). *"What does this word say? This says* me *and this says. . . ."*<br>Akira: *"My."*<br>• Set expectations for what student is to do on his own. *"And leave a space. . . . You don't need any more help. . . . Go back and read what you have and finish—keep writing, keep writing."*<br>• Celebrate. *"When you finish, I want you to bring it up because, guess what, we want to celebrate what you did, and I want to be able to call on you tomorrow to share."* | Find out what the student knows and is applying (so you know what to teach and can encourage independence):<br>• *"How do you spell* my*?"*<br>Akira: *"M."*<br>"My *is a word you should know. Is it on your word wall? Where could you find* my*?"*<br>[No response.]<br>• *"What do you hear at the end?* My.*"*<br>Akira: *"I hear /o/."*<br>Expect self-checking:<br>• *"OK, write it down. And then, let's see, is it on the. . . ."*<br>Mrs. McLean: *"It is on the word wall."*<br>Check that the student has learned what you taught:<br>• *"And so, how do you spell* my*?"*<br>Akira: *"M, y."*<br>*"Write it."* [Akira writes it correctly.] | • Why is it important to teach students to be as independent as possible right from the start? | • Recognize the difference between words and sentences.<br>• Identify words and their beginning and ending letters.<br>• Read selected sight words with automaticity.<br>• Use simple resources with teacher guidance (word wall).<br>• Decode words in isolation and in context. |
| **Using Publishing to Motivate a Reluctant Writer: Jacob (First Grader)**<br>(11:30 min.)<br>• Day 1: Scaffolded Conversation Before Writing | **NOTES**<br>First-grader Jacob had a talent for storytelling about his experiences, but that talent was not showing up in his writing. In October, when I met him in a writing residency, according to his classroom teacher, Chris Axel, "He was not producing much as a writer and was taking few risks."<br>In addition to the usual frontloading before students wrote, I showed the class copies of other first graders' published stories as models for their own storytelling and writing. We have just completed a couple of public scaffolded conversations, and I am giving last-minute instructions about choosing a real-life | Before I began teaching students in this classroom, I started with assessment (see chart at right). Notice how initial responses about what good writers do focus on neatness and correctness, which mirrors the writing they have been producing. With demonstrations and scaffolding, their knowledge grows and the chart list gets richer, as does their writing. | 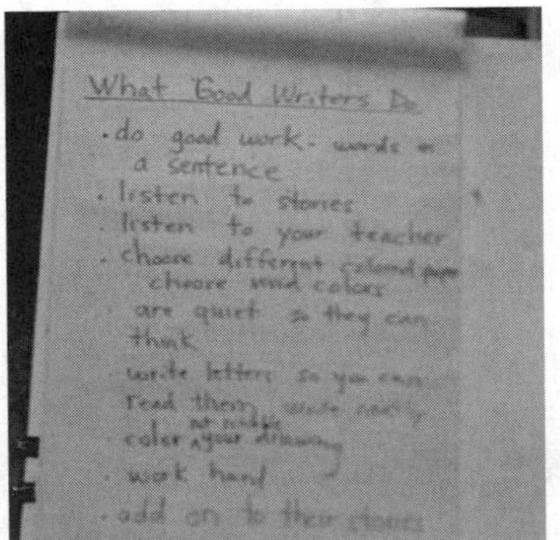 | |

continues

*Video* **SCENES**

**DEEPER UNDERSTANDING: Using Writing to Reach and Teach Struggling Learners**

| Setting, Notes, and Explicit Teaching Points<br>The What, Why, and How of Teaching | Ongoing Assessment<br>Informing Our Instruction | Questions/Reflections<br>For Professional Conversations | Learning Outcomes<br>What Students Know and Are Able to Do |
|---|---|---|---|

- Day 1: Scaffolded Conversation Before Writing *continued*

topic before sending students off to write. Because I am confused by Jacob's comment about wanting to write about ten houses, I invite him, on the spot, to have a public scaffolded conversation with me.

**TEACHING POINTS**

- Writers write for readers. *"So it has to be a really interesting story, because otherwise nobody's going to want to read it . . . be thinking about the best words you can use."*
- Give additional ideas for writing topics. *"You could write about a grandparent . . . a bicycle . . . spending time with your mom or your dad or your uncle . . . sports . . . losing teeth."*

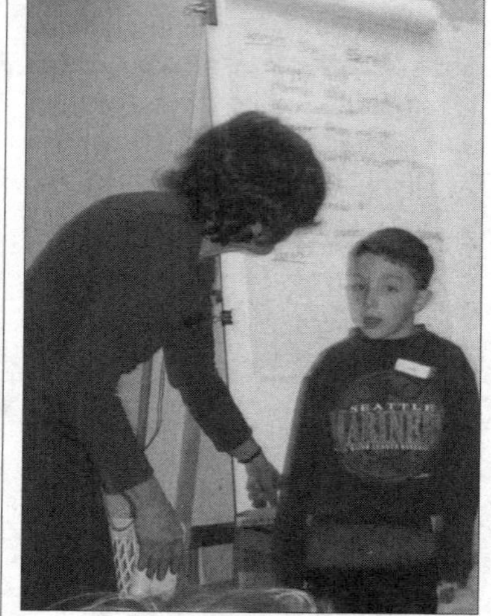

**My scaffolded conversation with Jacob.**

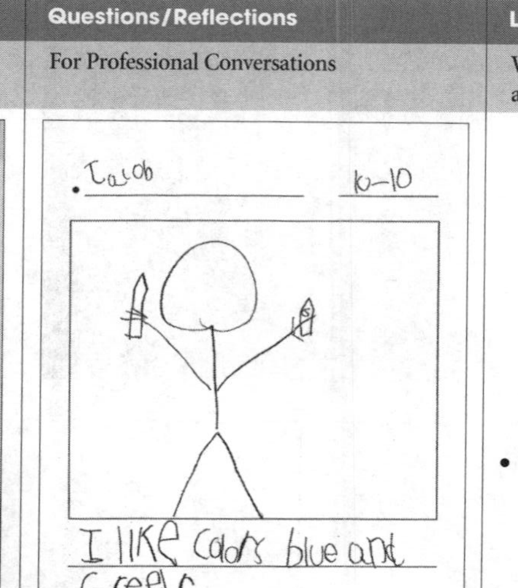

Jacob
10-10
I lIKE Colors blue and Green
Name Jacob
Date 10-3
I live ten HoSEES.


**Typical writing by Jacob before a writing demo and scaffolded conversation.**

- Participate orally in discussion about stories listened to and read (e.g., contribute who, what, when, where; in retells, contribute explanations; generate and answer questions; and/or make comparisons).

- Guide student to choose a new topic (when his topic doesn't make sense). *"What's something that you really are interested in . . . or that you know a lot about?"*
  Jacob: *"I lost a tooth."* *"How many teeth have you lost?"*
  Jacob: *"Four."*
- Encourage writing with detail (without labeling it detail). *"If you just say, 'I lost a tooth,' I want to hear about it. Did you have to twist it? Did the tooth fairy come? Was there blood? We want to hear what happened, everything that happened."*
- Use natural back-and-forth conversation to get students to elaborate on their story. *"Okay, can you tell us about what that was like? What happened the last time you lost a tooth? . . . Did you say something to Mom or someone in your family?"*
  Jacob: *"I told my dad, 'I've got a lose tooth.'"*
- Show how to write conversation in a story. *"I want to show you what that looks like* [I write 'I told my dad I have a loose tooth' on the chart]*."*

Pay attention to students' responses and provide more scaffolding, as needed.

- *"You want to write about ten houses."*
  Jacob: *"Yeah."*
  *"I don't know if I understand what that means."*
  Jacob: *"Houses, ten of them. Ten houses."*
  Mrs. Axel: *"He has been writing about ten houses."*

Confer with a student who is not ready to write (on an appropriate topic).

- *"Let's have you come up, Jacob. . . . By the way, the reason that I want Jacob to tell his story is because that's going to help some of you get some ideas. . . . You're not living in ten houses right? You're living in one house . . . ."*

- How does topic choice influence writing engagement and the quality of students' writing?

- Brainstorm, make lists, and sometimes formulate first sentence before writing.
- Write for self, family, friends, and teacher.
- Write to express own ideas.
- Develop and choose from a list of topics.
- Elaborate on ideas using descriptive words and phrases.

**Video SCENES**

**DEEPER UNDERSTANDING: Using Writing to Reach and Teach Struggling Learners**

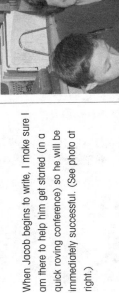

| | Setting, Notes, and Explicit Teaching Points<br>The What, Why, and How of Teaching | Ongoing Assessment<br>Informing Our Instruction | Questions/Reflections<br>For Professional Conversations | Learning Outcomes<br>What Students Know and Are Able to Do |
|---|---|---|---|---|
| | • Teach all students what you are teaching one. *"Watch this, kids, because this is something good writers do. They put talking in their story. 'I have a loose tooth'* [saying each word aloud as I write sentence on chart]*. . . . These are talking marks"* [adding quotation marks].<br>• Continue scaffolded conversation until you feel the student will be able to write beginning of story on his own. *"And what did Dad say?"*<br>Jacob: *"He said, 'We need to pull it out.'"*<br>*"Oh! He did? He said, 'We need to pull it out'"* [writing it on chart].<br>Jacob: *"Yeah."*<br>*". . . And did you let him?"*<br>Jacob: *"Yeah."*<br>*"So how did he pull it out? . . . Was there blood? . . . You were really, really brave."*<br>• Celebrate. *"Let's give Jacob a round of applause."* (Jacob and all students now have 15 minutes in which to write.) | Write down key words, phrases, and sentences (to remind student what he said, to encourage him to use his "smart language," and to assess and record what took place in the conference). Here, because many teachers are observing and I want them to see my jottings, I write on a chart. Usually, I write on sticky notes and give them to the student who adheres them to her or his writing. (Some teachers create/buy very small spiral notebooks for this purpose, so that these notes are all saved in one place.) | • What is the role of celebration in teaching and learning? <br>**A scaffolded conversation before writing.** | |
| • Day 2: Celebration Conference | **NOTES**<br>On Day 2, we celebrate before students write to affirm what they have done well, make teaching points to move them forward, and make suggestions to extend their writing and independence.<br><br>**TEACHING POINTS**<br>• Recognize and show a student's writing improvement (to recognize the student and show his peers what's possible). *"Jacob wrote on Oct 10th, 'I like colors blue and green,' and he's got perfect spelling. And before that. . . ."* (See p. 13–10.)<br>Jacob: *"I like ten houses."*<br>*"But yesterday, Jacob, you did your very best writing."* | When Jacob begins to write, I make sure I am there to help him get started (in a quick roving conference) so he will be immediately successful. (See photo at right.) |  **During roving conferences, try to get to your most struggling students first so they get off to a good start.** | • Share writing with others. |

*continues*

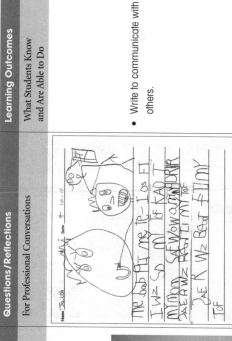

**DEEPER UNDERSTANDING: Using Writing to Reach and Teach Struggling Learners**

*Video* **SCENES**

- Day 2: Celebration Conference *continued*

### Setting, Notes, and Explicit Teaching Points
The What, Why, and How of Teaching

- Have student read his writing aloud (honors the child).
- Comment on everything student has done well (so his efforts are affirmed, so he will do it again, so others will do it). *"Let's go over this again, because that was really wonderful writing"* [reading it again and commenting on length, picture, language].
- Help student move forward (so he can continue to work independently).

  *"My tooth came out."*

  *"What happened then? What are you going to say next? Did Dad say anything?"*

  Jacob: *"My mom said something."*

  *"What did she say?"*

  Jacob: *"She said, 'Wow.'"*
- Demonstrate how and why to use quotation marks. *"Some of you are ready for this* [putting quotation marks around *Wow*] *. . . that lets us know that Mom said it."*
- Show how a writer learning to spell a longer word can put a dash within a word to designate unknown letters. *"He just put a dash here* [after writing T-E for tooth] *and that lets the reader know there are more letters."*
- Use responsive questioning to help student continue story.

  *"'My mom said, "Wow."' And then what happened?"*

  Jacob: *"And then my brother came out and he said, 'There's blood coming out of his mouth.'"*
- Post family words used in everyday writing. *"Let's add the word* brother *to our family words because a lot of you are using that"* [putting it on family words chart].
- Teach self-directing behavior for finding the spelling of a word on a posted chart. *"So you know what you can do, Jacob, when you're writing the word* brother*. You can pick yourself up and go over to the family words and copy down the word, OK?"*

### Ongoing Assessment
Informing Our Instruction

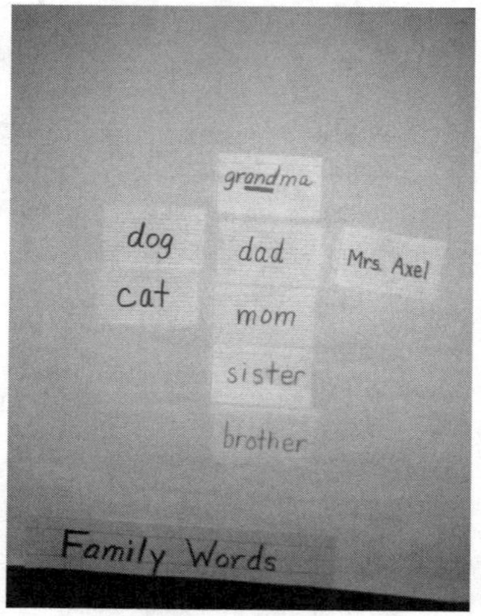


Check that students are using room resources to help spell words.

- *"Where can you find the spelling of mom . . . ?"*

  Student: *"Family words."*

Help students connect known parts of one word to other words.

- "Brother *ends just like* other, teacher. *What were those two letters? Who remembers?"*

  Student: *"E-r."*
- "Brother. *It has* other *in it. We had the word* other *this morning. . . . So if you know* other, *then we can do* brother."

### Questions/Reflections
For Professional Conversations

**Jacob's published draft:**

**My dad pulled my tooth.**
**I was afraid. I was sad.**
**My tooth came out!**
**My mom said, "WOW!"**
**My brother said there was blood on my tooth.**

- Why is it important to post high-frequency words and teach young writers how to access them?

### Learning Outcomes
What Students Know and Are Able to Do

- Write to communicate with others.
- Read own work and make some changes, especially punctuation.
- Edit shared text with teacher guidance.
- Read aloud familiar grade-level text with accuracy in a manner that sounds like natural speech.
- Read selected sight words with automaticity.

**Deeper Understanding: Using Writing to Reach and Teach Struggling Learners**

*Video* **SCENES**

- Day 3: From Draft to Published Book

| Setting, Notes, and Explicit Teaching Points | Ongoing Assessment | Questions/Reflections | Learning Outcomes |
|---|---|---|---|
| The What, Why, and How of Teaching | Informing Our Instruction | For Professional Conversations | What Students Know and Are Able to Do |

### Setting, Notes, and Explicit Teaching Points

**NOTES**

Because the loose tooth story is, by far, Jacob's best writing to date, we publish it immediately: to celebrate his success, to provide accessible reading text for him, and to use the publishing process to motivate other writers.

**TEACHING POINTS**

- Publish in a timely fashion (to recognize writers' efforts and show writing-to-reading connection). Mrs. Axel: *"Next week, everybody will be published."*
- Suggest that the writer might want to add a title to his story. *"Your book is about when your dad pulled your tooth out. What do you want to call it? You could call it 'Loose Tooth.'"* [No response.] *"We can add the title later."* [I reread Jacob's story.]
- Connect reading with writing. *"Can you read us this? Use your reading finger."*
- Discourage copying over writing (wastes time and takes energy that could go to writing). [Jacob has copied his story over twice.] *"You're working too hard. We want you to have fun with your writing . . . it just has to be neat enough so that you can read it."*
- Reread story to get an idea for the ending and the title. *"Tell us how you want to end it. . . . What's your whole story about?"*
- Help refine the title, if needed, but leave final choice to student. *"You want to call it 'My Teeth.' . . . Or do you want to call it 'My Tooth,' because it's really about just one tooth that came out? What do you think?"*

  Jacob: *"It would be good."*

  *"It can be the way you want it. You're OK with that?"*

  Jacob: *"Yeah."*
- Model the publishing process (so students know what to expect). *"Now watch what your teacher is doing. Everybody's going to get to do this."* [Mrs. Axel begins to scribe Jacob's title and story.]
- Publish side by side with the child and provide options for page layout. *"You get to decide . . . how you want it laid out* [reading some text]. *What do you think? Do you want that on your first page?"*

### Ongoing Assessment

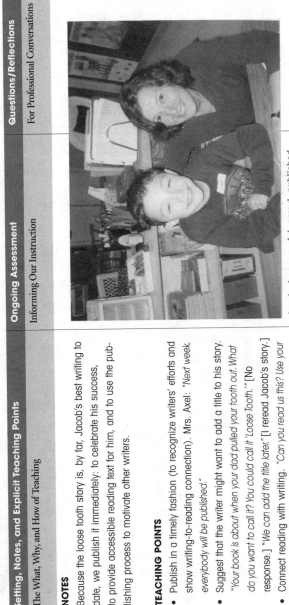

Jacob: A successful, proud, published writer.

Jacob makes decisions on how he wants his published book to look.

### Questions/Reflections

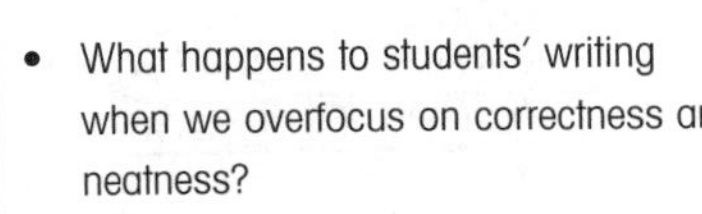

- What happens to students' writing when we overfocus on correctness and neatness?
- Because the writing-to-reading connection is so powerful, think about and plan how you might do more publishing with your students.

### Learning Outcomes

- Share writing in self-published texts.
- Identify the intended audience for a written piece.
- Use directionality when reading independently.
- Recognize that print represents spoken language.
- Recognize the difference between words and sentences.
- Select a title for a piece of writing.
- Share writing in self-published books.

continues

**DEEPER UNDERSTANDING: Using Writing to Reach and Teach Struggling Learners**

| *Video* SCENES | Setting, Notes, and Explicit Teaching Points<br>The What, Why, and How of Teaching | Ongoing Assessment<br>Informing Our Instruction | Questions/Reflections<br>For Professional Conversations | Learning Outcomes<br>What Students Know and Are Able to Do |
|---|---|---|---|---|
| • Day 3: From Draft to Published Book *continued* | Jacob: *"Yeah."*<br>*"Would the next page be . . . ?"*<br>• Explain that illustrations are important to support the text and perhaps to provide information not in the text. *"Maybe your writing is very short; you can have all kinds of stuff in your drawing, for the reader. . . ."* | | • What is the role of drawing and illustration in writing? When should it be emphasized? How much time should be spent on it? | • Illustrate work (e.g., drawings, computer graphics, collages). |
| **Turning a Child Into a Reader Through His Writing: Matt (First Grader)**<br>(4:36 min.)<br><br>• Day 1: Roving Conference | **NOTES**<br>By midyear in first grade, Matthew was not progressing as a reader in spite of high intelligence and superior verbal and listening skills. Because Matthew was not reading, he was about to be referred for evaluation. Matt's writing indicated good knowledge of letters and sounds and a great interest in nonfiction. I therefore suggested to his classroom teacher that we turn his daily writing into texts for reading before following through on the referral. We did, and Matthew took off as a reader! His solid interest in nonfiction, which fueled his desire to write, now motivated him to read his own word-processed stories. In independent reading, he focused on nonfiction, and that interest and knowledge carried over into his writing. By the end of the school year, he was a solid grade-level reader and was enjoying listening to Harry Potter being read aloud.<br>In this first brief scene, I look in on Matt as I am conducting brief, roving conferences in the classroom.<br><br>**TEACHING POINTS**<br>• Affirm what the writer has done well.<br>• Opening sentence. *"That is an amazing first sentence. 'Did you know that Ben Franklin was on the two-dollar bill?' Wow."*<br>Matt: *"And Lincoln's on the five."*<br>• Meaningful topic. *"So you're writing about money?"*<br>• Rereading. *"I could tell you were rereading because you've got those carets in there."*<br>• Writing with the reader in mind. *"Also, starting with a question like that really lets me know that you're thinking about the reader."*<br>• Celebrate. *"That's a great start. I'm going to definitely have you share."* | | • What are the advantages and disadvantages of quick, roving conferences? What role do such conferences play in the writing process? | Conferring with Matt.<br><br>See more samples of Matt's writing on pp. 13–6 and 13–7.<br><br>• Elaborate on ideas using descriptive words and phrases.<br>• Develop ideas from topics orally and visually.<br>• Write for an intended audience and purpose.<br>• Write to inform. |

**Deeper Understanding: Using Writing to Reach and Teach Struggling Learners**

# *Video* SCENES

| | Setting, Notes, and Explicit Teaching Points<br>The What, Why, and How of Teaching | Ongoing Assessment<br>Informing Our Instruction | Questions/Reflections<br>For Professional Conversations | Learning Outcomes<br>What Students Know and Are Able to Do |
|---|---|---|---|---|
| • Day 2: Public Conference: Celebrating the Writer | **TEACHING POINTS**<br>• Have student read his own writing and point to words as he reads (respects writer to have him read his writing; pointing to words while reading cements writing-to-reading connection).<br>• Face student's writing outward so class can see it (keeps students' attention and makes it easier to notice writing attributes).<br>• Reread student's writing (to get sense of whole, to decide what to comment on, for students to hear it clearly).<br>• State what writer has done well. [The initial question, spelling money *m-u-n-y* and then adding an *e*, title of story ("Money"), specific information about dollar bills.]<br>• Encourage the writer to add pertinent information. *"You might want to add that in there"* [after Matt says: *"They don't make them* (two-dollar bills) *anymore"*].<br>• Provide the help the writer/reader needs to move forward (in this case, having lines to write on and spacing words when writing).<br>• Explain why you're giving the particular help (so writer sees and values the purpose). *"You know why you're having a little trouble* [reading the writing]*? . . . the lines and the spacing . . . that will make it easier for everybody to hear your great words. . . . Tomorrow, right before you start writing, I'm going to help you just get your lines straight to make it easier for you."*<br>• Celebrate. *"Matt, I haven't seen anyone write like this in first grade. It's really great, isn't it. Let's give him a round of applause."* | Decide what the writer needs most to move forward as an independent writer. | • Think about/discuss the impact of commenting on content before conventions. What is the balance? | • Reread own work and make some revisions in response to teacher questions and peer feedback.<br>• Reread draft to self, peers, or adults.<br>• Write a draft that includes more than one sentence.<br>• Add detail and elaborate on ideas using descriptive words and phrases.<br>• Write for an audience and purpose. |
| • Day 3: Using Lines and Spacing to Make Writing Easier to Read | **NOTES**<br>Before Matt begins to write again, I have added lines on Matt's paper and directed him to use them. I also remind him to space his words so the reader (including Matt himself) can read them. I check in with Matt after he has been writing for 10 minutes.<br><br>**TEACHING POINTS**<br>• Provide necessary support before student begins to write. (ensures success and saves time later).<br>• Have the student read his writing.<br>• Focus on expectation previously set. *"Those lines helped you, didn't they? It was a lot easier."* | Money by Matthew Hebel<br>Did you know Ben Franklin is on the two dollar bill?<br>Did you know Abraham Lincoln is on the five dollar bill?<br>Some coins have eagles on the back of them. Did you know that?<br>Money is important because you will need a lot to buy a house.<br>**Four pages from Matt's 8-page published book, *Money*.** | | |

# *Video* SCENES

**DEEPER UNDERSTANDING: Using Writing to Reach and Teach Struggling Learners**

## SCENES WITH INTERMEDIATE STUDENTS

**Setting the Scene for Writing Success**

(1:09 min.)

### Setting, Notes, and Explicit Teaching Points
The What, Why, and How of Teaching

**NOTES**

Most of the students in this grade 4 classroom are writing about two years below grade level. They do not like writing much and do not see themselves as writers. Many of the students are struggling readers as well and receive their daily reading instruction through a pull-out intervention program that is commercially published, teacher-scripted, and focused on phonics skills that are taught in isolation.

The classroom teacher, Whitney Clark, has been teaching for five years, all of them in grade 4. Her daily writing program has included three days of journal writing with all students writing to the same prompt and two days of DOL (Daily Oral Language Exercises). For the residency focus, Whitney has requested we write personal narratives, and we write "life stories" that focus on a memorable childhood incident. Students have been immersed for several days in listening to life stories, such as *Marshfield Dreams* by Ralph Fletcher, and *Child Times* by Eloise Greenfield, and I have demonstrated my own first draft through writing and thinking aloud.

In this brief opening scene, I am reviewing and clarifying what might go in a good life story before students write. I want to ensure success for every writer.

**TEACHING POINTS**

- Read and listen to texts to get writing ideas from authors. *"…not only ideas of what you can put in your story, but how do they do it? How do they say it?"*
- Extend what students have noticed about what authors do (or reread and ask them what they notice). *"I noticed there was a lot of conversation…some humor…a lot of description… I wanted you to get a picture in your mind* [of the setting]*."*
- State or restate the purpose for reading aloud. *"I was reading you this* [book] *because I wanted you to get lots of ideas. I wanted you to see what it sounds like to write a story about your life.… You said 'lots of details.'"*

### Ongoing Assessment
Informing Our Instruction

We begin by charting "What Makes a Good Life Story?" and add on to our chart as students learn more.

Make sure students are clear on why they are doing what we are asking them to do:

- *"Why was I reading you stories from those books?"* (Meager response from students.)

Use student responses to adjust your teaching:

- [Addressing observing teachers] *"I didn't do a good enough job saying, 'When I'm reading these stories today I want you to listen for what the author is doing to get ideas.'"*
- *"What else did I want you to notice?"* Antonio: *"Ideas of what you could put in your story."*

### Questions/Reflections
For Professional Conversations

- Why is it especially important that our struggling students receive excellent and adequate frontloading before doing a literacy activity?

### Learning Outcomes
What Students Know and Are Able to Do

- Gather information from more than one resource and synthesize ideas to plan writing.
- Make decisions about writing based on feedback.
- Revise content based on new information.
- Write for different purposes.

# Video SCENES

**DEEPER UNDERSTANDING: Using Writing to Reach and Teach Struggling Learners**

| | Setting, Notes, and Explicit Teaching Points<br>The What, Why, and How of Teaching | Ongoing Assessment<br>Informing Our Instruction | Questions/Reflections<br>For Professional Conversations | Learning Outcomes<br>What Students Know and Are Able to Do |
|---|---|---|---|---|
| | • Clarify the use of details in writing. *"Sometimes adding details can actually make the writing worse, kids, if you just stick in words . . . it has to sound better."*<br>• Write for your reader: connect writing to reading. *"You want to write it in such an interesting way that the reader doesn't want to put your paper down. . . . I finished that book* [*Teacher Man*, by Frank McCourt] *in one day . . . because it was so good."* | | | • Select details relevant to the topic to elaborate.<br>• Use personal experiences, observation, and/or research to support opinions and ideas.<br>• Adjust voice for different audiences and purposes. |
| **A Public Scaffolded Conversation Before Writing: Tiara**<br>(4:41 min.)<br>• Tiara (Fourth Grader) | **NOTES**<br>Tiara has chosen to write about the first time she did gymnastics. The scaffolded conversation in the following scene helps her write a coherent, engaging story.<br><br>**TEACHING POINTS**<br>• Write down ideas on a sticky note. *"I'm going to be writing some things on a Post-it, and that is going to be to help Tiara remember some of the smart things that she's saying. And also when I come around* [during roving conferences], *it will also remind me of what we talked about."*<br>• Suggest a beginning for a story that builds on the student's language. *"You might start something like this: 'When I was five, I begged my mom to take gymnastics.'"*<br>• Ask questions that require elaboration and detail in the storytelling. *"And what did that room look like? . . . What else was there? . . . You want to give the reader a picture. . . . What do you mean by. . . ."*<br>• Slow down the storytelling. *"So what happened your first day? You walked in* [to the gym]. *Are you holding Mom's hand?* [Tiara nods.] *Tell us about that."*<br>• Suggest possible language, through questioning, that could go in the story. *"So you walk in. Are you feeling shy? Are you excited? Are you nervous?"*<br>Tiara: *"I was pretty scared, and I was nervous."*<br>• Build on what the student is trying to say. *"And what were you scared of?"*<br>*"Um, that people would laugh at me 'cause I didn't know how to do a cartwheel."*<br>*"So what happened?"* | Make sure students are ready to write:<br>• *"Who is ready with their story? . . . Tiara, what's yours going to be about?"*<br>Tiara: *"Gymnastics."*<br><br>Use responsive questioning to help a student "find" and elaborate upon her story:<br>• *"Where is this taking place?"*<br>• *"Did you kind of beg your mom to take you to gymnastics class, or did she just one day say, 'Tiara, I've signed you up for gymnastics'?"*<br>Tiara: *"I begged her."*<br>*"Okay, so what did you say to your mom?"*<br>Tiara: *"I said, 'Mom, can I go to gymnastics?' She said, 'No.' Then I kept on begging."* | **Tiara: Student Profile**<br>Tiara had difficulty organizing her writing, staying on topic, and writing with meaningful detail. Notice how a scaffolded conversation addresses those issues.<br><br>**A public scaffolded conversation with Tiara before she writes a "life story."** | • Use precise words.<br>• Write in own voice in personal narrative. |

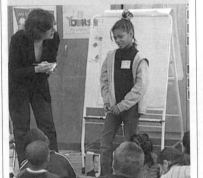

## DEEPER UNDERSTANDING: Using Writing to Reach and Teach Struggling Learners

*Video* **SCENES**

**Small-Group Support Before Writing**

(2:13 min.)

- Courtney (Fourth Grader)

### Setting, Notes, and Explicit Teaching Points
The What, Why, and How of Teaching

**NOTES**

Having additional scaffolded conversations with those students who are still having difficulty finding their life story topic despite lots of frontloading can have a big payoff. When those students do go off to write, they are more likely to succeed. Note that observing teachers have been advised not to look over kids' shoulders as they are writing but to do their own writing and/or reflect on their teaching of writing.

**TEACHING POINTS**

- Acknowledge difficulty of starting to write. *"Getting started for me is always the hardest part. OK, so let me help you with that."*
- Review the shared writing topics chart. *"Let's go over this list here—playing a game, a story about a new baby in your family or something that happened with a brother or sister, being sick . . . the first time you did something, a sport. . . ."*
- Help students uncover their topic, stay on the topic, and slow down the story. [Courtney has said she is sad that she doesn't get to see her mom much since her mom moved, but she recently saw her at Thanksgiving.] *"So you got to play with your mom. . . . What did she say to you? Did she sit close to you?"*
  Courtney: *"She gave me a hug and some kisses."*
  *"And what did you say to her? . . . Where are you with Mom? Are you in the living room? . . . Get that setting in."*
- Affirm student's language and story. *"I love the part when you said, 'She gave me hugs and kisses' and it was important to you because you don't get to see her much. It's a great story."*

### Ongoing Assessment
Informing Our Instruction

**Courtney: Student Profile**

Courtney is, according to her teacher, "a strong reader and one of the brighter students." She liked to write, but the quality of her writing was limited and did not match her reading. Telling a story that was important to her and talking it out before writing it helped her get her thoughts down.

### Questions/Reflections
For Professional Conversations

- How do effective scaffolded conversations make it possible for our most struggling writers to be successful? What does an effective scaffolded conversation encompass?
- Why is finding the "right" topic so critical for struggling writers?

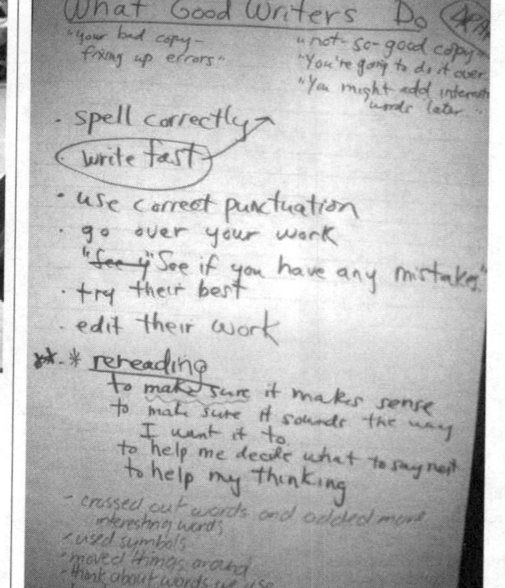


**Notice how our assessment chart documents students' limited knowledge about what good writers do, as well as their growing knowledge that has now moved beyond conventions.**

### Learning Outcomes
What Students Know and Are Able to Do

**Deeper Understanding: Using Writing to Reach and Teach Struggling Learners**

| *Video* **SCENES** | **Setting, Notes, and Explicit Teaching Points**<br>The What, Why, and How of Teaching | **Ongoing Assessment**<br>Informing Our Instruction | **Questions/Reflections**<br>For Professional Conversations | **Learning Outcomes**<br>What Students Know and Are Able to Do |
|---|---|---|---|---|
| • Antonio (Fourth Grader) | • Find out why the topic is important to the writer. (That's where the story is.) *"Why is that important that your mom had a baby?"*<br>Antonio: *"Because I can take care of her."*<br>*". . . So what do you do?"*<br>Antonio: *"Like carry her when she's crying."*<br>• Uncover the details. *"What do you do when the baby is crying to comfort it?"*<br>Antonio: *"Put her on her back."*<br>*"Do you rub her back? Do you talk to her?"*<br>Antonio: *"Yeah."*<br>*"What do you say to the baby?"*<br>Antonio: *"I say, 'Anaya, stop crying, please.'"*<br>*"What else do you do?"*<br>Antonio: *"Make her sleep."*<br>*"How do you help her go to sleep? . . . So you actually help her find a comfortable place to sleep. . . . What else do you do? Do you feed her?"*<br>• Affirm the writer. *"So that must make you feel pretty special. You're a big brother. OK, Antonio, you have a great story there."*<br>• Set expectation for writing. *"So get started, because you only have like 25 minutes. Don't waste a minute."* | **Antonio: Student Profile**<br>Antonio, according to his teacher, "did not see himself as a reader or writer. He was one of the lowest performing students in the classroom. He couldn't form sentences and struggled with basics, such as capital letters, grammar, and sentence fragments." He received his daily reading instruction in the pull-out, scripted intervention program.<br>The scaffolded conversations before writing helped him tell a coherent story that mattered to him. After he was genuinely celebrated in a public conference in front of everyone (students and observing teachers), his confidence was boosted for the rest of the school year. He worked harder, and his writing and reading improved a lot. See the *Teaching Essentials* website, Video Resources, Chapter 2. | • How do we get students to write with elaboration and detail in a meaningful way and not just "add details" to please us or meet the requirements on a rubric? | • Select details relevant to the topic.<br>• Use personal experiences and observations to support opinions and ideas. |
| **Writing Independently**<br>(0:19 sec.) | **NOTES**<br>Notice how silent the room is when kids are writing. All students (and teachers) get right to work. No one asks for extra help. | | | |
| **Celebration and Teaching Conference**<br>(5:58 min.)<br>• Antonio | **NOTES**<br>As Antonio is celebrated, he finally smiles. Always, my first concern is to focus on the writer, then the writing. Antonio reads his piece aloud; then I read it again and name everything Antonio has done well (so he will see himself as a writer). I comment on the title, first sentence, engaging the reader right at the start, the sound of his language, and use of interesting detail (*"I really like the way you . . ."*) before giving suggestions for improvement (*"Here are some things that might make it easier for the reader"*). | | • How can you add genuine celebration to all your writing conferences with students? Why is it necessary to include such celebration? | |

continues

## Video SCENES

**Celebration and Teaching Conference *continued***

**DEEPER UNDERSTANDING: Using Writing to Reach and Teach Struggling Learners**

| Setting, Notes, and Explicit Teaching Points | Ongoing Assessment | Questions/Reflections | Learning Outcomes |
|---|---|---|---|
| The What, Why, and How of Teaching | Informing Our Instruction | For Professional Conversations | What Students Know and Are Able to Do |
| **TEACHING POINTS**<br>• Clarify meaning. *"Tell us what you do when you pick her up."*<br>Antonio: *"You got to pat her on the back so she can calm down or she gets all mad."*<br>• Teach cutting and pasting. *"Is it okay if I cut this?* [Antonio nods.] *I want to show you a real easy way so you can add in and make your story even better* [demonstrating how to cut and paste]." And later: *"You had a skeleton here of a really good story. But now we're putting some meat on the bones. We're filling in all of those details that make it so interesting for the reader. . . . And so I'm going to give you more space here"* [showing cutting and pasting again].<br>• Connect ending punctuation to making meaning. *"But I really had a little bit of a hard time reading this because I wasn't sure where your sentences ended."*<br>• Give student the message: You can do this. I expect you to do this. *"Be sure you get those periods in there. You know where they go. Because that makes it much easier for the reader to follow."* And later: *"Now, I'm not going to do all of this for you because you're really smart."*<br>• Give genuine praise connected to what the writer has done. *"How do you feed her? What do you do?* [when you give her a bottle]"<br>Antonio: *"Like you got to put her back in her crib, and like she gots to be fixed in the right way, looking up."*<br>*"You know a lot of smart things about being a big brother."* | Check that student understands the role of ending punctuation:<br>• *"What do you need to add there?"*<br>Antonio: *"A period."*<br>• [Addressing teachers] *"It's very different to say to kids, 'You're missing a period at the end of every sentence.' 'So what?' students are thinking. 'My teacher will find it for me.'"* | • Why is it important (even with our struggling students) to put the responsibility on them to do the work after first providing adequate demonstrations and support? | • Revise at any stage of the writing process.<br>• Work on a draft over several days adjusting work to fit the time frame.<br><br>• Edit as needed at any stage of the writing process.<br>• Use punctuation rules from previous grades. |

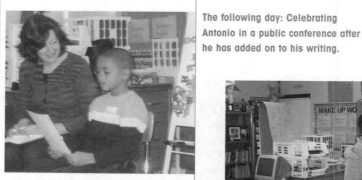

**The following day: Celebrating Antonio in a public conference after he has added on to his writing.**

**In one week Buba moves from a reluctant, unconfident writer to a successful one. (Also see the video of Buba on the website, *Teaching Essentials*, Video Resources, Chapter 1.)**

**Buba, a student who had not seen himself as a writer, gets right to work and writes uninterrupted and unaided for 30 minutes.**

**Video SCENES**

**Celebration and Teaching Conference *continued***

**DEEPER UNDERSTANDING: Using Writing to Reach and Teach Struggling Learners**

| Setting, Notes, and Explicit Teaching Points<br>The What, Why, and How of Teaching | Ongoing Assessment<br>Informing Our Instruction | Questions/Reflections<br>For Professional Conversations | Learning Outcomes<br>What Students Know and Are Able to Do |
|---|---|---|---|
| • Do whatever you can so that when the conference is over, the student is confident enough to go on writing. *"Did you know that you were a good writer?* [Inaudible response.] *You weren't sure. What do you think now?"*<br>Antonio: *"Now I think I am."* [I restate what Antonio is to do on his own when he goes back to his writing—add periods, add in information discussed in conference.]<br><br>**FINAL NOTE**<br>At the end of the week, students in this fourth-grade classroom, most of whom were severely struggling writers, saw themselves as writers and were initiating their own writing projects. Whitney Clark, the classroom teacher, said, "I saw a desire to write I hadn't seen before. It made my heart smile to see my most struggling writers praised for their writing and to have their ideas turned into readable sentences." | <br><br>Antonio (lower right) and his classmates. | | |

SESSION **13**

# **RESPONSE**NOTES

***Engage, Reflect, Assess, Celebrate!***

SESSION **14**

**Transforming** our **Teaching** through
**Reading/Writing Connections**

# Re-examining Our Beliefs and Celebration of Learning

**No Video**

## 1. Engage, Reflect, Assess

- *Small-Group Share*
  - Share with a partner or small group some teaching experiences you've had with one or more of your most struggling students. Show how you planned for and implemented immediate success in writing, and in reading the student-authored text, for those students.
  - Share, also, how you celebrated and published (if possible) a student's writing, and kept the focus on the student's strengths.

## 2. Discuss Professional Reading

- Discuss "Working with Struggling Readers" and "Teaching for Strategies" (*Conversations* excerpts, pp. 121–130, 130–136 and downloadable from the website).

**RESOURCES**

**In this Session**

- Regie Routman's Celebration Letter *14-3*
- Certificate of Appreciation (blank form) *14-4*
- List, Jot, Write Long (example) *14-5*
- List, Jot, Write Long (blank form) *14-6*

## 3. Goals

- Review how reading/writing instruction has changed as a result of the professional development program *Reading/Writing Connections.*
- Revise schoolwide beliefs and practices.
- Revisit goals set in Session 3 and note what has been accomplished.
- Celebrate learning.

## 4. Achieve a Deeper Understanding

- Display schoolwide revised belief statements from Session 3.
- Read and reflect on your beliefs from Session 3 as well as the goals you established at the start of this project.
- ***Whole-Group Share***
  - Share the highlights from the discussions you had with your small-group teams.
  - Share your revised beliefs with the whole group.
  - Identify the beliefs that the staff has in common:
    - Which beliefs are the same at all grade levels?
    - Which beliefs might be adopted as schoolwide beliefs?
    - Which beliefs need further discussion?
    - Which beliefs are no longer applicable?
  - Which schoolwide goals have been accomplished (or not)?

## 5. *Try It/Apply It* in the Classroom

- Explore and notice how schoolwide beliefs that were adopted at the beginning of the professional development program have changed and how those changes have impacted practices. Have the changes made your teaching lives easier? Harder? More satisfying? Perhaps write in your *Professional Development Notebook* an open-ended reflection or, perhaps, ***list, jot, and write long*** (see the example on p. 14–5) (Allen 2006).
  - **List** five ideas important to you and that we have talked about in the *Reading/Writing Connections* professional development program.
  - **Jot** down two more ideas for each idea and circle one you most want to try and apply to your teaching.
  - **Write long** (one paragraph) on one idea you circled.

## 6. Wrap-Up

- Read the enclosed Celebration Letter from Regie Routman.

- Choose a book to read for enjoyment. On the website, check out *What I'm Reading for Pleasure* for some possibilities.
- Please submit your session evaluation.

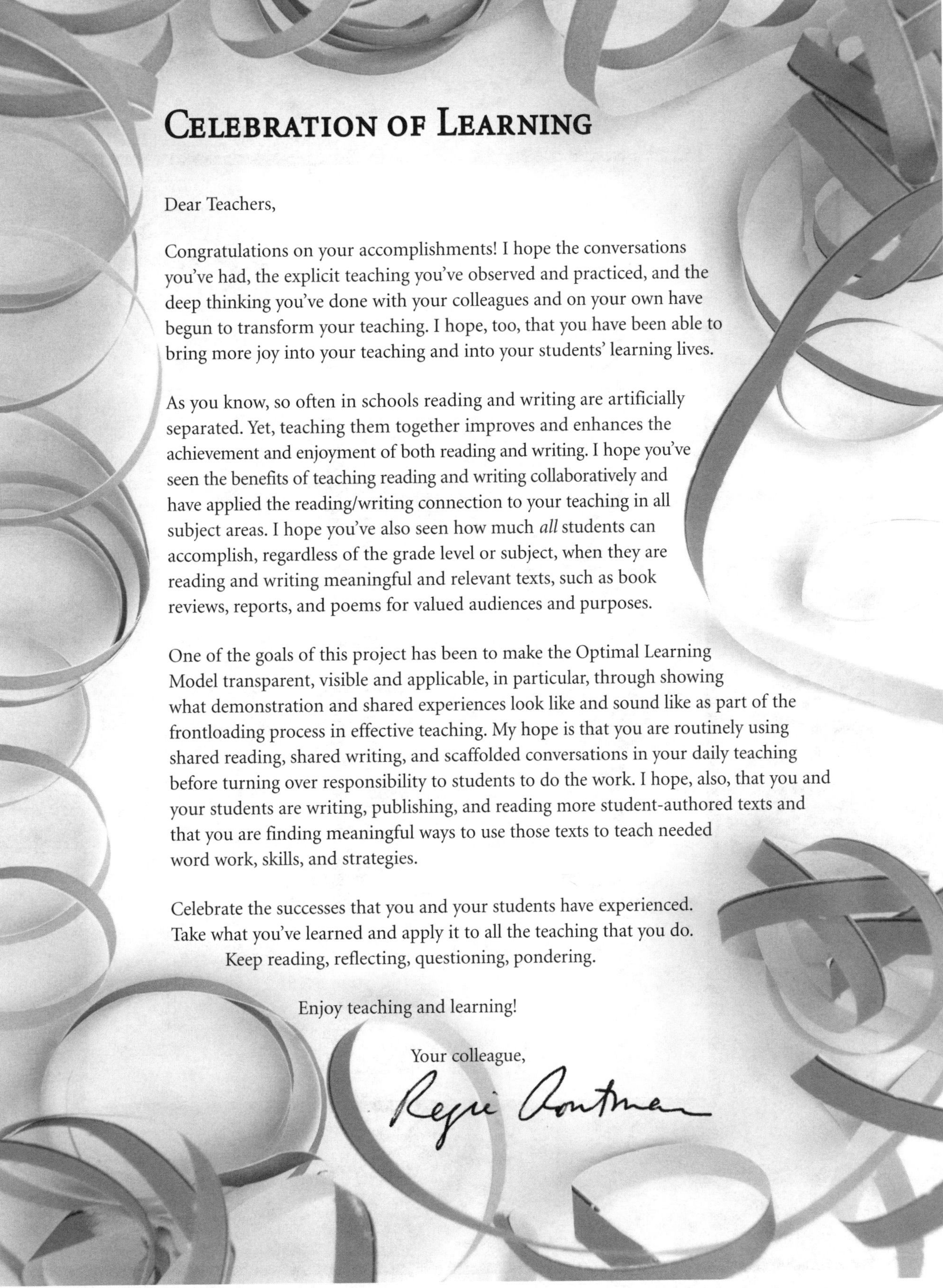

# Celebration of Learning

Dear Teachers,

Congratulations on your accomplishments! I hope the conversations you've had, the explicit teaching you've observed and practiced, and the deep thinking you've done with your colleagues and on your own have begun to transform your teaching. I hope, too, that you have been able to bring more joy into your teaching and into your students' learning lives.

As you know, so often in schools reading and writing are artificially separated. Yet, teaching them together improves and enhances the achievement and enjoyment of both reading and writing. I hope you've seen the benefits of teaching reading and writing collaboratively and have applied the reading/writing connection to your teaching in all subject areas. I hope you've also seen how much *all* students can accomplish, regardless of the grade level or subject, when they are reading and writing meaningful and relevant texts, such as book reviews, reports, and poems for valued audiences and purposes.

One of the goals of this project has been to make the Optimal Learning Model transparent, visible and applicable, in particular, through showing what demonstration and shared experiences look like and sound like as part of the frontloading process in effective teaching. My hope is that you are routinely using shared reading, shared writing, and scaffolded conversations in your daily teaching before turning over responsibility to students to do the work. I hope, also, that you and your students are writing, publishing, and reading more student-authored texts and that you are finding meaningful ways to use those texts to teach needed word work, skills, and strategies.

Celebrate the successes that you and your students have experienced. Take what you've learned and apply it to all the teaching that you do.
Keep reading, reflecting, questioning, pondering.

Enjoy teaching and learning!

Your colleague,

Regie Routman

Certificate of Appreciation

*is presented to*

*for taking part in the Regie Routman in Residence*

*Transforming Our Teaching Through Reading/Writing Connections*

*Regie Routman, Teacher and Writer*

*Principal*

# List, Jot, Write Long

## *(example)*

| **List**<br>(5 ideas important to you) | **Jot**<br>(Jot down 2 more ideas for each idea listed) |
|---|---|
| **1.** *Readers become better readers through writing.* | **1.** *Demonstrate for my students how I write and read for real-world purposes and audiences.*<br>**1.** *Support struggling readers in my classroom through writing and reading their own texts.* |
| **2.** | **2.**<br>**2.** |
| **3.** | **3.**<br>**3.** |
| **4.** | **4.**<br>**4.** |
| **5.** | **5.**<br>**5.** |

**Write Long**

(Circle one idea from above that you may want to write a paragraph about.)

Adapted from Allen, J. 2006. *Becoming a Literacy Leader: Supporting Learning and Change* (Stenhouse: Portland, ME).

# List, Jot, Write Long

| List<br>(5 ideas important to you) | Jot<br>(Jot down 2 more ideas for each idea listed) |
|---|---|
| 1. | 1.<br>1. |
| 2. | 2.<br>2. |
| 3. | 3.<br>3. |
| 4. | 4.<br>4. |
| 5. | 5.<br>5. |

| Write Long<br>(Circle one idea from above that you may want to write a paragraph about.) |
|---|
| |

Adapted from Allen, J. 2006. *Becoming a Literacy Leader: Supporting Learning and Change* (Stenhouse: Portland, ME).

SESSION **14**

# RESPONSENOTES

***Engage,***
***Reflect,***
***Assess,***
***Celebrate!***

SESSION 14

# RESPONSENOTES

***Engage, Reflect, Assess, Celebrate!***

SESSION 14

# RESPONSENOTES

***Engage,***
***Reflect,***
***Assess,***
***Celebrate!***

# RESPONSENOTES

# RESPONSENOTES

# RESPONSENOTES

ISBN-13: 978-0-325-01243-8
ISBN-10: 0-325-01243-1